Lecture Notes in Computer Science

Commenced Publication in 1973
Founding and Former Series Editors:
Gerhard Goos, Juris Hartmanis, and Jan van Leeuwen

Daqing Zhang   Marius Portmann
Ah-Hwee Tan   Jadwiga Indulska (Eds.)

Ubiquitous Intelligence and Computing

6th International Conference, UIC 2009
Brisbane, Australia, July 7-9, 2009
Proceedings

 Springer

Volume Editors

Daqing Zhang
Institut TELECOM & Management SudParis
Telecommunication Network and Services Department
HANDICOM Lab.
9, rue Charles Fourier, 91011 Evry Cedex, France
E-mail: daqing.zhang@it-sudparis.eu

Marius Portmann
Jadwiga Indulska
The University of Queensland
Australia's ICT Research Centre of Excellence (NICTA)
School of Information Technology and Electrical Engineering
Brisbane, QLD 4072, Australia
E-mail: marius@ieee.org; jaga@itee.uq.edu.au

Ah-Hwee Tan
Nanyang Technological University
School of Computer Engineering
Division of Information Systems
Blk N4-02A-26, Nanyang Avenue, 639798, Singapore
E-mail: asahtan@ntu.edu.sg

Library of Congress Control Number: 2009929393

CR Subject Classification (1998): H.4, C.2, H.5, K.4, I.5, H.5.2, H.3.5, H.5.3

LNCS Sublibrary: SL 3 – Information Systems and Application, incl. Internet/Web and HCI

ISSN 0302-9743

ISBN 978-3-642-02829-8 Springer Berlin Heidelberg New York

springer.com

© Springer-Verlag Berlin Heidelberg 2009

Typesetting: Camera-ready by author, data conversion by Scientific Publishing Services, Chennai, India
Printed on acid-free paper   SPIN: 12706440   06/3180   5 4 3 2 1 0

Preface

This volume contains the proceedings of UIC 2009, the 6th International Conference on Ubiquitous Intelligence and Computing: Building Smart Worlds in Real and Cyber Spaces. The UIC 2009 conference was technically co-sponsored by the IEEE and the IEEE Computer Society Technical Committee on Scalable Computing. The conference was also sponsored by the Australian Centre of Excellence in Information and Communication Technologies (NICTA). UIC 2009 was accompanied by six workshops on a variety of research challenges within the area of ubiquitous intelligence and computing. The conference was held in Brisbane, Australia, July 7–9, 2009.

The event was the sixth meeting of this conference series. USW 2005 (First International Workshop on Ubiquitous Smart World), held in March 2005 in Taiwan, was the first event in the series. This event was followed by UISW 2005 (Second International Symposium on Ubiquitous Intelligence and Smart Worlds) held in December 2005 in Japan. Since 2006, the conference has been held annually under the name UIC (International Conference on Ubiquitous Intelligence and Computing). UIC 2006 was held in September 2006 in Wuhan and Three Gorges, China, followed by UIC 2007 held in July 2007 in Hong Kong, and UIC 2008 held in June 2008 in Oslo, Norway.

Ubiquitous sensors, computers, networks and information are paving the way toward a smart world in which computational intelligence is distributed throughout the physical environment to provide reliable and relevant services to people. This ubiquitous intelligence will change the computing landscape because it will enable new breeds of applications and systems to be developed and the realm of computing possibilities will be significantly extended. By enhancing everyday objects with intelligence, many tasks and processes can be simplified, the physical spaces where people interact, like workplaces and homes, can become more efficient, safer and more enjoyable. Ubiquitous computing, or pervasive computing, uses these smart things to create smart environments. A smart thing can be endowed with different levels of intelligence, and may be context-aware, interactive, reactive, proactive, assistive, adaptive, automated, sentient, perceptual, cognitive and/or autonomic. Research on ubiquitous intelligence is an emerging research field covering many disciplines. A series of grand challenges exist to move from the current level of computing services to the smart world of adaptive and intelligent services.

The UIC 2009 conference offered a forum for researchers to exchange ideas and experiences in developing intelligent/smart objects, environments, and systems. This year, the technical program of UIC drew from a large number of submissions: 92 papers submitted from 23 countries representing four regions Asia Pacific, Europe, North and South America. Each paper was reviewed (as a full paper) by at least three reviewers, coordinated by the international Program Committee.

The Program Committee accepted 26 high-quality papers for presentation, which corresponds to a 28% acceptance rate. The accepted papers provide research contributions in a wide range of research topics that were grouped into the following seven conference sessions: Context Awareness, Middleware and Services, Routing and Sensor Networks, Ubiquitous Networks and Devices, Location-Based Services, Security and Privacy, and Ubiquitous Intelligence.

In addition to the refereed papers, the proceedings include the abstract of the keynote address by Mohan Kumar titled "Distributed Computing in Opportunistic Environments," and the keynote address by Tharam S. Dillon titled "Web of Things as a Framework for Ubiquitous Intelligence and Computing." Furthermore, the proceedings include an invited paper by Stephen Yau with the title "An Efficient Approach to Situation-Aware Service Discovery in Pervasive Service Computing Environments." We believe that the conference not only presented novel and interesting ideas, but also stimulated future research in the area of ubiquitous intelligence and computing.

Organization of conferences with a large number of submissions requires a lot of hard work and dedication from many people. We would like to take this opportunity to thank the numerous people whose work made this conference possible and ensured its high quality. First of all, we wish to thank the authors of submitted papers for their contribution to the technical program of the conference. We would further like to express our deepest gratitude to the Steering Committee Chairs, Jianhua Ma and Laurence T. Yang, for their timely advice and support during the whole process of the organization of UIC 2009. We also wish to express our greatest appreciation to the Vice Program Chairs (Yunhao Liu, Daniela Nicklas, Zhiwen Yu, Ramiro Liscano) for their hard work and commitment to quality during the paper selection process, and for their help with publicizing the conference. We would also like to thank all Program Committee members and external reviewers for their excellent job in reviewing papers, and the Advisory Committee for their continuous guidance.

We further acknowledge the excellent work of the Workshop Chairs (Robert C.H. Hsu, Mieso Denko) in organizing the six workshops, and Panel Chairs (Neil Bergmann, Max Muehlhaeuser) in organizing the UIC panel. Our thanks also go to the Publicity Chairs (Stephen J.H. Yang, Hassnaa Moustafa, Linda Jiang Xie, Evi Syukur, Sung-Bae Cho, Wenbin Jiang, Charalampos Z. Patrikakis) for advertising the conference and to the Web Chair (Peizhao Hu) for managing the conference website and helping with the editing of the conference proceedings. Last but not least, we would like to thank the NICTA Queensland Lab for its support, and The University of Queensland for hosting the conference.

July 2009

Daqing Zhang
Marius Portmann
Ah-Hwee Tan
Jadwiga Indulska

Organization

Executive Committee

General Chairs

Jadwiga Indulska	University of Queensland, Australia
Chris Scott	NICTA, Australia
Sumi Helal	University of Florida, USA

Program Chairs

Daqing Zhang	Institut Telecom SudParis, France
Marius Portmann	University of Queensland, Australia
Ah-Hwee Tan	Nanyang Technological University, Singapore

Program Vice Chairs

Yunhao Liu	Hong Kong University of Science and Technology, Hong Kong
Daniela Nicklas	Oldenburg University, Germany
Zhiwen Yu	Kyoto University, Japan
Ramiro Liscano	University of Ontario Institute of Technology, Canada

Advisory Committee Chairs

Stephen S. Yau	Arizona State University, USA
Norio Shiratori	Tohoku University, Japan

Steering Committee

Jianhua Ma (Chair)	Hosei University, Japan
Laurence T. Yang (Chair)	St. Francis Xavier University, Canada
Hai Jin	Huazhong University of Science and Technology, China
Jeffrey J.P. Tsai	University of Illinois at Chicago, USA
Theo Ungerer	University of Augsburg, Germany

Workshop Chairs

Robert C.H. Hsu	Chung Hua University, Hsinchu Taiwan, R.O.C.
Mieso Denko	University of Guelph, Canada

Publicity Chairs

Stephen J.H. Yang	National Central University, Taiwan, R.O.C.
Hassnaa Moustafa	France Telecom, France
Linda Jiang Xie	The University of North Carolina at Charlotte, USA
Evi Syukur	The University of New South Wales, Australia
Sung-Bae Cho	Yonsei University, Korea
Wenbin Jiang	HUST, China
Charalampos Z. Patrikakis	National Technical University of Athens, Greece

Panel Chairs

Neil Bergmann	The University of Queensland, Australia
Max Muehlhaeuser	Darmstadt University of Technology, Germany

International Liaison Chairs

Bernady O. Apduhan	Kyushu Sangyo University, Japan
Yo-Ping Huang	National Taipei University of Technology, Taiwan
Jong Hyuk Park	Kyungnam University, Korea

Industrial Liaison Chairs

Hakan Duman	British Telecom, UK
Nagula Sangary	RIM, Canada

Award Chairs

Frode Eika Sandnes	Oslo University College, Norway
Ohbyung Kwon	Kyunghee University, Korea

Web Administration Chair

Peizhao Hu	NICTA, Australia

Program Committee

Sebastien Ardon	NICTA Australia
Juan Carlos Augusto	University of Ulster, UK
Sasitharan Balasubramaniam	WIT, Ireland
Martin Bauer	NEC Heidelberg, Germany
Neil Bergmann	University of Queensland, Australia
Agustinus Borgy Waluyo	Institute for Infocomm Research, Singapore

Susanna Pirttikangas	Oulu University, Finland
Andry Rakotonirainy	Queensland University of Technology, Australia
Anand Ranganathan	IBM, USA
Michael Rohs	TU Berlin, Germany
Kurt Rothermel	University of Stuttgart, Germany
Gregor Schiele	Universität Mannheim, Germany
Isabelle Simplot-Ryl	University of Lille, France
Chiu C. Tan	College of William and Mary, USA
Bruce Thomas	University of South Australia, Australia
Jean-Yves Tigli	University of Nice Sophia Antipolis, France
Anand Tripathi	The University of Minnesota, USA
Sheng-De Wang	National Taiwan University, Taiwan
Athanasios Vasilakos	University of Western Macedonia, Greece
Zhijun Wang	Hong Kong Polytechnic University, Hong Kong
Ryan Wishart	National ICT Australia
Woontack Woo	Gwangju Institute of Science and Technology, South Korea
Hirozumi Yamaguchi	Osaka University, Japan
Tomoko Yonezawa	ATR, Japan
Zainab Zaidi	NICTA, Australia
Arkady Zaslavsky	Monash University, Australia
Justin Zhan	CMU, USA
Huaifeng Zhang	University of Technology Sydney, Australia
Jun Zhang	Dalian Maritime University, China
Bosheng Zhou	Queen's University, UK
Junyang Zhou	Hong Kong Baptist University, Hong Kong

Additional Reviewers

Wolfgang Blochinger
Remi Bosman
Yeong-Sheng Chen
Chen-Mou Cheng
Mario Ciampi
Alan Davoust
Frank Duerr
Christian Esposito
Klaus Herrmann
Guillaume Jourjon

Boris Koldehofe
Stéphane Lavirotte
Nan Li
Shijian Li
Kai Liu
Jean Martinet
Nathalie Mitton
Roberto Natella
Huan Jin Ng
William Niu

Andrés Muñoz Ortega
Generoso Paolillo
Nadia Qadri
Gaetan Rey
Fuk-hay Tang
Arvin Tsui
Bo Yan
Lin Yang
Yongtai Ye

Gold Sponsor

NICTA, Australia

Table of Contents

Keynote Speeches

Context Awareness

Middleware and Services

Routing and Sensor Networks

Ubiquitous Networks and Devices

Location-Based Services

Security and Privacy

Ubiquitous Intelligence

Distributed Computing in Opportunistic Environments

Mohan Kumar

The University of Texas at Arlington, USA

Abstract. Opportunistic networks have evolved from mobile ad hoc networking and the delayed tolerant networking paradigms and have quickly gained popularity in research and industry. In opportunistic networking, when pairs of devices come within each others communication range, opportunistically, short-lived links (or opportunistic links) are created. Opportunistic computing exploits the opportunistic links created by pair-wise contacts, to share information content, resources and services, leading to a wide variety of applications. In this talk we discuss the research challenges and issues in exploiting opportunistic contacts to create a delay tolerant distributed computing environment. Further more, the impact of social computing and networking paradigms for such problems as synchronization and trust will be investigated. Results of ongoing research work on information dissemination, collaboration and trust will be presented. The research work is supported through an NSF grant.

D. Zhang et al. (Eds.): UIC 2009, LNCS 5585, p. 1, 2009.

Web of Things as a Framework for Ubiquitous Intelligence and Computing

Tharam S. Dillon, Alex Talevski, Vidyasagar Potdar, and Elizabeth Chang

Digital Ecosystems and Business Intelligence Institute (DEBII)
Curtin University of Technology
GPO Box U1987
Perth, WA, 6845, Australia
{Tharam.Dillon,Alex.Talevski,Vidyasagar.Potdar,
Elizabeth.Chang}@cbs.curtin.edu.au

Abstract. In the last few years the web has evolved from just being a source of information to a platform for business applications. In parallel to this, wireless sensor network technologies have evolved to a stage where they are capable of connecting to the web. This amalgamation of technologies referred to as "Web of Things", has created new opportunities for intelligent application development. However, the "Web of Things" has brought interesting challenges like - efficiently utilizing online sensors, sensor composition for just in time application development and others that require urgent attention. In this paper, we propose a conceptual framework and reference architecture for embedding the notions of Ubiquitous Intelligence and Computing within the "Web of Things" and empowering their use in a broader context.

1 Introduction

The last few years have seen an explosive growth in the use of the web for many aspects of business and human endeavor. The web has evolved from its very early days where it was purely used for information dissemination, to application deployment, the read-write web with web 2.0 and progressively the provision of semantics on the web. In parallel with this development has been that of ubiquitous computing with the deployment of sensors and minimal computing devices on the person or in the environment of interest. These two trends have initially developed essentially on their own separate tracks. More recently there has been an increasing trend towards connecting these sensors and wearable devices to the internet leading to the formulation of the notion of the so called "Internet of Things". However, to be truly of the web rather then just being connected through it is necessary to have effective mechanisms for:

1. Locating these sensors.
2. Having a sharable interface description that is consistent with the developing web. Here it is important to remember that these sensors will not only have information but also some very limited computing capability.
3. Invoking and composing sensor data and functions.
4. Defining an architectural framework.

D. Zhang et al. (Eds.): UIC 2009, LNCS 5585, pp. 2–13, 2009.

A realization of this has led to the definition of the "Web of Things" which provides a framework for addressing these issues.

In this paper, we propose a conceptual framework and reference architecture for embedding the notions of Ubiquitous Intelligence and Computing within the "Web of Things" and empowering their use in a broader context. It also outlines some existing application areas.

2 Service-Oriented Architecture (SOA) vs. Resource Oriented Architecture (ROA)

In order to solve the UCDs and sensor integration problems, the supporting IT systems need to be simple and malleable. Research [1] has outlined the requirement for a service-based approach. Service-based approaches achieve loose coupling among interacting systems where disparate components may interact using a common interaction protocol and certain architectural and protocol constraints. By abstracting a component's internals through an interface, components become well isolated and standardized. Such architectures define component location, integration, management, monitoring and security in a straightforward way. Tailorable systems may then be rapidly adapted to satisfy specialized and evolving requirements. Tailorable system architectures require specific tools and significant technological support. We have identified the following categories and features that must be investigated when developing architectures for the "Web of Things" to allow composition, Interaction and collaboration and these are:

- **Context independence** - Identifying the clear decompositions in such a system is a key to developing a hierarchical system architecture where systems are built from building blocks.
- **Service Model or a Resource Model** – A service or Resource model ensures that disparate devices which reside on different platforms, can interoperate.
- **Accessibility** - Services and Resources must be accessible by clients that are implemented using different technologies, and are distributed over a network.
- **Data Exchange** – A data exchange model is a communication protocol that enables components to interact and transfer data in a standardized way.
- **Location Transparency** - To achieve location transparency and seamless interoperability, a piece of wrapping middleware code lies between components that make interactions transparent.
- **Contracts** – An interaction contract guarantees that an interface exists, and provides its advertised services.
- **Plug and Play** - The use of stable, published interfaces represented in a sharable standardized representation enables assembly or integration of applications from disparate sources. In this way, components can be reconfigured, added, removed, or replaced after system deployment.
- **Automation** – The use of macros and scripts that are implemented to facilitate dynamic discovery, interaction and integration of reusable components at runtime [2][3].

In order to perform UCD and sensor service composition and application reconfiguration within a dynamically changing operation environment, UCD and sensor software and middleware systems need to be simple and malleable. A service based approach for sensor systems facilitate dynamic system self configuration, adaptation and adhoc network routing protocols. Service-based approaches may achieve loose coupling among interacting sensors and devices. Tailorable architectures allow generic sensors and devices to be rapidly adapted to satisfy the specialized, rapidly changing, unclear and / or evolving system requirements through hierarchical and iterative service composition. They provides a means for the straightforward creation and modification of application solutions from provided sensor and device services. Using a reconfigurable approach as a basis for the creation and modification of sensor applications, it possible to construct, customize, integrate and evolve software solutions as a response to production requirements. Such a service framework and platform are directed at increasing software quality and performance, reducing software development and maintenance costs and easing runtime software modification.

In exploring reference architectures we review the potential of SOA and ROA as potential candidates as a reference architecture for the "Web of Things".

Service-Oriented Computing (SOA) in general and Web services in particular have recently received tremendous momentum because the encapsulation, componentization, decentralization, and integration capability provided by SOC. Web services are substantial; they provide both architectural principles and software specifications to connect computers and devices using standardized protocols across the Internet. SOA is a reference architectural style that defines a set of constraints on how service-oriented applications interact with each other in order to achieve high degree of flexibility and dynamicity [4]. Here by reference architecture [5] we mean it is the principal architecture that determines the overall software system behavior such as flexibility and dynamicity which are two important requirements for the Web of Things. As an architectural style [6] SOA, through its "publish-find-bind" triangle, achieves loose-coupling which facilitates the dynamicity and flexibility. Web services technology realizes SOA through providing one with an implementation that builds a one-to-one mapping between the SOA architecture and the implementation. For example, matchmaker in SOA is implemented as the UDDI registry/repository in Web services. Service capability information is described using the WSDL (Web Services Description Language) documents. Service consumers and providers can be realized as SOAP (Simple Object Access Protocol) clients and servers that communicate via SOAP messages over the Internet. From the technological viewpoint, a Web service is "an interface that describes a collection of operations that are network accessible through standardized XML messaging" [7]. The standardized interface differentiates Web services from other distributed object technologies (e.g. CORBA, DCOM, etc.), in which interfaces are not defined using open standards and tools. Standardized interfaces represent 'a shared understanding towards implementation independence'; a key element for building loosely-coupled distributed applications through interoperability. This implementation independence has made Web services a technology of choice for building complex applications in a loosely-coupled manner across distributed environments. Two types of Web service interfaces are common: the traditional Big Web services (WSDL, SOAP, and UDDI) and the RESTful Web services which treat

HTTP as a semantically capable application protocol rather than just as a transport protocol which is the case in SOAP.

Resource-Oriented Architecture (ROA) was first proposed in [8], in which four key concepts were defined for a ROA: Resources, URL, Representation, and Links. The key properties of ROA compliant software architecture is: addressability, stateless-ness, connectedness, and a uniform interface.   A useful paradigm here is termed as Resource-Oriented Computing (ROC). ROC is an emerging simplified paradigm to perform computational tasks.   In ROC, everything (e.g. processes, data, business logic, etc) is treated as a logic resource that is an abstract set of information. ROC provides a high-level view towards computation, which abstracts away from low-level data and objects situated at the physical layer. One of the unique uses of identity (URI) in ROC is that URI is used for both identity and for representing a functional program. This property is of crucial importance for the Web of Things.

3 Architectural Framework for the Web of Things

The "Web of Things" uses a standardized protocol HTTP as an application protocol instead of just as a transport protocol to provide connection of sensors with the inter-net. This relies on the so-called "Restful Services" discussed above. Within this framework, the "Web of Things" refers to the next generation of network and web where each and every object on the globe will be identifiable, interactive and a part of an adhoc network. The "Web of Things" relies on the numerous electronic devices or sensors, which form a collaborative system. The important aspect of these Ubiquitous Computing Devices (UCD) is that they can measure quantities and events and provide information on these and also carryout some very limited logic operations or compu-tations. We choose to represent a UCD as a resource. We use the following definition from [9] namely a resource, is "*a thing that has a universal identifier, a name, may have reasonable representations and which can be said to be owned*". Note this defi-nition allows a Web services resource to be universally identifiable through the Web, thus permitting discovery, selection, and invocation desirable of a Web services iden-tified by the URL on the Web. We distinguish between a *Web service resource* and a *Web resource* in that the former one does not necessarily encode information about the "state" of the resource i.e it is stateless whilst the *Web resource* may have state even though it does not maintain any state information this is encoded in the represen-tation sent back to the resource requester.

This "Web of Things" thus provides an integrated framework for Ubiquitous In-telligence and Computation. The "Web of Things" envisions a network implementa-tion (which is frequently wireless) for its sheer ubiquity. "Web of Things" brings enormous challenges on the conceptual and technical levels which must be resolved to produce a successful "Web of things " strategy for ubiquitous intelligence and computation and these include:

- Abstractions for sensor and event representations
- Compositions of sensors to deliver particular information

- Semantics for compositions of sensors and events
- Robust wireless devices and networks
- The storage, structure and retrieval of the tsunami of wireless sensor data
- User interfaces for visualizing, configuring, monitoring and controlling such networks and their outputs
- Middleware to seamlessly integrate and tailor adhoc devices and the "Web of Things" network
- Convergence of technologies to deliver truly synchronized wireless voice, video and data.
- Wireless network and device security

When these are combined with wearable devices and sensors associated with the immediacy of a person, it leads to the concept of "Human Space Computing". Human Space Computing (HSC) refers to an end user or consumer interacting with technology-based system(s) or embedded computer devices through interactive protocols or modalities such as audio, video, hearing, feeling, vision, touching, sound, voice, vibrating, reading, writing, tagging, blogging, binding etc.. all human sensations [10].

The distinction between this and Human Computer Interaction (HCI) lies in the definition of what the Human interacts with; system or computers, - what are the differences between the two; the interaction protocols and what do they include. It is obvious that Human Space Computing requires a much larger scale of emphasis and automation on 'system' and 'interaction' and it is where the challenges are.

4 Abstractions for Ubiquitous Computing Devices (UCD) and Event Representations

The first challenge with the deployment of the "Web of Things" is to abstract the UCD information for event representation and information representation. As mentioned earlier "Web of Things" envisions many items on this globe would transmit data (such as identity, temperature, location, etc.) from UCDs such as sensor data on a regular basis which give us information on an object or the state of a particular ambient environment. This data requires processing to generate information which can then be used for event identification and representation. As both individual UCDs and individual events are really UCD instances and event instances we need abstractions for these. Abstracting UCD and event representations is a challenging task that requires frameworks that can deal with this problem in its entirety. At the first level as mentioned above, UCDs can be represented as resources which associate a unique identifier that allows them to be located in the "Web of Things" space. At the next level, it is important to develop the notion of

1. UCD classes which represent collections of UCD instances with particular properties. e.g. a temperature UCD monitor and alarm class. This class could consist of several instances. To allow for mobility, this class would have both location and time as two amongst other properties.
2. Event classes which represent collections of event instances with particular properties. e.g. an intrusion event detection class which could consist of

several event instances. Event classes too would have location and time (or at least position in a sequence in time) as two amongst other properties. This need for developing event abstractions has also been put forward by Ramesh Jain in his "Web of Events" keynote delivered in the 2008 Keynote at the Semantics, Knowledge and Grid Conference.

In addition, there will be relationships between these classes, which will allow for representation of generalization/specialization, composition and associations.

It would be useful to record the sensor data in a portable format like XML or UCDML so that it can seamlessly integrate with high level applications. This will allow us to meet the following challenges:

- Manage how raw sensor data is kept, maintained and exported by disparate sources.
- Interpreting events associated with particular sensor configurations and outputs.
- Transforming system level knowledge from distinct sensors or UCDs into higher-level management applications.
- The fact that the abstract level representation of the UCDs or sensors is implemented will allow substitution of new UCDs or sensors as technology progresses by keeping the interfaces standardized.

5   Compositions of UCDs and Events to Address Complex Requirements

The second challenge with the deployment of the "Web of Things" is to provide an ability to compose data from multiple sensors based upon the requirements laid by a particular application scenario. This has its own set of challenges that again require a dedicated framework on how information from multiple sensors is composed and correlated for meeting the QoS requirements of a particular scenario.

Here we will need a decomposition technique which will allow for the decomposition of complex functionality that is required into lower level resources which can then be met by specific UCDs or Events. Here we distinguish between

1. Decomposition into aggregations of simpler resources.
2. Decomposition of complex events into aggregations of simpler events.

It has to be clearly understood that this decomposition requires one to specify the items in the aggregation as well as their dynamic sequence of execution or arrangement. To model the dynamics, it has often been suggested that workflows specified in a language such as BPEL would be appropriate. An alternative, particularly for resources (but also suitable for services particularly Restful services) is the use of Mashups which allow easier configuration of these workflows. Our preferred approach is to utilize Mashups for this representation of the workflows.

The "Web of Things" envisions that all the items would be tagged with sensors, with or without having a prior idea of how this sensed information would be utilized. For example, a set of things could be tagged with a generic sensor that could monitor external phenomenon. Now it is up to the middleware or different application to decide how this sensor data can be used to suit application specific requirements. However, many challenges in composing sensor data remain. The composition of events remains a challenging issue with a focus on sequencing them to produce a composite event.

6 Semantics for Compositions of Sensors and Events

The third challenge with the deployment of the "Web of Things" is to provide semantics during the sensor composition phase so that automatic sensor discovery, selection and composition can happen. Semantics here is the study of the meaning of Things (Resources that represent UCDs or sensors) and Events. It represents the definitions of the meaning of elements, as opposed to the rules for encoding or representation. Semantics describe the relationship between the syntactical elements and the model of computation. It is used to define what entities mean with respect to their roles in a system. This includes capabilities, or features that are available within a system.

Ontologies are formal, explicit specifications of a shared semantic conceptualization that are machine-understandable and abstract models of consensual knowledge. We merge Gruber's [11], Borst's [12], and Studer's [13] definitions of an ontology as a basis for our discussion here. Using such an ontology, it is possible to define concepts through uniquely identifying their specifications and their dynamic and static properties. Concepts, their details and their interconnections are defined as an ontology specification. Ontology compositions are typically formed from many interconnected ontology artifacts that are constructed in an iteratively layered and hierarchical manner. It is necessary to use a graphical representation of ontologies at a higher level of abstraction to make it easier for the domain experts to capture the semantic richness of the defined ontology.

The ontology-based architecture is grounded on the notion of a base ontology, subontologies [14] and/or commitments [15]. These sub-ontologies are used as independent systems (in functionality) for the various decentralized users. This would allow for a very versatile and scalable base of operation. Numerous sub-ontologies provide custom portals for different expert groups to access information and communicate with other groups [16][17].

They are concerned with all processes of sensor and device operation. They define concepts, abstractions, relationships and interactions as domain concepts and instantiations for manual or automated reasoning. These ontologies signify information which evolves to reflect the operational environment. Reaching such a formal consensus of understanding is of benefit in an environment that deals with self-contained, distributed and heterogeneous sensors and devices. In general the following system properties can be defined:

- **Information and Communication** - refers to the basic ability to gather and exchange information between the parties involved.
- **Integrability** - relates to the ability of sensors and devices from different sources to mesh relatively seamlessly and the ability to integrate these sensors to build the final solution in a straightforward way.

- **Coordination** - focuses on scheduling and ordering tasks performed by these parties.
- **Awareness and Cooperation** - refer to the implicit knowledge of the operation process that is being performed and the state of the system.

The integration of a number of ontologies can be used to augment the functionality of any framework namely;

- **Process Ontology** - develops a representation of the different types of processes involved in an operation.
- **Resource Ontology** - provides a representation of all the resources involved in the operation activity at the different levels of granularity. As each large granularity the composite resource is likely to consist of sub resources itself, it is important that these are all represented within the ontology.
- **Outputs Ontology** - represents the different types of outputs or units that will result from the operation activity. They involve classification of the outputs and its features.

Each defined ontology conceptually represents the perceived domain knowledge through its concepts, attributes, taxonomies, relationships, and instances for operations.

Two approaches to the representation of semantics here would be (1) use of ontologies (2) lightweight semantic annotations. The choice of a method that would be suitable will depend on the circumstances. For representing the knowledge in a given domain ontologies and for adding semantics to individual resources annotation may suffice. A special challenge here is developing ontologies for events.

7 Robust Wireless Devices and Networks

A key element of the "Web of Things" is the ability to deploy sensors with flexibility and mobility.   An important technology here is WSN technology. Recent advances in wireless technology have enabled the development of wireless solutions capable of robust and reliable communication in various environments. International standards such as the IEEE 802.11a/b/g/n for wireless local area networks and the IEEE 802.15.4 for low-rate wireless personal area networks, as well as numerous RFID (radio-frequency identification) specifications, have enabled applications such as wireless networking, sensing, monitoring, control, and asset tracking. Such wireless sensing technologies have the potential to be beneficial in both domestic and industry applications in a number of ways. Introducing these technologies can contribute to;

- The monitoring of the working and living environment, systems and devices
- Reduced installation, integration, operation and maintenance costs
- Speedy installation and removal
- Mobile and temporary installations
- Up-to-date information services are available at anytime, anywhere
- Enhanced visualization, foresight, forecasting and maintenance schedules
- Determine certain patterns and characteristics of our everyday lives

- Safe living and working environment and optimized processes
- Effective and efficient operation

The challenge with the deployment of the "Web of Things" is to provide robust wireless sensing devices and extremely reliable communication networks. This is the most challenging task so far as there are many parameters that need to be considered. The key challenges when we consider deploying "Web of Things" using wireless devices can be categorized as follows:

- Restricted size, shape, construction and certification.
- Make do with limited processing power, memory, storage, battery consumption and screen real-estate resources.
- Self contained. When possible, devices should generate their own power or, contain battery packs with extended battery life of many years to reduce maintenance.
- Operate in a difficult wireless environment both in terms of radio noise and obstructions but also where certain restrictions on such radio devices are present (such as flammable areas).
- Operate in a hostile areas where environmental conditions may be difficult.
- Embedded platforms.
- Implement complex network algorithms with real-time requirements and adaptive routing protocols.
- Contribute in a simplified ad-hoc and multi-hop network.
- Seamlessly integrate with existing IT solutions.
- Self re-configurable, dynamic and adaptive.
- Provide services within a dynamically changing system environment.
- Exhibit fault tolerance and recovery (self-healing, robust and reliable).
- Based on open, international standards.
- Operate in the unlicensed portions of the frequency spectrum.
- Low maintenance.
- Implement strict encryption, transmitter authentication and data consistency validation.
- Clearly defined operational reliability and availability of the wireless network within the operational environment.

8   The Tsunami of Information in the "Web of Things"

IP traffic will nearly double every two years through to 2012 [18]. Therefore, total IP traffic will increase by a factor of six from 2007 to 2012. High-definition video, audio and other high-resolution, high update streaming data such as that produced by cctv cameras and sensors over high-speed connections will be the main driver behind the 46%pa IP growth in the coming years. Such streaming data may now account for approximately one-quarter of all Intranet traffic. Streaming data grew from 12 percent in 2006 to 32 percent in 2008 [18]. The rapid growth of the use of high resolution devices on our networks has produced a significant challenge in dealing with such a tsunami of data.

We may utilize 1000s of streaming sensors and cameras to monitor certain conditions. These sensors will become an integral part of the safe and high performance operations. These sensors produce significant amounts of unstructured and unclassified data that is simply used to momentary visualize conditions. It is essential that sensor systems have sufficient network bandwidth, processing power and storage capacity to cater for the tsunami of data that is experienced.

9 Application Areas

There are many application areas of the above such as;
- Oil, gas, resources and manufacturing industries
- Vehicle, road, traffic and transportation
- Human space technologies, smart appliances and wearable devices
- Social Networking
- Convergence

For reasons of space we will only discuss one of these below.

9.1 Oil, Gas, Resources and Manufacturing Industries

Oil, gas and resource production plants use a variety of sensors that produce a visual representation of the just-in-time plant operational state. Such sensors are particularly important when the platform functions are operated remotely. The use of sensor data supports the move from "Decision Support" operations to true "Remote Operations. Many technologies have not yet become mature to successfully facilitate remote operations. A requirement for large remotely operated oil, gas and resources plants is for the engineers and technical personnel to be remotely distributed, while plant operators are located on-site. This physical distance can becomes a crucial issue if remote interactions are incomplete and/or ambiguous; problematic and/or potentially dangerous events may occur. Therefore, the need for a formal remote operation strategy has considerable significance. Operations ontologies may foster domain knowledge, process knowledge, standards and procedures, plant architecture, components, composition and systems, staff and resources, projects and schedules, stakeholders, and supply chain (vendors, suppliers). There is even ongoing research projects in the oil and gas industry looking into the development of completely unmanned production platforms. For such a scheme to be successful, it is essential that cctv cameras, microphones, communications, control systems and other data that is transmitted is synchronized and converged.

Existing sensor output handling has many deficiencies in information processing and presentation. System operators are often presented with large amounts of data that must be processed quickly and decisively. However, the amount of information required to be digested is quite large when crucial decisions need to be made within a constrained timeframe. This can leave the system operator suffering from cognitive overload when decisions have the greatest impact. This problem requires sources of sensor data, methods of obtaining that sensor data, and methods of interpreting the sensor data and producing a relevant message to be investigated. Expert system approaches have been quite useful in the areas of sensor output processing. There are a number of problems that cannot be practically solved and result in inadequate results because of several difficulties. The continuing increase in the size and complexity of oil, gas and resources platforms and production has led to monitoring and control involving a significantly extensive and complex data set. This is further complicated in emergency situations when rapid decisions are required. Sensor output processing is a problem which has been investigated for quite some time. Various problems associated with such processing techniques such as system complexity, output relationships, response time, reasoning, incomplete and incorrect data have been investigated. Expert system approaches have been useful in the areas of sensor output processing. However, several issues have not been addressed. The integration of Expert Systems and Artificial Neural Networks to solve many sensor output processing problems have proved to be quite successful n addressing a large set of problems in the power system [19]. However, the use of such techniques in oil, gas and resource production are seldom discussed or effectively employed.

10 Conclusion

In this paper we explored the use of the "Web of Things" as a framework for Ubiquitous Intelligence and Computing. Several issues that need to be resolved were identified and some solutions were proposed. Several open questions that must be addressed were also identified for future research.

References

[1] Schutte, R.: SOA is changing software (2003),
    http://www4.gartner.com/resources/111900/111987/111987.pdf
[2] Chang, E., Annal, D., Grunta, F.: A Large Scale Distributed Object Architecture – CORBA & COM for Real Time Systems. In: Proceedings of the Third IEEE Conference on Object Oriented Real Time Distributed Systems, Newport Beach, California (March 2000)
[3] Annal, D.: NetCaptain Client Architecture. In: System Development Document. Philips Public Communications Pty. Ltd, Australia (1999)
[4] Dillon, T.S., Wu, C., Chang, E.: Reference Architectural Styles for Service-Oriented Computing. Springer, Heidelberg (2008)
[5] Barber, K.S., Graser, T.J., Holt, J.: Evolution of Requirements and Architectures: An Empirical-based Analysis. In: 1st International Workshop on Model-based Requirements Engineering, San Diego, CA (2001)
[6] Perry, D.E., Wolf, A.L.: Foundations for the Study of Software Architecture. Software Engineering Notes, ACM SIGSOFT 17(4), 40–52 (1992)
[7] Kreger, H.: Fulfilling the web services promise. Communications of the ACM 46(6), 29–34 (2003)
[8] Richardson, L., Ruby, S.: RESTful Web Services. O'Reilly, Sebastopol (May 2007)
[9] Booth, D., Haas, H., McCabe, F., Newcomer, E., Champion, M., Ferris, C., Orchard, D.: Web services architecture, W3C Working Group, Hewlett-Packard, Software AG, IBM, Fujitsu Labs of America, Iona, BEA Systems, W3C (2004)

[10] Chang, E., Dillon, T., Calder, D.: Human system interaction with confident computing. The mega trend. In: Proceedings of Conference on Human System Interaction, Poland (2008)

[11] Gruber, T.R.: A translation approach to portable ontology specification. In: Knowledge Acquisition (1993)

[12] Borst, W.: Construction of Engineering Ontologies, Centre of Telematica and Information Technology, University of Tweenty, Enschede, The Netherlands (1997)

[13] Studer, R., Fensel, D.: Knowledge Engineering: Principles and Methods. IEEE Transactions on Data and Knowledge Engineering (1998)

[14] Jarrar, M., Meersman, R.: Formal Ontology Engineering in the DOGMA Approach. In: Proc. Intl. Conf. on Ontologies, Databases, and Applications of Semantics, pp. 1238–1254 (2002)

[15] Spynus, P., Meersman, R., Mustafa, J.: Data Modeling versus Ontology Engineering. In: Proc. 21st ACM SIGMOD Intl. Conf. on Management of Data, pp. 14–19 (2002)

[16] Klein, M., Fensel, D., Kiryakov, A., Ognyanov, D.: Ontology versioning and change detection on the web. In: Gómez-Pérez, A., Benjamins, V.R. (eds.) EKAW 2002. LNCS, vol. 2473, pp. 197–212. Springer, Heidelberg (2002)

[17] Wouters, C., Dillon, T.S., Rahayu, W., Chang, E., Meersman, R.: A Practical Approach To The Derivation of A Materialized Ontology View. In: Taniar, D., Rahayu, W. (eds.) Web Information Systems, pp. 191–226. Idea Group Press, Melbourne (2004)

[18] Cisco, Visual Networking Index – Forecast and Methodology 2007–2012 (2009), http://www.cisco.com/

[19] Dillon, T.S., Morsztyn, K., Phua, K.: Short-Term Load Foercasting Using Adaptive Pattern Recognition and Self-Organising Techniques. In: Proceedings of the Power System Computation Conference, Cambridge, UK (March 1975)

Inferring Human Interactions in Meetings: A Multimodal Approach

Zhiwen Yu[1], Zhiyong Yu[1], Yusa Ko[2], Xingshe Zhou[1], and Yuichi Nakamura[2]

[1] School of Computer Science, Northwestern Polytechnical University, P.R. China
zhiwenyu@nwpu.edu.cn
[2] Academic Center for Computing and Media Studies, Kyoto University, Japan
yuichi@media.kyoto-u.ac.jp

Abstract. Social dynamics, such as human interaction is important for understanding how a conclusion was reached in a meeting and determining whether the meeting was well organized. In this paper, a multimodal approach is proposed to infer human semantic interactions in meeting discussions. The human interaction, such as proposing an idea, giving comments, expressing a positive opinion, etc., implies user role, attitude, or intention toward a topic. Our approach infers human interactions based on a variety of audiovisual and high-level features, e.g., gestures, attention, speech tone, speaking time, interaction occasion, and information about the previous interaction. Four different inference models including Support Vector Machine (SVM), Bayesian Net, Naïve Bayes, and Decision Tree are selected and compared in human interaction recognition. Our experimental results show that SVM outperforms other inference models, we can successfully infer human interactions with a recognition rate around 80%, and our multimodal approach achieves robust and reliable results by leveraging on the characteristics of each single modality.

Keywords: human interaction; smart meeting; multimodal recognition.

1 Introduction

In recent years, smart meeting systems have attracted much attention from researchers in the areas of image/speech processing, computer vision, human–computer interaction, and ubiquitous computing [1]. Many systems have been developed that can assist people in a variety of tasks, such as scheduling meetings, preparing meetings, taking notes, sharing files, and browsing minutes after a meeting [2, 3, 4, 5, 6, 7, 8, 9]. However, to date, little research has been conducted on social aspects. Meeting is intrinsically a human collaboration process that encapsulates a large amount of social and communication information. Such kind of information is particularly important for understanding how a conclusion was reached, e.g., whether all members agreed on the outcome, who did not give his opinion, who spoke a little or a lot. In this paper, we aim to infer human *semantic* interactions in meetings, which are defined as social behaviors among meeting participants with respect to a particular topic, such as proposing an idea, giving comments, expressing a positive opinion, and requesting

D. Zhang et al. (Eds.): UIC 2009, LNCS 5585, pp. 14–24, 2009.

information. As a kind of semantic information extracted from raw meeting data, human interactions are useful for meeting participants, organizers, and sponsors.

- For meeting participants: The information helps meeting members be aware of their own and others' behavior in a discussion (e.g., one person proposes or comments a lot, and one person is always critical), and then make adjustments to increase the satisfaction of the group with the discussion process. Social dynamic information could assist group in understanding and improving its interaction [10].
- For meeting organizers: Knowing the current status of the meeting (e.g., did all members agree on the outcome, who was quiet, who was extroverted, etc.), the organizer can conduct adjustments to make the meeting more efficient, such as encouraging speaking and suggesting related interesting topics for discussion.
- For meeting sponsors: Meeting sponsors are those who steer a meeting, care about its conclusions, and might sponsor its decisions (e.g., plan or activity). Hence human interactions are valuable for them to determine whether the meeting was well organized and the conclusion well reasoned.

Due to its dynamic and complex characteristics, human semantic interaction is challenging to detect. Through image processing, we may be able to recognize physical interactions, e.g., who was talking to whom [11]. But it is difficult to clearly distinguish the participant's intention or attitude toward a particular topic. Speech transcription can determine implicit actions (e.g., agreement or disagreement) regarding a topic. However, the accuracy of speech transcription in meeting is not satisfactory due to highly conversational and noisy nature of meetings, and lack of domain specific training data [12]. Furthermore, it ignores other nonverbal information, e.g., body movement, which may be important in identifying human attitude. For instance, nodding or shaking of the head is thought of as something that communicates to other people.

To achieve robust and reliable results, in this paper we propose a multimodal approach for inferring human interactions in meetings. Audiovisual and high-level features such as gestures, attention, speech tone, speaking time, interaction occasion (spontaneous or reactive), and information about the previous interaction are utilized so as to recognize human interaction from multiple aspects. Four different classification models including Support Vector Machine (SVM), Bayesian Net, Naïve Bayes, and Decision Tree are selected to infer human interaction. The effectiveness of the four different inference algorithms, effect of different features and feature combinations are studied in the experiments.

The rest of this paper is organized as follows. In Section 2, we discuss related works. Section 3 introduces the multimodal approach for interaction inference, including human interaction definition, feature extraction, and inference models. In Section 4, the evaluation method and experimental results are presented. Finally, we conclude the paper in Section 5.

2 Related Work

Many smart meeting systems have been implemented in the past decade (see [1] for a full review). They can be roughly divided into two main categories. One is about providing adaptive services and relevant information in a meeting room by using ubiquitous sensors and context-awareness techniques, such as the Conference Assistant [2], EasyMeeting [3], and SMeet [4]. The other class aims at meeting capture and view, such as the MeetingAssistant [5], TeamSpace [6], the FXPAL's conference room [7], the ICSI's Meeting Corpus [8], and Junuzovic et al's 3D meeting viewer [9]. Unlike these systems, our study focuses on detecting human interactions and understanding their semantic meaning in meeting discussion.

Much research has been conducted on recognizing physical interactions in meetings. Stiefelhagen et al [11] proposed an approach for estimating who was talking to whom, based on tracked head poses of the participants. Otsuka et al [13] used gaze, head gestures, and utterances in determining interactions regarding who responds to whom in multiparty face-to-face conversations. The AMI project [14, 15] deals with interaction issues, including turn-taking and gaze behavior. Sumi et al [16] analyzed user interactions (e.g., gazing at an object, joint attention, and conversation) during poster presentation in an exhibition room. In general, the above-mentioned systems mainly focus on analyzing physical interactions between participants without any relation to the topics; in other words, they do not include semantic meanings in the analysis. Therefore, they cannot determine clearly a participant's attitude or role in a discussion.

A few systems attempted to analyze semantic information in meeting interactions. Hillard et al [17] proposed a classifier for the recognition of an individual's agreement or disagreement utterances using lexical and prosodic cues. The Discussion Ontology [18] was proposed for obtaining knowledge such as a statement's intention and the discussion flow in meetings. The Meeting Mediator at MIT [19] detects dominance in a meeting using sociometric feedback. Garg et al [20] proposed an approach to recognize participant roles in meetings. Our system differs in two aspects. First, besides inferring positive or negative opinions, we analyze more types of human semantic interactions in topic discussion such as proposing an idea, requesting information, and commenting on a topic. Second, our system adopts a multimodal approach for interaction inference by considering a variety of contexts (e.g., gestures, face orientation, speech tone), which provides robustness and reliability.

3   Multimodal Approach for Inferring Interaction

3.1   Human Interaction Definition

Human semantic interactions are defined as social behaviors among meeting participants corresponding to the current topic. Various interactions imply different user roles, attitudes, and intentions about a topic during a discussion. We created a set of interaction types including: *propose, comment, acknowledgement, requestInfo, askOpinion, posOpinion,* and *negOpinion.* The detailed meanings are as follows: *propose*—a user proposes an idea with respect to a topic; *comment*—a user comments on a proposal, or answers a question; *acknowledgement*—a user confirms someone else's comment or explanation, e.g., "yeah," "uh huh," and "OK"; *requestInfo*—a user requests unknown information about a topic; *askOpinion*—a user asks someone else's opinion about a proposal; *posOpinion*—a user expresses a positive opinion, i.e., supports a proposal; and *negOpinion*—a user expresses a negative opinion, i.e., disagrees with a proposal.

3.2 Feature Extraction

Our interaction inference is based on such features as head gestures, attention from others, speech tone, speaking time, interaction occasion, and the type of the previous interaction. These features are extracted from raw audio–visual and motion data recorded with video cameras, microphones, and motion sensors [21].

Head gesture. Head gestures (e.g., nodding and shaking of the head) are very common, and are often used in detecting human response (acknowledgement, agreement, or disagreement).

We determine nodding through the vertical component of the face vector calculated from the position data. We first determine the maximum and minimum values of the vertical component of the face vector in a time window (here, we set one second). Next, we calculate θ_1 (the difference between the maximum and minimum values) and θ_2 (the difference between the current value and the minimum). Then the nodding score is calculated as: $Score = (\theta_1/11.5) \times (\theta_2/11.5)$. Here, 11.5 is empirically set as the normalization constant. If the calculated score is above a preset threshold (e.g., 0.80), we consider the head gesture to be nodding.

Head-shaking is detected through the horizontal component of the face vector. We first calculate a projection vector of the face vector on the horizontal plane. To distinguish head-shaking from normal changes in facial orientation, we count the switchback points of the projection vector's movement in a time window (e.g., 2 s). If the number of switchback points is larger than the preset threshold (e.g., 2), we consider that it is a shaking action.

Attention from others. Attention from others is an important determinant of human interaction. For example, when a user is proposing an idea, he is usually being looked at by most of the participants. The number of people looking at the target user during the interaction can be determined by their face orientation. We measure the angles between the reference vectors (from the target person's head to the other persons' heads) and the target user's real face vector (calculated from the position data). Face orientation is determined as the one whose vector makes the smallest angle.

Speech tone and speaking time. Speech tone indicates whether an utterance is a question or a non-question statement. Speaking time is another important indicator in detecting the type of interaction. When a user puts forward a proposal, it usually takes a relatively longer time, but it takes a short time to acknowledge or ask a question. Speech tone and speaking time are automatically determined using the Julius speech recognition engine [22], which segments the input sound data into speech durations by detecting silence intervals longer than 0.3 s. We classify segments as questions or non-questions using the pitch pattern of the speech based on Hidden Markov Models [23] trained with each person's speech data. The speaking time is derived from the duration of a segment.

Interaction occasion. Interaction occasion is a binary variable that indicates whether an interaction is spontaneous or reactive. In the former case, the interaction is initiated spontaneously by a person (e.g., proposing an idea or asking a question). The latter denotes an interaction triggered in response to another interaction. Discussion tags [18] can be used to explicitly indicate the interaction occasion. We manually label this feature in our current system. Automatic extraction method will be explored in our future research.

Type of the previous interaction. The type of the previous interaction also plays an important role in detecting the current interaction. It is intuitive that certain patterns or flows frequently occur in the course of a discussion in a meeting. For instance, *propose* and *requestInfo* are usually followed by a *comment*. This feature can be obtained from the recognition result of the previous interaction.

3.3 Inference Model

Four kinds of classification models, including Support Vector Machine (SVM), Bayesian Net, Naïve Bayes, and Decision Tree are selected to infer the type of each interaction. In our system, the LIBSVM library [24] is used for SVM (RBF kernel) classifier implementation while Weka 3.5 toolkit [25] is adopted to implement Bayesian Net, Naïve Bayes, and Decision Tree (REPTree).

Before learning and inference, we need to represent each data instance as a vector of real numbers. For the attributes with continuous values (e.g., speaking time and attention from others), we use their original values in the vector. If an attribute has categorical values (e.g., head gesture and speech tone), we use linear numbers to represent it. For instance, head gesture is a three-category attribute {nodding, shaking, normal}, which is represented as 0, 1, and 2. The learning and testing data is prepared with the format that LIBSVM and Weka can process.

The meeting content is first segmented into a sequence of interactions. Sample interactions are selected and fed into the classifiers as learning data, while others are used as a testing set. We will compare the performance of these four inference models in the experiments.

4   Experiments

In this section, we first describe the experiment method including experiment schema, meeting capture, and evaluation metrics. We then report detailed experimental results with corresponding discussions.

4.1 Experimental Method

Fig. 1 shows the schema of our experiment. It includes five steps: meeting capture, segmentation, feature extraction, interaction inference, and evaluation. Segmentation is performed according to speech signal. Feature extraction and interaction inference have been depicted in Section 3. We here focus on the meeting data capture and evaluation methods.

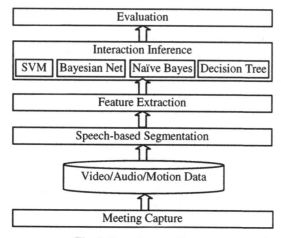

Fig. 1. Experiment schema

Meeting capture. We use multiple devices such as video cameras, microphones, and motion sensors for capturing human interactions. Please refer to our earlier paper [21] for details about meeting capture.

We captured a total of four meetings, one PC purchase meeting (26 min, discussing about PCs to be ordered for the laboratory, such as types, configuration, size, weight, manufacturer, etc.), one trip planning meeting (18 min, discussing time, place, activities, and transportation for a summer trip), one soccer preparation meeting (23 min, talking about the players and their roles and positions in an upcoming match), and one job selection meeting (10 min, talking about factors that will be considered in seeking a job, such as salary, working place, employer, position, interest, etc.). Each meeting had four participants seated around a table. In the former three meetings, one of the participants played as a main speaker by showing slides on a screen. The participants in the PC purchase meeting were different from those in the trip planning and soccer preparation meetings. No slides were used in the job selection meeting and all participants were freely and equally discussing. We aim to enrich our experimental data by capturing meetings with different persons and styles.

Evaluation metrics. We would like to test the effectiveness of the four different inference algorithms, effect of meeting diversity, accuracy of different interaction types, effect of different features and feature combinations, etc.. With respect to the inference accuracy of interaction, we use the typical evaluation criteria of recognition rate by number (R_N):

$$R_N = \frac{m}{N}$$

where N stands for the total number of the interactions after being partitioned by a segmentation method while m denotes the number of interactions our approach correctly infers their types.

4.2 Results

Experiment 1: Comparison of different inference models. We used the four inference models to learn and test interaction types. The inference accuracy is shown in Fig. 2. In this experiment, all of the four meetings were used. We utilized the same meeting data for learning and testing, i.e., part of a particular meeting (e.g., trip meeting) was fed into the inference models as training data, while the other data of the same meeting (e.g., trip meeting) was used as the testing set. All of the four inference algorithms can correctly recognize over 65 percentage interactions with respect to all the four meetings. If we take the four meetings into account, we can see the SVM outperforms other models. It got recognition rates above 80% corresponding to the PC-purchase meeting and job-selection meeting, while the other meetings' rate around 75%. The performance of Bayesian Net is very close to the SVM. It even performs better in recognizing interactions in the PC-purchase meeting, but worse in the other three meetings. The Naïve Bayes is the worst. Consequently, we used the SVM inference model in the following experiments.

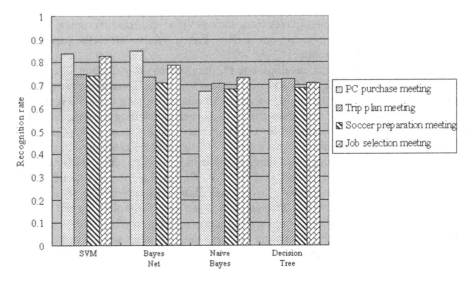

Fig. 2. Recognition rate of different inference models

Experiment 2: Effect of training with different meetings. In this experiment, we used different meeting data for training and testing (e.g., using trip meeting to test soccer meeting). The experimental results are depicted in Table 1. The SVM inference model was adopted. The element in position (i, j) is the recognition accuracy of testing meeting j by using meeting i as training data. For instance, the table shows that by using the training data from the soccer meeting to test the trip meeting, it achieved an accuracy of 0.726. We can observe that the accuracies of using the same meeting data for training and testing are usually higher than those of training with different meeting data. But the differences are not substantial. The results indicate that our model can be trained once and used to test other meetings. Also different meeting participants and styles do not have much influence on the results. To our surprise, training soccer meeting to test PC-purchase meeting is better than to test itself (0.775 vs. 0.743). We expect the values of (i, i) elements to be the largest in the same line and column. So far we have no satisfactory explanation for this exception but we plan to investigate this further in detail in future study.

Table 1. Recognition accuracy by training with different meetings

	PC	Trip	Soccer	Job
PC	**0.838**	0.747	0.689	0.718
Trip	0.713	0.747	0.676	0.709
Soccer	**0.775**	0.726	0.743	0.742
Job	0.740	0.632	0.610	0.826

Experiment 3: Evaluation of different interaction types. We test the effectiveness of the SVM inference model in recognizing different interaction types in this experiment. The PC-purchase meeting data is selected, within which 189 interactions were chosen as the learning set, and the other 80 were used for testing. Table 2 shows the inference results for different interactions. We can observe that the algorithm performs well in recognizing the categories of *comment, acknowledgment, reqestInfo*, and *posOpinion*. This also indicates that these four types of interactions can be easily detected with the current feature setting. The other three categories (*propose, askOpinion*, and *negOpinion*) are difficult to recognize. In particular, all the *propose* interactions were wrongly classified into the category of *comment*, and the *askOpinion* was often confused with the category of *reqestInfo*. Surprisingly, recognition was much better in detecting *posOpinion* than *negOpinion*. We would have expected the *negOpinion* class to perform well, as we used head shaking to signal disagreement. However, there were very few shaking actions during the meeting. The participants usually expressed their positive opinions explicitly but indicated disagreement implicitly.

Table 2. Recognition results for different interactions

Interaction type	Recognition accuracy
propose	0.000
comment	**0.875**
acknowledgment	**0.966**
reqestInfo	**0.889**
askOpinion	0.500
posOpinion	0.667
negOpinion	0.000

Experiment 4: Single feature exploration. In this experiment we examined the contribution of each of the six features to the interaction inference. Table 3 shows the result of each feature in stand-alone discriminating the seven interaction types. The SVM model

and PC-purchase meeting data were utilized. As we can see, head gesture and speaking time outperform other features, and attention from others and the type of previous interaction also show their advantages over speech tone and interaction occasion.

Table 3. Interaction recognition accuracy using each feature alone

Feature	Recognition accuracy
Head gesture	**0.638**
Attention from others	0.600
Speech tone	0.500
Speaking time	0.625
Interaction occasion	0.550
Type of previous interaction	0.600

Experiment 5: Effect of different feature combinations. To test the effect of different feature combinations on interaction inference, different feature subsets were configured and fed into the SVM inference model. In this test, the PC-purchase meeting data was used. The feature set configuration and recognition results are presented in Table 4. There are a total of six different feature subsets in this experiment. Set 1 contains features about head movement (i.e., head gesture and attention from others), Set 2 includes speech related features (i.e., speech tone and speaking time), and Set 3 consists of high-level features about occasion and previous interaction. Then Sets 4, 5, 6 are combinations of basic feature subsets, Sets 1 and 2, Sets 1 and 3, and Sets 2 and 3, respectively. From the results shown in Table 4, first we can observe that the basic combination of speech features (Set 2) is more effective than that of head movement (Set 1) and occasion and previous interaction (Set 3). On the other hand, by combining head movement and speech features (Set 4), speech, occasion and previous

Table 4. Interaction recognition results with different feature subsets (f1: head gesture, f2: attention from others, f3: speech tone, f4: speaking time, f5: interaction occasion, f6: type of previous interaction)

Feature sets	Recognition accuracy
Set 1 – features about head movement: {f1, f2 }	0.650
Set 2 – features about speech: {f3, f4}	0.713
Set 3 – features about occasion and previous interaction: {f5, f6}	0.700
Set 4 – features about head movement and speech: {f1, f2, f3, f4}	**0.788**
Set 5 – features about head movement, occasion and previous interaction: {f1, f2, f5, f6}	0.675
Set 6 – features about speech, occasion and previous interaction: {f3, f4, f5, f6}	**0.788**

interaction (Set 6), we scored the same high accuracy (i.e., 0.788). However, adding head movement to occasion and previous interaction (Set 5), we could not improve the inference performance as we expected, but degrade by 0.025 in accuracy (from 0.700 to 0.675). This might be caused by the correlation between features of head movement and interaction occasion as well as previous interaction. We need to investigate our inference model and features further, and also enrich the experimental data to learn a more robust model. According to the results derived from Experiments 4 and 5, combinations of more features, roughly speaking, outperform those of fewer features, showing that multimodal fusion can be successful.

5 Conclusion and Future Work

In this paper, we proposed a multimodal approach to infer human interactions in meetings based on a variety of features. Our work would be helpful for understanding how people are interacting in a meeting discussion. We evaluated our approach using four real meetings lasting around 80 minutes. The experimental result showed that SVM outperformed other inference models in interaction recognition. It also verified that our multimodal approach achieved robust and reliable results by overcoming single modality limitations and difficulties in recognition.

We envision several enhancements to our approach. First, in our current system, the high-level feature of interaction occasion (spontaneous or reactive) is extracted manually, which might reduce the usability of the approach in real-life settings. We plan to recognize it automatically based on several basic features, e.g., gaze and speaking time. For instance, when a person gives a spontaneous interaction, he or she usually looks through most participants in the meeting and speaks relatively long. Second, to improve the interaction inference accuracy, we will incorporate more contexts (e.g., lexical cues) into the detection process.

Acknowledgments. This work was partially supported by the National Natural Science Foundation of China (No. 60803044), the Specialized Research Fund for the Doctoral Program of Higher Education (No. 20070699014), the Doctorate Foundation of Northwestern Polytechnical University of China (No. CX200814), and the Ministry of Education, Culture, Sports, Science and Technology, Japan under the project of "Cyber Infrastructure for the Information-explosion Era".

References

1. Yu, Z., Nakamura, Y.: Smart Meeting Systems: A Survey of State-of-the-Art and Open Issues. ACM Computing Surveys 41(3) (2009)
2. Dey, A.K., Salber, D., Abowd, G.D., Futakawa, M.: The Conference Assistant: Combining Context-Awareness with Wearable Computing. In: Proc. ISWC 1999, pp. 21–28 (1999)
3. Chen, H., Finin, T., Joshi, A.: A Context Broker for Building Smart Meeting Rooms. In: Proc. of the Knowledge Representation and Ontology for autonomous systems symposium (AAAI spring symposium), pp. 53–60 (2004)
4. Kim, N., Han, S., Kim, J.W.: Design of Software Architecture for Smart Meeting Space. In: Proc. PerCom 2008, pp. 543–547 (2008)

5. Yu, Z., Ozeki, M., Fujii, Y., Nakamura, Y.: Towards Smart Meeting: Enabling Technologies and a Real-World Application. In: Proc. ICMI 2007, pp. 86–93 (2007)
6. Geyer, W., Richter, H., Abowd, G.D.: Towards a Smarter Meeting Record – Capture and Access of Meetings Revisited. Multimedia Tools and Applications 27(3), 393–410 (2005)
7. Chiu, P., Kapuskar, A., Reitmeier, S., Wilcox, L.: Room with a Rear View: Meeting Capture in a Multimedia Conference Room. IEEE Multimedia 7(4), 48–54 (2000)
8. Janin, A., et al.: The ICSI Meeting Project: Resources and Research. In: Proc. of NIST ICASSP Meeting Recognition Workshop (2004)
9. Junuzovic, S., Hegde, R., Zhang, Z., Chou, P.A., Liu, Z., Zhang, C.: Requirements and Recommendations for an Enhanced Meeting Viewing Experience. In: Proc. ACM Multimedia 2008, pp. 539–548 (2008)
10. DiMicco, J.M., et al.: The Impact of Increased Awareness While Face-to-Face. Human-Computer Interaction 22(1), 47–96 (2007)
11. Stiefelhagen, R., Chen, X., Yang, J.: Capturing Interactions in Meetings with Omnidirectional Cameras. International Journal of Distance Education Technologies 3(3), 34–47 (2005)
12. Yu, H., Finke, M., Waibel, A.: Progress in Automatic Meeting Transcription. In: Proc. of 6th European Conference on Speech Communication and Technology (Eurospeech-1999), vol. 2, pp. 695–698 (1999)
13. Otsuka, K., Sawada, H., Yamato, J.: Automatic Inference of Cross-modal Nonverbal Interactions in Multiparty Conversations. In: Proc. ICMI 2007, pp. 255–262 (2007)
14. Nijholt, A., Rienks, R.J., Zwiers, J., Reidsma, D.: Online and Off-line Visualization of Meeting Information and Meeting Support. The Visual Computer 22(12), 965–976 (2006)
15. Nijholt, A., Zwiers, J., Peciva, J.: Mixed reality participants in smart meeting rooms and smart home environments. Personal and Ubiquitous Computing 13(1), 85–94 (2009)
16. Sumi, Y., et al.: Collaborative capturing, interpreting, and sharing of experiences. Personal and Ubiquitous Computing 11(4), 265–271 (2007)
17. Hillard, D., Ostendorf, M., Shriberg, E.: Detection of Agreement vs. Disagreement in Meetings: Training with Unlabeled Data. In: Proc. HLT-NAACL 2003, pp. 34–36 (2003)
18. Tomobe, H., Nagao, K.: Discussion Ontology: Knowledge Discovery from Human Activities in Meetings. In: Washio, T., Satoh, K., Takeda, H., Inokuchi, A. (eds.) JSAI 2006. LNCS, vol. 4384, pp. 33–41. Springer, Heidelberg (2007)
19. Kim, T., Chang, A., Holland, L., Pentland, A.: Meeting Mediator: Enhancing Group Collaboration using Sociometric Feedback. In: Proc. CSCW 2008, pp. 457–466 (2008)
20. Garg, N.P., Favre, S., Salamin, H., Tur, D.H., Vinciarelli, A.: Role Recognition for Meeting Participants: an Approach Based on Lexical Information and Social Network Analysis. In: Proc. ACM Multimedia 2008, pp. 693–696 (2008)
21. Yu, Z., Aoyama, H., Ozeki, M., Nakamura, Y.: Collaborative Capturing and Detection of Human Interactions in Meetings. In: Adjunct Proc. of PERVASIVE 2008, pp. 65–69 (2008)
22. Julius speech recognition engine (2008), http://julius.sourceforge.jp/en/
23. Rabiner, L.: A tutorial on Hidden Markov Models and selected applications in speech recognition. Proc. IEEE 77(2), 257–286 (1989)
24. Chang, C.C., Lin, C.J.: LIBSVM: a library for support vector machines (2001), http://www.csie.ntu.edu.tw/~cjlin/libsvm
25. Weka (2008), http://www.cs.waikato.ac.nz/ml/weka/

Gesture Recognition with a 3-D Accelerometer

Jiahui Wu[1], Gang Pan[1], Daqing Zhang[2], Guande Qi[1], and Shijian Li[1]

[1] Department of Computer Science
Zhejiang University, Hangzhou, 310027, China
{cat_ng,gpan,shijianli}@zju.edu.cn
[2] Handicom Lab, Institut TELECOM SudParis, France
daqing.zhang@it-sudparis.eu

Abstract. Gesture-based interaction, as a natural way for human-computer interaction, has a wide range of applications in ubiquitous computing environment. This paper presents an acceleration-based gesture recognition approach, called *FDSVM* (Frame-based Descriptor and multi-class SVM), which needs only a wearable 3-dimensional accelerometer. With FDSVM, firstly, the acceleration data of a gesture is collected and represented by a frame-based descriptor, to extract the discriminative information. Then a SVM-based multi-class gesture classifier is built for recognition in the nonlinear gesture feature space. Extensive experimental results on a data set with 3360 gesture samples of 12 gestures over weeks demonstrate that the proposed FDSVM approach significantly outperforms other four methods: DTW, Naïve Bayes, C4.5 and HMM. In the user-dependent case, FDSVM achieves the recognition rate of 99.38% for the 4 direction gestures and 95.21% for all the 12 gestures. In the user-independent case, it obtains the recognition rate of 98.93% for 4 gestures and 89.29% for 12 gestures. Compared to other accelerometer-based gesture recognition approaches reported in literature FDSVM gives the best resulrs for both user-dependent and user-independent cases.

1 Introduction

As computation is getting to play an important role in enhancing the quality of life, more and more research has been directed towards natural human-computer interaction. In a smart environment, people usually hope to use the most natural and convenient ways to express their intentions and interact with the environment. Button pressing, often used in the remote control panel, provides the most traditional means of giving commands to household appliances. Such kind of operation, however, is not natural and sometimes even inconvenient, especially for elders or visually disabled people who are not able to distinguish the buttons on the device. In this regard, gesture-based interaction offers an alternative way in a smart environment.

Most of previous work on gesture recognition has been based on computer vision techniques [12]. However, the performance of such vision-based approaches depends strongly on the lighting condition and camera facing angles, which greatly restricts its applications in the smart environments. Suppose you are enjoying movies in your home theater with all the lights off. If you intend to change the volume of TV with gesture, it turns out to be rather difficult to accurately recognize the gesture under poor lighting condition using a camera based system. In addition, it is also uncomfortable

D. Zhang et al. (Eds.): UIC 2009, LNCS 5585, pp. 25–38, 2009.
© Springer-Verlag Berlin Heidelberg 2009

and inconvenient if you are always required to face the camera directly to complete a gesture.

Gesture recognition from accelerometer data is an emerging technique for gesture-based interaction, which suits well the requirements in ubiquitous computing environments. With the rapid development of the MEMS (Micro Electrical Mechanical System) technology, people can wear/carry one or more accelerometer-equipped devices in daily life, for example, Apple iPhone [21], Nintendo Wiimote [22]. These wireless-enabled mobile/wearable devices provide new possibilities for interacting with a wide range of applications, such as home appliances, mixed reality, etc.

The first step of accelerometer-based gesture recognition system is to get the time series of a gesture motion. Previous studies have adopted specific devices to capture acceleration data of a gesture. For example, TUB-Sensor Glove [23] can collect hand orientation and acceleration, and finger joint angles. Tsukada [2] designed a finger-based gesture input device with IR transmitter, touch sensor, bend sensor and acceleration sensor. Mäntyjärvi [4] put a sensor box into a phone in order to detect 3-axis acceleration of users' hand motion. Now most accelerometers can capture three-axis acceleration data, i.e. 3D accelerometers, which convey more motion information than 2D accelerometers. They have been embedded into several commercial products such as iPhone [21] and Wiimote [22]. This paper employs Wiimote as the gesture input device for experimental set-up and performance evaluation.

To recognize a gesture from the captured data, researchers have applied diverse machine learning and pattern recognition techniques. The main algorithms in the literature are DTW (dynamic time warping)-based approach [17,18,20] and HMM (hidden Markov model) -based approach [1,5,6,7,24]. Both sets of algorithms process the acceleration data in the time domain. For example, in the seminal work of acceleration-based gesture recognition [7], the acceleration data is fed to HMM immediately after vector quantization. The DTW-based approach also exploited the acceleration data directly without doing feature extraction. Besides, Cho[16] utilizes Bayesian Networks using local maxima and minima as features to identify the majority of the selected gestures and further adopts binary-class SVM to discriminate the confusion gesture pair. Most of previous work on accelerometer-based gesture recognition performed matching or modeling in time domain, there is no feature extraction stage, which may result in sensitiveness of noise and variation of gesture data. We believe that a good feature extraction method can not only give a compact informative representation of a gesture, but also reduce the noise and variation of a gesture data to improve the recognition performance.

There are usually two ways to evaluate the performance of the gesture recognition algorithms: *user-dependent* and *user-independent*. Previous work focuses more on user-dependent gesture recognition [1,6,18], in which each user is required to perform a couple of gestures as training/template samples before using the system. One of the solutions to this problem is to reduce the user efforts in training by adding artificial noise to the original gesture data to augment the training data [5]. The user-independent gesture recognition does not require a user to enroll any gesture samples for the system before using it, where the model for classification has been well-trained before and the algorithm does not depend on users. The user-independent gesture recognition is more difficult than the user-dependent one since there is much more variation for each same gesture.

This paper addresses the gesture recognition problem using only one three-axis accelerometer. In order to reduce the effect of the intra-class variation and noise, we introduce a frame-based feature extraction stage to accelerometer-based gesture recognition. A gesture descriptor combining spectral features and temporal features is presented. The SVM-based gesture classification is proposed to deal with the highly nonlinear gesture space issue and the limited sample size problem. To evaluate our method, we conduct both the user-dependent experiments and the user-independent ones.

2 Frame-Based Gesture Descriptor

2.1 Frame-based Gesture Descriptor

An accelerometer can sense discretely the acceleration data of three spatial orthogonal axes in each gesture in a certain sampling frequency. We can denote a gesture as:

$$G = (a_x, a_y, a_z) \tag{1}$$

where $a_T = (a_T^0, a_T^1, ..., a_T^{L-1})$, $T = x, y, z$, is the acceleration vector of an axis and L is the length of the temporal sequence.

To describe the whole gesture but distinguish the periods from each other, we divide a gesture into $N+1$ segments identical in length, and then every two adjunct segments make up a *frame* (cf. Fig. 1), which thus can be represented as R_k as follows:

$$R_k = (r_{x,k}, r_{y,k}, r_{z,k}), k = 0, ..., N-1, \tag{2}$$

$$r_{T,k} = (r_{T,k}^0, r_{T,k}^1, ..., r_{T,k}^{L_s \cdot 2 - 1}), T = x, y, z, \tag{3}$$

$$r_{T,k}^n = a_T^{L_s \cdot k + n}, n = 0, ..., L_s \cdot 2 - 1, \tag{4}$$

where $L_s = \lfloor L/(N+1) \rfloor$ is the length of a segment. Each two adjunct frames have a segment-length overlap, as shown in Fig.1.

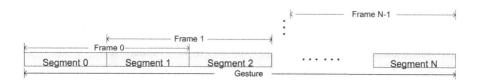

Fig. 1. Illustration of segments and frames for a gesture

Given a feature-type set $\mathscr{F}$ which describe the characteristics of a signal sequence, we can select a subset $F = \{f^{(i)}\}$, $i = 1, ..., n$, $f^{(i)} \in \mathscr{F}$ to describe one frame of a gesture based on a single axis. Since there are 3 axes and totally N frames per gesture, we combine all features to form a vector, whose dimension is $d=3 \cdot n \cdot N$. More specifically, a gesture can be represented as:

$$
\tau = (f_{x,0}^{(1)}, \quad f_{y,0}^{(1)}, \quad f_{z,0}^{(1)}, \quad f_{x,0}^{(2)}, \quad f_{y,0}^{(2)}, \quad f_{z,0}^{(2)}, \cdots, \quad f_{x,0}^{(n)}, f_{y,0}^{(n)}, f_{z,0}^{(n)},
$$
$$
\cdots \cdots
$$
$$
f_{x,N-1}^{(1)}, f_{y,N-1}^{(1)}, f_{z,N-1}^{(1)}, f_{x,N-1}^{(2)}, f_{y,N-1}^{(2)}, f_{z,N-1}^{(2)}, \cdots, f_{x,N-1}^{(n)}, f_{y,N-1}^{(n)}, f_{z,N-1}^{(n)}). \tag{5}
$$

Intuitively, more frames a gesture is broken up into, more details we know about the gesture. However, it may lead to the over-fitting problem if the frame number N becomes large. It will also increase the dimension of the feature space, which increases computational complexity. We will conduct an experiment to determine the optimal frame number N later.

2.2 Features for One Frame

According to the signal processing theory, features in the frequency domain have rich information about the signal. Hence not only the temporal features but also spectral features should be included in the feature-type set $\mathscr{F}$ to describe a single frame. In this paper, we make up the feature-type set $\mathscr{F}$ by combining the *mean μ, energy ε* and *entropy δ* in frequency domain and *standard deviation σ* of the amplitude and *correlation γ* among the axes in time-space domain, whose subsets will be utilized to describe a gesture:

$$
\mathscr{F}=\{\mu, \varepsilon, \delta, \sigma, \gamma\}. \tag{6}
$$

To obtain the features in frequency domain, we firstly employ a discrete Fourier transform (DFT) on each frame per axis to build a spectrum-based gesture representation:

$$
t_{T,k}^m = \sum_{n=0}^{L_s \cdot 2-1} r_{T,k}^n e^{-\frac{2\pi i}{L_s \cdot 2-1}kn},
$$
$$
T = x, y, z,
$$
$$
k = 0, \dots, N-1, \tag{7}
$$
$$
m = 0, \dots, L_s \cdot 2 - 1
$$

Afterwards, three spectral features are extracted from a frame: Mean μ , Energy ε and Entropy σ. Bao et al.[19] have successfully applied these three features in activity recognition. The mean feature is the DC component of the frequency domain over the frame:

$$
\mu_{T,k} = t_{T,k}^0 \tag{8}
$$

The energy feature is the sum of all the squared DFT component magnitudes except the DC component of the signal, for the DC component has be used as an individual feature μ. The sum is divided by the number of the components for the purpose of normalization:

$$\varepsilon_{T,k} = \frac{\sum_{n=1}^{L_s \cdot 2 - 1} |t_{T,k}^n|^2}{|L_s \cdot 2 - 1|} \tag{9}$$

The entropy feature is the normalized information entropy of the DFT component magnitudes, where the DC component is also excluded:

$$\delta_{T,k} = \sum_{m=1}^{L_s \cdot 2 - 1} p_{T,k}^m \log(\frac{1}{p_{T,k}^m}) \tag{10}$$

$$p_{T,k}^m = \frac{|t_{T,k}^m|}{\sum_{n=1}^{L_s \cdot 2 - 1} |t_{T,k}^n|} \tag{11}$$

In the time domain, two features, i.e., standard deviation σ and correlation γ are obtained. Standard deviation of a gesture indicates the amplitude variability of a gesture, whose magnitude is equivalent with the other features compared with deviation:

$$\sigma_{T,k} = \sqrt{\sum_{n=0}^{L_s \cdot 2 - 1} (r_{T,k}^n - \bar{r}_{T,k}^n)^2} \tag{12}$$

$$\bar{r}_{T,k}^n = \frac{r_{T,k}^n}{\sum_{n=0}^{L_s \cdot 2 - 1} r_{T,k}^i} \tag{13}$$

The correlation feature implies the strength of a linear relationship between two axis:

$$\gamma_{T_1 \sim T_2, k} = \frac{v_{T_1 \sim T_2, k}^n - \bar{r}_{T_1, k}^n \cdot \bar{r}_{T_2, k}^n}{\sqrt{v_{T_1 \sim T_1, k}^n - (\bar{r}_{T_1, k}^n)^2} \cdot \sqrt{v_{T_2 \sim T_2, k}^n - (\bar{r}_{T_2, k}^n)^2}} \tag{14}$$

$$v_{T_1 \sim T_2, k}^n = \frac{\sum_{n=0}^{L_s \cdot 2 - 1} |r_{T_1, k}^n \cdot r_{T_2, k}^n|}{L_s \cdot 2} \tag{15}$$

$$T_1, T_2 = x, y, z$$

3 SVM-Based Gesture Classification

The Support Vector Machine (SVM) [11] is a small sample size method based on statistic learning theory. It is a new method to deal with the highly nonlinear classification and regression problems. SVM has been widely used in various applications, for example, gender classification [14], face detection [15], activity recognition [8].

When there are limited training data available, SVM usually outperforms the traditional parameter estimation methods which are based on Law of Large Numbers, since it benefits from structural risk minimization principle and avoidance of over-fitting by its soft margin. SVM originally is used to solve the binary-class classification problems in the sense that it aims at finding the maximum-margin hyperplane that separates two classes of samples in the feature space.

Suppose there are two type of gestures $GTR1$, $GTR2$ needed to be classified. We denote the training set with n samples as

$$\{(\tau_i, g_i)\}, \quad i=1,\ldots,n \tag{16}$$

where $\tau_i \in R^d$ represents a feature vector of a gesture like (5) and

$$g_i = \begin{cases} +1, & if \ \tau_i \ belongs \ to \ GTR1 \\ -1, & if \ \tau_i \ belongs \ to \ GTR2 \end{cases} \tag{17}$$

A separating plane can be written as

$$w \cdot \tau + b = 0. \tag{18}$$

The dual representation of margin maximum problem is:

Maximize: $W(\alpha) = \sum_{i=1}^{n} \alpha_i - \frac{1}{2}\sum_{i,j=1}^{n} g_i g_j \alpha_i \alpha_j K(\tau_i, \tau_j)$ $\qquad$ (19)

s.t. $\sum_{i=1}^{n} g_i \alpha_i = 0$ $\qquad\qquad\qquad\qquad\qquad\qquad$ (20)

$$0 \leq \alpha_i \leq C \qquad i=1,\ldots,n \tag{21}$$

where α_i is the Lagrange factor and $K(\tau_i, \tau_j)$ is the kernel function [11]. Then the classification function would be:

$$f(x) = \text{sgn}(h(x)), \tag{22}$$

$$h(x) = \sum_{i=1}^{n} \alpha_i^* g_i K(\tau_i, \tau_j) + b^* \tag{23}$$

where α_i^*, b^* is the optimal solution of (19).

A gesture recognition system is supposed to recognize more than two types of gestures. For this reason, a multi-class SVM is required. The predominant approach is to convert a multi-class problem into several binary-class problems. Two typical strategies are available to build up a multi-class classifier: one-versus-one and one-versus-all (cf. Fig. 2). The former is to distinguish every pair of gestures and select the winner with more votes; the latter is to distinguish each type from the rest and select the one with largest output $|h(x)|$ in Equation (23). Figure 2 demonstrates the two strategies in classification of four types of gestures. For convenience of visualization, each gesture is represented by a 2D mean feature -- X-mean and Y-mean as shown in Equation (8).

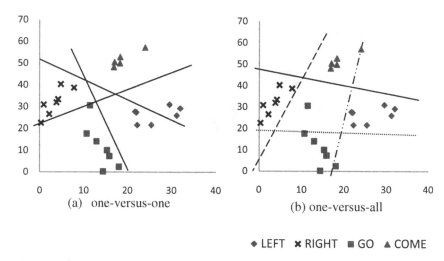

(a) one-versus-one   (b) one-versus-all

♦ LEFT ✕ RIGHT ■ GO ▲ COME

Fig. 2. Illustration of SVM classification of the four gestures LEFT, RIGHT, GO, COME. For visualization simplicity, each gesture is represented by a 2D mean feature. (a) illustrates the one-versus-one strategy by giving the separating lines between COME and one of the other three gestures. (b) shows the one-versus-all strategy by giving the separating lines between a gesture and the rest three ones.

4 Experiments

To evaluate the presented gesture recognition approach FDSVM, we implemented the gesture recognition system and collected a data set with 12 gestures of 10 individuals over two weeks. Three experiments were designed and reported in this section: the first one aimed at determining the optimal frame number N ; the second and the third ones were to evaluate the recognition performance for user-dependent and user-independent gesture recognition respectively.

4.1 Data Collection

To evaluate our system, we collected a gesture acceleration data set with 12 gestures of 10 individuals. We adopted *Wiimote*, the controller of Nintendo Wii equipped with a 3D accelerometer, to acquire gesture acceleration data. It can transmit users' gesture motion acceleration data via Bluetooth. The accelerometer samples at a rate of nearly 100Hz. The start and end of a gesture were labeled by pressing the A button on the Wiimote during data acquisition. Figure 3 illustrates the acquisition devices.

In order to evaluate our gesture recognition algorithm, we choose three kinds of typical gestures: 4 direction gestures, 3 shape gestures, 5 one-stroke alphabet letters (the other 4 one-stroke letters, "O, L, U, M", are not included since 'O' is similar to CIRCLE, 'L' is similar to RIGHT-ANGLE, 'U' is similar to 'V', and 'W' is close to 'M'), as illustrated in Fig.4. These twelve gestures are divided into four groups (cf. Table 1) for evaluating the recognition performance. The first group is for direction gestures, the second for direction gestures plus shape gestures, the third is for one-stroke letters, and the last group is for all 12 gestures.

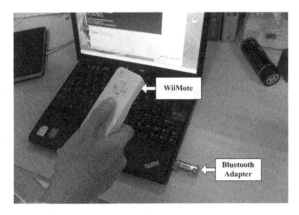

Fig. 3. Acquisition devices of gesture acceleration data

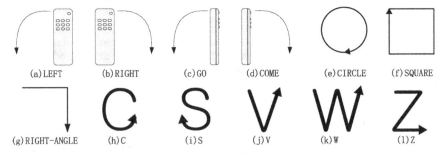

Fig. 4. Twelve gestures in the data set. (a) – (d) describe the gestures to swing the remote to left, right, forward or backward centered at the bottom point of the remote. (e) – (l) describe the gestures to draw a shape or letter.

Ten people participated in the data collection, including two female and eight male students aged between 21 and 25. Each student was asked to perform each gesture for 28 times over two weeks, namely 336 gesture samples in total. Every 12 different gestures performed sequentially was regarded as one set of gesture data. In order to consider variability of user performance, a participant was not allowed to perform more than two sets each time and not more than twice per day. Some acceleration data samples of the same gesture from a single participant are depicted in Fig.5, which obviously demonstrate the large variation of a gesture.

Table 1. Twelve gestures are divided into 4 groups for extensive evaluation

No.	Group Name	Included Gestures
1	Direction	LEFT, RIGHT, GO, COME
2	Direction+Shape	LEFT, RIGHT, GO, COME, CIRCLE, SQUARE, RIGHT-ANGLE
3	One-stroke Letter	C, S, V, W, Z, CIRCLE(O), RIGHT-ANGLE(L)
4	All	LEFT, RIGHT, GO, COME, CIRCLE, SQUARE, RIGHT-ANGLE, C, S, V, W, Z

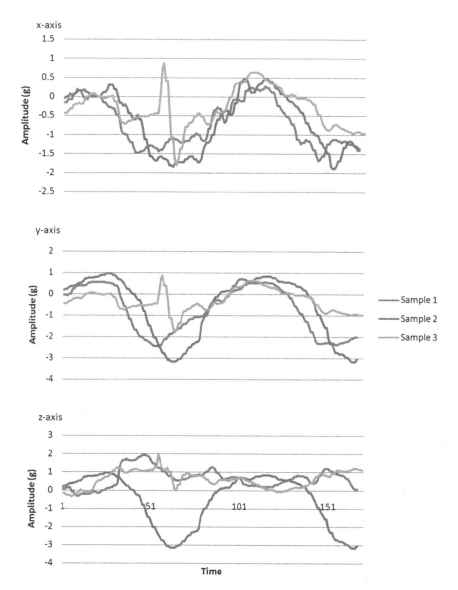

Fig. 5. Variation of a gesture for the same person . The three acceleration samples are from the gesture 'W' of the same person, shown in x-axis, y-axis, z-axis respectively. The three samples were performed at different time.

We employed the *4-fold cross validation* for the user-dependent case and the *leave-one-person-out cross validation* for the user-independent case. For the 4-fold cross validation, we divided 28 samples of the same gesture into four partitions, namely 7 samples per partition. At each time, one of the four partitions is for testing; the other three partitions are for training. We repeated it four times and finally took the average recognition rate. For the leave-one-person-out cross validation, the samples from one participant of ten are used as the testing data and the other nine participants' data as the training data.

4.2 Implementation of the System

The gesture recognition system has four main components: acceleration data acquisition, feature extraction, training phase, and recognition phase, as shown in Fig. 6. The *Acceleration Data Acquisition* is conducted with a Wiimote device, followed by the data transfer to a PC through Bluetooth. The continuous data streams are divided into individual gesture according to the A-button pressing label.

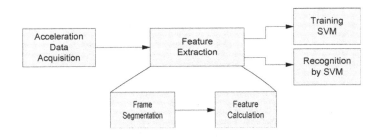

Fig. 6. Major components of the gesture recognition system

For the *feature extraction* of each gesture, firstly, it is divided into N frames (see Section 2). *Fourier transformation* is then employed on each frame, which uses an open source software package of FFTW [9]. Features *mean, energy, entropy, correlation,* and *standard deviation* of individual axis in one frame are calculated using equation (7)-(15), combined as a feature vector using (9).

The feature vector is eventually put into a classifier in order to train an SVM model or retrieve a recognized gesture type. The SVM component utilizes the open source package SVM$^{multi-class}$[10].

4.3 Experiment 1: Effect of Frame Number N

The purpose of analyzing a gesture in frames rather than in a whole is to describe its local characteristics corresponding to time span. The frame count N indicates the precision we know about a gesture. Yet increasing the number N results in higher computational complexity. This experiment is to examine the effect of varing N.

Figure 7 shows the experimental result for varying frame number N using the data set of Group 4. As it is shown, higher-rating occurs at the center in both curves, and lower-rating at both ends. The result supports our assumption that the feature will convey little discriminative information when N is too small, and the over-fitting problem will occur when N is too large. The recognition accuracy is obviously lower than the rest when N is 2. The two curves are nearly flat when N is between 5 and 11. In the following experiments, we will choose $N = 9$.

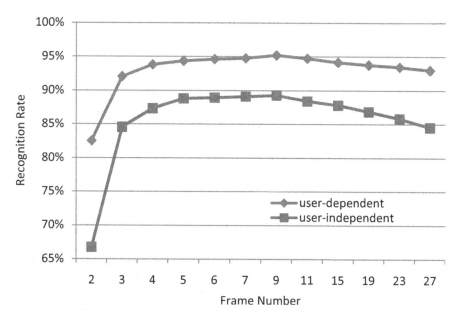

Fig. 7. The experimental result for various frame number N

4.4 Experiment 2: User-Dependent Gesture Recognition

In this experiment, to demonstrate the performance of our method, we compare it with four methods: decision tree C4.5, Naïve Bayes, DTW, and the HMM algorithm implemented by the package *WiiGee* [1] (which is an HMM-based method derived from [24]). We employed the implementation of C4.5 by Quinlan [13] and the WiiGee system developed by the authors of [1] for comparison purpose..

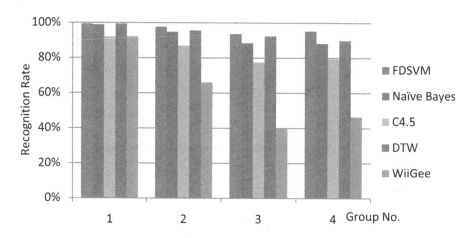

Fig. 8. The experimental results for the user-dependent case

We carried out the experiments and comparison tests on the four groups of data set respectively. The comparison results are shown in Fig.8. When recognizing the four gestures of Group 1, the recognition rate of the five approaches are all more than 90%, where our proposed FDSVM achieved 99.38%. From the figure, the performance of WiiGee decreases significantly when the number of gesture type increase. In contrast, our FDSVM method performs well even in recognizing all the 12 gestures, with the recognition rate of 95.21%. DTW is slightly better than Naïve Bayes while it is still outperformed by our FDSVM for Group tests 2/3/4.

4.5 Experiment 3: User-Independent Gesture Recognition

User-independent case means that the system is well-trained before users use it. Such implementation avoids users' efforts to perform several gestures as training data. The results of user-independent gesture recognition test and comparison are shown in Fig. 9. Obviously, the recognition rate of user-independent gesture recognition is lower than that of user-dependent one. Our FDSVM significantly outperforms the others. It obtains the recognition rate of 98.93% for 4 gestures of Group 1 and 89.29% for 12 gestures of Group 4. DTW and Naïve Bayes achieve recognition rate of 99.20% and 98.30% respectively for Group 1, very close to the performance of FDSVM. However, our FDSVM significantly outperforms DTW and Naïve Bayes for 7 gestures of Group 2, 7 gestures of Group 3, and 12 gestures of Group 4. The result reveals that our FDSVM has good generalization capability when the gesture type increases.

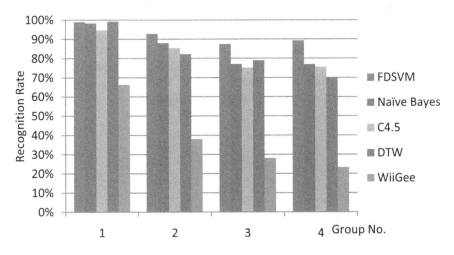

Fig. 9. The experimental result for the user-independent case

5 Conclusions

In this paper, an accelerometer-based gesture recognition method, called FDSVM, is presented and implemented. Different from the popular accelerometer-based gesture recognition approaches in the literature such as HMM and DTW, which don't include feature extraction explicitly this paper proposes a frame-based gesture descriptor for recognition, which combines spectral features and temporal features together. This explicit feature exaction stage effectively reduces the intra-class variation and noise of gestures. To tackle the issue of high nonlinearity of the gesture feature space, a multi-class SVM-based gesture classifier is built.

The extensive experiments on a data set with 3360 gesture samples of 12 gestures over time demonstrate that our approach FDSVM achieves the best recognition performance both in the user-dependent case and in the user-independent case, exceeding other four methods, DTW, HMM, Naïve Bayes and C4.5. In particular, the perfect user-independent performance of FDSVM on the large dataset, the high recognition rate of 98.93% for 4 gestures and 89.29% for 12 gestures hints us that the practical user-independent gesture recognition could be possible in the near future.

The future work is planned in three folds: new applications of the accelerometer-based gesture recognition, new approaches to improve the user-independent performance, and the continuous gestures recognition

Acknowledgements

This work is supported in part by the National High-Tech Research and Development (863) Program of China (No. 2008AA01Z132, 2009AA010000), the Natural Science Fund of China (No. 60525202, 60533040). The authors would thank anonymous reviewers for their valuable comments. The corresponding author is Dr. Gang Pan.

References

1. Schlömer, T., Poppinga, B., Henze, N., Boll, S.: Gesture Recognition with a Wii Controller. In: International Conference on Tangible and Embedded Interaction (TEI 2008), Bonn Germany, Feburary 18-20, pp. 11–14 (2008)
2. Tsukada, K., Yasumura, M.: Ubi-Finger: Gesture Input Device for Mobile Use. In: Proceedings of APCHI 2002, vol. 1, pp. 388–400 (2002)
3. Sawada, H., Hashimoto, S.: Gesture Recognition Using an Accelerometer Sensor and Its Application to Musical Performance Control. Electronics and Communications in Japan Part 3, 9–17 (2000)
4. Mäntylä, V.-M., Mäntyjärvi, J., Seppänen, T., Tuulari, E.: Hand Gesture Recognition of a Mobile Device User. In: Proceedings of the International IEEE Conference on Multimedia and Expo., pp. 281–284 (2000)
5. Mäntyjärvi, J., Kela, J., Korpipää, P., Kallio, S.: Enabling fast and effortless customization in accelerometer based gesture interaction. In: Proceedings of the 3rd International Conference on Mobile and Ubiquitous Multimedia (MUM 2004), October 27-29, pp. 25–31. ACM Press, New York (2004)
6. Mäntylä, V.-M.: Discrete Hidden Markov Models with Application to Isolated User-Dependent Hand Gesture Recognition. VTT publications (2001)
7. Hofmann, F.G., Heyer, P., Hommel, G.: Velocity profile based recognition of dynamic gestures with discrete hidden markov models. In: Wachsmuth, I., Fröhlich, M. (eds.) GW 1997. LNCS, vol. 1371, pp. 81–95. Springer, Heidelberg (1998)

8. Ravi, N., Dandekar, N., Musore, P., Littman, M.: Activity Recognition from Accelerometer Data. In: Proceedings of IAAI 2008, July 2005, pp. 11–18 (2005)
9. Frigo, M., Johnson, S.G.: The Design and implementation of FFTW3. Proceedings of the IEEE 93(2) (2005)
10. Joachims, T.: Making large-Scale SVM Learning Practical. In: Schöllkopf, B., Burges, C., Smola, A. (eds.) Advances in Kernel Methods – Support Vector Learning. MIT-Press, Cambridge (1999)
11. Christanini, J., Taylor, J.S.: An Introduction to Support Vector Machines and other Kernel-based Methods. Cambridge University Press, Cambridge (2000)
12. Mitra, S., Acharya, T.: Gesture Recognition: A Survey. IEEE Trans. Systems, Man, and Cybernetics, Part C 37(3), 311–324 (2007)
13. Quinlan, J.R.: Improved use of continuous attributes in c4.5. Journal of Artificial Intelligence Research 4, 77–90 (1996)
14. Moghaddam, B., Yang, M.-H.: Learning Gender with Support Faces, IEEE Trans. Pattern Analysis and Machine Intelligence 24(5), 707–711 (2002)
15. Osuna, E., Freund, R., Girosi, F.: Training Support Vector Machines: An Application to Face Detection. In: Proc. IEEE Computer Soc. Conf. Computer Vision and Pattern Recognition, pp. 130–136 (1997)
16. Cho, S.-J., Choi, E., Bang, W.-C., Yang, J., Sohn, J., Kim, D.Y., Lee, Y.-B., Kim, S.: Two-stage Recognition of Raw Acceleration Signals for 3D-Gesture-Understanding Cell Phones. In: 10th International Workshop on Frontiers in Handwriting Recognition (2006)
17. Niezen, G., Hancke, G.P.: Gesture recognition as ubiquitous input for mobile phones. In: International Workshop on Devices that Alter Perception (DAP 2008), conjunction with Ubicomp 2008 (2008)
18. Liu, J., Wang, Z., Zhong, L., Wickramasuriya, J., Vasudevan, V.: uWave: Accelerometer-based Personalized Gesture Recognition and Its Applications. In: IEEE PerCom 2009 (2009)
19. Bao, L., Intille, S.S.: Activity recognition from user-annotated acceleration data. In: Ferscha, A., Mattern, F. (eds.) PERVASIVE 2004. LNCS, vol. 3001, pp. 1–17. Springer, Heidelberg (2004)
20. Wilson, D.H., Wilson, A.: Gesture Recognition using the XWand, Technical Report CMU-RI-TR-04-57, CMU Robotics Institute (2004)
21. Apple iPhone, http://www.apple.com/iphone
22. Nintendo Wii, http://www.nintendo.com/wii
23. Hommel, G., Hofmann, F.G., Henz, J.: The TU Berlin High-Precision Sensor Glove. In: Proceedings of the WWDU 1994, Fourth International Scientific Conference, vol. 2, pp. 47–49. University of Milan, Milan (1994)
24. Kela, J., Korpipaa, P., Mantyjarvi, J., Kallio, S., Savino, G., Jozzo, L., Marca, D.: Accelerometer-based gesture control for a design environment. Personal Ubiquitous Computing 10, 285–299 (2006)

Context-Aware Activity Recognition through a Combination of Ontological and Statistical Reasoning

Daniele Riboni and Claudio Bettini

EveryWare Lab, D.I.Co., Università di Milano
{riboni,bettini}@dico.unimi.it

Abstract. In the last years, techniques for activity recognition have attracted increasing attention. Among many applications, a special interest is in the pervasive e-Health domain where automatic activity recognition is used in rehabilitation systems, chronic disease management, monitoring of the elderly, as well as in personal well being applications. Research in this field has mainly adopted techniques based on supervised learning algorithms to recognize activities based on contextual conditions (e.g., location, surrounding environment, used objects) and data retrieved from body-worn sensors. Since these systems rely on a sufficiently large amount of training data which is hard to collect, scalability with respect to the number of considered activities and contextual data is a major issue. In this paper, we propose the use of ontologies and ontological reasoning combined with statistical inferencing to address this problem. Our technique relies on the use of semantic relationships that express the feasibility of performing a given activity in a given context. The proposed technique neither increases the obtrusiveness of the statistical activity recognition system, nor introduces significant computational overhead to real-time activity recognition. The results of extensive experiments with data collected from sensors worn by a group of volunteers performing activities both indoor and outdoor show the superiority of the combined technique with respect to a solely statistical approach. To the best of our knowledge, this is the first work that systematically investigates the integration of statistical and ontological reasoning for activity recognition.

1 Introduction

There is a general consensus on the fact that effective automatic recognition of user activities would greatly enhance the ability of a pervasive system to properly react and adapt to the circumstances. Among many applications of activity recognition, a special interest is in the pervasive e-Health domain where automatic activity recognition is used in rehabilitation systems, chronic disease management, monitoring of the elderly, as well as in personal well being applications (see, e.g., [1,2,3]).

Example 1. Consider the case of Alice, an elderly person undergoing rehabilitation after having been hospitalized for a minor heart attack. In order to help Alice

D. Zhang et al. (Eds.): UIC 2009, LNCS 5585, pp. 39–53, 2009.

in correctly following the practitioners' prescriptions about the physical activities to perform during rehabilitation, the hospital center provides her with a monitoring system that continuously keeps track of her physiological data as well as of her activities. In particular, physiological data (e.g., heart rate and blood pressure) are acquired by wearable sensors that transmit them through a wireless link to the monitoring application hosted on her mobile phone. Similarly, accelerometer data provided by a smartwatch are transmitted to the monitoring application and merged with those provided by the accelerometer integrated in her mobile phone to automatically infer her current physical activity. On the basis of physiological data and performed activities, the monitoring application provides Alice with alerts and suggestions to better follow her rehabilitation plan (e.g., "please consider to take a walk this morning", or "take some rest now"). Moreover, those data are reported to the medical center on a daily basis for further processing.

Of course, for such a system to be effective, the activity recognition module must provide very accurate results. In fact, if activities are wrongly recognized, the monitoring system may draw erroneous conclusions about the actual adherence of the patient to the practitioners' prescriptions, as well as provide error-prone statistics about the health status of the patient.

A research direction consists in devising techniques to recognize activities using cameras with the help of sound, image and scene recognition software (see, e.g., [4,5]), but this is limited to very confined environments and often subject to serious privacy concerns, clearly perceived by the monitored users.

Alternative activity recognition techniques are based on data acquired from body-worn sensors (e.g., motion tracking and inertial sensors, cardio-frequency meters, etc) and on the application of statistical learning methods. Early attempts in this sense were mainly based on the use of data acquired from multiple body-worn accelerometers (e.g., [6,7]). One of the main limitations of these early systems relied on the fact that they did not consider contextual information (such as current location, environmental conditions, surrounding objects) that could be usefully exploited to derive the user's activity (for simplicity, in the rest of this paper we refer to this kind of data as *context*). As a consequence, later approaches were aimed at devising activity recognition systems taking into account the user's context. For instance, in [8] a method is proposed to classify physical activities by considering not only data retrieved from a body-worn accelerometer, but also environmental data acquired from several other sensors (sound, humidity, acceleration, orientation, barometric pressure, . . .). Spatio-temporal traces are used in [9] to derive high-level activities such as *shopping* or *dining out*. Observations regarding the user's surrounding environment (in particular, objects' use), possibly coupled with body-worn sensor data, are the basis of many other activity recognition systems (e.g., [10,11]).

Most of these systems rely on the application of supervised learning algorithms that, in order to perform well, need to be trained with a sufficiently large amount of labeled data. Indeed, with an insufficient set of training data, to consider a wide set of context data would be ineffective, if not counterproductive, since the classifier could draw erroneous predictions due to the problem of overfitting. For instance, in [8] some available context data are discarded in order to avoid this problem, that is one of the main reasons why activity recognition systems do not perform well out of the laboratory. Since training data are very hard to acquire, systems relying on supervised learning are prone to serious scalability issues the more activities and the more context data are considered. For instance, suppose to consider as the only context data the user's current symbolic location (e.g., *kitchen, dining room, mall, park,* etc). Even in this simple case, in order to gain good recognition results a sufficiently large set of training data should be acquired for each activity in any considered location. Of course, such a large set of training data is very hard to obtain. Moreover, when we consider as context not only location but also environmental conditions and surrounding objects, the task of collecting a sufficient amount of training data is very likely to become unmanageable, since training data should be acquired in any possible contextual condition. This challenging issue has been addressed (e.g., in [12]) by means of a combination of supervised and unsupervised learning techniques. Even if similar techniques can be adopted to mitigate the problem, it is unlikely that they can provide a definitive solution. In this paper we investigate the use of ontological reasoning coupled with statistical reasoning in order to address the above-mentioned problem. The intuition behind our solution is that very useful hints about the possible activities performed by a user based on her context can be obtained by exploiting symbolic reasoning without the need of any training data. Besides, statistical inferencing can be performed based on raw data retrieved from body-worn sensors (e.g., accelerometers) without the need to acquire them under different context conditions during the training phase; indeed, given a performed activity, these data are mainly independent from the user's context. Hence, by coupling symbolic reasoning with statistical inferencing it is possible to perform activity recognition using a comprehensive set of information in a sufficiently scalable way.

In particular, our technique consists in the use of semantic relationships and constraints to express the feasibility of performing a given activity in a given context. For this reason we have defined an ontology that models activities, artifacts, persons, communication routes, and symbolic locations, and that expresses relations and constraints between these entities. To the best of our knowledge this is the first work that systematically investigates the integration of statistical and ontological reasoning for activity recognition. Extensive experimental results with data collected by volunteers show the superiority of the proposed technique with respect to a solely statistical approach.

The rest of the paper is organized as follows: Section 2 presents an overview of the proposed activity recognition system; Section 3 illustrates the technique for combining ontological reasoning and statistical activity recognition; Section 4 presents experimental results; Section 5 concludes the paper.

2   The *COSAR* Activity Recognition System

The proposed activity recognition system is graphically depicted in Figure 1. The lower layer (SENSORS) includes body-worn sensors (providing data such as

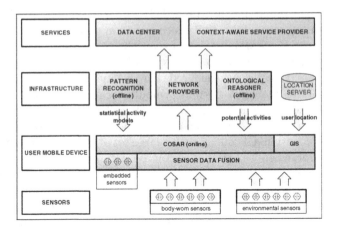

Fig. 1. The *COSAR* system

accelerometer readings and physiological parameters) and sensors spread in the environment.

Data provided by environmental and body-worn sensors are communicated through a wireless connection to the USER MOBILE DEVICE, and merged with sensor data retrieved by the device itself (e.g., data provided by an embedded accelerometer) to build a *feature vector* that will be used to predict the user's activity. The device also continuously keeps track of the current physical location provided by a GPS receiver. When the GPS reading is not available or not sufficiently accurate (e.g., indoor), localization is performed by an external LOCATION SERVER (e.g., a GSM triangulation system provided by the network operator, or an RFID system). The GIS module is in charge of mapping the physical location reading to the most specific symbolic location that correspond to that physical location. This information will be used by the COMBINED ONTO-LOGICAL/STATISTICAL ACTIVITY RECOGNITION module (COSAR) to refine the statistical predictions.

The INFRASTRUCTURE layer includes a PATTERN RECOGNITION module that is in charge of deriving a statistical model of the considered activities, which is communicated offline to the COSAR module. This layer is also in charge of performing ontological reasoning to calculate the set of activities that can be potentially performed in a given context. This set is also communicated offline to the COSAR module. In addition, the infrastructure layer includes a network provider offering the connectivity necessary to exchange data between modules at different layers, and, in particular, to communicate activity information to remote data centers or context-aware service providers. With respect to efficiency issues, we point out that the most computationally expensive tasks (i.e., ontological reasoning and pattern recognition to build a statistical model of activities) are executed offline. Note that privacy issues are of paramount importance in this domain; however, their treatment is outside the scope of this paper. Preliminary work on integrating privacy preservation in a context-aware middleware can be found in [13].

3 Combining Ontological Reasoning and Statistical Activity Recognition

In this section we illustrate how ontological reasoning is coupled with statistical inferencing in order to recognize the user's activity.

3.1 Statistical Activity Recognition with a Temporal *voted* Variant

As illustrated in the introduction, the most common approach to activity recognition is to make use of supervised statistical learning methods. Roughly speaking, these methods rely on a set of preclassified activity instances that are used in a training phase to learn a statistical model of a given set of activities. The obtained model is then used to automatically classify new activity instances.

Activity instances are characterized by a *duration*; i.e., the temporal resolution at which activity instances are considered. Each activity instance is represented by means of a *feature vector*, in which each feature corresponds to a given measure (typically, a statistics about some measurements retrieved from a sensor or from a set of sensors during the duration of the activity instance).

Even if significant exceptions exist (e.g., Hidden Markov Models and Linear Dynamical Systems [14]), it is worth to note that most models adopted by statistical learning algorithms implicitly assume independence between each pair of instances to be classified. As a consequence, the prediction of an instance i_2 does not depend on the prediction of another instance i_1. However, when considering activity instances the above-mentioned assumption does not hold. In fact, persons do not continuously switch among different activities; instead, they tend to perform the same activity for a certain lapse of time before changing activity. Similarly to other approaches in the literature, we exploit this characteristic to improve the classification result of statistical activity recognition systems by introducing a *voted* variant. Since a thorough description of this variant is outside the scope of this paper, we only mention that it is based on a time window to classify each activity instance considering some of the previous activity instances; this technique can be applied to a large class of statistical learning algorithms.

3.2 Ontological Reasoning to Identify Potential Activities Based on Context

Even if our technique can be applied to any kind of context data, in the rest of this paper we concentrate on location information. Indeed, location is an important case of context information, and the current symbolic location of a user can give useful hints about which activities she can or cannot perform. Moreover, from a practical perspective, localization technologies are more and more integrated in mobile devices and buildings; hence, differently from other context data, location information is available in many situations.

Rationale. Even if in theory the set of possible activities that can be performed in a given symbolic location could be manually specified by a domain expert,

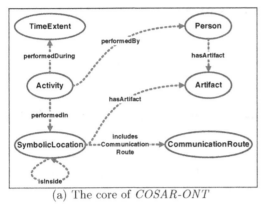

(a) The core of *COSAR-ONT*

Class	Descendants
Activity	35
Artifact	43
CommunicationRoute	14
Person	4
SymbolicLocation	30
TimeExtent	11

(b) Number of classes

Fig. 2. The *COSAR-ONT* ontology

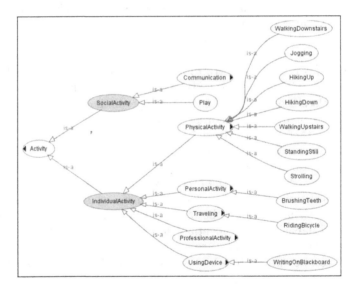

Fig. 3. Part of the *COSAR-ONT* activities

this method would be clearly impractical. Indeed, even considering a few tens of activities and symbolic locations, the number of their combinations would quickly render this task unmanageable. Moreover, this task should be repeated each time the characteristics of a symbolic location change (e.g., when an artifact is added to or removed from a room).

Our solution is based on the use of an OWL-DL [15] ontology to represent activities, symbolic locations, communication routes, artifacts, persons and time granularities, as well as relations among them. To this aim we have developed a novel ontology, named *COSAR-ONT*, whose main classes and properties are graphically depicted in Figure 2(a). Figure 2(b) shows the number of descendants of the main classes of the ontology. In particular, COSAR-ONT includes 30 symbolic locations and 35 activities. Figure 3 shows part of the activities modeled by our ontology; the rightmost activities in the figure are those used in the experimental evaluation of our system (Section 4). The set of locations and activities in our ontology is obviously non exhaustive; however, we believe that this ontology can be profitably used to model many health care scenarios. Moreover, the ontology is easily extensible to address additional application domains. In order to illustrate our technique we introduce the following example.

Example 2. Consider the activity BrushingTeeth, and the task of automatically inferring the set of symbolic locations in which such activity can reasonably be performed. One possible definition of the considered activity is the following:

BrushingTeeth $\sqsubseteq$ PersonalActivity $\sqcap$ $\forall$ performedIn. ($\exists$ hasArtifact.Sink) $\sqcap$ ...

According to the above definition, BrushingTeeth is a subclass of PersonalActivity that can be performed only in locations that contain a Sink (that is defined as a subclass of WaterFixture); other restrictions may follow, but they are not considered here for simplicity. Now consider two symbolic locations, namely RestRoom and LivingRoom, defined as follows:

RestRoom $\sqsubseteq$ Room $\sqcap$ $\exists$ hasArtifact.Sink $\sqcap$ ...

LivingRoom $\sqsubseteq$ Room $\sqcap$ $\neg\exists$ hasArtifact.WaterFixture $\sqcap$ ...

According to the above definitions, RestRoom is a Room that contains a sink, while LivingRoom is a Room that does not contain any WaterFixture (once again, other details about the definition of these classes are omitted)[1]. Given those ontological definitions it is possible to automatically derive through ontological reasoning the set of symbolic locations in which the activity BrushingTeeth can be performed. To this aim, the following assertions are stated and added to the assertional part of the ontology (called *ABox*):

BrushingTeeth(CURR_ACT); RestRoom(CURR_LOC_1); LivingRoom(CURR_LOC_2)

The above assertions create an instance of activity BrushingTeeth identified as CURR_ACT, an instance of location RestRoom identified as CURR_LOC_1, and an instance of location LivingRoom identified as CURR_LOC_2. Then, in order to understand if a given activity instance a can be performed in a given location l it is sufficient to add an assertion to the ABox stating that activity a is performed in location l, and then to check if the ABox is consistent with respect to the terminological part of the ontology by performing a *consistency checking* reasoning task:

performedIn(CURR_ACT,CURR_LOC_1); isABoxConsistent()

---

[1] Note that, due to the open-world assumption of description logic systems [16] and, consequently, of OWL-DL, it is necessary to explicitly state those artifacts that are not present in a given location. This is simplified by considering in the definition of symbolic locations only artifacts that characterize the activities to be discriminated and using the artifact ontology to exclude whole classes of artifacts, as done in the LivingRoom example with WaterFixture.

The above statements are used to verify if activity BrushingTeeth can be performed in location RestRoom. In this case the consistency check succeeds, since the declared constraints on the execution of BrushingTeeth (i.e., the presence of a sink) are satisfied by the considered location. The same statements, substituting CURR_LOC_1 with CURR_LOC_2 verify if activity BrushingTeeth can be performed in location LivingRoom. In this case the consistency check does not succeed, since the definition of LivingRoom states that no WaterFixture is present in that location. As a consequence, since Sink has been defined as a subclass of WaterFixture, the ontological reasoner infers that no sink is present in LivingRoom, thus violating the constraints for the execution of activity BrushingTeeth.

Algorithm for the Derivation of Possible Activities (*DPA*). The DPA algorithm takes as input an empty ABox and the terminological part of the ontology (called TBox) that describes classes and their properties. The output of the algorithm is a matrix M whose rows correspond to symbolic locations in the TBox, columns correspond to activities in the TBox, and $M_{i,j}$ equals to 1 if activity corresponding to column j is a possible activity in location corresponding to row i according to the TBox; $M_{i,j}$ equals to 0 otherwise.

As a first step, the terminological part of the ontology is classified to compute the hierarchy of the atomic concepts of the TBox. Then for each pair $\langle l_i, a_j \rangle$, where l_i is a symbolic location and a_j is an activity in TBox, the algorithm creates three assertions $s_1 = $ "$a_j(\mathcal{A})$", $s_2 = $ "$l_i(\mathcal{L})$", and $s_3 = $ "performedIn$(\mathcal{A}, \mathcal{L})$" to state that activity a_j is performed in location l_i, and adds them to the ABox. Then, the ABox is checked for consistency, and $M_{i,j}$ is set with the result of the test (1 if the check succeeds, 0 otherwise). Finally, assertions s_1, s_2 and s_3 are retracted from the ABox in order to remove the possible inconsistency that would affect the result of future consistency checks.

An example of the output of the DPA algorithm with a subset of locations and activities modeled by COSAR-ONT is given in Table 1.

3.3 Coupling Ontological Reasoning with Statistical Inferencing

Rationale. We illustrate our technique by means of an example.

Table 1. Part of the M matrix of potential activities

	1	2	3	4	5	6	7	8	9	10
Garden	0	0	0	1	1	1	1	0	0	0
HospitalBuilding	1	0	0	0	0	1	0	1	1	1
Kitchen	1	0	0	0	0	1	0	0	0	1
Laboratory	0	0	0	0	0	1	0	0	0	1
LivingRoom	0	0	0	0	0	1	0	0	0	0
Meadow	0	0	0	1	1	1	1	0	0	0
RestRoom	1	0	0	0	0	1	0	0	0	0
UrbanArea	0	0	0	1	1	1	1	1	1	0
Wood	0	1	1	1	1	1	1	0	0	0

Columns: 1=brushingTeeth; 2=hikingUp; 3=hikingDown; 4=ridingBycicle; 5=jogging; 6=standingStill; 7=strolling; 8=walkingDownstairs; 9=walkingUpstairs; 10=writingOnBlackboard

Example 3. Suppose that user Alice is taking a stroll on a path that goes across the wood near home wearing the sensor equipment of the monitoring system. As explained before, the system (deployed on her mobile phone) continuously keeps track of her current activity, as well as of her current symbolic location (that in this case is Wood). The system also knows the matrix M that was calculated offline by the DPA algorithm.

Considering a single activity instance i and the statistical model of m different activities $a_1, \ldots, a_m$, the statistical classifier of the system returns a m-length *confidence vector* $\vec{s}_i$ in which the jth element $\vec{s}_i^{(j)}$ corresponds to activity a_j and its value corresponds to the *confidence* of the classifier regarding the associa-tion of i to a_j, such that $0 \leq \vec{s}_i^{(j)} \leq 1$ and $\sum_{j=1}^{m}(\vec{s}^{(j)}) = 1$. For instance, suppose that the considered activities are those shown in Table 1 (the jth column of the table corresponds to activity a_j), and that $\vec{s}_i = \langle 0, 0, 0.16, 0, 0, 0, 0.39, 0.45, 0, 0 \rangle$. In this case, the maximum confidence value (0.45) corresponds to activity Walk-ingDownstairs, followed by Strolling (0.39) and hikingDown (0.16). The con-fidence value corresponding to the other seven activities is 0. Hence, considering the statistical prediction alone, the classifier would erroneously conclude that user Alice is walking downstairs.

However, looking at matrix M one can note that WalkingDownstairs is not a feasible activity in the current location of Alice. The rationale of the COSAR technique is to discard those elements of $\vec{s}_i$ that correspond to un-feasible activities according to M, and to choose the activity having maximum confidence among the remaining elements (or one such activity at random if the maximum confidence corresponds to more than one activity). In this case, the COSAR technique consists in discarding activities BrushingTeeth, Walk-ingDownstairs, WalkingUpstairs and WritingOnBlackboard, and in choosing activity Strolling, since it is the one that corresponds to the maximum confi-dence among the remaining activities. Hence, in this case the COSAR technique correctly recognizes Alice's activity.

Handling location uncertainty. Every localization technology is character-ized by a certain level of inaccuracy. As a consequence, the mapping of a physical location reading to a symbolic location is prone to uncertainty. For instance, if the physical location is retrieved from a GSM cell identification system, the area including the user may correspond to different symbolic locations, such as a HomeBuilding, a HospitalBuilding and a Park.

Uncertainty in location is taken into account by our system. In particu-lar, if the user's physical location corresponds to n possible symbolic locations $l_1, \ldots, l_n$, the possible activities that can be performed by the user are calculated as those that can be performed in at least one location belonging to $\{l_1, \ldots, l_n\}$.

Example 4. Suppose that Alice forgot her GPS receiver at home. Consequently she relies on a GSM cell identification service, which provides coarse-grained lo-cation information. In particular, the service localizes Alice within an area that includes both a Wood and a UrbanArea. Hence, our system calculates the set of

Alice's possible activities as the union of the set of activities that can be performed in woods and the set of activities that can be performed in urban areas. Considering matrix M derived by the DPA algorithm and shown in Table 1, possible activities for Alice are those that correspond to columns 2 to 9, included. Therefore, with respect to the scenario depicted in Example 3, in this case WalkingDownstairs and WalkingUpstairs are possible activities (since urban areas may include steps).

The *COSAR-voted* algorithm. At first, the vector of predictions $\vec{C}'$ is initialized. Then, the process of actual activity recognition starts. For each activity instance to be recognized, the LOCATION SERVER is queried to obtain the symbolic location corresponding to the current physical location $\vec{l}_i$ of the user. Note that, if the location server provides location information at a coarse grain, more than one symbolic location can correspond to the user's physical location. Then, sensor data are retrieved from sensors and a feature vector f_i is build by the SENSOR DATA FUSION module. The feature vector is used to classify the corresponding activity instance according to the statistical model provided by the PATTERN RECOGNITION module, obtaining a confidence vector $\vec{s}_i$. According to $\vec{s}_i$, to the possible symbolic locations $\vec{l}_i$, and to the matrix M obtained by the DPA algorithm, the combined ontological-statistical prediction $\bar{c}_i$ is calculated; as explained before, $\bar{c}_i$ is the possible activity according to M having highest confidence in $\vec{s}_i$. Finally, the voted variant is applied to obtain the voted prediction $\bar{c}'_i$ considering $\bar{c}_i$ and the bag of (non-voted) predictions $\{\bar{c}_{i-1}, \ldots, \bar{c}_{i-k}\}$ of the k most recently classified activity instances. In particular, $\bar{c}'_i$ is set to the prediction having the maximum multiplicity in $\{\bar{c}_i, \bar{c}_{i-1}, \ldots, \bar{c}_{i-k}\}$. If multiple predictions exist which have the maximum multiplicity, one of them is chosen at random. Then, prediction $\bar{c}'_i$ is added to the vector of predictions $\vec{C}'$.

4   Experimental Evaluation

In order to validate our solution we performed an extensive experimental evaluation comparing our technique with a purely statistical one. We point out that the symbolic location is used as a feature only in the experiments performed with the purely statistical technique (named *statistical* and *statistical-voted* in the following). In the experiments with the COSAR technique (named *COSAR* and *COSAR-voted*) location is not used as a feature by the statistical classifier; instead, it is used by the ontological module only.

4.1   Experimental Setup

The experiments concerned the recognition of 10 different activities performed both indoor and outdoor by 6 volunteers (3 men and 3 women, ages ranging from 30 to 60) having different attitude to physical activities. While performing activities, volunteers wore one sensor on their left pocket and one sensor on their right wrist to collect accelerometer data, plus a GPS receiver to track

Fig. 4. Sensors used for the experiments

their current physical location. This setup reproduces the situation in which data are acquired from an accelerometer embedded in a fitness watch, and from an accelerometer and a GPS receiver embedded in a mobile phone. Since in the current implementation of our system the GIS module is only simulated, physical locations were manually mapped to symbolic locations.

Each activity was performed by 4 different volunteers for 450 seconds each. Overall, each activity was performed for 30 minutes; hence, the dataset is composed of 5 hours of activity data. The dataset is published on the web site of our project[2] and can be freely used to reproduce the experiments, or as a testbed for evaluating other techniques.

Accelerometer data were retrieved using *Small Programmable Object Technology (SPOT)* by Sun® Microsystems. SPOTs (shown in Figure 4 together with the used GPS receiver) are sensor devices programmable in Java Micro Edition; they are equipped with a 180 MHz 32 bit processor, 512K RAM/4M Flash memory, and IEEE 802.15.4 radio with integrated antenna. They mount a 3-axis accelerometer, and sensors for light intensity and temperature.

Samples from accelerometers were taken at 16Hz, and the time extent of each activity instance was 1 second; hence, the dataset is composed of 18000 activity instances. For each activity instance, accelerometer readings were merged to build a feature vector composed of 148 features, including means, variances, correlations, kurtosis, and other statistical measures. Preliminary experiments (not reported here for lack of space) suggest that in our case feature selection does not improve classification accuracy; however, feature selection can still be useful to reduce CPU usage at run time, hence we will consider this issue in future work.

Statistical classification was performed using *Weka*[3], a Java-based toolkit that provides APIs for implementing several machine learning algorithms. The COSAR ontology was developed using *Protégé*[4], while *RacerPro*[5] was used to perform ontological reasoning. Since the sensor devices we used lacked a

---

[2] http://everywarelab.dico.unimi.it/palspot
[3] http://www.cs.waikato.ac.nz/ml/weka/
[4] .http://protege.stanford.edu/
[5] http://www.racer-systems.com/

Table 2. Summary of experimental results

(a) Evaluation of statistical classifiers

Classifier	Accuracy
Bayesian Network	72.95%
C4.5 Decision Tree	66.23%
Multiclass Logistic Regression	80.21%
Naive Bayes	68.55%
SVM	71.81%

(b) Overall accuracy

Classifier	Accuracy
statistical	80.21%
statistical-voted	84.72%
COSAR	89.20%
COSAR-voted	93.44%

(c) Error reduction

versus →	statistical	statistical-voted	COSAR
statistical-voted	22.79%		
COSAR	45.43%	29.32%	
COSAR-voted	66.85%	57.07%	39.26%

Bluetooth interface we could not establish a direct connection between a mobile device and the sensor devices themselves. For this reason experiments were executed on a desktop workstation. However, at the time of writing we are working on the implementation of the COSAR-voted algorithm for devices supporting Java Micro Edition.

In order to evaluate recognition rates we performed 4-folds cross validation, dividing the dataset in 4 subsamples such that each subsample contains 450 instances for each activity. Ideally, an out-of-the-box activity recognition system should be able to recognize one person's activities without the need of being trained on that person. Hence, in order to avoid the use of activity data of the same user for both training and testing we ensured that activity instances regarding a given volunteer did not appear in more that one subsample.

4.2   Results

Exp. 1) Statistical classification algorithms: The first set of experiments was only aimed at choosing a statistical classification algorithm to be used in the subsequent experiments. In general, since in many applications activity recognition must be performed on-line, the choice of a classification algorithm should privilege not only good recognition performance, but also very efficient classification procedures. Indeed, in many cases, the activity recognition algorithm must be executed on a resource-constrained mobile device.

In this first experiment we compared classification techniques belonging to different classes of pattern recognition algorithms (i.e., Bayesian approaches, decision trees, probabilistic discriminative models and kernel machines). Experimental results on our data (shown in Table 2(a)) show that, among the considered techniques, Multiclass Logistic Regression with a ridge estimator (MLR), outperform the other techniques, gaining recognition rates higher than 80%. Hence, our choice for the statistical classification algorithm was to use MLR [17], a classification technique belonging to the class of probabilistic discriminative models [14], having the advantage of being particularly computationally efficient at classification time.

Table 3. Results for the statistical classifier

(a) Confusion matrix

(b) Precision / recall

classified as →	1	2	3	4	5	6	7	8	9	10	prec.	recall
1	1336	4	1	11	8	304	0	33	2	101	95,43%	74,22%
2	4	1551	219	5	14	0	1	1	5	0	76,93%	86,17%
3	0	382	1376	4	3	1	31	2	1	0	80,66%	76,44%
4	1	5	10	1738	23	0	0	23	0	0	96,61%	96,56%
5	13	3	17	21	1664	1	7	73	1	0	71,94%	92,44%
6	32	5	3	0	290	1254	17	34	126	39	61,20%	69,67%
7	0	0	78	0	304	3	917	383	115	0	92,53%	50,94%
8	0	0	1	0	0	0	2	1762	35	0	71,74%	97,89%
9	0	5	0	4	0	1	16	144	1629	1	84,89%	90,50%
10	14	61	1	16	7	485	0	1	5	1210	89,56%	67,22%

Columns: 1=brushingTeeth;   2=hikingUp;   3=hikingDown;   4=ridingBycicle;
5=jogging;   6=standingStill;   7=strolling;   8=walkingDownstairs;   9=walkingUpstairs;
10=writingOnBlackboard

Exp. 2) Statistical technique: Table 3 shows the confusion matrix and precision/recall measures for the statistical technique evaluated in the first set of experiments. As expected, when data from accelerometers are used and the symbolic location is used as a feature, many misclassifications occur between activities that involve similar body movements; e.g., instances of *strolling* are often classified as instances of *walking downstairs*.

Exp. 3) Statistical-voted technique: We evaluated the *voted* variant of the statistical classification algorithm by simulating the case in which a user performs each activity for 7.5 minutes before changing activity. With this technique, the accuracy of activity recognition is 84.72% (see Table 2(b)), which results in an error reduction rate of 22.79% with respect to the statistical technique (see Table 2(c)). Due to lack of space we do not report the confusion matrix and precision/recall measures for this experiment; however, this technique does not significantly reduce the number of misclassifications between activities involving similar movements.

Table 4. Results for the COSAR classifier

(a) Confusion matrix

(b) Precision / recall

classified as →	1	2	3	4	5	6	7	8	9	10	prec.	recall
1	1622	0	0	0	0	178	0	0	0	0	98,30%	90,11%
2	0	1443	171	19	34	14	119	0	0	0	83,99%	80,17%
3	0	268	1284	22	2	13	211	0	0	0	87,82%	71,33%
4	0	4	7	1787	1	1	0	0	0	0	86,87%	99,28%
5	0	0	0	134	1640	9	6	8	3	0	96,76%	91,11%
6	0	3	0	26	9	1738	21	1	2	0	76,06%	96,56%
7	0	0	0	69	9	54	1597	67	4	0	81,73%	88,72%
8	4	0	0	0	0	1	0	1753	42	0	90,55%	97,39%
9	24	0	0	0	0	26	0	107	1643	0	96,99%	91,28%
10	0	0	0	0	0	251	0	0	0	1549	100,00%	86,06%

Columns: 1=brushingTeeth;   2=hikingUp;   3=hikingDown;   4=ridingBycicle;
5=jogging;   6=standingStill;   7=strolling;   8=walkingDownstairs;   9=walkingUpstairs;
10=writingOnBlackboard

Exp. 4) COSAR technique: The use of the COSAR technique considerably improves the recognition rate with respect to the solely statistical techniques. In particular, the recognition rate of COSAR is 89.2%, which results in an error reduction of 45.43% with respect to the statistical technique, and of 29.32% with respect to the statistical-voted technique. Looking at the confusion matrix (Table 4), we note that COSAR avoids many misclassifications between activities characterized by similar body movements but different locations in which they are typically performed (e.g., *brushing teeth* versus *writing on a blackboard*, and *strolling* versus *walking up/downstairs*).

Exp. 5) COSAR-voted technique: Finally, the voted variant of COSAR (evaluated with the same setup as in *Exp. 3*) further improves classification results, gaining a recognition rate of 93.44%, an error reduction of 39.26% with respect to the COSAR technique, and of 66.85% with respect to the statistical technique.

5   Conclusions and Future Work

In this paper we proposed the integration of statistical and ontological reasoning for activity recognition. Our technique relies on modeling context data in ontologies and using derived semantic relationships expressing the feasibility of performing a given activity in a given context. Results from extensive experiments with data acquired by volunteers confirm the effectiveness of our technique.

Even if in the current implementation of our system we focused on location data to enact ontological reasoning, our technique can be easily extended to consider a wider class of context data. In particular, future work includes an extension of our technique to consider the temporal characterization of activities (e.g., duration), as well as their temporal relationships (i.e., the probability that a given activity a_i is followed by an activity a_j). To this aim we plan to design a temporal extension of our ontology, and to investigate the use of a probabilistic framework such as Hidden Markov Models. Moreover, since in many situations available context data may be insufficient to unambiguously determine the activity performed by a user, we are investigating the use of fuzzy ontologies to cope with uncertainty and fuzziness.

Acknowledgments

This work has been partially supported by a grant from Sun® Microsystems. The authors would like to thank the volunteers that collaborated to the collection of data used in our experiments.

References

1. Chang, K.H., Liu, S.Y., Chu, H.H., Hsu, J.Y.J., Chen, C., Lin, T.Y., Chen, C.Y., Huang, P.: The Diet-Aware Dining Table: Observing Dietary Behaviors over a Tabletop Surface. In: Fishkin, K.P., Schiele, B., Nixon, P., Quigley, A. (eds.) PERVASIVE 2006. LNCS, vol. 3968, pp. 366–382. Springer, Heidelberg (2006)

2. Tentori, M., Favela, J.: Activity-Aware Computing for Healthcare. IEEE Pervasive Computing 7(2), 51–57 (2008)
3. Amft, O., Tröster, G.: Recognition of dietary activity events using on-body sensors. Artificial Intelligence in Medicine 42(2), 121–136 (2008)
4. Oliver, N., Horvitz, E., Garg, A.: Layered Representations for Human Activity Recognition. In: Proc. of ICMI-2002, IEEE Comp. Soc., pp. 3–8 (2002)
5. Brdiczka, O., Crowley, J.L., Reignier, P.: Learning Situation Models for Providing Context-Aware Services. In: Stephanidis, C. (ed.) UAHCI 2007 (Part II). LNCS, vol. 4555, pp. 23–32. Springer, Heidelberg (2007)
6. Golding, A.R., Lesh, N.: Indoor Navigation Using a Diverse Set of Cheap, Wearable Sensors. In: Proc. of ISWC-1999, IEEE Comp. Soc., pp. 29–36 (1999)
7. Kern, N., Schiele, B., Schmidt, A.: Multi-sensor Activity Context Detection for Wearable Computing. In: Aarts, E., Collier, R.W., van Loenen, E., de Ruyter, B. (eds.) EUSAI 2003. LNCS, vol. 2875, pp. 220–232. Springer, Heidelberg (2003)
8. Lester, J., Choudhury, T., Kern, N., Borriello, G., Hannaford, B.: A Hybrid Discriminative/Generative Approach for Modeling Human Activities. In: Proc. of IJCAI-2005, P.B.C., pp. 766–772 (2005)
9. Liao, L., Fox, D., Kautz, H.A.: Location-Based Activity Recognition using Relational Markov Networks. In: Proc. of IJCAI-2005, P.B.C, pp. 773–778 (2005)
10. Wang, S., Pentney, W., Popescu, A.M., Choudhury, T., Philipose, M.: Common Sense Based Joint Training of Human Activity Recognizers. In: Proc. of IJCAI-2007, pp. 2237–2242 (2007)
11. Stikic, M., Huynh, T., Laerhoven, K.V., Schiele, B.: ADL Recognition Based on the Combination of RFID and Accelerometer Sensing. In: Proc. of Pervasive Health 2008, IEEE Comp. Soc., pp. 2237–2242 (2008)
12. Huynh, T., Schiele, B.: Towards Less Supervision in Activity Recognition from Wearable Sensors. In: Proc. of ISWC 2006, IEEE Comp. Soc., pp. 3–10 (2006)
13. Pareschi, L., Riboni, D., Agostini, A., Bettini, C.: Composition and Generalization of Context Data for Privacy Preservation. In: Proc. of PerCom 2008 Workshops, IEEE Comp. Soc., pp. 429–433 (2008)
14. Bishop, C.M.: Pattern Recognition and Machine Learning. Springer, Heidelberg (2008)
15. Horrocks, I., Patel-Schneider, P.F., van Harmelen, F.: From SHIQ and RDF to OWL: The making of a Web Ontology Language. Journal of Web Semantics 1(1), 7–26 (2003)
16. Baader, F., Calvanese, D., McGuinness, D.L., Nardi, D., Patel-Schneider, P.F. (eds.): The Description Logic Handbook: Theory, Implementation, and Applications. Cambridge University Press, Cambridge (2003)
17. Le Cessie, S., van Houwelingen, J.: Ridge Estimators in Logistic Regression. Applied Statistics 41(1), 191–201 (1992)

Context-Aware Path Planning in Ubiquitous Network

Chiung-Ying Wang and Ren-Hung Hwang

Dept. of Computer Science and Information Engineering,
National Chung-Cheng University, Taiwan, R.O.C
{wjy,rhhwang}@cs.ccu.edu.tw

Abstract. A ubiquitous network aims to provide users intelligent human-centric context-aware services at anytime anywhere. Path planning in a ubiquitous network considers users' needs and surrounding context to plan the best path which is very different from that of car navigation or mobile robot research currently available. In this paper, we propose a context-aware path planning mechanism based on spatial conceptual map (SCM) and genetic algorithm (GA), referred to as UbiPaPaGo. SCM model is adopted to represent the real map of the surrounding environment. GA is a robust heuristic algorithm that devotes to UbiPaPaGo to plan the optimal path. The goal of UbiPaPaGo is to automatically find the best-fitting path that satisfies multiple requirements of individual user. A prototype of the UbiPaPaGo has been implemented to show its feasibility. Our numerical results also indicate that the proposed UbiPaPaGo is very efficient.

Keywords: Ubiquitous network, human-centered computing, context-awareness, path planning, genetic algorithm, spatial conceptual map.

1 Introduction

In recent years, along with rapid development of wireless and communication technologies, the demand for intelligent navigation applications in path finding has grown tremendously, such as PaPaGo [1] and TomTom [2]. These systems provide mobile users, such as car drivers, intelligent path planning, routing and navigation services and direct users to their destination with the help of electronic map and Global Position System (GPS). However, these systems are computer-centric, unable to achieve the vision of Mark Weiser [3] which describes a ubiquitous environment with human-centric systems and applications. Context-aware is the key concept to human-centric applications in ubiquitous networks. The key feature of context-aware application is to extract, interpret and use context and adapt its functionality automatically to the current context of individual user. Consequently, mobile users are able to use context to automatically plan the "best-fitting" path.

Path planning problem has been investigated extensively in the past, but most of the attentions have concentrated on mobile robot [4-7] in grid map, transportation system [8], and game system [9, 10]. These proposed planning path algorithms emphasized on features such as collision avoidance, and easy to be tracked. Although information of road, obstacle and map are taken into consideration, their solutions are

D. Zhang et al. (Eds.): UIC 2009, LNCS 5585, pp. 54–67, 2009.

not adaptive to user's situation. Recently, the context-aware approach for path finding (moving path) has been addressed. However, most of the attentions focus on context-aware path prediction [11-13]. These approaches use context, such as use's preference, location, history data, and map data to reason the future moving path in advance. These results are useful for many context-aware applications, e.g. if the moving path is determined, the handoff process can be prepared such that seamless handoff can be better achieved. However, the preferable or habitual moving path may not the optimal path regarding of user's objective. Therefore, our goal is to plan a path based on user's surrounding context which best fits user's needs, such as network connectivity, bandwidth, and path length.

To help address the problem and our solution, we sketch a scenario of finding Mary's optimal path that satisfies multiple requirements. Mary needs to go to the classroom as soon as possible because she is late. Before arriving classroom, Mary uses her PDA with wireless interface to download handouts from an on-line e-learning system. Moreover, Mary remembered that she needs to hand in a hard copy assignment today. In this situation, Mary needs to find a short path to the classroom while keeping the connectivity with the e-learning system and printing out her assignment by the way. Therefore, in this case, the optimal path needs to take into account the distance, received signal strength (RSS), available bandwidth of WiFi Access Point (AP) or 3G Base Station (BS) and available printing service. The problem to be addressed herein is formally defined as how to plan an optimal path for individual user based on his requirement and context of his surrounding environment, such as user's preference, location, time, network status, network bandwidth, service availability.

The context is very important for inferring the optimal path. The path planning framework relies on rich context acquired from various sensing sources. The collected contexts are stored in a distributed context management server [14], referred to as U-gate which is responsible for context acquisition, context representation, context retrieval, and context inference. U-gate is an open framework for ubiquitous environment. Context considered includes user's context, such as personal information and active applications, as well as environment's context, such as map information, available networks. On the other hand, context could be classified into static and dynamic context. The static context, such as user's identification, does not change while dynamic context may change frequently and has correlation with each other. For example, list of accessible AP/BS changes according to the user's location. In the proposed framework, U-gate acquires dynamic context frequently and infers new context based on rules defined by services.

The solution proposed is based on spatial conceptual map and genetic algorithm, referred to as UbiPaPago. In our solution, we first proposed a modified Spatial Conceptual Map (SCM) [15] to model the real world map and related environment context. Based on this model, a path planning map is then generated. Finally, Genetic Algorithm (GA) [16, 17] is adopted to find the optimal path. Chromosomes are encoded based on the method proposed in [18] while the fitness function is carefully designed to fit user's multiple requirements. Prototyping as well as simulations are conducted to show the feasibility and efficiency of the proposed UbiPaPago.

The remainder of this paper is organized as follows. Section 2 presents the SCM model. The design of context-aware path planning mechanism based on GA is described in Section 3. A prototype implementation is shown in Section 4. Section 5 then presents the experimental results of UbiPaPaGo. Conclusions are finally drawn in Section 6, along with recommendations for future research.

2   Spatial Conceptual Map Model

In this section, the trajectory map and environment context are represented using a Spatial Conceptual Map (SCM) model. SCM is an abstraction of real map representation containing of a set of landmark objects (Oj), a set of medium objects (Wy) and influence areas of those objects. In [15], the landmark objects define those areas, such as buildings or user's target destination. The medium objects (also called Ways) define those areas, such as streets, roads, trajectories and virtual connections between objects. A way object is further partitioned into continuous blocks, called Way Elementary Areas (WEAs).

To encode more context information, a new approach of partitioning a way object is proposed as follows. In [15], a WEA may be landmark object (Oj) or a crossing point of two or more ways. In our scenario, more contexts, such as received signal strength (RSS) of AP/BS and available bandwidth are needed. Thus, besides partitioning a way object based on crossings, characteristics of AP/BS, such as RSS, are also considered. Specifically, a way object is partitioned into several continuous blocks (WEAs) such that the RSS of an AP/BS within each WEA is roughly at the same level. For example, Figure 1 shows a portion of Chung Cheng University (CCU) campus map and Figure 2 shows its SCM representation, respectively.

Fig. 1. A portion of Chung Cheng University (CCU) Campus Map

We use a Matrix of Orientation and Adjacency and Characteristic (MOAC) [11] to represent the WEAs of the SCM. MOAC contains characteristic information of each WEA and landmark object, relative information and displacement direction between two WEAs. A portion of MOAC of Figure 2 is shown in Figure 3. The cell (x, x) represents the characteristics, i.e. context, of WEA α_x. The cell (x,y), where $x \neq y$, represents characteristics of relative direction between α_x and α_y in terms of east (E), west (W), south (S) and north (N). For example, α_{19} is on the east side of α_{18}. According to MOAC, we can infer the list of blocks along a moving path, along with moving direction and all required context information.

The characteristic function $Co()$ describes several characteristics of an object. Specifically, $Co(O_j)$ and $Co(\alpha_i)$ describe the context information of a landmark object and a WEA, respectively. Moreover, since state information of APs is also considered in this work, each AP is also associated with a characteristic function $Co(AP_i)$. For example, if O_1 is a library, the characteristic function represents the characteristics in terms of name, location, opening time and closing time. Thus an example of $Co(O_1)$ could be {c1=library, c2=α_8, c3=9:00AM, c4=9:00PM}. Similarly, WEA α_2 is covered by two APs and provides two services, the characteristic function of $Co(\alpha_2)$ is then denoted by {c1={AP_1, AP_2}, c2={printer, fax}}. The characteristics of AP are described in terms of available bandwidth (c(1)), RSS (c(2)) and distance (c(3)). Therefore, an example of $Co(AP_1)$ could be { c1=11 Mbps, c2=4, c3=5 meter}.

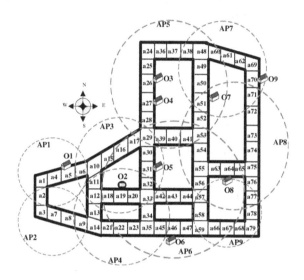

Fig. 2. SCM Representation of CU Campus Map

	α_{18}	α_{19}	α_{20}	α_{21}	α_{22}	α_{23}
α_{18}	Co(α_{18}) Co(AP₃) Co(AP₄) Co(AP₆)	E				
α_{19}	W	Co(α_{19}) Co(O₂) Co(AP₃) Co(AP₄) Co(AP₆)	E			
α_{20}		W	Co(α_{20}) Co(AP₃) Co(AP₄) Co(AP₆)			
α_{21}				Co(α_{21}) Co(AP₄)	E	
α_{22}				W	Co(α_{22}) Co(AP₄) Co(AP₆)	E
α_{23}					W	Co(α_{23}) Co(AP₄) Co(AP₆)

Fig. 3. A portion of MOAC of Fig. 2

3 Context-Aware Path Planning Mechanism

In this section, we present our context-aware plan planning mechanism, referred to as UbiPaPaGo. UbiPaPaGo is based on GA and its procedure is shown in Figure 4. Before applying the GA procedure, the SCM model obtained in section II is converted to path planning map first, as shown in Figure 5, where node α_i presents an object or a crossing in Figure 2. In other words, only objects and crossings are considered in the path planning map to reduce the length of chromosome. However, the computation of the fitness function of a chromosome is still based on all WEAs and their characteristic functions, as we will describe later.

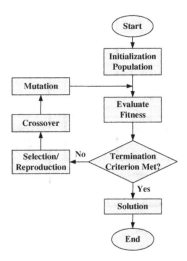

Fig. 4. The procedure of GA

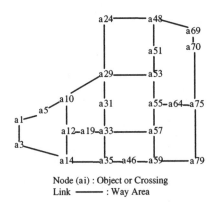

Fig. 5. Path planning map

3.1 Chromosome Coding Method and Initialization

Encoding a solution as a chromosome is the critical operation for GA. In this paper, we adopt the encoding method proposed in [18] where all chromosomes have the same length to facilitate simple crossover operation. As shown in Figure 6, the upper sequence is the locus number and the lower one is the chromosome. Every locus of the chromosome represents the order of node ID in a map. Chromosome is represented by a sequence of integer number. Each number, which corresponds to a gene, represents the node ID it passes through. To encode a path that consists of an edge from node X to node Y, node Y is put in the Xth locus of the chromosome. For the locus is not along path, its corresponding gene is filled with a neighboring node randomly selected from the set of its neighboring nodes. For example, the chromosome in Figure 6 represents a path from α_{19} to α_{51}, passes through α_{33}, α_{31}, α_{29}, α_{24} and α_{48}.

locus

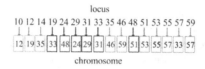

Fig. 6. Example of encoding path from α_{19} to α_{51}

Initial population is very important because it affects the convergence speed and the quality of solution. Random and heuristic initializations are the most commonly used mechanism to generate candidate solutions. However, random initialization possible leads to large computing overhead and loop path and heuristic initialization [19] is hard to find global optimal. Note that heuristic initialization explores a small part of solution space, so it is faster. We adopt a probability network approach [20] which combines the features of random and heuristic initializations to generate initial candidate paths in the gene pool. An initial chromosome is generated as follows. Starting with the source node, it selects the next node from its directly connected neighbors. In order to reduce the convergence speed, each neighboring node is assigned with a different selection probability. If the neighboring node is located at forwarding direction to the destination, it is assigned with a higher probability. The selected next node is then becomes the gene of the source node's locus. The next node then repeats the above procedure until the path reaches the destination node. Moreover, to avoid looping problem, a node will not be visited twice on the same path during the next node selection procedure. Consider the example shown in Figure 6 in which α_{29} has four neighboring nodes, α_{10}, α_{24}, α_{31} and α_{53} as shown in Figure 5. Based on the proposed initialization mechanism, α_{24} and α_{53} have higher probability to be chosen for α_{29} because they are located at forwarding direction to α_{51} and do not appear on the path before. For locus that is not on the path under consideration, its neighboring node is randomly selected. For example, any one of α_5, α_{12} and α_{29} can be selected for the locus α_{10}.

3.2 Evaluation Operation

The fitness function is derived to measure the quality of the chromosome. In this paper, qualify of a path depends on characteristics of each block of the path, include received signal strength (RSS), available bandwidth (B), distance (D) and available service (AS). Since these four qualities of service (QoS) metrics are not compatible to each other, quantification and normalization are required. Furthermore, some of the metrics have minimum requirement to ensure smooth operations of applications, such as RSS and bandwidth, thresholds are set for these metrics. In the following, we show how quantification and normalization are done and thresholds are set in defining these metrics. In Table 1, we show the quantification of these metrics. Equations (1) and (2) then define the quantities of RSS and bandwidth with consideration the minimum requirement for smooth operations of services. The rationale is that when the quality is better than the minimum threshold, quantities are not discounted. Otherwise, the quantities are inversely proportional the shortage of the metric. If the quality is lower than another threshold, the quantity is set to zero. Finally, based on in [21], equation (3) to (5) normalized these three metrics to fall between 0 and 1. Since some metrics are the larger the better, such as RSS and bandwidth, while others are the smaller the better, such as delay. When performing the normalization, we also make sure that the higher the quantity, the better the quality. Specifically, the normalization of RSS, RSS*, is shown in equation (3), where u_{RSS} and l_{RSS} are upper bound and lower bound of RSS for each block, respectively. Similar to RSS*, equation (4) defines the normalization of B, B*. Finally, let $D(P_k)$ denote the end-to-end distance of the kth feasible path in the gene pool. The normalization of $D(P_k)$, $D(P_k)$*, is given in equation (5), where the u_D and l_D are upper bound and lower bound of total distance for each path in the gene pool.

$$RSS(\alpha_i) = \begin{cases} RSS(\alpha_i), & RSS(\alpha_i) \geq threshold_{RSS} \\ \dfrac{1}{threshold_{RSS} - RSS(\alpha_i)}, & 1 \leq RSS(\alpha_i) < threshold_{RSS} \\ 0, & RSS(\alpha_i) < 1 \end{cases} \quad (1)$$

$$B(\alpha_i) = \begin{cases} B(\alpha_i), & B(\alpha_i) \geq threshold_B \\ \dfrac{1}{threshold_B - B(\alpha_i)}, & 1 \leq B(\alpha_i) < threshold_B \\ 0, & B(\alpha_i) < 1 \end{cases} \quad (2)$$

$$RSS*(\alpha_i) = 1 - \frac{|RSS(\alpha_i) - u_{RSS}|}{u_{RSS} - l_{RSS}} \quad (3)$$

$$B*(\alpha_i) = 1 - \frac{|B(\alpha_i) - u_B|}{u_B - l_B} \quad (4)$$

$$D*(P_k) = 1 - \frac{|D(P_k) - l_D|}{u_D - l_D} \quad (5)$$

Table 1. Gene Type and Quantification

Gene Type	Notation	Quantification
Received Signal Strength	RSS	$1 \xleftarrow{\text{Weak}} \xrightarrow{\text{Strong}} 5$
Available Bandwidth	B	X Mbps
Distance	D	K meter
Available Service	AS	0, if required service is **not** available
		1, if required service is available

The fitness function of each a chromosome measures the objective cost function. The fitness function F of a feasible path is evaluated as equation (6), where the relative values of w_{RSS}, w_B and w_D represent the weighting (preference or importance) of these three metrics. Note that as long as the available service exists in all blocks of a path, the path is feasible. As aforementioned, when applying the fitness function, all blocks on the path are considered. For example, if the path in Figure 5 is $\alpha_5 \to \alpha_{10} \to \alpha_{29} \to \alpha_{31}$ the corresponding path in Figure 4 is $\alpha_5 \to \alpha_6 \to \alpha_{10} \to \alpha_{15} \to \alpha_{16} \to \alpha_{17} \to \alpha_{29} \to \alpha_{30} \to \alpha_{31}$. Therefore, the fitness function evaluates the cost of each block on path $\alpha_5 \to \alpha_6 \to \alpha_{10} \to \alpha_{15} \to \alpha_{16} \to \alpha_{17} \to \alpha_{29} \to \alpha_{30} \to \alpha_{31}$ as shown in equation (7).

$$F = (w_{RSS} \cdot \frac{\sum_{i=1}^{n} RSS * (\alpha_i)}{n} + w_B \cdot \frac{\sum_{i=1}^{n} B * (\alpha_i)}{n} + w_D \cdot D * (P_i)) \cdot (\overset{n}{\underset{i=1}{Max}} (f (AS (\alpha_i)))) \quad (6)$$

$$, w_{RSS} + w_B + w_D = 1$$

$$F = w_{RSS} \cdot \frac{(RSS^*(\alpha_5) + RSS^*(\alpha_6) + RSS^*(\alpha_{10}) + RSS^*(\alpha_{15}) + RSS^*(\alpha_{16}) + RSS^*(\alpha_{17}) + RSS^*(\alpha_{29}) + RSS^*(\alpha_{30}) + RSS^*(\alpha_{31}))}{9}$$

$$+ w_B \cdot \frac{(B^*(\alpha_5) + B^*(\alpha_6) + B^*(\alpha_{10}) + B^*(\alpha_{15}) + B^*(\alpha_{16}) + B^*(\alpha_{17}) + B^*(\alpha_{29}) + B^*(\alpha_{30}) + B^*(\alpha_{31}))}{9}$$

$$+ w_D \cdot \frac{(D^*(\alpha_5) + D^*(\alpha_6) + D^*(\alpha_{10}) + D^*(\alpha_{15}) + D^*(\alpha_{16}) + D^*(\alpha_{17}) + D^*(\alpha_{29}) + D^*(\alpha_{30}) + D^*(\alpha_{31}))}{9} \quad (7)$$

$$+ w_{AS} \cdot (Max((f(S(\alpha_5)), f(S(\alpha_5)), f(S(\alpha_{10})), f(S(\alpha_{15})), f(S(\alpha_{16})), f(S(\alpha_{17})), f(S(\alpha_{29})), f(S(\alpha_{30})), f(S(\alpha_{31}))))$$

3.3 Selection and Reproduction Operation

Some of chromosomes are stochastically selected by roulette wheel selection to reproduce more offspring of the next generation through crossover and mutation operations. We use the most common type - roulette wheel selection in which chromosomes are given a probability of being selected that is directly proportional to their fitness. Two chromosomes are then chosen randomly based on the probabilities and reproduce a new offspring. A new offspring is then evaluated by fitness function, and chromosomes with higher fitness value will continue onto the next generation in the gene pool. Otherwise, the chromosomes with lower fitness value will die out.

3.4 Crossover Operation

Crossover operation combines two chromosomes (called parents) to produce a new chromosome (called offspring). In this paper, we adopt the uniform crossover method proposed in [18]. Moreover, our crossover operation is carefully designed to avoid the path looping problem. The crossover operation is performed as follows. Two parent chromosomes are randomly selected from the gene pool. To generate the new offspring through crossover, we start with the gene in the locus of the source node. If the genes of the locus of two parents are the same, then just copy the gene to the offspring. Otherwise, we will prefer to select the gene (node) that has not been appeared (visited) before. Tie is broken by random selection. After the selection of gene of the current locus, we move to the locus of the next node (i.e., the gene we just selected), and the procedure repeats until the destination node is reached as the gene of current locus. An example of crossover operation is shown in Figure 7. We assume the chromosome of parent 1 corresponds to the path $\alpha_{19} \rightarrow \alpha_{33} \rightarrow \alpha_{57} \rightarrow \alpha_{55} \rightarrow \alpha_{53} \rightarrow \alpha_{51}$ and that of parent 2 is $\alpha_{19} \rightarrow \alpha_{33} \rightarrow \alpha_{31} \rightarrow \alpha_{29} \rightarrow \alpha_{24} \rightarrow \alpha_{48} \rightarrow \alpha_{51}$. Since the genes of locus 19 of both parent chromosomes are 33, the offspring also starts the 33 in its locus 19. For the locus 33, we randomly select α_{57} or α_{31} as they are not visited before. Assume α_{31} is selected, then we consider locus 31. For locus 31, we select α_{29} as α_{33} has been visited passed before. The operation then is repeated until the destination node is reached. After the crossover operation, the new offspring $\alpha_{19} \rightarrow \alpha_{33} \rightarrow \alpha_{31} \rightarrow \alpha_{29} \rightarrow \alpha_{53} \rightarrow \alpha_{51}$ is generated. Note that for the locus of nodes which are not passed through, such as 10, the gene in the new chromosome is randomly select form the two genes of two parents, e.g α_{12} in locus 10.

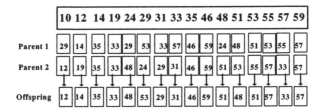

Fig. 7. An example of crossover operation

3.5 Mutation Operation

With a given probability, mutation introduces variations into the chromosome to change partial chromosomes to avoid local optimal. A random node (mutation node), which is neither source nor destination node, along path is chosen for mutation. The new gene value is randomly chosen from directly connected nodes of the mutation node. An example of mutation operation is shown in Figure 8. The α_{33} is randomly chosen for mutation gene. After mutation operation, the new path is $\alpha_{19} \rightarrow \alpha_{33} \rightarrow \alpha_{35} \rightarrow \alpha_{46} \rightarrow \alpha_{59} \rightarrow \alpha_{57} \rightarrow \alpha_{55} \rightarrow \alpha_{53} \rightarrow \alpha_{51}$.

After crossover and mutation operations are completed, the chromosomes are once again evaluated by fitness function for another round of reproduction until a termination condition has been satisfied.

Before: *19->33->57->55->53 ->51*
After: *19->33->35->46->59->57->55->53->51*

Fig. 8. An example of mutation operator

4 Prototype Implementation

In this section, we demonstrate the feasibility of the UbiPaPaGo via prototyping a real system in U-gate. Our demonstration scenario is made up with user using EeePC with

(a) User connects to Service Provider and uses UbiPaPago Service (Service Provider IP:140.123.105.8)

(b) UbiPaPaGo Service Provider receives the request from user

Fig. 9. The Demonstration of UbiPaPaGo

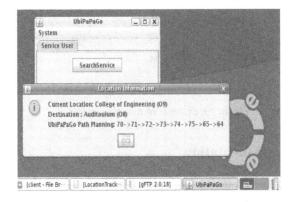

(c) The path planning result

Fig. 9. (*Continued*)

WiFi, RFID. The scenario is demonstrated that the user uses UbiPaPaGo service in EeePC to connect UbiPaPaGo service provider, as shown in Figure 9 (a) and (b) to plan path form college of engineering (O_9) to auditorium (O_8). U-Gate collects the contexts of user's current location, requirement, ID, schedule and SCM map to infer path planning result as shown in Figure 9 (c). Readers are referred to [22] for the detailed implementation.

5   Experimental Results

In this section, the proposed UbiPaPaGo is implemented by Java code program and evaluated by computer simulations. In this experiment, the population size is set to 20, the crossover rate is set to 0.8 and the mutation probability is set to 0.1. The generation number varies from 10 to 100. To obtain the results as shown in the following figures, 20 simulation runs were conducted.

Figure 10 (a) and (b) show the optimal paths (red dotted lines) found for the indicated source (O_1) and destination (O_6). We can observe that the result computed by the proposed UbiPaPaGo in Figure 10 (a) coincides with optimal path in Figure 10 (b).

Figure 11 compares the effect of the average fitness value under various generation numbers for UbiPaPaGo and random approach. The random approach differs from UbiPaPaGo by the fact that pure random approach is adopted in the initialization and crossover operations such that some chromosomes may contain loops. We observe that the proposed UbiPaPaGo converges faster than the random approach. The results indicate that avoiding looping in initialization and crossover operations when selecting the next hop of a path does improves the convergence speed.

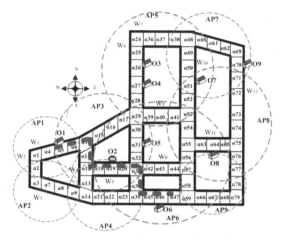

(a)   Results of UbiPaPaGo

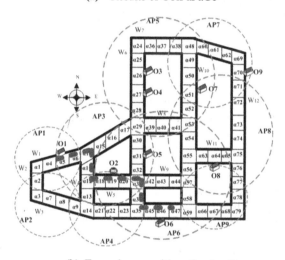

(b) Example map with optimal path

Fig. 10. Comparison results for the path found by each mechanism

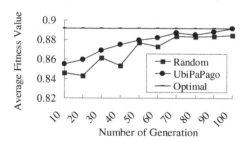

Fig. 11. Average fitness value under various population sizes

6 Conclusion and Future Works

In this paper, we have proposed an intelligent navigation application, UbiPaPaGo, which focuses on providing human-centric context-aware path planning mechanism in ubiquitous networks. Specifically, UbiPaPaGo takes into account multiple requirements and context of users and environment when planning the best-fitting path. Experimental results show that the proposed UbiPaPaGo efficiently finds the best-fitting path which guarantees RSS, bandwidth, available service and shorter distance simultaneously.

Several issues of the proposed UbiPaPaGo need future research. In this paper, the destination is assumed to be given by inferring to user's personal context, such as schedule. If the destination of the path is uncertain or unknown, how to predict the destination from related context becomes a priori problem. Besides, we only consider how to plan a good path for a user; issues like vertical handoff between AP and BS, resource reservation along the path in advance to guarantee quality of service of the path are still under investigation. Finally, security and privacy issues also need further investigation. A general framework for preserving privacy shall be deployed in the future.

Acknowledgment

The research is supported by the NSC 96-2219-E-194-006, NSC 97-2221-E-194-011-MY3 and NSC 97-2221-E-194-012-MY3, National Science Council, ROC.

References

1. PAPAGO, http://www.papago.com.tw/
2. TomTom International, http://www.tomtom.com/
3. Weiser, M.: The Computer for the Twenty-First Century. Scientific American, 94–104 (1991)
4. Li, Q., Zhang, W., Yin, Y., Zhang, W., Liu, G.: An Improved Genetic Algorithm of Optimum Path Planning for Mobile Robots. In: The Sixth International Conference on Intelligent Systems Design and Applications, pp. 637–642 (2006)
5. Tu, J., Yang, S.: Genetic Algorithm based Path Planning for a Mobile Robot. In: IEEE International Conference on Robotics and Automation, Taipei, pp. 1221–1226 (2003)
6. Castilho, O., Trujilo, L.: Multiple Objective Optimization Genetic Algorithms for Path Planning In Autonomous Mobile Robots. International Journal of Computers, Systems and Signals 6(1), 48–63 (2005)
7. Lei, L., Wang, H., Wu, Q.: Improved Genetic Algorithms Based Path planning of Mobile Robot Under Dynamic Unknown Environment. In: IEEE International Conference on Mechatronics and Automation, June 2006, pp. 1728–1732 (2006)
8. Li, Q., Liu, G., Zhang, W., Zhao, C., Yin, Y., Wang, Z.: A Specific Genetic Algorithm for Optimum Path Planning in Intelligent Transportation System. In: 6th International Conference on ITS Telecommunications, June 2006, pp. 140–143 (2006)

9. Wan, T.R., Chen, H., Earnshaw, R.: Real-time Path Planning for Navigation in Unknown Environment. In: Theory and Practice of Computer Graphics, June 2003, pp. 138–145 (2003)
10. Arikan, O., Chenney, S., Forsyth, D.A.: Efficient Multi-Agent Path Planning. In: Eurographic Workshop on Computer Animation and Simulation, Manchester, UK, September 2001, pp. 151–162 (2001)
11. Samaan, N., Karmouch, A.: A Mobility Prediction Architecture Based on Contextual Knowledge and Spatial Conceptual Maps. IEEE Transactions on Mobile Computing 4(6), 537–551 (2005)
12. Sigg, S., Haseloff, S., David, K.: A novel approach to context prediction in ubicomp environments. In: 17th Annual IEEE International Symposium on Personal, Indoor and Mobile Radio Communications (PIMRC 2006), September 2006, pp. 1–5 (2006)
13. Anagnostopoulos, T., Anagnostopoulos, C., Hadjiefthymiades, S., Kalousis, A., Kyriakakos, M.: Path Prediction through Data Mining. In: IEEE International Conference on Pervasive Services (ICPS), Istanbul, Turkey, July 2007, pp. 128–135 (2007)
14. Lu, J.H., Hwang, R.H.: An Open Framework for Distributed Context Management in Ubiquitous Environment. In: National Symposium on Telecommunications, Session B4-3 (2008)
15. Kettani, D., Moulin, B.: A Spatial Model Based on the Notions of Spatial Conceptual Map and of Object's Influence Areas. In: Freksa, C., Mark, D.M. (eds.) COSIT 1999. LNCS, vol. 1661, pp. 401–416. Springer, Heidelberg (1999)
16. Holland-I, H.: Adaptation in Natural and Artificial Systems. University of Michigan Press, Ann Arbor (1975)
17. David, E., Goldberg: Genetic Algorithms in Search, Optimization, and Machine Learning. Addison-Wesley, Massachusetts (1989)
18. Inagaki, J., Haseyama, M., Kitajima, H.: A Genetic Algorithm for Determining Multiple Routes and Its Applications. In: IEEE International Symposium (ISCAS 1999), pp. 137–140 (1999)
19. Hue, X.: Genetic Algorithms for Optimization: Background and Applications. In: Edinburg Parallel Computing Centre, Ver. 1.0, Feburary 1997. University of Edinburg, Edinburg (1997)
20. Lauritzen, S.L., Spiegelhalter, D.J.: Local Computations with Probabilities on Graphical Structures and Their Application to Expert Systems. J. Royal Stat. Soc. (B) 50, 157–224 (1988)
21. Charilas, D., Markaki, O., Nikitopoulos, D., Theologou, M.E.: Packet-switched Network Selection with the Highest QoS in 4G Networks. Computer Networks 52(1), 248–258 (2008)
22. Huwang, H.Y., Wang, C.Y., Hwang, R.H.: Context-awareness Access Point Planning in Ubiquitous Network. In: National Symposium on Telecommunications, Session B4-6 (2008)

An Efficient Approach to Situation-Aware Service Discovery in Pervasive Service Computing Environments

Stephen S. Yau and Gautam G. Pohare

Department of Computer Science and Engineering
Arizona State University
Tempe, AZ 85287-8809, USA
{yau,gautam.pohare}@asu.edu

Abstract. Service discovery, which is an important required function for service-based systems (SBS), affects the performance of SBS, especially in pervasive service computing environments. In this paper, an efficient approach to service discovery in multi-hop pervasive service computing environments is presented. This approach is situation-aware and based on group-based service discovery protocol. In a pervasive computing environment, the situation, including available service resources, users' preferences and the physical environment, changes more dynamically. Our service discovery approach exploits the network asymmetry and incorporates situational information while keeping low network overhead. Our simulation results show that our approach discovers services efficiently.

Keywords: Pervasive service computing environments, situation-aware service discovery, service resources, and users' preferences.

1 Introduction

Service-based systems (SBS), which are based on Service-Oriented Architecture (SOA) [1], are rapidly becoming popular for distributed applications. In a SBS, various organizations in different domains provide various capabilities in the form of services to their users. With increasing availability of small computing devices and low-cost wireless networking hardware, pervasive computing is becoming common.

Pervasive computing environments usually comprise various heterogeneous computing devices, some of which are resource-rich, such as desktops and laptops, and others are resource-constrained, such as handheld, wearable and embedded computers connected by wireless ad-hoc networks and wireless infrastructure-based networks. The SBS in pervasive computing environments facilitate collaboration among users. In a collaborative multi-hop SBS pervasive computing environment, users collaborating on a task may demand as well as provide services. In order to use the services available in such an environment, service discovery is required. Due to the inherent dynamism, heterogeneity and network asymmetry in pervasive computing environments, service discovery needs to be efficient and situation-aware. The situation awareness (SAW) capability of a system is that the system is aware of situation changes and adapting its behavior due to situation changes [2, 3]. A *situation* is a set

D. Zhang et al. (Eds.): UIC 2009, LNCS 5585, pp. 68–82, 2009.

of contexts in an application over a period of time that affects future system behavior. A *context* is any instantaneous, detectable, and relevant property of the environment, system, or users, such as location, available bandwidth, and remaining power. SAW is needed for efficient service discovery in order to satisfy various quality of service (QoS) for pervasive service computing [2 - 6].

A service discovery approach is efficient if it creates little network overhead, which includes handling service discovery messages, such as service requests, replies and announcements while finding available services in the network. In this paper, we will present an efficient situation-aware service discovery approach in multi-hop pervasive service computing environments based on group-based service discovery (GSD) protocol [7]. In this approach, the network is organized into a two-level hierarchy such that resource-rich nodes, called *Ultrapeers* [8], participate more in the dissemination of service discovery messages than resource-constrained nodes, called *leaves*. Our approach has the following major advantages: (i) It creates less network overhead than existing approaches due to efficient aggregation, dissemination and real-time updates of service related information. (ii) It facilitates users to use services that satisfy service-related resource and situational constraints. (iii) Resource-constrained nodes can share data for a longer time than existing approaches because the system resources of the nodes in the network are considered in our approach. Our approach has a limitation which is every domain provides services from unique set of service groups (SGs). This limitation is less serious because our approach does not limit the number of SGs in the network.

2 Related Work

Service discovery approaches can be classified into four categories: (i) centralized or semi-centralized, (ii) hash based, (iii) hierarchical or directory based, and (iv) directory-less. The centralized or semi-centralized approaches [9 – 16] assume the network is stable or wired, and hence they are unsuitable for dynamic pervasive computing environments. The hash based approaches [17 - 21] hash service descriptions, names or operations to a key or filter. They restrict dynamic updates whenever changes are made to service descriptions, names or operations. In Chord [17] and INS/Twine [18], the overhead for a node to join or leave a dynamic network is quite large. In [19 - 21], bloom-filters [22] are used to encapsulate service information, but users are assumed to know the required service descriptions, keywords or names in order to search for the services in the network. Hence, the hash based approaches are unsuitable for dynamic environments. Hierarchical or directory-based service discovery approaches [23 - 26] are unsuitable for the pervasive service computing environments because (i) they cause very large overhead in a dynamic network, (ii) they have the same shortcomings as the approaches [17 - 21], or (iii) they use flooding to disseminate service requests. The directory-less service discovery approaches [7, 27 - 30] are unsuitable for pervasive service computing environments because (i) they assume the network supported multicasting, (ii) they put heavy burden on the network resources for service advertisement broadcasts and service request flooding, (iii) they can be used only in single-hop environments, (iv) they use periodic broadcasts of service advertisements which creates large network overhead, or (v) they broadcast service requests when no service match is found. Due to these limitations, we need to have an efficient situation-aware service discovery approach.

3 An Example Scenario

To illustrate the importance of situation-aware service discovery in multi-hop pervasive computing environment, let us consider an example with patrons attending a runners' marathon exhibition and registration event on an open site as shown in Fig.1. This event allows runners to (a) get photographed, (b) obtain timing-chip and schedule its demonstration video, (c) register for a marathon, and (d) purchase marathon-related products from various independent vendors. For illustration purpose, assume that we have four entities at the event on the site: Registration facility (RF), shoes vendor (SV), running equipment vendor (REV) and medical information facility (MIF). Because there are many runners for the event, these entities facilitate the runners to quickly complete their marathon registration and marathon-related equipment purchases by providing data services to everyone on site. Each of these four entities has its own separate network domain with laptops or desktops in their designated area for their workers. These entities form a network to enable the users to discover the services in the network. The users have portable devices, such as handhelds or Tablet-PCs through which they discover and use the services in order to finish their marathon registration and purchase products on-site.

As shown in Fig. 1, the open site has various domains to form a two-tier hierarchical network of nodes. In this network, the resource-rich nodes are selected as ultrapeers (UPs) and resource-constrained nodes become leaves (LFs). The UPs act as web service (WS) proxies to their LFs. Both the UPs and LFs have lightweight situation-aware middleware [2 - 6] to provide situation-aware support for situation-aware services.

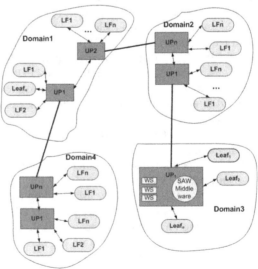

Fig. 1. Network Diagram

A user may request a situation-aware service from any entity in the network. The UPs connected to other UPs discover the service for the user. Table 1 shows a brief description of some services provided by RF and SV to its users, and the photograph service and the timing-chip demonstration service are situation-aware. The service discovery approach in the given environment needs to satisfy both the service requests and the service-related resource and situational constraints.

Table 1. The service information table for the example

Service Name	Service Group (SG) Name	SG No.	Service Providing Domain	Service Functionality
Timing-chip Demonstration Service (TCDS)	Timing-chip	1	Registration Facility	Schedule the timing chip video demonstration based on situational parameters, such as ambient sound
Registration Service (RS)	Registration	2	Registration Facility	Register a runner for the marathon race
Photograph Service (PS)	Photograph	3	Registration Facility	Schedule a photograph time based on the number of patrons already scheduled and situational parameters, such as ambient light and temperature
Shoes Purchase(SP)	Shoes	4	Shoes Vendor	Reserve and purchase a specific size running-shoes

4 Overview of Our Approach

Without loss of generality, we assume the following: (i) Each wireless node in the network has an omni-directional antenna, all the network links are bi-directional and the network is connected. (ii) The application has assigned a unique number between 1 to N to represent each service group in the network, where N is the total number of service groups for the application. A service group (SG) is a group of similar services based on their functionality.

In our approach, the UPs act as web service (WS) proxies to their LFs. Both the UPs and LFs may provide data services. We use the GSD's technique [7] to classify services into groups to selectively forward service requests (SRs). Unlike GSD, only the resource-rich UPs participate in routing, caching, service discovery and network maintenance; and service descriptions (SDs) and service group information (SGI) are not periodically broadcasted. After network formation, SDs and highly compacted SGI are sent by LFs to their UPs, which exchange their SGI with other UPs after a UP to UP connection is formed. The UPs in a domain select the most resource-rich UP among themselves to be their domain SD-Keeper (SDK), which stores all SDs in its domain sent by the intra-domain UPs. To reduce the network overhead, the SDs in different domains are not exchanged. Because SDs may be modified by the service providers, UPs update SGI and SDs based on SGI-change and SD-change events. In order to quickly and efficiently aggregate various SGI received by UPs and to reduce the size of the SGI, we convert and store SGI at UPs in a compact service-group bitmap (SG-BMP). Depending on whether a particular SG is already present in the SG-BMP at an UP, an emergence or disappearance of a service may not result in a SGI-change event among UPs, and thus saving additional update messages. Because the SGI and SDs are kept latest through SGI-change and SD-change events, unlike GSD, we do not broadcast service request (SR) when it cannot be satisfied at a forwarding node, and thus saving additional overhead.

To maintain the network connectivity, all nodes use 1-hop periodic broadcast for a short hello message. Service-related situational information, including local resources, may change dynamically for pervasive computing applications. To discover the requested service that matches the SR and satisfies service-related resource and situational constraints, the service providers include the resource and situational information in their hello messages. During SR processing, UPs take the service-related constraints into account to find the correct service. To facilitate a LF to switch its connection to another UP in the network based on the LF's resource requirements, the UPs include their resource values in their hello messages. In order to reduce the overhead associated with periodic hellos of every node, the frequency of the hellos is based on a node's stability and situational information. Depending on the dynamism of the environment, an application may specify lower and upper bounds for hello message intervals.

Our approach can be summarized in the following five steps:

S1) Network formation
S2) Vertical and horizontal aggregation and dissemination of SGI
S3) Consolidation of service descriptions at respective SDKs
S4) Event-based SGI and SD updates
S5) Processing of service requests

In Sections 5 to 7, we will present Steps *S2)*, *S3)* and *S4)* and then present the implementation of our approach in Section 8, including Steps *S1)* and *S5)*.

5   Vertical and Horizontal Aggregation and Dissemination of SGI

It is necessary to efficiently disseminate SGI in the network and hence we reduce the number and size of the SGI messages. To reduce the size of the SGI messages and to quickly and efficiently aggregate and disseminate SGI in the network, we convert and store SGI at UPs in a compact SG-BMP in which every bit of the SG-BMP represents one service group (SG). To reduce the number of SGI messages, we do not periodically broadcasts SGI in the network. In our approach, we assume that every domain provides services from unique set of SGs.

Consider the example in Section 3, the "registration facility" domain provides three services from SGs 1 to 3. Assume that the timing-chip demonstration service (SG 1) and photograph service (SG 3) are provided by LF1 and LF2, respectively, and that the registration service (SG 2) is provided by their UP1 in that domain. Assume that we have 16 SGs in the given example, and then a 2-byte (16 bits) data structure will suffice to hold all the SGI in the network. Fig. 2 shows the initial SG-BMPs and the vertically aggregated SGI at the UP. We refer this as vertical aggregation and dissemination of SGI because LFs (at a lower level in the network) send their SGI to their UPs (at a higher level), where all the individual SGI is aggregated and com-pacted to the SG-BMP as shown from Fig. 2(a) to Fig.2(b) . During horizontal SGI aggregation and dissemination, the UPs at the same level exchange, aggregate and disseminate the SGIs to each other in the network.

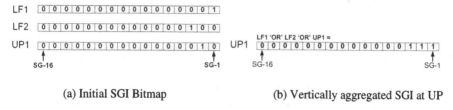

(a) Initial SGI Bitmap   (b) Vertically aggregated SGI at UP

Fig. 2. Vertical aggregation of SGI

Every UP has the following three types of SGI-BMPs:

(i) *Cluster-SGI*: A combined SGI-BMP of all services provided by a UP and its di-rectly connected LFs.
(ii) Intra-domain SGI or *own-SGI*: A combined SGI-BMP of all services provided in its own domain
(iii) Inter-domain SGI or *other-SGI*: A combined SGI-BMP of all services provided in all other domains.

Step *S2)* exploits both the SGI uniformity and the two-tier network by combining, compacting and reducing the size of SGI packets. It minimizes the SGI packets in the network when combined with event-based SGI updates. It increases the possibility of discovering a service because it eliminates the need for having a limiting factor – "the number of hops" that a SGI packet can traverse in the network. Depending on whether a particular SG is already present in the cluster-SGI or own-SGI bitmap at a UP, an emergence or disappearance of a service *may not result in a SGI-change event* among UPs, and thus saving additional update messages.

Hence, *S2)* can be summarized as follows:

S2.1) The LFs connected to one UP and providing services send their SGI and SD in a single- packet to the UP. The UP stores each of its LF's SGI and SD in a table, called *neighbor table (NT)*.

S2.2) The UP aggregates all the LFs' SGI, including its own, to create a compact SG-BMP using a quick bitwise 'OR' operation. The UP stores this combined SGI-BMP as its own "cluster-SGI".

S2.3) Each UP sends the following two types of SGI-exchange messages for a few times until no new SGI is received:

Intra-domain-SGI-exchange: UPs send this message only to directly connected in-tra-domain UPs. This message contains

<ID of sender UP, domain ID, cluster-SGI, own-SGI, other-SGI>.

Inter-domain-SGI-exchange: UPs send this message only to directly connected in-ter-domain UPs. This message contains

<ID of sender UP, domain ID, own-SGI, and other-SGI>.

S2.4) Depending on whether the received SGI-BMP has intra-domain or inter-domain SGI, a UP aggregates it with its existing own-SGI with intra-domain SGI or other-SGI with inter-domain SGI using "OR" operation. The cluster-SGI, own-SGI and other-SGI received from a neighbor-UP are stored in NT to avoid sending the same information back to the neighbor-UP.

6 Consolidation of Service Descriptions at Respective SDKs

To reduce the network overhead associated with the dissemination of SDs, we consolidate the SDs within a domain. We first define a *SD-set as a* set of SDs belonging to one SG. We also define the *SD-table as a* table at SDK containing all SD-sets in the SDK's domain. Each entry in the SD-table has the following fields:

<SG of the SD-set, the SD-set, hash of the SD-set,

source UP for this SD-set, expiration-time>.

A SD-set can be very large because it contains many service descriptions. The hash of a SD-set can be very small (for example, 32-bits using Cyclic Redundancy Check) compared to the SD-set itself. There may be multiple source UPs for a SD-set.

The SD-set hash is utilized to reduce the size and the number of SD-set related messages between a UP and its SDK. During SR processing, while a UP obtains a SD-set from its SDK, the SD-set is cached by any forwarding UP in the domain. The UPs use the cached SD-set until the SD-set's expiration time or until the SD-set is dynamically updated due to SD-change event. This process provides the latest SD to all the forwarding UPs in the domain and hence the network overhead of our approach is smaller than that of periodic and large SD broadcasts [7].

Hence, *S3)* can be summarized as follows:

S3.1) Every UP combines all of the SDs of the UP's LFs, including the UP's own. Every UP sends all the combined SDs to the SDK in the domain of the UP

S3.2) The SDK in the domain classifies the received SDs according to their SGs to form SD-sets (including the hash code, expiration time, and source UP of the SD-set) to be stored in the SD-table.

S3.3) If a service provider changes its SD, the SD is updated on SD-change event.

7 Event-Based SGI and SD Updates

In a dynamic environment, a service provider may become unavailable or re-available resulting in a change in SGI and SDs at the service provider's UP. A service provider may change or update its SDs. Hence, it is necessary to have the latest SGI and SDs at a UP to correctly process service requests. After Steps *S2)* and *S3)*, the changed SGI and SDs are updated when SGI-change and SD-change events are detected, respectively.

A SGI-change event may occur at a UP when the UP detects that an existing service is no longer available or a new service has become available on the UP. Depending on whether a particular SG is already present in the cluster-SGI at a UP, an emergence or disappearance of a service may not result in a SGI-change event and SGI updates. An SD-change event may occur at a UP when it detects an updated SD or the emergence or disappearance of a service. Step *S4)* can be summarized as follow:

S4.1) Event-based SGI update: If a UP detects a SGI-change on the UP, the UP updates its SGI as follows: The UP calculates its cluster-SGI and own-SGI using *S2.2)* to *S2.4)*. This updating process applies to all the UPs having SGI-change.

S4.2) Event-based SD update: If a UP detects a changed SD on the UP, the UP sends the changed SD to the SDK of the UP's domain. Using the SDK's SD-table, the SDK replaces the old SD in the SD-set and received from the same UP in *S3.1)*, with the changed SD. The SDK stores the updated SD-set, including the modified hash and expiration time, in the SDK's SD-table.

8   Implementation of Our Approach

In a pervasive service computing environment, nodes use 1-hop periodic broadcast of short hello messages to establish and maintain connections. The hello message contains

$$<ID, UP, domain, SI_t, Cn_t, RVi_t, i=1, 2, ... n>$$

where ID, UP and domain are the node's address, the UP address and domain address, respectively; SI_t is the situation of the node at time t; Cn_t is the number of directly connected nodes of the node at time t; $RVi_t, i = 1, 2, ..., n$, is a set of 1-byte resource variables at time t of the contexts, such as CPU power, network bandwidth, and memory.

A node may not know its domain address at beginning, in which case the node knows the domain address when the node joins the network. SI_t is included in hellos if the change of the situation of the node exceeds its constraint. The UPs utilize RVi_ts and SI_t during SR processing to find a service that meets both the user requirements under the situational constraints. The Cn_t, which is applicable to the UPs only, is used by LFs to decide whether to select a particular UP.

The "Network Formation" in Step *S1)* can be summarized as follows:

S1.1) Nodes utilize 1-hop periodic broadcast of hellos to discover each other. Each node stores the latest hello message received from the node's neighbors in the node's NT.

S1.2) After a specified time, a resource-rich node chooses to be a UP itself if the RVi_ts, Cn, the number of nearby UPs in 1-hop range, and signal strength of the node satisfy the minimum system requirements of the application. Each resource-constrained node compares the following three values of each of the UPs in its neighborhood: (i) RVi_ts, (ii) Cn, and (iii) the received signal strength (RSS) of the UP from which the hello message is received. As long as a UP has the three values above the thresholds of the minimum system requirements, the UP can be selected by the resource-constrained node. After applying this step to all the nodes, all the LFs are connected to UPs.

S1.3) After a specified time, each UP broadcasts a 1-hop UP-connection message. Any UP in the 1-hop range of the node broadcasting the UP-connection message establishes a UP-to-UP connection with its neighbor UPs. The UPs in a domain select the most resource-rich UP among themselves to be the SDK of their domain.

S1.4) The LF creates passive connection to one and only one neighboring UP as its backup UP. Each UP, including the SDK, selects the most resource-rich LF in the UP's cluster as a backup UP to take over the current UP when the UP ceases to exist. Based on the SDK's stability, the SDK may store its SD-sets on the SDK's backup UP and inform the address of the SDK's backup UP to all the intra-domain UPs. Connections between any pair of directly connected nodes are maintained using the 1-hop periodic hellos. The frequency of hellos is low if a node is stable. At the end of step *S1)*, the network is formed containing UPs, LFs and SDKs.

Once the network is formed, the UPs aggregate and disseminate SGI and SDs in the network as described in Steps *S2)* and *S3)*. Subsequent changes in SGI and SD are handled with event-based SGI and SD updates described in Step *S4)*.

In Step *S5)*, we will present how the UPs in the network will process the SRs. A SR can be represented by

<Packet-type, SR-Num, Sender's ID, Sender's Domain ID, SG, SD, SR-Path>,

where SR-Num is the request number used by the service requester, and SR-Path is the path followed by this SR. The SR-Num and SR-Path are used to check duplicates and SRs already processed. The user may include service-related resource requirements in the SD field of the SR. In order to find a matched service reply (SRP) regardless of any RVi_ts or SI_t values, a user may specify no service-related resource requirements.

A SRP contains

<Packet-type, Service Replier's ID, Service Requester's ID, SG, SD, SRP-Path> ,

where SG and SD are the service group and service description of the matched service, respectively, and SRP-Path is the reversed SR-path.

Step *S5)* can be summarized as follows:

S5.1). If the SR is from LF, the LF sends the SR to the LF's current UP.

S5.2) This UP first checks its cluster-SGI and SD cache to find a matching service on the UP. Service matching can be done using existing service matching approaches [31, 32]. If a matched service is found, go to *S5.5)*.

S5.3) If the UP's own-SGI has the required SG and

(a) If the UP does not have a SD-set associated with the required SG, the UP obtains the SD-set from the SDK of the UP's domain. Or

(b) If the UP has a cached but expired SD-set associated with the required SG. the UP sends the required SG and the hash of the UP's SD-set associated with the required SG to the UP's SDK. Because in *S3.2)* the SDK has stored each SD-set associated with one SG in the SDK's SD-table, the SDK compares the hash received from the UP with the corresponding hash of the SD-set stored in the SDK's SD-table.

(b.1) If the two hashes do not match, it implies the SD-set in the SDK's SD-table is newer than the SD-set present on the UP. The SDK sends the latest SD-set to the requesting UP. While forwarding the SD-set from the SDK to the requesting UP, the intra-domain UPs cache the SD-set.

(b.2) If the two hashes match, the SDK sends no reply to the requesting UP which proceeds after a short specified wait period.

The UP finds a matched service using the SDs in the SD-set. If a matched service is found, go to *S5.5)*.

S5.4) If the UP's other-SGI has the required SG, the UP selectively forwards the SR to a UP from which the required SG was received. The SR reaches at a UP where the service from the required SG may be present. Each UP, that selectively forwards the SR using the UP's SGI, checks for a service match using the SGI and SDs at the UP. If a service match occurs at a UP, go to *S5.5)*. If no service match occurs at a UP, then no SRP is sent. If the three SGI-BMPs i.e. cluster-SGI, own-SGI and other-SGI at a UP does not have the required SG, then the SR is not transmitted further.

S5.5) The UP checks (i) whether the SI_t value of the service provider is below the situational constraint for the service needed by the SR, and (ii) whether the RVi_ts of the UP meets the service-related resource requirements in the SR. If both (i) and (ii) are met, the UP sends a (positive) SRP to the user.

9 An Illustrative Example

In this section, we will use the example in Section 3 to illustrate our approach. Let domains 1, 2, 3 and 4 be registration facility (RF), shoes vendor (SV), running equipment vendor (REV) and medical information facility (MIF), respectively. On the open site for the marathon exhibition and registration event, these domains are created ad-hoc. Assume that there are many runners carrying PDAs on site. In order to quickly complete the marathon registration and equipment purchases, the workers in the RF, SV, REV and MIF areas have laptops to provide data services. Assume that a runner named Raj, who has entered the site near the SV area, wants to complete his marathon registration. Table 1 shows the service information of services provided by RF and SV to the users. In order to complete the marathon registration, a runner must schedule a timing-chip video demonstration. From Table 1, the timing-chip demonstration service (TCDS) and registration service (RS) is classified to timing-chip (SG 1) and registration (SG 2) service groups, respectively. For illustration purpose, we assume that each service group has only one service as shown in Table 1. According to Fig. 1 and Table 1, TCDS, RS, PS and SP services reside on LF1 connected to UP1 in RF, UP1 in RF, LF2 in RF, and UP1 in SV respectively. Let Raj's PDA be LF1 in the SV domain. We will illustrate how to use our approach to discover the TCDS service,

S1) All nodes broadcast 1-hop hellos, store received hellos in their NT and search for UPs in their domains. Assume the UPs in domain1 select UP2 as the SDK of the domain and the UPs in domain 2 select UP1 as the SDK. Raj's PDA, which is LF1 in domain 2, selects the UP1 as its UP.

S2) Fig. 2 shows the SGI-BMP of LF1, LF2, UP1 and the combined cluster-SGI of UP1 in domain 1. The UPs receive the SGI from all domains by sending SGI-exchange messages to their neighboring UPs. Fig. 3 shows the three SGI bitmaps of all the UPs in the network after vertical and horizontal SGI aggregation and dissemination. Due to limited space, we show only the lower order bits of the bitmap relevant to our example.

S3) LF1 and LF2 send the SDs of their services to the UP1 in domain 1. The UP1 combines the two SDs with its own SD and sends the combined SDs to the UP2 in the same domain. The UP2 in RF is the SDK of domain 1. In domain 2, no LFs provide services, and the UP1, which provides the SP service, is the SDK of domain 2. Each SDK classifies the received SDs according to their SGs to form SD-sets to be stored in the SD-table.

S4) Due to limited space, we omit the illustration of event-based updates here.

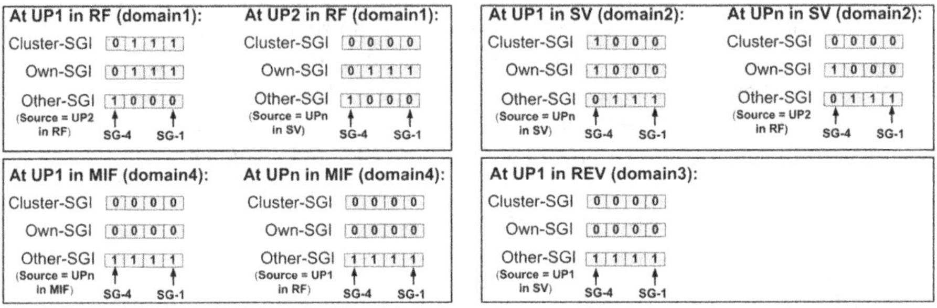

```
At UP1 in RF (domain1):        At UP2 in RF (domain1):
Cluster-SGI  [0|1|1|1]         Cluster-SGI  [0|0|0|0]
Own-SGI      [0|1|1|1]         Own-SGI      [0|1|1|1]
Other-SGI    [1|0|0|0]         Other-SGI    [1|0|0|0]
(Source = UP2                  (Source = UPn
 in RF)      SG-4   SG-1        in SV)      SG-4   SG-1

At UP1 in SV (domain2):        At UPn in SV (domain2):
Cluster-SGI  [1|0|0|0]         Cluster-SGI  [0|0|0|0]
Own-SGI      [1|0|0|0]         Own-SGI      [1|0|0|0]
Other-SGI    [0|1|1|1]         Other-SGI    [0|1|1|1]
(Source = UPn                  (Source = UP2
 in SV)      SG-4   SG-1        in RF)      SG-4   SG-1

At UP1 in MIF (domain4):       At UPn in MIF (domain4):      At UP1 in REV (domain3):
Cluster-SGI  [0|0|0|0]         Cluster-SGI  [0|0|0|0]        Cluster-SGI  [0|0|0|0]
Own-SGI      [0|0|0|0]         Own-SGI      [0|0|0|0]        Own-SGI      [0|0|0|0]
Other-SGI    [1|1|1|1]         Other-SGI    [1|1|1|1]        Other-SGI    [1|1|1|1]
(Source = UPn                  (Source = UP1                 (Source = UP1
 in MIF)     SG-4   SG-1        in RF)      SG-4   SG-1        in SV)      SG-4   SG-1
```

Fig. 3. SGI information at the UPs in the network after vertical and horizontal SGI aggregation and dissemination

S5) In his PDA, Raj enters the service description, service requirements and service group, which is "Timing-chip", to discover the TCDS service. Because the LF1 in domain 2 knows the SG number for each SG, LF1 generates the SR with SG as 1. Raj's PDA, which is LF1 in domain 2, sends the SR to the UP1 in domain 2. According to Fig. 3, the UP1 in domain 2 has SG-1 in other-SGI with source UP of other-SGI as UPn in domain 2. Hence, the UP1 in domain 2 forwards the SR to UPn in domain 2. The UPn has SG-1 in other-SGI with source UP as UP2 in domain 1. UPn forwards the SR to the UP2 in domain 1. The UP2 in domain 1 has SG-1 in own-SGI which means an intra-domain UP may have the required service. Hence, the UP2 finds from its own NT table that the SG-1 is part of cluster-SGI of the UP1 in domain 1 and was received from the UP1 in domain 1. The UP2 in domain 1 forwards the SR to the UP1 in domain 1. The UP1 in domain 1 discovers that the SD of the TCDS service, which is provided by the UP1's LF1, matches SR of the user Raj. Based on the latest RVi_ts and SI_t values of the UP1's LF1, the UP1 in domain 1 checks whether the two conditions of *S5.5)* are satisfied. If the two conditions are satisfied then the UP1 in domain 1 sends a SRP to Raj.

10   Simulation Results

In this section, we evaluate the efficiency of our approach and compare it with that of GSD. Both GSD [7] and CNPGSDP [30] periodically broadcast service advertisements containing much information in a network. In both approaches, when no matched SG is found, the SR is broadcasted in the network. In the two-level hierarchic network of nodes, LFs connected to one UP may have services from the required SG. In such a case, CNPGSDP will not reduce the number of SRs because all the cluster-nodes are on the potential list of SR receivers, regardless whether they contain a matched service. Hence, we compare the network overhead of our approach with that of GSD. To do so, we have implemented both our approach and GSD in the NS-2 simulator [33]. For evaluation purposes, we use the following metrics: (i) the total number of packets transmitted by all nodes in the network, (ii) the total number of bytes transmitted by all nodes, (iii) the total numbers of SRs and SRPs sent, forwarded and received by all nodes, and. (iv) the average number of SRs processed per node. In addition, we present the success ratio of our approach.

Due to limited resources, simulations were carried out with a topology comprising 96 nodes, simulation time up to 1000 seconds and a relatively stable mobile environment with nodes' instability and mobility simulated by turning the nodes OFF and ON to make them unavailable or re-available. The SRs were generated at the application layer at regular time intervals. The rate of change of SGI and SDs was 4 seconds. The period for sending hello messages was 1-second for all nodes. Based on the stability and situation of a node, the probability of switching the hello period from 1 second to a maximum 2 seconds was 0.5. In the simulation, we used 30 SGs numbered from 1 to 30. The size of a SD was 200 bytes. For GSD, the advertisement diameter was 1-hop, so the broadcasted advertisements were restricted to 1-hop only. Table 2 shows the common simulator parameters used for the experiment.

Table 2. Simulation Parameters

Parameter	Value	Parameter	Value
Network area	1000m by 1000m	Max. packets in ifq	50
No. of nodes	96	Seed	0.0
Propagation Model	Two Ray Ground	Routing Layer	AODV
Mac Layer	802.11	Simulation-time	200 to 1000s
Interface queue (ifq)	Droptail/PriQueue	SGI-Change-Rate	4 seconds
Antenna	OmniAntenna	SD-Change-Rate	4 seconds

Fig. 4 shows the simulation results: Fig. 4(a) shows that the total number of packets transmitted is lower for our approach than GSD. Fig. 4(b) shows that the total number of bytes transmitted in GSD is much higher than our approach. Fig. 4(c) shows that the total number of SRs and SRPs processed by all nodes in GSD is much higher than our approach. Fig. 4(d) shows that the average number of SRs processed per node in GSD is much higher than our approach. All these results confirm that our approach has much lower overhead than GSD. These improvements are due to efficient dissemination of service discovery messages in our approach, no periodical broadcast of service information, and only the UPs processing the service discovery messages. In addition to the functional requirements of a user, a UP can satisfy a SR more efficiently by taking the service-related resources and situational constraints into account. Moreover, the frequency of hellos is reduced with the consideration of the resource and situational information of a node.

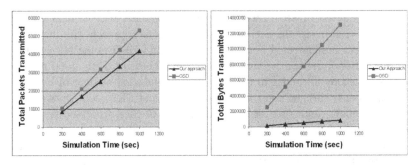

(a) Total number of packets transmitted   (b) Total number of bytes transmitted

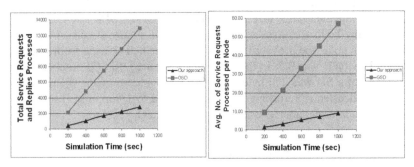

(c) Total service requests and replies   (d) Average number of service requests proc-
processed   essed per node

Fig. 4. Simulation over various time-periods

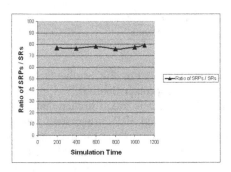

Fig. 5. Ratio of SRPs / SRs in our approach

Fig. 5 shows the ratio of SRPs / SRs, which represents the success rate of discovering matched services. In our approach, about 79% of SRs get matched service responses. This success rate can be considered good because each response indicates
that the matched services are more usable due to the fact that both the user requirements and service-related situational constraints are taken into consideration.

11 Conclusion

In this paper, we have presented an efficient approach to situation-aware service discovery for pervasive service computing environments. Our approach is situation-aware and causes smaller overhead. In addition, the services discovered by our approach are more usable because the resources and situation of the application systems are considered. Additional research in this area which needs to be done includes considering the resource constraints and situations at intermediate nodes in the multi-hop service discovery environments.

Acknowledgement

This work was supported by the National Science Foundation under grant number ITR-CYBERTRUST 0430565.

References

[1] Web Services Architecture, http://www.w3.org/TR/ws-arch/
[2] Yau, S.S., Karim, F., Wang, Y., Wang, B.: Reconfigurable Context-Sensitive Middleware for Pervasive Computing. IEEE Pervasive Computing 1(3), 33–40 (2002)
[3] Yau, S.S., Wang, Y., Karim, F.: Development of Situation-Aware Application Software for Ubiquitous Computing Environments. In: Proc. 26th IEEE Int'l Conf. on Computer Software and Applications, pp. 233–238 (2002)
[4] Yau, S.S., Huang, D., Gong, H., Yao, Y.: Support for Situation-Awareness in Trustworthy Ubiquitous Computing Application Software. Jour. Software Practice and Experience 36(9), 893–921 (2006)
[5] Yau, S.S., Yao, Y., Banga, V.: Situation-Aware Access Control for Service-Oriented Autonomous Decentralized Systems. In: Proc. 7th Int'l Symp. on Autonomous Decentralized Systems, pp. 17–24 (2005)
[6] Yau, S.S., Liu, J.: Incorporating Situation Awareness in Service Specifications. In: Proc. 9th IEEE Int'l Symp. on Object and Component-Oriented Real-Time Distributed Computing, pp. 287–294 (2006)
[7] Chakraborty, D., Joshi, A., Yesha, Y., Finin, T.: Toward Distributed service discovery in pervasive computing environments. IEEE Trans. on Mobile Computing 5(2), 97–112 (2006)
[8] Singla, A., Rohrs, C.: Ultrapeers: Another step towards Gnutella Scalability (2002), http://www.limewire.com/developer/Ultrapeers.html
[9] Sun Microsystems: Jini Technology, http://www.sun.com/jini
[10] Salutation Consortium: Salutation Architecture Specification, http://www.salutation.org
[11] Guttman, E., Perkins, C., Viezades, J., Day, M.: Service Location Protocol Version 2. IETF RFC 2608, http://www.ietf.org/rfc/rfc2608.txt
[12] UPnP Forum, http://www.upnp.org
[13] Universal Description Discovery and Integration Platform, http://www.uddi.org
[14] Paolucci, M., Kawamura, T., Payne, T., Sycara, K.: Semantic Matching of Web Services Capabilities. In: Proc. IEEE Int'l Symp. on Wearable Computers, pp. 333–347 (2002)
[15] Paolucci, M., Soudry, J., Srinivasan, N., Sycara, K.: A Broker for OWL-S Webservices. In: American Association for Artificial Intelligence Spring Symp. Series on Semantic Web Services, pp. 92–99 (2004)

[16] Trastour, D., Bartolini, C., Gonzalez-Castillo, J.: Semantic Web Approach to Service Description for Matchmaking of Services. In: Proc. Int'l Semantic Web Working Symp., pp. 447–461 (2001)

[17] Stoica, I., Morris, R., Karger, D., Kaashoek, M., Balakrishnan, H.: Chord: A Scalable P2P Lookup Service for Internet Applications. In: Proc. ACM Special Interest Group on Data Communications, vol. 31(4), pp. 149–160 (2001)

[18] Balazinska, M., Balakrishnan, H., Karger, D.: INS/Twine: Scalable P2P Architecture for Intentional Resource discovery. In: Mattern, F., Naghshineh, M. (eds.) PERVASIVE 2002. LNCS, vol. 2414, pp. 195–210. Springer, Heidelberg (2002)

[19] Lv, Q., Cao, Q.: Service Discovery Using Hybrid Bloom Filters in Ad-Hoc Networks. In: Proc. Int'l Conf. on Wireless Communications, Networking and Mobile Computing, pp. 1542–1545 (2007)

[20] Goering, P., Heijenk, G.: Service Discovery using Bloom Filters. In: Proc. Conf. of Advanced School for Computing and Imaging, pp. 219–227 (2006)

[21] Lee, C., Yoon, S., Kim, E., Helal, A.: An efficient service propagation scheme for large-scale MANETs. In: Proc. Int'l Workshop on Middleware for Pervasive and Ad-Hoc Computing, pp. 9–13 (2006)

[22] Bloom, B.: Space/time trade-offs in hash coding with allowable errors. Communication of the ACM 13(7), 422–426 (1970)

[23] Artail, H., Safa, H., Hamze, H., Mershad, K.: A Cluster Based Service Discovery Model for Mobile Ad Hoc Networks. In: Proc. Int'l Conf. on Wireless and Mobile Computing, Networking and Communications, pp. 57–64 (2007)

[24] Klein, M., Konig-Ries, B., Obreiter, P.: Service rings - a semantic overlay for service discovery in ad hoc networks. In: Proc. Int'l Workshop on Database and Expert Systems Applications, pp. 180–185 (2003)

[25] Sailhan, F., Issarny, V.: Scalable Service Discovery for MANET. In: Proc. IEEE Int'l Conf. on Pervasive Computing and Communications, pp. 235–244 (2005)

[26] Schiele, G., Becker, C., Rothermel, K.: Energy-efficient cluster-based service discovery for Ubiquitous Computing. In: Proc. 11th Workshop on ACM SIGOPS European (2004)

[27] Helal, S., Desai, N., Verma, V., Lee, C.: Konark – A Service Discovery and Delivery Protocol for Ad-hoc Networks. In: Proc. IEEE Conf. on Wireless Communications and Networking, vol. 3, pp. 2107–2113 (2003)

[28] Harbird, R., Hailes, S., Mascolo, C.: Adaptive resource discovery for ubiquitous computing. In: Proc. ACM Workshop on Middleware for Pervasive and Ad-hoc Computing, pp. 155–160 (2004)

[29] Nidd, M.: Service Discovery in DEAPspace. IEEE Personal Communications 8(4), 39–45 (2001)

[30] Gao, Z., Wang, L., Yang, M., Yang, X.: CNPGSDP: an efficient group-based service discovery protocol for MANETs. Computer Networks 50(16), 3165–3182 (2006)

[31] Jaeger, M., Goldmann, R., Liebetruth, C., Mühl, G., Geihs, J.: Ranked Matching for Service Descriptions Using OWL-S. Communication in Distributed Systems (Kommunikation in Verteilten Systemen), 91–102 (2005)

[32] Yau, S.S., Liu, J.: Functionality-based Service Matchmaking for Service-Oriented Architecture. In: Proc. Int'l Symp. on Autonomous Decentralized Systems, pp. 147–154 (2007)

[33] The Network Simulator (NS2), http://www.isi.edu/nsnam

Printing in Ubiquitous Computing Environments

Athanasios Karapantelakis[1,2], Alisa Devlic[1,3], Mohammad Zarify[4],
and Saltanat Khamit[1]

[1] Royal Institute of Technology (KTH), Stockholm, Sweden
[2] Ericsson AB, Stockholm, Sweden
[3] Appear Networks AB, Kista Science Tower, Sweden
[4] University of Twente, Enschede, Netherlands
{athkar,devlic}@kth.se, M.Zarifi@utwente.nl,
saltanat.khamit@radio.kth.se

Abstract. Document printing has long been considered an indispensable part of the workspace. While this process is considered trivial and simple for environments where resources are ample (e.g. desktop computers connected to printers within a corporate network), it becomes complicated when applied in a mobile context. Contemporary mobile devices have the computational resources required for document processing and are affordable enough for an increasingly large number of users. Therefore, document printing using mobile devices is now both technically feasible and relevant to users' needs. In this study, we present an infrastructure for document printing using mobile devices. In order to realize the vision, we utilize an existing set of network protocols, a set of common programming languages, standard concepts of ubiquitous computing, and machine learning, in order to automate the printing process.

Keywords: Ubiquitous printing, SIP/SIMPLE, SNMP, PJL.

1 Introduction

Over the last decades printing devices have continuously improved, keeping pace with customer expectations. Monitoring of annual print outputs from various academic institutions [1] [2] indicates a trend towards increased printer utilization. Wright suggests that printing will continue to increase as public interest shifts towards the enormous volume of information available on the World Wide Web [3].

To realize the customer demand for printing services, printer manufacturers and operating system authors have tried to improve interoperability between printers (hardware) and workstations (software) [4]. Although such efforts have been successful in solving technical issues, such as a common page layout description (i.e. page description languages such as PCL and PostScript), standardized communication interfaces (e.g. IEEE 802.11, Ethernet, Bluetooth, parallel, USB ports), and a consistent way for the user to parameterize a print request (printing protocols and APIs), there has been little improvement in processing and interpretation of printer *semantics*. Traditionally, the user visually monitors the progress of their print request on a display. If the printing process halts due to an error, (for example need for paper

D. Zhang et al. (Eds.): UIC 2009, LNCS 5585, pp. 83–98, 2009.

refill/ink replacement), the responsibility for fixing the issue and resuming printing is the user's. Another common case is that certain document types may require special hardware capabilities (e.g. a color, high resolution printer) for optimal results. The lack of a resource aware infrastructure wastes time, a critical factor for academic and corporate environments.

Additionally, in office environments increasingly users use their personal mobile devices for common tasks such as reading/composing e-mails, accessing the corporate directory, browsing the web, etc. These devices are also used for document editing and storage, but generally lack the software to interface with printers: due to their heterogeneous nature (different processor architectures, hardware specifications), printer vendors have not written device drivers for all of these mobile devices.

Our solution addresses mobile printing by providing a universal printer access interface based on *open* protocols. Additionally, exploiting awareness of all the printers in the environment it chooses the most suitable printer to serve the current print request, thus making printing more time-effective and transparent for users.

Our implementation approximates the definition of the *Ubiquitous Computing Environment*, as defined by McGarth *et al.* [5]. We consider users with mobile devices as autonomous, heterogeneous entities, with no prior knowledge of the infrastructure. Similarly the printing infrastructure has no knowledge of potential users.

This paper is organized into five sections. Section 2 provides an overview of published relevant work. In section 3, we describe the theoretical scope of our work, introducing data models and decision algorithms. This section also includes a technical overview of the system. Section 4 presents and evaluates a set of measurements. We conclude in section 5, with a recapitulation of the key aspects of our work, and suggest some future work.

2 Related Work

Mobile printing is a relatively new concept since mobile devices have only recently acquired the necessary network interfaces (e.g. Bluetooth and IEEE 802.11) to interact with printers – other than via a point-to-point IRDA link. Burke specifies two general methods for mobile printing, namely serverless printing i.e. directly through the utilization of device drivers, and print by reference [6].

Mobile device drivers render the files locally on the device using a page description language, and subsequently send this data to the printer over a network interface. Printer manufacturers (such as HP [7]) and mobile device manufacturers (such as Nokia [8]) have developed printing drivers for specific models of devices. SonyEricsson's camera phones have adopted the PictBridge standard [9], which allows images to be printed directly to the printer without the presence of a computer. Additionally, third party developers have implemented their own solutions for mobile printing [10]. In an effort to disambiguate the complex issue of implementing serverless mobile printing, the Mobile Imaging and Printing Consortium (MIPC) publishes technical documentation in a developer guideline format [11]. Their document distinguishes between different network interfaces that mobile devices may potentially be equipped with, and addresses each case separately (see figure 1). However, although serverless printing can function as an integrated solution on specific pairs of mobile devices and printers, it does not scale well for environments where the hardware specifications are not fixed *a priori*.

One constrain is that there must be a network path from the network interface (typically via a WLAN, USB, and/or wide area wireless network interface) of the mobile device to the printer. Statistically, the majority of mobile devices today have a wireless network interface, whereas most network printers still use Ethernet as their network interface of choice. However, MIPC's serverless printing implies a direct connection between the mobile device and the printer. An additional disadvantage is the vertical implementation of the current serverless printing solutions, which leads to poor code reusability and increased costs for maintenance.

In order to render a file, the corresponding application has to decode its contents, encode it (in a page description language), and send it to the printer. Although most mobile devices support common file formats (e.g. for text, spreadsheets, and images), this software lacks features available in desktop applications. Therefore, files edited with specialized desktop applications (e.g. architectural drawings, 3d models, mathematical workspaces, etc), are unlikely to be able to be directly printed, since the mobile device does not know how to decode the document and encode it for printing.

Printing by reference is another method that moves the computational complexity, file format decoding and page layout from the mobile device and delegates this responsibility to the printer [6]. In this case, a mobile device transmits only the URI of the document to a printer. Subsequently, the printer fetches the document and prints it. The rendering resources required can be implemented by a server attached to the network or software in the printer itself. Since the mobile device only provides a link to the document there is no requirement for printer drivers on the mobile device. However, there is need for a network attached document repository, where documents will be stored (after being sent from the mobile device prior to printing or already stored).

We propose a third method that improves on concepts from both the previously mentioned methods while effectively addressing their disadvantages (see section 3.1) for a networked printer environment with heterogeneous sets of mobile devices. Specifically we seek to exploit device mobility and context in our design of a mobile printing infrastructure. The service provided by our solution can be summarized in a sentence: For a user trying to print, this infrastructure automatically selects the *nearest suitable* printer.

A distributed algorithm that accepts printing requests handles the selection process. It uses the user's location, printer status, and document type as input parameters. The algorithm quantifies the possible printer states according to the severity of their impact on the selection process. Similarly the relative location of each printer with respect to the user is considered. Thus, for each printer in the infrastructure, the algorithm calculates a printer suitability index. Subsequently, these indexes are compared and the largest value indicates the most suitable printer for this request.

3   System Overview

Figure 1 illustrates the operating environment of the system we deployed in our lab. Printers are scattered around an indoor workspace, consisting of different rooms and corridors. Printing Point Services (PPS) provide printer context (see section 3.2).

Additionally, user location context is provided from RFID tag readers, when available[1]. The context broker is the centerpiece of our architecture, and plays a double role: It functions both as a context repository and also implements the aforementioned decision algorithm (see section 2). Each of the system components is described in detail in the following subsections. This section concludes with a description of the operating phases of the system.

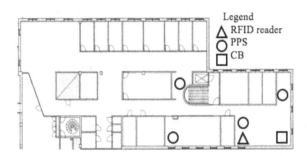

Fig. 1. Deployed system topology. A context broker ("CB") acts as a repository of context information coming from Printing Point Services – "PPS" (printer status and capabilities), as well as RFID readers – "R" (user location). The CB is also responsible for handling printing requests from mobile users by designating suitable a suitable printer.

3.1 Context Broker

The context broker is a host with network connectivity to every PPS and mobile terminal. Our software solution builts upon the open source SIP Express Router (SER) [12] and is responsible for registering new mobile terminals and handling print requests. We extended the functionality of SER by implementing three modules for context handling, user presence , and resource discovery.

The context broker incorporates the Service Locator, a separate resource discovery mechanism which uses the Service Location Protocol (SLP) [13] in order to discover available Printing Point Services in the infrastructure (see section 3.2). Resource discovery takes place not only during bootstrapping, but also during normal system operation. This allows for installation of new PPSs at any time. Pairs of <PPSid, IPaddress> are stored inside a "printer pool" table in a MySQL database (The PPSId is a unique identifier of a given PPS and is assigned by the Service Locator).

The context aggregation module receives and stores location updates from the location service infrastructure, as well as printer status updates from the PPSs. We are using SIP/SIMPLE messages to transfer event updates to SER [14]. These events are transferred as a PUBLISH message payload and are modeled after the Presence Information Data Format (PIDF) XML Schema [15]. SIP messages, as well as the functional role of the presence server, are defined in the SIP/SIMPLE protocol [16].

The user presence module registers mobile terminals with the infrastructure. Registration can be automatic (if the devices are detected by the RFID readers), or

---

[1] The user's location could be provided by any location system, with room level resolution.

by an explicit registration request. A mobile terminal initially subscribes to the printing service by sending a SUBSCRIBE request message to the context broker. SER processes these requests and registers the mobile terminal in a database (see figure 2).

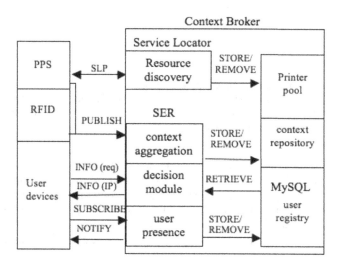

Fig. 2. Architecture of the Context Broker and interoperability with the user terminals and context providers. Context providers (PPSs and RFID readers) transmit PUBLISH messages to the aggregator, with XML-encoded context as payload. Users register with the CB using SIP SUBSCRIBE messages. After subscribing, clients are eligible to place print requests using INFO messages. The decision module uses the context stored by the context aggregator to deduce a suitable printer and returns its IP address to the requestor. The Context Broker automatically discovers printing resources using the Service Location Protocol.

In order to renew their registration, mobile terminals have to periodically transmit SUBSCRIBE requests. In addition to handling subscriptions, the presence module also transmits NOTIFY messages to subscribed devices. These responses concern feedback about printing sessions (i.e., documents remaining in the queue and current printer status) or location information (see section 3.3). The presence module interoperates with the context aggregation module, in order to provide this information to the terminals. Together these modules implement a *presence server*, a logical entity capable of acquiring, storing, and transmitting context.

After establishing a subscription to the context broker, a mobile terminal is able to send printing requests. This is done by sending SIP INFO messages to the context broker [17]. Acceptance and processing of printing requests is handled by the decision module, which collects relevant context stored in the database, and responds by returning the IP address of a suitable printer to the requestor (see figure 3).

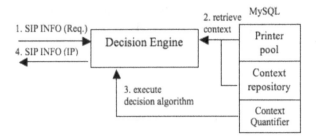

Fig. 3. Handling of printing requests in the decision module of the context broker. An incoming request triggers the execution of the decision algorithm, which in turn uses information stored in the database to select a PPS. Subsequently, it sends a response with the PPS's IP address to the requestor. Responses and requests are carried as SIP INFO payloads.

The module includes a decision algorithm, which estimates the *suitability index* (SI) of each of the PPSs, based on the retrieved context information. Our solution is based on printer status quantifiers, where each state is assigned a *weight*. The larger the value of the weight, the greater its contribution is to the SI. The same approach is employed for user location. In this case, there is an inverse relationship between the value of the weight and the SI. For our proof of concept system, we have hardcoded

Table 1. List of parameters contributing to suitability index

Location Status	$L(p_i)$	Description
Distance from PPS	$\dfrac{1}{d_i}$	d_i: Distance from PPS in meters (hardcoded into the database).
Insufficient RFID reader data.	0	No RFID footprint of the user's device on any of the readers for the last 60 seconds.

User Preferences	$U(t_i)$	Description
Color printout	$c_i = \begin{matrix} 0.5 \text{ supported} \\ 0 \text{ not supported} \end{matrix}$	d_i: Distance from PPS in meters (hardcoded into the database).
Resolution	$d_{res} = 0.25 \cdot \dfrac{a_{dpi}}{b_{dpi}}$	a_{dpi} resolution of printer, r_{dpi} requested resolution
Double-sided printing	$ds_i = \begin{matrix} 0.5 \text{ supported} \\ 0 \text{ not supported} \end{matrix}$	True/false operation

Printer Status	$S(p_i)$	Description
Busy	$\dfrac{0.5}{q_i}$	q_i: Number of pending print jobs in the PPS.
Idle	0	True/False operation
Offline – Permanent	-1	Errors can be: network connection (PPS does not respond to keepalive requests), paper jam (communicated from the PPS).
Offline - Temporary	-0.5	Printer in PPS may require user intervention to resume printing (no paper, low toner)

the weights into a database table called *Context Quantifier*. The SI for a given PPS is the sum of the status, location, and user preference weights. The algorithm returns the IP address of the PPS with the largest SI.

Table 1 gives some example weights for user location and printer status. It is important to note that the formulae in this table are representative of the operating environment of our system (see figure 2), coupled with the average user requirements for this environment. Future versions of the broker will allow for customization of the Context Quantifier. Note that these weights are fixed at the time of system initialization.

When referencing the table of weights, the SI for each printer p_i, given a print request from a terminal t_i, is computed using the equation $SI = S(p_i) + L(p_i) + u(t_i)$.

For example, assume that a user wants to print a color photograph. Initially, the user configures their printing requirements via the client application in their mobile terminal (see section 3.4). This information is propagated to the Decision Engine, as payload in a SIP INFO request message (see figure 4). The decision engine retrieves printer and location context from the local database, aggregates the user preferences and executes the decision algorithm. The algorithm consults the list of available printers and evaluates their SI, returning the IP address of the printer with the largest SI value (see table 2 for this example).

Table 2. Example of calculated weights for printer, user and location context

Printer 1		Printer 2	
Context	Weight	Context	Weight
$S(p_i)$: Printer status: Busy (1 document pending)	0.5	$S(p_i)$: Printer status: Idle	1
$L(p_{ii})$: 15m from printer (recorded 20 seconds ago)	0.066	$L(p_i)$: 30m from printer (recorded 20 seconds ago)	0.033
$u(t_i)$: Printer supports color, 1200 dpi resolution (requested 2000dpi)	0.65	$u(t_i)$: Printer black and white, 2000 dpi resolution (requested 2000dpi)	1
SI	1.216	SI	2.033

3.2 Printing Point Services

Printing Point Services combine a Service Agent (SA) with a physical connection to a printer. This SA is software that acts as an intermediary between users and printers. This software runs on a computer that is connected to a printer, and has network reachability from the various clients (i.e., the applications run by users to print files). This SA plays a double role: (1) processing requests to print documents (from the users) and (2) acquiring and providing printer context to the context broker. The SA is highly configurable and scalable and may support more than one network interfaces, a wide range of printers (either network-attached printers, or printers directly connected to the SA).

The SA builds on standards, both for printer context aggregation, and for printing. We have defined a simple communication protocol for negotiating with devices. In our architecture, we propose to use *tight coupling* between a service agent and a printer (see figure 4). We believe that a single interface to the printer enhances the role of the service agent as a gateway for providing print services (e.g. it allows for policy-based control of printing and is more secure).

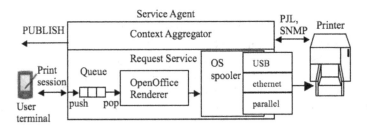

Fig. 4. Block structure of a Printing Point Service. Tight coupling of printer and service agent allows for control of printing requests. In addition, support of multiple interfaces allows for use of a wide range of printers.

In order to successfully support printer awareness, a service agent needs to successfully retrieve static and real-time information from a printer (see section 2.2). In this study, we have used HP's Printer Job Language (PJL) to get static information about the printer [18]. PJL was developed in order to support printer status reading from the printer to the host computer, and has been adopted by all major printer manufacturers. In our system, static information inquiries are only done during start-up of the SA. As soon as the necessary information has been gathered, an SLP message is sent to the context broker, informing it of the URI address of the service agent, as well as the retrieved printer information as attributes (see table 3).

Table 3. Construction of an SLP message using information obtained through PJL commands

PJL command, as issued from Service Agent	Reply from the printer	SLP Message
PJL INQUIRE RESOLUTION	1200	
PJL INFO ID	LJ 4M	URI:service:printer:lpr://192.168.1.12 Attributes:(printer-model=*LJ4M*),(printer-document-format-supported=*application/ postscript*),(printer-color–supported= *false*), (printer-resolution-supported=*1200*)
PJL INQUIRE RENDERMODE	GREYSCALE	
PJL INFO LANGUAGES	POSTSCRIPT	

Although PJL has a status command, tests in our lab indicated that some printers are slow to respond to PJL commands. However, response time is a critical factor when retrieving printer status, therefore, in order to collect real ‑ time information, we make use of managed objects (defined here as printer information resources). Such objects are stored inside a database known as Management Information Base (MIB). Inside each MIB the objects are organised hierarchically and are accessed using a network - management protocol such as SNMP. The identity of each object is known as an object identifier. RFC1759 indicates that proper combination of information from printer objects, leads to an accurate printer status inference [19]. We distinguish between four printer states: busy, idle, alert, and offline. Alerts (low toner and low paper) indicate that future print requests are likely to generate error messages. An offline state conveys irreversible errors, requiring human intervention (out of paper, jammed, paper tray open, and network error).

The status is encoded in an XML document and periodically transmitted to the context broker. The document is modeled after the Printer Working Group (PWG) semantic model, with a collection of documents extending the XML Schema and describing printer characteristics (The PWG schema is currently a candidate standard.) [20]

In addition to the printer's status, information about the printer's location and name are transmitted, as well as the IP address of the SA. Additional information necessary for the communication between the mobile clients and the SA is appended. We chose to transmit this information in real-time, because it may change (for example, a SA might change its IP address, the printer may be relocated, a new printer might replace an existing printer, etc.). In many of these cases, a restart of the SA is not required, as the broker will be notified about the changes automatically.

The negotiation process for printing a document occurs between the device and the service agent, after the discovery phase, on a per-request basis. Note that this process starts immediately after the user terminal receives the IP address of an available PPS, from the context broker (see section 3.1). For this negotiation we implemented a simple UDP protocol. After receiving an IP address from the context broker (see section 3.1), the client sends a UDP request to print to the PPS. Based upon the relevant policies, the identity of the user, the status of the printer, etc., the service agent chooses whether to allow or deny the printing request. If the request is allowed, the client starts an FTP session with the service agent in order to transfer the document.

The printing queue of the service agent is a queue: a process monitors the queue and while there are pending jobs, it extracts the first job from the queue and sends it to the printer. Note that in some cases, it is permissible to prioritize one job over another based on criteria other than the time of arrival of the document. Therefore, the queue also includes a prioritize function, which is used by the decision module.

Once a document is dequeued it is ready to be sent to the printer. Note that contemporary printers generally expect Adobe's PostScript®, a page description language [21]. In order to convert the file to this format (if necessary), we use Open Office, an open source office suite, which can print all major file formats (documents, spreadsheets, images, etc.). Therefore, the document to be printed is sent to the corresponding open office application (i.e. there is a different application for spreadsheets, presentations and documents), which in turn outputs the document in PostScript format.

The service agent makes use of printing profiles. These profiles correspond to different settings for the same printer. Parameters that can be set are the number of pages per sheet, number of copies of the document, printing quality, colour printing (if supported), and others. The idea is that printing profiles fine-tune the printing, thus enhancing the user's experience. Profiles can be customized to specific users and are created by the service agent, based on the feedback from the previous choices of each user. We plan to show that in the long term, such profiles can accommodate the printing preferences of the users, without users having to tweak their printing preferences every time that they want to print something (see section 3.4).

3.3 RFID Infrastructure

Acquiring location information in a mobile computing environment is not a trivial task. Hazas, et al. overview different location sensing technologies and show that they differ in accuracy and deployment feasibility [22]. Based on this study, we chose RFID as a technology for inferring user location, as it addresses our accuracy, scalability, and availability requirements.

RFID readers in proximity of the RFID tag can read the tag and report having seen this tag to the context broker. Such readers are strategically placed throughout the context-aware environment.

The TagMaster AB LR-6 readers used for our proof of concept system were running an embedded version of the Linux operating system. This enabled us to create our own software which enables the reader to act as a context provider, i.e., the reader sends a PUBLISH message to the context broker, containing the MAC address of the mobile device. The reader locally stores an internal table of <tagID, MAC> pairs, which is used to match authenticated tags against the MAC address of the device they belong to. This mapping between tag number and device ID is done locally on the TagMaster device in order to avoid transmitting the tag ID, thus protecting the privacy of the users.

3.4 Mobile Application

A proof-of-concept application was written in C# and runs on Windows Mobile 2003 platform (both PDAs and smartphones). It requires some form of IP connectivity (e.g. Wi-Fi) and reachability to the service agents and the SIP proxy (in the case of the subscription-based approach). Since printing is usertriggered, the user starts the application, selects a document, and waits for feedback from the system.

The application itself is designed to proactively adjust to the user's preferences. Initially the user browses the filesystem of their mobile device and selects a file to print. The application automatically makes a rudimentary match of the file to one of three categories: Presentation, Document, or Photo. This match is currently based on the extension of the file's name. However, future versions of the application should allow for recognition of the file type, based on a file header signature [23].

Depending on the category and the capabilities of the printer, different printing options are available. For example when printing presentation slides, the user selects how many slides per page he/she wants to print. There is also an option for double-sided printing. For documents, additional options are color printing, and a printing speed/quality adjustment. For pictures, the user gets a preview of the picture he/she wants to print (the default choice in this case is to print the picture using the highest quality settings, so there is no adjustment for printing quality, as there is on the documents). All categories include a number of copies setting.

The long-term objective is to minimize user input; therefore the application stores a history of selected printing options, aggregating them into a dataset. This implies that there is a training period, in order for the application to have sufficient data. During this period the user is presented with all the printing options. We found that the number of samples in the dataset required to reach a statistically safe decision may vary depending on the user (see section 4).

Using past behavior and the category of the file to print, we apply a probabilistic algorithm to make an informed decisions about the printing options to present to the user. The algorithm is based on the principle that *given a new print request, a print option "O", "n" number of previous requests, and "d" times of previously selected option "O", calculate the likelihood that the user chooses option "O" for this request.* Mathematically, this can be expressed as the probability $P(O) = d/n$. On every iteration, the algorithm calculates P(O) for every printing option, then classifies the options in order of previous occurrence. This step also determines which options will be visible to the user (see section 4.1) for hiding these options. Options are presented to the user in such a way so that the ones more likely to be chosen are shown in a more visually prominent position in the client's application window (see figure 5)

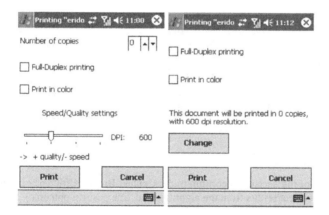

Fig. 5. Options presented to the user from the client application when printing a document: Each option O_i is presented in its own visual space (i.e. a different "line") on the client window. When $P(O_i)$ is above a certain threshold, the designated option is visible. Upon initial use of the application, all options are visible (a). However after a period of use, it is possible that some options are preselected automatically, depending on the frequency they are chosen by the user (b). This limits the amount of input required, therefore accelerating the printing process.

4 Measurements

In order to properly monitor the system in real-world operating conditions, we deployed a prototype in our lab and monitored the system for a period of five consecutive (working) days. In an effort to promote user diversity (as it would occur in real-world situations), six different clients were given access to the system, during working hours. In order to establish the efficiency of the decision algorithm of the context broker, we measure the ratio of "true positive" versus the total number of print sessions. A true positive result occurs when the decision algorithm works as expected, i.e. the user is able to print to a printer best approximating a preset, prioritized set of requirements (see section 3.1).

Figure 6 illustrates the performance of the decision algorithm as a histogram. The results represent the collective percentage of true positive occurrences for the period of five days. The true positive occurrences are at least 80% of the total. This 20% error margin is attributed to false parameter estimations due to synchronization errors: as some service agents did not report the current status of the printer in time to the context broker.

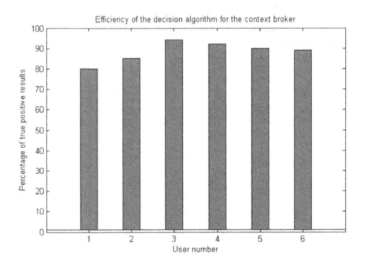

Fig. 6. Efficiency of the decision algorithm in the Context Broker. Efficiency is determined by the percentage of correct results from the algorithm (i.e. true positive outcome)

When evaluating the performance of the decision algorithm in the user application, the question was how large should the training set be for this algorithm, i.e. how many print sessions are required a priori, in order for the algorithm to generate statistically safe decisions.

Figure 8 illustrates an experiment in which we executed the decision algorithm for every client, with a different dataset size each time. In this case, a true positive result indicates that all desired options were visible to the user beforehand (i.e. the user did not have to push the "change" button as seen in figure 7). Overall we conducted 8 different measurements, with an increase in 5 print sessions per step. The results indicated a large improvement for a dataset size up to 35 (which corresponds to an approximate 83.8 % average of true positive occurrences). After this point, the gains are not substantial enough to justify a further increase in the number of samples; therefore the default size was set to 35. It is important to note that in these empirical measurements, we are not concerned about absolute values but rather simply observing trends in user behaviour.

We have conducted a series of measurements concerning various aspects of performance of the context broker, the centrepiece of this system's architecture. Initially, we monitored the average response time, from when an incoming SIP INFO message is received, until the response is sent in another INFO message. Note that this value is also influenced by external factors such as printer availability, user preferences, and location (in these measurements the propagation delay over the carrier network is not taken under account, since we assume that there is sufficient capacity to serve all the requests). In practical terms this is an important measurement because it indicates how long the user has to wait in order to access a printer. In a typical working environment, prompt handling of print requests is vital.

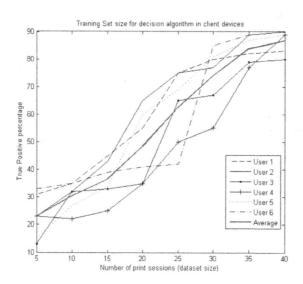

Fig. 7. Determining the optimal dataset size for statistically safe decisions

In general, we found that the demand was higher during working hours (typically in the middle of a day), and that the response times were between approximately 0.5 and 0.8 seconds (see figure 8). This can be interpreted as a positive outcome, since there were no prominent delays observed.

We also subjected the system to a number of stress tests. This helped to identify the thresholds of stable operation. This is important when the system is deployed on a large-scale, with many resources and users. Our test involved testing the context aggregation module (see section 3.1). In particular we wanted to learn the maximum frequency of PUBLISH messages that this module is able to accept and successfully

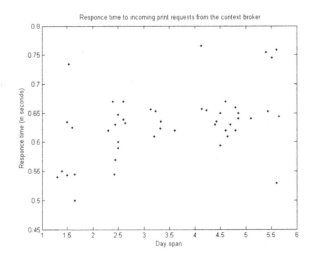

Fig. 8. This scatter plot showing responce times to print requests made from the users to the Context Broker for all 5 days of our experiment

store the updated presence information in the database. We created a virtual RFID reader, which sends PUBLISH updates to the presence server. Figure 9 illustrates the error rate observed for a given frequency of incoming PUBLISH updates. Beyond 400 messages/sec, we observe a gradual increase in the error rate, which is very prominent after 1200 messages/sec mark. This means that our CB in its present form can sustain up to 400 presence user agents (assuming that these agents send periodic updates every second); larger systems have to distribute the handling of PUBLISH messages between multiple CBs.

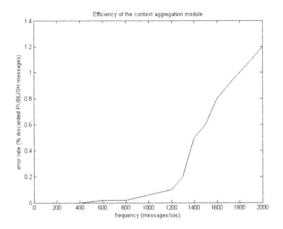

Fig. 9. This plot showing the percentage of discarded PUBLISH messages from the CB, depending on the volume of incoming messages

5 Conclusion

In this paper we proposed a mobile printing solution for workspace environments. This solution implements a policy-based decision algorithm for forwarding print requests from mobile devices to appropriate printers. The objective was to provide the user with a transparent printing service allowing him/her to print the files on his/her mobile device. We have currently tested the solution in our research lab, but plan to extend testing to a corporate environment.

We are also working on a security module for the context broker which works both for the service agents (which first have to obtain a digital certificate from the module, in order to communicate), and for the mobile terminals (which first have to form an SSL tunnel to securely interface with a service agent). Note that much of the proposed infrastructure is compatible with the 3GPP IP Multimedia System (IMS), so an area of future work is to further evaluate the integration of such a context aware approach with IMS.

Finally, although this paper presented a printing service, our ambition is to use the same infrastructure (i.e. the context broker and RFID readers) to provide more services in the future. Examples of such services include automatic presentation arrangement, meeting room reservations, information guides, etc.

References

[1] Blando, P.: Printing statistics from University of Davis in California (annual from 1996 to 2004), http://clm.ucdavis.edu/pubs/labrep/summer2004/stats/print.html (visited July 8, 2008)

[2] Minnesota State University Technical Services Group, Annual statistics from various sites at Minnesota State University (annual from 2004 to 2007), http://mavdisk.mnsu.edu/bryan/mavprintstats07.htm (visited July 8, 2008)

[3] Wright, D.: The ubiquity of print. Lexmark Technical Report, http://www.w3.org/2006/02/slides/wright.pdf (visited July 8, 2008)

[4] Microsoft Knowledge Base, Agreement between Microsoft and IHVs (Independent Hardware Vendors), http://support.microsoft.com/kb/156082 (visited July 8, 2008)

[5] McGrath, R.E., Ranganathan, A., Campbell, R.H., Mickunas, M.D.: Incorporating semantic discovery into ubiquitous computing infrastructure. In: Proceedings of System Support for Ubiquitous Computing Workshop at the Fifth Annual Conference on Ubiquitous Computing (UbiComp 2003) (October 2003)

[6] Burke, P.: Mobile Printing. In: W3C Mobile Web Initiative Workshop, Barcelona, Spain, November 18-19 (2004)

[7] HP mobile printing SDK for mobile devices (discontinued), http://h20000.www2.hp.com/bizsupport/TechSupport/Home.jsp?lang=en&cc=se&prodTypeId=18972&prodSeriesId=352517&lang=sv&cc=se (visited July 8, 2008)

[8] Nokia, Xpress print, http://europe.nokia.com/xpressprint (visited July 8, 2008)

[9] Camera and Imaging Products Association (CIPA), Digital Photo Solutions for Imaging Devices, whitepaper (February 2003),
     `http://www.cipa.jp/english/pictbridge/DPS_WhitePaper_E.pdf`
     (visited July 8, 2008)

[10] WestTek, JETCET Print application for Windows CE,
     `http://www.westtek.com/pocketpc/jetcet/` (visited July 8, 2008)

[11] Mobile Imaging and Printing Consortium: Implementation Guidelines for Printing with Mobile Terminals, version 2.1,
     `http://www.mobileprinting.org/developers/guidelines/`
     (visited July 8, 2008)

[12] Iptel. org., SIP Express router - high-performance, configurable, free SIP server licensed under the open source GNU license, `http://www.iptel.org/ser/` (visited July 8, 2008)

[13] Eslami, M.Z.: A Presence Server for Context-Aware Applications. Masters Thesis, Royal Institute of Technology (KTH), Stockholm, Sweden (December 2007)

[14] Niemi, A. (ed.): RFC3903, Session Initiation Protocol (SIP) Extension for Event State Publication (October 2004), `http://www.ietf.org/rfc/rfc3903.txt` (visited July 8, 2008)

[15] Sugano, H., Fujimoto, S., Klye, G., Bateman, A., Carr, W., Peterson, J.: RFC 3863, Presence Information Data Format (PIDF) (August. 2004),
     `http://www.ietf.org/rfc/rfc3863.txt` (visited July 8, 2008)

[16] Rosenberg, J.: RFC 3856, A Presence Event Package for the Session Initiation Protocol (SIP) (August 2004), `http://www.ietf.org/rfc/rfc3856.txt` (visited July 8, 2008)

[17] Donovan, S.: RFC 2976, The SIP INFO Method (October 2000),
     `http://www.ietf.org/rfc/rfc2976.txt` (visited July 8, 2008)

[18] HP, PCL/PJL reference - Printer Job Language Technical Reference Manual,
     `http://h20000.www2.hp.com/bc/docs/support/SupportManual/bpl13208/bpl13208.pdf` (visited July 8, 2008)

[19] Smith, R., Wright, F., Hastings, T., Zilles, S., Gyllenskog, J.: RFC1759, Printer MIB, section 2.2.13.2, `http://www.ietf.org/rfc/rfc1759.txt` (visited July 8, 2008)

[20] Printer Working Group (PWG) Semantic Model – Candidate standard, `ftp://ftp.pwg.org/pub/pwg/candidates/cs-sm10-20040120-5105.1.pdf`
     (visited July 8, 2008)

[21] Adobe Systems Incorporated, Postscript Language Reference, 3rd edn.,
     `http://www.adobe.com/products/postscript/pdfs/PLRM.pdf`
     (visited July 8, 2008)

[22] Hazas, M., Scott, J., Krumm, J.: Location-Aware Computing Comes of Age. IEEE Computer 37(2), 95–97 (2004)

[23] Kessler, G.: File signatures table,
     `http://www.garykessler.net/library/file_sigs.html` (visited July 8, 2008)

The Å Publish/Subscribe Framework

Clint Heyer

Strategic R&D for Oil, Gas and Petrochemicals,
ABB Oslo, Norway
clint.heyer@no.abb.com

Abstract. This paper describes the design and implementation of a novel decentralized publish/subscribe framework. The primary goal of the design was for a high level of end-developer and user accessibility and simplicity. Furthermore, it was desired to have strong support for occasionally-connected clients and support for mobile and web-based systems. Content-based event patterns can be defined using scripts, with many common script languages supported. Script-based, stateful event patterns permit rich expressiveness, simplify client development and reduce network usage. The framework also offers event persistence, caching and publisher quenching. We also describe a number of applications already built on the framework, for example publishers to support location and presence awareness and ambient visualizations of financial data.

Keywords: Publish/subscribe, distributed applications, middleware, pervasive computing, ubiquitous computing.

1 Introduction

Å was designed and developed as middleware to support rapid prototyping of pervasive computing applications for an industrial workplace. We desired a content-based publish/subscribe paradigm following on from our earlier experiences and success in using a preexisting publish/subscribe system for a similar purpose [1]. As publicly available publish/subscribe systems did not suit the requirements of the current research project, we designed and developed our own implementation.

Publish/subscribe systems are well suited for mobile usage [2]. Mobile devices tend to have unstable and variable network connectivity, for example a device might transition from a high-speed WiFi-equipped space to an outdoors area with lower-speed cellular data connectivity to a subway with no connectivity at all. Publish/subscribe systems generally hide connectivity issues, for example seamlessly rediscovering new, local routers and resubscribing, or publishing events that have been queued during a period of disconnection.

This paper is structured as follows. In section 2 we introduce the publish/subscribe paradigm for the unfamiliar reader. Section 3 outlines the requirements we devised for the system, followed by Section 4 with a description and discussion of the design and implementation of the Å framework. Section 5 describes some prototype applications we have already built on top of the framework, while Section 6 outlines plans for

D. Zhang et al. (Eds.): UIC 2009, LNCS 5585, pp. 99–110, 2009.
© Springer-Verlag Berlin Heidelberg 2009

future work. Section 7 concludes the paper, summarizing the framework's features and relating them to the initial design requirements.

2 Publish/Subscribe

Publish/subscribe systems allow *publishers* to send *events* (also referred to as *notifications*) to an event *router* (also known as a *dispatcher*) which is then responsible for distributing events to interested *subscribers*. *Subscribers* register their interest in particular events through the use of *event patterns*, which can be dynamically registered and deregistered. When an event is received, it is checked against registered event patterns and forwarded to the matching subscribers. Events usually consist of a collection of key-value pairs, with typed or opaque blob value types. One alternative approach is a tree-based structure for events, such as an XML-based format [3]. Traditionally the router was a single daemon [4], well-known to both publishers and subscribers but most contemporary systems use a distributed network of routers to improve reliability, scalability and performance [5; 6]. Publishers and subscribers are logical entities; in practice a single application can exhibit publisher or subscriber behavior, or some combination thereof.

The primary benefit of the publish/subscribe paradigm is the loose coupling of publishers and subscribers. Publishers produce events without prior knowledge of how the event will be distributed or to whom. Subscribers can consume events that they are interested in without prior knowledge of where the event came from or who produced it. Essentially, publishers send events into a cloud, and subscribers receive events from cloud. Communication takes place asynchronously with no requirement for coordination between publishers and subscribers, although coordination logic can be built on top of the eventing layer. Disruptions in communication are usually hidden, for example if a particular publisher is offline, subscribers will not necessarily be aware of it or affected by it – the absence of received events can be caused by any number of factors.

There is, however, a weak coupling in that subscribers usually need some prior knowledge of the format of events that the publisher produces. For example, a subscriber will not receive stock price notifications for symbol "XYZ" if it subscribes to the pattern StockSymbol = "XYZ" yet the publisher produces events such as Symbol = "XYZ"; Price = 23.09. Issues associated with event schema mismatches can be resolved by using *adapters*, which republish events with an alternative schema. This allows preexisting publishers and subscribers to be linked without modification or strengthened coupling. Publishing events with 'fuzzy' or higher-semantic values is also a potential approach. For example, a publisher sending events for person's current location might not only include latitude and longitude, but also the building, suburb, city and country or the fact that the person is in an office rather than outside. Subscribers interested in a person's location then have a variety of ways of expressing that interest, for example a region defined by latitude-longitude coordinates or perhaps they only care when someone is outside in a particular suburb.

Publish/subscribe event patterns are generally either subject-based, which uses broad groups or channels to determine event delivery, or content-based, whereby event patterns are used to filter events. The content-based approach permits subscribers to have fine-grained control over what messages they will receive based on the content of the events. Typically, this is accomplished using a simple logical expression that must evaluate to true based on event values. Expressions are, in effect, parsed and compiled and then executed against each incoming event to determine whether to deliver the message to the subscriber. Systems will often support basic functions which can perform value transformation and thus increase the expressive power of the pattern, such as accessing a particular sub-range of a string or converting a timestamp to elapsed time. Subscriptions are usually evaluated in a stateless environment, however some work has investigated stateful evaluation [7; 8].

For some kinds of publishers, the production of individual events may be a costly process so it would be beneficial to only publish events that matched current subscriber's event patterns. This process is called *quenching,* and allows the publisher to determine when there is some entity interested in its events, so that event production can be adapted accordingly.

3 System Requirements

We had a number of requirements for the system which were not satisfied by available publish/subscribe implementations. Our primary goal was for end-developer and user accessibility and simplicity. It needs to be as straightforward as possible to write applications that take advantage of the framework, applications should have minimal configuration requirements, be reliable and easy to deploy. Our secondary goal was to support loose-coupling, not only between applications built on the framework (as is usually the case with publish/subscribe systems), but also between applications and publish/subscribe system itself.

In addition to the two main goals, several other requirements shaped the design of the framework. Since the applications to be built on top of the framework were to emerge as part of an exploratory research process, it was critical that the framework was open and flexible enough to support a variety of uses. The Microsoft .NET framework is the predominate programming environment in our laboratory, so it was a requirement that the framework was accessible to .NET-based applications and followed API design conventions for that platform. However, as we intended on using the framework from a number of different environments, such as the web and embedded and mobile devices, it also needed to be programmatically interacted with it in a simple, open, standardized manner.

There were also a number of characteristics of many publish/subscribe implementations that we did not deem salient for our prototype applications. We did not for example, anticipate requiring any guarantees of ordered, reliable or timely event delivery, nor did the system need to be able to route messages with a high throughput or scale to millions of nodes. These relaxed requirements are contrary to the focus of numerous research efforts [9; 10; 11; 12; 13], however they suited our applications and allowed us to focus our implementation efforts appropriately.

4 Architecture and Implementation

This section describes the architecture and implementation of the framework and relates it to the literature. The distributed, decentralized network topology is described, in which clients connect to a router, which is a member of an interconnected mesh network. Events in the framework are typed key-value pairs. Each event has associated metadata which can be used in event patterns or extracted by subscribers, and is set by publishers and the router mesh. Subscribers can use a XML-based query language or scripts to define which events they receive. Script-based event patterns are a novel feature of the framework, and support a high level of expressiveness, reduced network traffic and simplified client implementation. Basic quenching support is provided so that publishers can be aware when a subscriber exists that is interested in their events, and perhaps adjust event production accordingly. Publishers can opt to have their events persisted in a mesh-based store which is transparent to subscribers. The mesh itself additionally caches events transparently to publishers, and clients can request their own mesh-based caching of particular events. These event storage and caching features permit occasionally-connected subscribers to still make use of events which occurred before they connected and removes the need for publishers to be continually connected. Client development is supported by a .NET API, tools and services. Mobile and non .NET-based usage is provided by a standards-based HTTP endpoint.

4.1 Peer-to-Peer Topology

We took a distributed, decentralized approach to event routing. Routers discover and connect to each other forming an interconnected peer-to-peer mesh, around which all events are distributed. Clients (publishers and subscribers) connect to a router within the mesh, forming leaf nodes (Fig. 1). If one router receives an event from a connected subscriber, it distributes it to all routers it has a connection to and so the process continues until the event has passed through all routers or its time-to-live hop counter has expired. Events are marked with globally-unique identifier when first received from a client, which is used to ignore duplicate forwarded events. Router nodes with multiple network interfaces automatically behave as network gateways, allowing individual Å entities to communicate transparently across network boundaries.

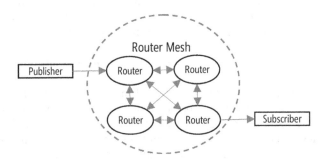

Fig. 1. Example network structure. Arrows indicate potential event flow

Our peer-to-peer event forwarding approach is less sophisticated than other work, for example some implementations only forward events that the connected router has expressed an interest in [14], or use an optimized peer-to-peer connectivity topology [5]. As we did not expect to scale the system to thousands of routers or have a high throughput of events, we preferred the naive approach for its simplicity and reliability.

Routers maintain the mesh by continually looking for new router nodes to incorporate and exchanging addresses of known routers. Discovery takes place by broadcasting UDP packets on available or predefined network subnets and by attempting to connect to well-known router endpoints if they are defined. Mesh topology information is periodically persisted to disk so the router can quickly re-integrate into the mesh should it restart. When a connection to a router is lost, or an exception otherwise occurs during a communication, it is added to a "poison" list. Subsequent connection attempts occur in exponentially increasing intervals – thus a faulty node is increasingly marginalized the more frequently it fails, up until a maximum interval. The same discovery, persistence and poison list processes are followed in the client API used by publishers and subscribers. Once connected to a router (and thus, a leaf node of the mesh) clients periodically request alternative router endpoints which are attempted in case of disconnection to the discovered router. Together, these processes allow routers and clients to operate requiring zero or only minimal configuration.

Router nodes have three modes of execution: 1) a system service, managed by the operating system, 2) a console program, or 3) by referencing the router library, embedded in any .NET application. This flexibility allows nodes to be easily deployed and managed. In our environment, most nodes are run as system services, with scheduled tasks to automatically update router software.

4.2 Events

Events in the Å framework are essentially dictionaries, a collection of typed name-value pairs. Each event also has associated metadata, also a collection of name-value pairs. Publishers can use metadata to set per-event parameters which can be acted upon by routers or the receiving subscriber. On receiving an event from a client, the router will set metadata such as the client's unique identifier, whether the client has authenticated itself and so on. As events are forwarded around the mesh, metadata is used to track which routers the event has already passed through and also the time-to-live hop counter, which is decremented with each forward, both of which prevent infinite forwarding. Events can also have a *type identifier*, the value of which is treated as opaque by routers, but allows publishers to declare that particular events are of the same type, or group. For example, a publisher might send sensor readings every minute, and use event types to group events from a particular source sensor. Types can be used by the persistent store (described in section 4.5), used in event patterns, or extracted by subscribers when they receive an event.

4.3 Event Patterns

Å uses a pluggable event pattern system to support alternative pattern evaluation kernels. Currently, there are two implemented kernels: script and XPath. The latter executes XPath [15] queries against events which have been transformed into an XML structure, however it adds additional overhead due to the XML transformation.

Script event patterns support a rich expressiveness and powerful filtering capabilities. Subscribers register patterns on a router simply by sending the text syntax of the script, its format, and the well-known language identifier. The pattern format determines if the script is evaluated as a simple logical expression or interpreted as a structured script which potentially could include functions and types. We leverage the Microsoft Dynamic Language Runtime (DLR), thus event patterns can be written in Python, Ruby, JavaScript or any other language with a DLR provider. Patterns have the full capability of the language they are written in, with all the in-built functions and supporting types available. Developers and users can therefore leverage existing knowledge of common scripting languages instead of learning and working within the confines of bespoke pattern syntax.

Rather than the typical approach of a pattern being able to only access individual event values, isolated from other events and the system as a whole, Å's novel script-based approach allows patterns to optionally incorporate a rich, broad awareness of the publish/subscribe environment. An object model is exposed so that the script can access and manipulate the event in a structured manner, maintain state, and access properties and functions of the script's host router.

With support for sophisticated pattern logic, subscribers can be simplified, reducing the need for additional client-side filtering logic. Moreover, executing logic "close" to the data and stateful subscriptions can reduce network traffic and offload computational work from the client. In turn, this enables subscribers to run in resource-impoverished environments like a mobile phone or embedded system. For example, a subscriber might start an alarm when a sensor reaches a high temperature. A traditional stateless event pattern, such as `Temperature > 100` would result in the subscriber receiving events continuously while the temperature is above 100. A stateful event pattern on the other hand could be used so that the subscriber only receives an event once the high temperature is reached, such as:

```
   if (Temperature > 100)
     if (!highAlarm) { highAlarm = true; ForwardEvent(e); }
 else highAlarm = false;
```

Loosely-coupled coordination of distributed subscribers is also possible. For each router, only one instance of a particular pattern syntax is used. All subscribers who register the same pattern are associated with the single pattern instance, forming an ad-hoc group based on this shared interest. By utilizing the additional logic afforded by script-based patterns, the pattern might, for example, notify its subscriber pool in a round-robin fashion to distribute load.

4.4 Quenching

A basic form of quenching is supported so publishers can be notified when a subscriber registers for their events. Publishers can request to receive quench notifications by registering an event as an *event prototype* with the router. Routers in turn forward registrations around the mesh and ensure newly-joined routers are updated. On the initial quench notification registration, each router examines its list of subscriptions and sends a notification to the publisher for each subscription that matches the prototype. Any subsequent subscription within the mesh is checked against registered prototypes and generates the same notifications. The publisher is also notified if a matching subscription is removed or expires. Publishers are thus informed when there is an entity interested in their events and can alter publishing behavior accordingly, such as stopping or slowing. For example, an embedded device might measure snow depths in a remote valley, reporting readings over an expensive cellular data network. Reducing data transmissions would be beneficial, so the publisher can use quenching and only transmit events when there is an interested subscriber.

This approach is limited in that subscriber's event patterns need to be sufficiently broad in order to match the publisher's registered event prototype. Consider the aforementioned snow depth publisher. If a subscription has an event pattern of `SnowDepth == 80` and the publisher uses a quench event prototype of `SnowDepth-Sensor = True; SnowDepth = 50` the subscription would not match, the publisher would not receive the quench notification and thus events would never be sent. Alternatively, if the subscriber were to use an event pattern of `SnowDepthSensor == true`, the quench event prototype would match, resulting in the expected behavior. This, however, would require the subscriber to perform additional filtering if they are indeed only interested in events where the snow depth is 80 and increase the coupling between publisher and subscriber, as they now rely on the shared value of `SnowDepthSensor`. In our current usage of the framework, we consider this trade-off to be acceptable if quenching is required.

4.5 Event Persistence and Caching

Each router maintains a persistent event store, used to store events when requested by publishers. As events get forwarded around the mesh, they are replicated at each node, ensuring redundancy. Publishers can use event metadata to specify a combination of time or quantity-based store expiry policies. For example, a publisher could specify that the router should remove events after three hours and only keep a maximum of five events of that type. When a subscriber first registers an event pattern, the store is queried for matching historical events, which are sent to the subscriber as normal events (albeit with metadata identifying it as historical). The persistent store is particularly useful for publishers that run infrequently, send events infrequently or anticipate loss of connectivity which would preclude periodic sending.

Subscribers who might benefit from such a store (such as those that have intermittent mesh connectivity) need to rely on publishers to set the persistency option for events they send. This can introduce unnecessary coupling between publishers and subscribers if a publisher needs to be modified for the benefit of an occasionally-connected subscriber. Å has two techniques to address this problem: the mesh event cache, and the client event cache.

The mesh event cache functions like the event store, differing in four ways: 1) cached events are not transparently returned to subscribers, they must be specifically requested; 2) publishers have no control over expiration policy, only whether to opt-out entirely; 3) cached events are not persisted to disk, only stored in memory; and 4) it is opt-out rather than opt-in.

The client event cache allows clients to set their own caching policy, as they are not able to influence what is kept in the store or mesh cache. It is identical to the mesh event cache except that clients have ownership and control. This cache is maintained on per-client basis when requested, and replicated across the mesh so that it is still available even if a client reconnects to a different router node. Clients specify an event pattern and expiry policy, and are responsible for periodically sending keep-alive requests to prevent the cache being removed. Like the mesh event cache, events must be specifically requested – they are not returned as part of a normal subscription. Clients can also perform basic manipulations such as altering the caching policy and clearing it.

4.6 Security

Only basic security mechanisms are included in the current implementation of the framework. Events received by a router are marked with the publisher's network address so the event can be traced to a particular host if required. Publishers can optionally send a certificate after establishing a connection to the router. Routers inspect the certificate and if it was signed by the same root certificate authority as the router's own certificate, the publisher's events are marked with the username contained in the certificate. This identifier can be used in event patterns by subscribers, for example opting to only receive events from trusted sources. Routers can also be configured to only accept mesh or client connections from certain network address ranges.

4.7 Client API, Services and Tools

A .NET client API has been implemented to simplify building applications on the Å framework. It hides protocol details, provides useful data structures and performs management tasks such as mesh discovery. Using the API allows a simple publisher or subscriber to be written in as little three lines of code.

The framework includes a basic container service which can run as a console application or operating system service and hosts one or more add-ins. Developing Å components as add-ins simplifies their implementation and deployment as well as reducing system load. Deployment of add-ins is accomplished simply by copying them to the container service's directory and restarting the service. Event adapters and producers are well-suited as container service add-ins.

Command line tools are included so the framework can be interacted with directly and to support operating system scripting. Events can be sent or subscribed to, mesh metadata queried and simple per-event received actions can be performed, such as starting a program or appending to the system event log.

4.8 Mobility and HTTP Access

To support mobile access and improve accessibility of the framework, each router node also exposes a XML-over-HTTP web service endpoint in addition to the binary TCP endpoints used for normal communication. HTTP communication and XML manipulation is supported by most modern programming environments and has a wide variety of supporting tools. Moreover, HTTP is permitted in many network environments which block traffic on non-standard ports. The endpoint uses a RESTful paradigm [16] well-suited for use not only from sophisticated applications but also command line scripts and web-based scripts and applets. HTTP-based access is included in the client API, which can also run from Windows Mobile-based mobile devices and simplifies development by hiding protocol specifics.

HTTP-orientated subscribers register event patterns in a similar fashion as binary-orientated subscribers. However, because of HTTP's stateless nature and the assumption that the client has only limited capabilities, it is not possible for the router to forward events as they are received and processed. Instead, for HTTP clients, the router implicitly enables the client event cache (discussed in section 4.5) so that events are stored on the mesh. Clients periodically query the HTTP endpoint which returns queued events in a standard Atom syndication format [17] XML stream. Mesh-side event caching is particularly useful for mobile clients as they can receive events even for periods that they did not have network access.

5 Applications

We have built a number of applications using the Å framework within our laboratory. All employees in our organization use notebook computers as their primary computing resource, and often operate in an occasionally-connected manner. The framework has proven to be reliable and robust in these situations, automatically discovering and connecting the mesh when it is available, and consuming little resources when unavailable.

Container service-hosted publisher add-ins run on a number of servers, workstations and notebook computers. Basic publishers have been written to produce events relating to financial data, current and forecast weather conditions, shared file storage usage, nearby WiFi or Bluetooth radios and instant messaging status. An application which runs on Windows Mobile devices sends similar network and location events, however also leverages in-built GPS receivers and cellular tower information. A wrapper around the Phidget[1] API allows a wide variety of hardware sensors (such as light, force, proximity, touch and so on) to produce Å events. Three industrial robots have also been augmented to produce events based on their current activity and status.

Adapters also run to "remix" events into alternative translations or add additional semantics. For example, a location adapter transforms radio proximity and network information events into location events, for example inferring that if a node is close to a particular WiFi access point, it must be in a certain building, and thus in a certain geographical location. Presence events are produced by a presence adapter, which asserts that if two separate nodes are detecting similar radios or have similar network properties, they are co-located or in close proximity. Because these adapters run on single server, matching logic can be easily altered without requiring updating individual nodes which produce the events.

Subscribers (mostly running on end-user notebook computers) make use of the events produced by publishers and adapters. A telepresence ambient visualization uses a LED bar to light a white wall with different colors based on activity occurring in the remote robot lab. This has been a useful mechanism for people working in the office space to be aware of their colleague's activity in the robot lab, located in a separate building. Another ambient visualization uses financial data events and Phidget servo-motors to articulate a sheet of satin. The sheet represents market index activity, while a LED bar behind the sheet colors it depending on the organization's stock price activity. The visualization thus provides focus, a company's stock price,

---

[1] http://www.phidgets.com

and also the context, the wider market's activity. It has proven to be a popular in the office place, spurring conversation and raising awareness of the company's financial performance. Nabaztag/tag[2] rabbits can be controlled by sending events, for example moving ears, displaying light patterns or speaking aloud text. This is currently used for informal office place announcements. More sophisticated applications are currently under development, for example a location and presence awareness system which utilises location and presence events and sensors.

Rapid development of prototypes was possible as the client API hides much of the implementation specifics, allowing them to operate without regard to connections, queuing, resources, authentication and so on. For a subscriber, data is simply put into a dictionary-like data structure and sent; for a publisher, after sending a subscription event pattern, data is received using standard callback mechanisms. Using the framework made network-enabling a data source such as a sensor straightforward, as well as implementing a remote client to make use of the data. Loose-coupling meant that there are few issues with versioning or coordination and has also allowed us to reappropriate event data without requiring modification of the publisher or existing subscribers. The container service speeded component development as scaffolding and lifecycle management code did not need to be written. The framework's open-ended event format allowed a variety of data to be exchanged and the sophisticated event pattern functionality allows subscribers exert fine-grained control over which events are received. Decentralized architecture eased configuration and increased reliability, as the system could still function even with unstable routers or clients. Having a unified event distribution mesh not only allows disparate components to communicate, but permits rich aggregation and translation of the disparate events, such as producing context inferences from numerous independent data sources.

6 Future Work

While the framework fulfils our current requirements, we are interested in advancing certain aspects of its functionality and conducting an evaluation and improvement of its performance.

Particularly of interest is to extend the script event pattern model to offer more sophisticated capabilities and better performance (rough benchmarking show that the script kernel can process several hundred events per second for a single basic expression). For example, scripts can be precompiled into intermediate bytecode to increase execution speed. If arbitrary bytecode can be used as subscriptions, this model could be further extended so that subscribers could send complete, precompiled modules for high-performance and rich mesh-side event filtering or to act as general purpose add-ins to the mesh. For example, an occasionally-connected client might inject a module to perform event adaption on the mesh itself. In-built .NET execution isolation sandboxes can also be leveraged so scripts run in restricted environments and unable to cause router instability. This would introduce significant additional complexity as remotely-loaded add-ins would need to be managed across the distributed mesh.

---

[2] http://www.nabaztag.com

To further simply development from non .NET platforms, a JavaScript API could be developed to simplify access of the HTTP endpoint. Providing mechanisms for HTTP endpoint discovery is also a priority.

7 Conclusion

This paper described the design and implementation of the Å framework, a novel approach to the decentralized publish/subscribe paradigm which emphasises accessibility, simplicity and loose-coupling. The framework uses stateful, content-based event patterns, which can be defined as rich scripts, using a number of popular scripting languages. This permits a high level of expressiveness and allows clients to place more of their logic close to the data, improving performance and simplifying client implementation.

The primary design goal was for end-developer and user accessibility and simplicity. This is achieved through a powerful client API, automatic mesh discovery and maintenance, rich stateful event pattern expressiveness and event caching and persistency options. The secondary goal was to support loose-coupling between publishers and subscribers as well as framework components. Å provides additional support for loose-coupling through the use of caches, quenching and rich event patterns. Occasionally-connected clients such as mobile devices are well supported through the use of the aforementioned features. Å systems (clients or router nodes) are entirely self-hosting, and do not require any external services or infrastructure (apart from necessary basic network services) and are thus easily deployed and maintained. Tertiary design goals were for an open, flexible interface for non-.NET systems. This is provided using a HTTP-based endpoint which uses common web standards and protocols, and is thus accessible to most programming and network environments.

The paper also briefly describes a number of applications already built on the framework, such as presence and location publishers and ambient visualization systems and outlines plans for future work.

Acknowledgements. The authors wish to acknowledge the support of the Norwegian Research Council and the TAIL IO project for their continued funding and support for this research. The TAIL IO project is an international cooperative research project led by StatoilHydro and an R&D consortium consisting of ABB, IBM, Aker Solutions and SKF.

References

1. Sutton, P., Brereton, B., Heyer, C., MacColl, I.: Ambient Interaction Framework: Software infrastructure for the rapid development of pervasive computing environments. In: Proc. of the Asia Pacific Forum on Pervasive Computing, pp. 1–8. Australian Computer Society (2002)
2. Muhl, G., Ulbrich, A., Herman, K.: Disseminating information to mobile clients using publish-subscribe. IEEE Internet Computing 8(3), 46–53 (2004)

3. Tian, F., Reinwald, B., Pirahesh, H., Mayr, T., Myllymaki, J.: Implementing a scalable XML publish/subscribe system using relational database systems. In: Proc. of the ACM SIGMOD international Conference on Management of Data, pp. 479–490. ACM Press, New York (2004)
4. Segall, B., Arnold, D.: Elvin has left the building: A publish/subscribe notification service with quenching. In: Proc. of AUUG 1997 (1997)
5. Chand, R., Felber, P.A.: A Scalable Protocol for Content-Based Routing in Overlay Networks. In: Proc. of the Int'l Symposium on Network Computing and Applications. IEEE, Los Alamitos (2003)
6. Carzaniga, A., Rosenblum, D.S., Wolf, A.L.: Achieving scalability and expressiveness in an Internet-scale event notification service. In: Proc. of the ACM Symposium on Principles of Distributed Computing, pp. 219–227. ACM Press, New York (2000)
7. Leung, H.K.: Subject space: a state-persistent model for publish/subscribe systems. In: Proc. of the Conf. of the Centre for Advanced Studies on Collaborative Research. IBM Press, Toronto, Canada (2002)
8. Ionescu, M., Marsic, I.: Stateful publish-subscribe for mobile environments. In: Proc. of the W'shop on Wireless Mobile Applications and Services on WLAN Hotspots, pp. 21–28. ACM Press, New York (2004)
9. Pereira, J., Fabret, F., Jacobsen, H.-A., Llirbat, F., Preotiuc-Preito, R., Ross, K., et al.: Publish/Subscribe on the Web at Extreme Speed. In: Proc. of ACM SIGMOD Conf. on Management of Data, pp. 627–630. ACM, New York (2000)
10. Triantafillou, P., Economides, A.: Subscription Summarization: A New Paradigm for Efficient Publish/Subscribe Systems. In: Proc. of the I'tnl Conf. on Distributed Computing Systems (ICDCS 2004), pp. 562–571. IEEE Press, Los Alamitos (2004)
11. Fabret, F., Jacobsen, H.A., Llirbat, F., Pereira, J., Ross, K.A., Shasha, D.: Filtering algorithms and implementation for very fast publish/subscribe systems. In: Proc. of the SIGMOD Int'l Conf. on Managment of Data, pp. 115–126. ACM Press, New York (2001)
12. Aguilera, M.K., Strom, R.E., Sturman, D.C., Astley, M., Chandra, T.D.: Matching events in a content-based subscription system. In: Proc. of the ACM Symposium on Principles of Distributed Computing, pp. 53–61. ACM Press, New York (1999)
13. Eisenhauer, G., Schwan, K., Bustamante, F.: Publish-Subscribe for High-Performance Computing. IEEE Internet Computing 10(1), 40–47 (2006)
14. Cugola, G., Di Nitto, E., Fuggetta, A.: The JEDI event-based infrastructure and its application to the development of the OPSS WFMS. IEEE Trans. on Software Engineering 27, 827–850 (2001)
15. Clark, J., DeRose, S.: XML Path Language (XPath). W3C (1999)
16. Richardson, L., Ruby, S.: RESTful Web Services. O'Reilly, Sebastopol (2007)
17. Nottingham, M., Sayre, R.: RFC 4287 Atom Syndication Format. IETF Network Working Group (2005)

Mining and Visualizing Mobile Social Network
Based on Bayesian Probabilistic Model

Jun-Ki Min, Su-Hyung Jang, and Sung-Bae Cho

Department of Computer Science, Yonsei University
262 Seongsanno, Seodaemun-gu, Seoul 120-749, Korea
{loomlike,neogates}@sclab.yonsei.ac.kr, sbcho@cs.yonsei.ac.kr

Abstract. Social networking has provided powerful new ways to find people, organize groups, and share information. Recently, the potential functionalities of the ubiquitous infrastructure let users form a mobile social network (MSN) which is discriminative against the previous social networks based on the Internet. Since a mobile phone is used in a much wider range of situations and is carried by the user at all times, it easily collects personal information and can be customized to fit the user's preference. In this paper, we presented MSN mining model which estimates the social contexts like closeness and relationship from uncertain phone logs using a Bayesian network. The mining results were then used for recommending callees or representing the state of social relationships. We have implemented the phonebook application that displays the contexts as network or graph style, and have performed a subjectivity test. As a result, we have confirmed that the visualizing of the MSN is useful as an interface for social networking services.

Keywords: Mobile social network, Bayesian network, context visualization.

1 Introduction

A social network is a group of people connected by common features such as interests, ideas, and friendships. Social networking has grown dramatically more popular since the Internet emerged which provides an easy means for interacting with someone else through web, e-mail, and instant messaging services [1]. MySpace (myspace.com) and Facebook (facebook.com), for example, are the most well-known web based social networks, and are now successfully evolved into the ubiquitous environment with innovations in mobile technologies. Therefore, users now can send emails to friends and access the community information through their mobile devices just the same as before via the Internet [2, 3].

The current mobile social network (MSN) services, however, still have limitations since they keep their concepts of original web-services rather than utilize the ubiquitous features. A mobile device can collect everyday information effectively because it is used in a much wider range of situations and is carried by a user at all times. Especially, a mobile phone is promising to support the social networking because it can easily model the user's social connections based on the relationship between a caller and a callee. Eagle and Pentland, in the Reality Mining project at the MIT Media Lab,

D. Zhang et al. (Eds.): UIC 2009, LNCS 5585, pp. 111–120, 2009.

observed the interactions among 100 users with Bluetooth-enabled mobile phones, and recognized the friendship by using Gaussian mixture model [4].

In this paper, we propose a social contexts mining model that automatically generates MSN. Using Bayesian networks (BNs), the proposed method infers meaningful information like closeness and personal relationships from uncertain mobile logs, and then it visualizes the context in order to provide useful information for social networking such as personal relationship management. Here, user's call patterns including time, frequency, and place are exploited as the mobile logs. For the experimental test, we implemented a mobile phonebook interface using the proposed method.

2 Background

With advances in sensor technologies, context-based applications on a mobile phone are becoming available which give users more convenience by reducing the amount of human attention needed to provide the service. Cao et al. introduced a mobile tourist guide which considers spatiotemporal information of the device and community contexts together [5]. They specified a community by the members' profiles such as contact information and traveling history, and used rule-based context reasoning engine. Lee et al. developed an emoticon transformation service on mobile devices which infers the user's emotion and transfers the corresponding emoticon to other users in the network [6]. They estimated the emotion using the predefined rules with bio-signals like heartbeat, galvanic skin response, and skin temperature.

Context awareness, however, is difficult to achieve because of the environmental uncertainties like user's behavioral irregularity and sensors' inaccuracy [7]. Since a BN is one of efficient tools to handle the uncertainties, it has been widely used for context modeling. Park et al. trained user's preference with BNs by using context information like location, time, weather, and user request collected from the mobile device in order to provide a map-based recommendation system [8]. Cho et al. used BNs designed by experts to find memorable events and summarize in a cartoon-style diary from a user's daily life logs [9]. In this paper, we exploit BNs to infer social contexts from the mobile logs.

3 Mining and Visualizing Mobile Social Network

Mobile social contexts, such as interact with whom in a specific place or at a certain time of a day, are very useful information in terms of social networking services. It can be a criterion for grouping people or improves the performance of mobile systems [4, 10]. The proposed method models and visualizes the MSN according to the social contexts which helps a user to manage his/her personal relationships. Fig. 1 shows an overview of the proposed system. We implemented each module runs on the platform of MS Windows Mobile 2003 SE Pocket PC with a small global positioning system (GPS) receiver that transfers data with Bluetooth to the phone (It is described more specifically at experimental results section).

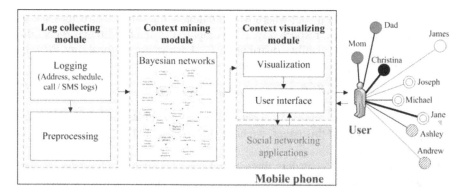

Fig. 1. An overview of the proposed system. It provides a user the information of social relationships as graphs or a network. These kinds of visualized features can be used as an interface of other mobile social networking applications.

3.1 Log Collection and Preprocessing

A mobile phone enables various types of communication like a voice conversation (call) and a short message service (SMS). It also can perceive people's encounter with each other using Bluetooth signal. Moreover, it continuously records the user's location (GPS) and other personal or social context. These spatiotemporal patterns of interactions can be adopted for mining the social connections like relationships or closeness. Table 1 lists the mobile phone logs related to the social interactions.

After collecting logs, our system preprocesses them to be informative and usable for BNs. Some values are discretized by using simple rules based on statistical analysis (For example, the state of "the number of recent calls" is defined as "many" if there are more than five calls in "the recent time period," otherwise "few"). The coordinates gathered by using GPS are converted to the semantic labels. Here, we have only considered three semantic locations of home, workplace, and others.

Table 1. Mobile phone logs used for mining the social contexts. Among the four types of interactions, in this paper, only *call* log was used.

Type	Information
Address book	Name, phone number, e-mail address, home address, workplace address, ...
Interaction logs	Call, short message, nearby person by Bluetooth, data transfer
Device logs	Spatial information (latitude, longitude, speed) by GPS, temporal information (duration, time, day of week)

3.2 Social Context Mining

Bayesian probabilistic inference is the efficient model to handle the uncertain information, and also easily utilizes an expert's pre-knowledge for its structure or parameters [11]. In this regard, we have employed BNs for mining the social context.

Let $G(B_s, \theta)$ be the BN model where B_s and θ denote the network structure and the set of network parameters, respectively. θ is composed of the conditional probability table B_Φ and the prior probability distribution B_p. For the prior probability $P(\theta)$, the knowledge discovery process is as follows:

$$P(Z_T, Y_T, \theta) = P(Y_T \mid Z_T, B_\Phi) P(Z_T \mid B_p) \tag{1}$$

where $Z_T = \{z_1, z_2, \ldots, z_T\}$ represents a set of T states variables, and Y_T is the corresponding observations. In this paper, we have specified B_s and θ manually based on the domain knowledge.

The proposed method considers three social contexts such as closeness, related-activity and relationship. Each context is described more specifically in Table 2.

Table 2. Four social contexts used in this paper

Social context	BN node state	Meaning
Closeness	{close, distant}	Whether the user has contact with him/her closely or not
Related activity	{move, work, study, rest, play, eat}	Which activity the user has been normally performing with him/her
Relationship	{family, lover, friend, colleague, acquaintance, etc}	Type of relationship

BN designed for this problem includes 19 variables and 24 dependencies as shown in Fig. 2. The design methodologies of the BN in terms of the target contexts are as follows:

Degree of closeness. People who contact frequently with each other or spend long time together are regarded as close. They often tend to meet/call at personal time like evening, weekends, and holiday. The activity on phone call is related with the closeness either. It is because he/she would not want to be interrupted by unfamiliar person during resting or playing.

Relationship. Personal information which can be gained from the mobile address book is useful to extract the relationship. For example, persons with same last name or home address probably are family. Here, we simply matched the personal information (within the Address book) between a user and the other for calculating their similarity. Since people commonly meet their colleagues at workplace and friends at the outside, the contact place also used for inferring the relationship.

Activity during contact. It is tightly correlated with closeness and relationships. For instance, people have more chances to interact with colleagues than friends or families when they are working. On the other hand, they will contact with friends for playing. The activity inference part was designed by using spatio-temporal information with general knowledge such as "People work at workplace during daytime" or "They eat at lunch or dinner time".

High level contexts explained so far should be estimated for all the persons who are contained in the address book and updated whenever the user makes a contact with him/her.

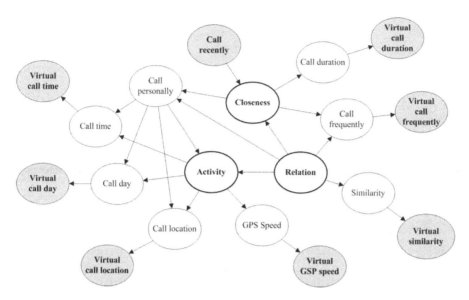

Fig. 2. The Bayesian network designed for mining social contexts. In order to use continuous variables as evidences (*gray nodes*), we have made virtual nodes and dynamically changed their conditional probabilities.

Since conditional probabilities of a BN are based on discrete variables, continuous values need to be discretized. In principle, it will result in some loss of information. For example, the 'Call recently' node in Fig. 2, which represents "How much time has passed since the last contact," has to be defined as finite states like {within three days, from three to five, from six to eight, more than nine days}. In order to address this problem, the proposed method changes the probability table dynamically so that can express the continuous variables such as likelihood ratio that represent the observer's strength of confidence toward the observed event or statistical observations. For the previous example, the propose method only takes two states of 'Recent' and 'Long ago,' and substitutes their probabilities for each observation by fuzzy membership values instead of selecting the evidence by a specific state (see upper image of Fig. 3). It is possible because the node is a root that has no prior conditions. If the node is, however, not a root such as the 'Call time' in Fig. 2, then the evidence should be specified to a state for updating the belief with the observations. In this case, our model attaches a virtual node [12], which has binary states of *Yes/No* with all variables of its parent's states, to the target node. The conditional probabilities of *Yes* state are then set based on the statistics of observations. The lower image of Fig. 3 shows an example where a user has called someone eight per 10 at night and one per 10 at morning.

3.3 Social Context Visualization

In order to help the user to understand his/her condition of social relationships, the proposed method represents social structures by a network in terms of nodes (individuals) and ties (relationships), and visualizes social contexts as graphs or descriptive texts.

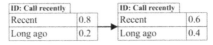

ID: Call recently	
Recent	0.8
Long ago	0.2

ID: Call recently	
Recent	0.6
Long ago	0.4

In case the evidence node is **a root**

ID: Virtual-Call time	Morning	Afternoon	Night	Dawn
Yes	0.05	0.05	0.8	0.1
No	0.95	0.95	0.2	0.9

Never used ◄ ─── Ensure the row sum to be **one**

In case the evidence node is **not a root**

Fig. 3. Examples of specifying evidence with continuous variables like fuzzy membership variables or statistics of observations (both row and column sums to be one)

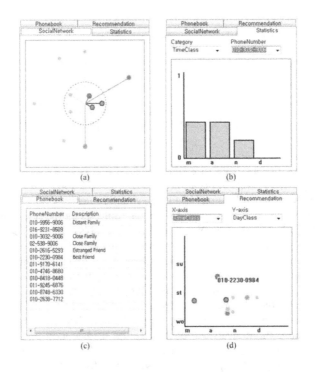

(a)   (b)   (c)   (d)

Fig. 4. Phonebook interface based on the proposed method which visualizes the (a) social structure, (b) contact pattern in terms of context category, (c) description of relationship, and (d) correlation among contexts

For the network, as shown in Fig. 4(a), three contexts such as recently contact, closeness, and relationship are expressed as edge length, edge color (with gray level), and node color, respectively. People intimate with a user are marked as dark gray line, while estranged people are represented as lighter gray line, and more distant persons are not presented on the network. The edge becomes longer as time passed since the user contacted with the corresponding person lastly. Here, the user can set the 'circle of relationship' which means the boundary of friendship (see the dotted line in Fig. 4(a)). The proposed method then recommends an estranged friendly person (a node on outside of boundary with a dark gray edge) to the user for making contact with. After the user called him/her, the corresponding edge is shrunk into the boundary.

In addition to the network, the proposed method visualizes the user's contact tendency in terms of various contexts such as day, time, and location (Fig. 4(b)), describes the relational information of the user and others on the phonebook (Fig. 4(c)), and shows the correlations of two different contexts which can be used to the callee recommendation (For example, if current time is Sunday *su* afternoon *a*, then the system recommends 010-2220-0984 whom the user have made phone call with at Sunday afternoon as shown in Fig. 4(d)).

4   Experimental Results

Experiments on real user data have been performed to validate the proposed method. We have implemented the agents on the platform of MS Windows Mobile 2003 SE Pocket PC and collected the logs of ten university student over about a month using the Samsung SPH-M4650 smart phone device with a small GPS receiver that transfers data with Bluetooth to the phone as shown in Fig. 5.

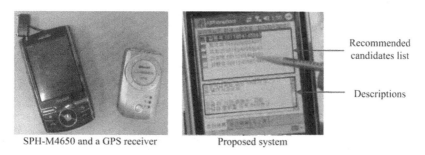

SPH-M4650 and a GPS receiver   Proposed system

Fig. 5. Mobile devices and the proposed system implemented on mobile phone

We have analyzed the social contexts extracted by the proposed method. Figure 6 shows examples of the BN for a user's two callees. The upper person had been personally and closely connected with the user, and their personal information was similar for each other. Therefore, their relationship was inferred as *family*. In case of the lower person, their relationship was *friend* since they had called for each other frequently and personally while they neither contacted recently nor closely.

We have compared the extracted relationships with the actual labels tagged by users, and achieved about 60~70% accuracies. There were several reasons for the low performance. Firstly, the lack of personal information in the address book caused the confusion between *friend* and *lover*. The occupation of subject also made the problem difficult. Since they were all students, *coworker* is quite ambiguous type of relationship. Finally and mostly, our four weeks logs were insufficient to model the user's relationship exactly. Friends whom the users never called were regarded as acquaintances after all. Yet, the inferred contexts including the relationship can be useful information for characterizing groups on social network.

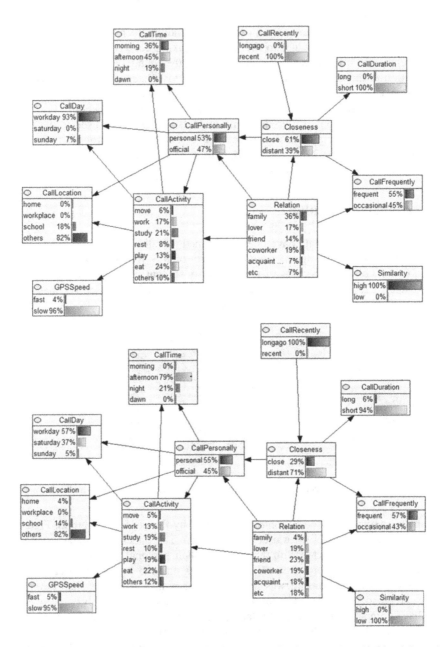

Fig. 6. Examples of the BN inference results for a user's family (upper) and a friend (lower)

In order to validate the usefulness of the proposed method, we performed a subjectivity test about the implemented application for ten users based on the System Usability Scale (SUS) questionnaires. The SUS is a simple, ten-item scale giving a global view of subjective assessments of usability where its score has a range of zero

Table 3. Modified questionnaires of the System Usability Scale

		Strongly disagree				Strongly agree
1.	I think I would like to use this application frequently	1	2	3	4	5
2.	I found the application unnecessarily complex	1	2	3	4	5
3.	I thought the application was easy to use	1	2	3	4	5
4.	I think that I would need the support of a technical person to be able to use this application	1	2	3	4	5
5.	I found the various functions in this application were well integrated	1	2	3	4	5
6.	I thought there was too much inconsistency in this application	1	2	3	4	5
7.	I would imagine that most people would learn to use this application very quickly	1	2	3	4	5
8.	I found the application very cumbersome to use	1	2	3	4	5
9.	I felt very confident using the application	1	2	3	4	5
10.	I needed to learn a lot of things before I could get going with this application	1	2	3	4	5

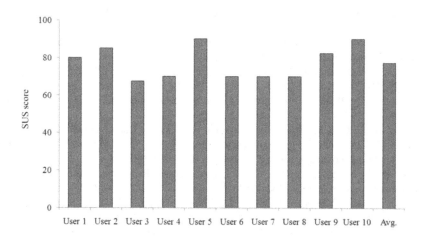

Fig. 7. SUS scores for the proposed system

to 100 [13]. In this paper, we modified the questionnaires by replacing the word *system* with *application* as shown in Table 3. As shown in Fig. 7, the SUS test results indicated that the visualization provides effective ways to manage the MSN services.

5 Conclusions

This paper presents the social contexts' mining and visualizing method. It infers the user's contexts from uncertain mobile logs using Bayesian networks and provides useful information for MSN services such as relationship management by recommending estranged friends. It also visualizes user's social contexts or contact patterns using various types of graphs or descriptive text. There are, however, still many issues to be solved such as mining more kinds of social context or testing on the realistic environment where many users interact with each other. As a future work, we will exploit various types of interactions among multiple users including physical meeting (acquired from Bluetooth) in order to make more realistic and accurate model. We will also perform the accuracy test of the extracted contexts such as relationship and activity.

Acknowledgement. This work was supported by MKE, Korea under ITRC IITA-2009-(C1090-0902-0011).

References

1. Staab, S., et al.: Social Networks Applied. IEEE Intelligent Systems 20(1), 80–93 (2005)
2. Chen, Y., Xie, X., Ma, W.-Y., Zhang, H.-J.: Adapting Web Pages for Small-Screen Devices. IEEE Internet Computing 9(1), 50–56 (2005)
3. Bottazzi, D., Montanari, R., Toninelli, A.: Context-Aware Middleware for Anytime, Anywhere Social Networks. IEEE Intelligent Systems 22(5), 23–32 (2007)
4. Eagle, N., Pentland, A.: Reality Mining: Sensing Complex Social Systems. Personal and Ubiquitous Computing 10(4), 255–268 (2006)
5. Cao, Y., Klamma, R., Hou, M., Jarke, M.: Follow Me, Follow You-Spatiotemporal Community Context Modeling and Adaptation for Mobile Information Systems. In: IEEE International Conference on Mobile Data Management, pp. 108–115 (2008)
6. Lee, H., Park, J., Ko, E., Lee, J.: An Agent-Based Context-Aware System on Handheld Computers. In: IEEE International Conference on Consumer Electronics, pp. 229–230 (2006)
7. Hwang, K.-S., Cho, S.-B.: Modular Bayesian Network for Uncertainty Handling on Mobile Device. In: International Conference on Information Processing and Management of Uncertainty in Knowledge-Based Systems, pp. 402–408 (2008)
8. Park, M.-H., Hong, J.-H., Cho, S.-B.: Location-Based Recommendation System Using Bayesian User's Preference Model in Mobile Devices. In: Indulska, J., Ma, J., Yang, L.T., Ungerer, T., Cao, J. (eds.) UIC 2007. LNCS, vol. 4611, pp. 1130–1139. Springer, Heidelberg (2007)
9. Cho, S.-B., Kim, K.-J., Hwang, K.-S., Song, I.-J.: AniDiary: Daily Cartoon-Style Diary Exploits Bayesian Networks. IEEE Pervasive Computing 6(3), 66–75 (2007)
10. Miklas, A.G., Gollu, K.K., Chan, K.K.W., Saroiu, S., Gummadi, K.P., de Lara, E.: Exploiting Social Interactions in Mobile Systems. In: Krumm, J., Abowd, G.D., Seneviratne, A., Strang, T. (eds.) UbiComp 2007. LNCS, vol. 4717, pp. 409–428. Springer, Heidelberg (2007)
11. Jensen, F.V.: Introduction to Bayesian Networks. Springer, New York (1996)
12. Pearl, J.: Probabilistic Reasoning in Intelligent Systems: Networks of Plausible Inference. Morgan Kaufman, San Mateo (1988)
13. Brooke, J.: SUS: A Quick and Dirty Usability Scale. In: Jordan, P.W., et al. (eds.) Usability Evaluation in Industry, Taylor and Francis, London (1996)

SMSR: A Scalable Multipath Source Routing Protocol for Wireless Sensor Networks[*]

Sutaek Oh[1], Dongkyun Kim[2,**], Hyunwoo Kang[3], and Hong-Jong Jeong[2]

[1] IDIS corporation, Korea
stoh@idis.co.kr
[2] Dept. of Computer Engineering, Kyungpook National University, Korea
dongkyun@knu.ac.kr, hjjeong@monet.knu.ac.kr
[3] Electronics and Telecommunications Research Institute (ETRI), Korea
hwkang@etri.re.kr

Abstract. In wireless sensor networks (WSNs), providing resilience (fault tolerance) is a challenging issue. A lot of multipath routing protocols, therefore, have been proposed to achieve the goal; however, they usually suffer from control message overhead or a lack of scalability. Although some protocols utilize partially disjoint paths or longer alternate paths in order to reduce such overhead, they cannot guarantee resilience, because a single failure on a shared node breaks all the paths. In this paper, we therefore propose a scalable multipath source routing (SMSR) protocol. In SMSR, a sink node collects each sensor node's one-hop upstream neighbor information during an initialization phase which the sink node then uses in order to construct several shortest node-disjoint downstream (sink-to-sensor) paths. When transmitting downstream packets, the source routing technique is exploited. On the other hand, each sensor node forwards upstream (sensor-to-sink) packets to one of its upstream neighbors, through the concept of gradient-based routing. The initialization phase depends on only one-time flooding and n (network size) times unicasting, and each sensor node manages only one-hop upstream neighbor information. In this sense, SMSR is scalable in terms of the overhead and the size of routing tables in sensor nodes. Particularly, since SMSR provides several node-disjoint paths with low overhead, it can guarantee resilience efficiently. Through experiments using both ns-2 simulation and our real world test-bed, we verify that SMSR achieves the goal better than other existing routing protocols.

1 Introduction

In wireless sensor networks (WSNs), the failure of sensor nodes, caused by depletion of their limited energy, results in frequent topology changes. Therefore, it is challenging to provide a resilient service. A lot of multipath routing protocols

---

[*] This work was supported by Electronics and Telecommunications Research Institute (ETRI).
[**] The corresponding author is Dongkyun Kim. dongkyun@knu.ac.kr

D. Zhang et al. (Eds.): UIC 2009, LNCS 5585, pp. 121–135, 2009.
© Springer-Verlag Berlin Heidelberg 2009

have been proposed in order to ensure the resilience of wireless multihop networks such as mobile ad hoc networks (MANETs) or wireless mesh networks (WMNs). They are applicable to WSNs, because the networks have similar characteristics with WSNs. In particular, one major approach that is widely adopted in multipath routing protocols is distributed on-demand route discovery [12][13][14]. When applied to WSNs, however, it suffers from control message overhead and a lack of scalability due to its dependence on flooding. This overhead results in setting-up suboptimal paths due to the loss of broadcasted packets. To address this problem, a lot of protocols utilize partially node-disjoint paths or longer alternate paths. However, these protocols still cannot avoid inefficiency; when a shared node of partial disjoint paths fails, all paths which include the node are broken. In addition to this, it is clear that transmitting packets over a longer alternate path consumes more resources.

The distributed on-demand route discovery has an additional drawback as follows. The arrival time of the flooded route request may affect the number of shortest disjoint paths that can be found. For example in Figure 1(a); there are two shortest node-disjoint paths between the sink node S and the sensor node 7, S-1-3-6-7 and S-2-4-5-7. However, if a route request through S-1-3-5-7 first arrives (i.e. the primary path is S-1-3-5-7), on-demand route discovery protocols cannot find any node-disjoint alternate paths at node 7. Besides, although the primary path has been constructed through S-1-3-6-7, a node-disjoint alternate path still cannot be found when the route request through S-1-3 first arrives at node 5. In this case, the node 5 forwards only the route request coming from S-1-3, not the route request from S-2-4. In order to have more alternate paths, some routing protocols forward every route request. However, they cannot avoid the above-mentioned control overhead.

In this paper, we therefore propose a scalable multipath source routing (SMSR) protocol in order to address the two problems mentioned above. In addition, a sink node is assumed to usually have more resources than sensor nodes, and most applications in WSNs usually require communications between a sink node and sensor nodes, rather than those between sensor nodes, which SMSR also assumes. In SMSR, therefore, upstream paths are established utilizing the concept of gradient-based routing as in [4]. For downstream paths, a sink node constructs several shortest node-disjoint paths between itself and a sensor node through a heuristic algorithm and then packets are transmitted via the source routing technique. SMSR only requires a one-time flooding of control messages and n (network size) times unicasting to construct both upstream and downstream paths; this enables SMSR to achieve scalability in terms of control message overhead. In particular, intermediate sensor nodes do not have to maintain their routing table; instead, they only manage their one-hop upstream neighbor nodes.

- **Design of Scalable Multipath Source Routing (SMSR).** SMSR belongs to a class of multipath routing protocol for WSNs. Based on the fact that WSNs usually have a centralized node (i.e. sink node), SMSR can find the larger number of shortest node-disjoint paths than other on-demand multipath routing protocols, which are achieved at the sink node in a centralized manner. SMSR also provides route maintenance mechanisms with low control overhead.

- **Real world implementation.** Performance of most proposed routing protocols has been evaluated by using simulation techniques. However, simulations cannot reflect real world environment. Thus, in order to give insight into the behavior of SMSR in real world, we implemented SMSR into sensor mote and investigated its performance.

The rest of this paper is organized as follows: Section II introduces some multipath routing protocols. In Section III, our proposed scalable multipath source routing protocol is presented in detail. Section IV shows the experimental results from both ns-2 simulation and a real world sensor test-bed. Finally, some conclusion remarks are given in Section V.

2 Related Work

An extensive survey on routing protocols for WSNs and their motivation can be found in [2]. In this section, a brief survey of several multipath routing protocols which have similar objectives with SMSR is provided.

A multipath routing protocol based on Directed Diffusion [4] was proposed in [3]. The authors argue that even though disjoint paths are attractive, it is inefficient to construct them in terms of energy efficiency. It is because the alternative disjoint path may be longer than the primary path. Thus, they construct k braided paths, i.e. partially disjoint paths, by using k reinforcement message. Although braided paths can reduce the energy consumption and control overhead, it is fragile with a single node failure causing widespead failure.

A multipath extension of dynamic source routing (DSR) for MANETs was proposed in [6] (called MDSR in this paper for simplicity). Based on the fact that multiple copies of a route discovery message arrive through multiple paths, MDSR allows the destination node to still reply to route discovery messages which arrive later if they are link-disjoint with the primary path. However, if packets have already been transmitted over a broken link, they will be lost. To address this problem, the destination replies to all nodes in the primary path with an alternate disjoint path towards itself. MSR [7] exploits similar concept with MDSR for route discovery. MSR also employs a load balancing technique by measuring round trip time of packets. Although the route cache of MDSR and MSR significantly reduces control message overhead, the overhead is still significant and they usually cannot find a sufficient number of shortest node-disjoint paths due to their route discovery mechanism.

AOMDV [8] also belongs to on-demand multipath routing protocols. As an extension to AODV [14], it constructs multiple link-disjoint paths and provides new rules for loop avoidance. The authors argue that although the link-disjointedness is less resilient than node-disjointedness since the link-disjointedness is useful only when links fail independently, the number of node-disjoint paths makes itself less efficient. However, this problem, which occurs in both MDSR and AOMDV, comes from the reason that have been mentioned in Section 1 and can be overcome by SMSR.

3   Our Proposed Protocol: SMSR

3.1   Overview of SMSR

Here, we overview our proposed scalable multipath source routing (SMSR) protocol. In our targeted application model, a sink node collects a periodic sensing data from sensor nodes and transmits control messages to the sensor nodes occasionally. In case of address centric routing protocols, each sensor node should maintain its routing table in order to relay data packets to the destination. Hence, the size of routing table increases in proportion to the number of sensor nodes in the network. This leads to a scalability problem.

Our proposed SMSR exploits the concept of gradient-based routing, which is widely adopted in wireless sensor networks, as its basic forwarding technique from sensor nodes to a sink node (upstream path). On the other hand, the occasional packet delivery from sink to sensor nodes (downstream path) is performed by a source routing technique that enables the routing header to contain intermediate nodes from source to destination. Hence, SMSR can reduce the routing protocol overhead that each sensor node should maintain its routing table, since it manages only one-hop upstream neighbor information towards a sink node for upstream packets.

In order to set up the upstream path, a sink node floods an initialization request (IREQ) message in the network. On receiving IREQ messages through different paths, each sensor node sets up the multiple paths towards the sink node. As a response to IREQ messages, the sensor node sends an initialization reply (IREP) message to the sink node. The sink node collects IREP messages from all of the sensor nodes and calculates multiple source routes to the sensor nodes using a heuristic algorithm described in section 3.3. In this section, we first describe upstream and downstream path setup algorithm and path recovery process.

3.2   Upstream Path Setup

To set up gradient paths, a sink node floods an initialization request (IREQ) message towards all sensor nodes. The IREQ message contains the sink node's address and hop-distance (i.e. hop count) to the sink node. It also contains a sequence number in order to avoid routing loops. Each node listens to the IREQ message for a certain time duration t. During the duration t, upon receiving the IREQ messages, each sensor node records the address of a sink node and addresses of the upstream neighbor nodes (predecessor nodes which have the shortest hop-distance towards the sink node). See Algorithm 1. After t, each sensor node replies with an initialization reply (IREP) message to the sink node. The IREP message contains the sensor node's address, hop-distance from the sensor node to the sink node, and a list of the IREP originator's upstream neighbor nodes. From this information, the sink node fills up its routing table, which is modeled as a directional acyclic graph as shown in Figure 1. Note that the IREP unicasting from all sensor nodes may cause a large amount of control traffic. To alleviate this overhead, transmission of these IREPs can be randomly distributed over time t and IREPs should be aggregated. That is, if a sensor node which did not send its own IREP yet receives IREPs from other sensor nodes, it aggregates its own IREP and the received IREPs into a single IREP message and unicasts it towards the sink node.

As mentioned before, when a sensor node has a packet to send to the sink node, it basically uses the gradient routing technique. It first chooses one of its upstream neighbor nodes and forwards the packet. Various metrics can be utilized to select its upstream neighbor. For simplicity, however, a random selection is assumed in this paper. The upstream neighbor node which receives a packet to forward also repeats this procedure until the packet reaches the sink node.

Algorithm 1. Algorithm for IREQ processing

1: $IREQ.sender$: address of the IREQ originator.
2: $NewSeqNum$: sequence number of current IREQ.
3: $LastSeqNum$: sequence number of previous IREQ (default 0).
4: $NewHopCnt$: hop-distance of current IREQ.
5: $LastHopCnt$: hop-distance of previous IREQ (default ∞).
6:
7: **if** $NewSeqNum < LastSeqNum$ **then**
8:     **return**
9: **else if** $NewSeqNum > LastSeqNum$ **then**
10:     Initialize upstream neighbor list and LastHopCnt;
11: **end if**
12:
13: $NewHopCnt := NewHopCnt + 1$;
14:
15: **if** $NewHopCnt == LastHopCnt$ **then**
16:     Add $IREQ.sender$ to upstream neighbor list;
17: **else if** $NewHopCnt < LastHopCnt$ **then**
18:     Initialize upstream neighbor list;
19:     $LastHopCnt := NewHopCnt$;
20:     Add $IREQ.sender$ to upstream neighbor list;
21:     Broadcast $IREQ$ with $IREQ.sender$ set to its own address;
22: **end if**

3.3   Downstream Path Calculation

When a sink node has a packet to transmit to one of sensor nodes, it first creates a path from itself to the destination node, as described in this section. This path information is carried in the packet using the source route technique and the packet is forwarded along a given source route. Since the route is calculated by the sink node, routing loops can be easily avoided.

Finding disjoint paths in a graph is a graph is a well-investigated subject in the literature [9] - [11]. However, most of the proposals have high computational complexity and some of them attempt to find the shortest pairs of disjoint paths or k-disjoint paths, rather than all the shortest disjoint paths. In this section, a heuristic algorithm is proposed which finds the shortest disjoint paths as many as possible. The algorithm has low computational complexity and it can be easily implemented in low-capacity devices.

This idea is based on the breadth first search (BFS) algorithm starting at the destination node. However, the default behavior of BFS cannot find the sufficient number of the shortest node-disjoint paths. Thus, the BFS algorithm was modified to use a priority queue. The priority is defined by a pair of (hop_dist, $num\_neighbor$) where hop_dist and $num\_neighbor$ represent the hop-distance and the number of upstream neighbor nodes, respectively. In other words, a larger hop_dist and the smaller $num\_neighbor$ represent higher priority. For the same hop_dist, $num\_neighbor$ breaks the tie. With this priority, a node which has the insufficient number of upstream neighbor nodes is given the opportunity to select its forwarding upstream neighbor node prior to the node that has the sufficient number of upstream neighbor nodes. For example in Figure 1, node 7 (destination node) is first visited. Then, node 5 with priority (3, 2) and node 6 with priority (3, 1) will be inserted into the priority queue. Thus, the algorithm first selects node 6 prior to node 5, while the basic BFS algorithm selects node 5. This enables the heuristic to find two node-disjoint paths (i.e. S - 1 - 3 - 6 - 7 and S - 2 - 4 - 5 - 7). However, the basic BFS algorithm finds only a single path (i.e. S - 1 - 3 - 5 - 7). Figure 2 shows two node-disjoint multipaths which

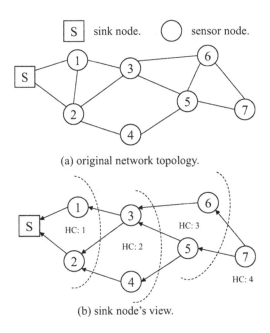

(a) original network topology.

(b) sink node's view.

Fig. 1. A directional acyclic graph constructed in a sink node

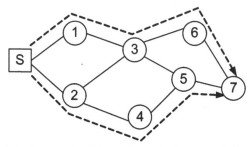

(a) an example of downstream paths to node 7

dest.	HC	active	neighbor 1	neighbor 2
1	1	true	sink	none
2	1	true	sink	none
3	2	true	1	2
4	2	true	2	none
5	3	true	3	4
6	3	true	3	none
7	4	true	5	6

(b) an example of routing table of sink node

Fig. 2. An example of downstream paths and routing table of sink node

are calculated using our algorithm. Refer Algorithm 2 for detail. The algorithm runs in $O(n + e)$ time, where n is the number of nodes and e is the sum of the number of each node's upstream neighbors. It requires only $O(n)$ bytes of memory space to trace the BFS-traversed path.

Note that this path calculation is performed on demand, i.e. node-disjoint paths are constructed when the sink node has a packet to send or the sink node receives an RREQ from a sensor node. This on-demand nature allows the computational overhead to be distributed over time. Furthermore, once the paths are constructed, they can be cached for future use until the corresponding routing table entries are changed.

3.4 Path Recovery

In WSNs, frequent changes of network topology occur due to node failures. Thus, SMSR has two path recovery mechanisms; upstream path recovery and downstream path recovery.

Upstream path recovery. In the upstream path recovery mechanism, when a node which has packets to send cannot reach an upstream neighbor node, it simply chooses another upstream neighbor node and removes (or decreases the selection priority of) the unreachable upstream node from its upstream neighbor list. In order to inform a sink node that the upstream node cannot be reached, the node which detects the link breakage unicasts a node unreachable error (NERR) message towards the sink node. However, it is possible that a node cannot reach all of its upstream neighbor nodes. In this case, it initializes its

Algorithm 2. Algorithm for Downstream Path Calculation

1: *dest*: address of the destination.
2: *PQ*: priority queue.
3: *PL*: precursor list. (default NULL)
4:
5: *PQ*.enqueue *dest* with priority (*hop_dist*, *num_neighbor*)
6: **while** *PQ* is not empty **do**
7:   *u* =*PQ*.dequeue();
8:   visit *u*;
9:   **for all** *v* that has incomming edges from *u* and not visited **do**
10:     *PQ*.enqueue *v* with priority;
11:     *PL(v) = u*;
12:   **end for**
13: **end while**
14: construct node-disjoint paths using *PL*;

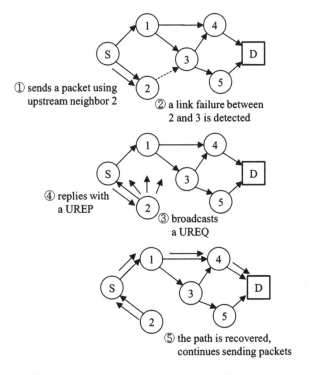

Fig. 3. An example of upstream path recovery

last-known hop-distance towards the sink node as well as the sink node's last-known sequence number, and then the node broadcasts an upstream path request (UREQ) message towards its one-hop neighbor nodes.

Upon receiving the UREQ message, a node first removes the UREQ originator address, if it exists, from its upstream neighbor table because it cannot reach the sink node through the UREQ originator any more. Next, the node checks whether it can still reach the sink node using another upstream neighbor. If so, it unicasts an upstream path reply (UREP) message towards the UREQ originator with its upstream neighbor list, hop-distance towards the sink node and the sink node's sequence number. The UREQ originator may receive one or more UREP messages. In this case, it processes them according to Algorithm 1. And then, the sink node will be informed this by receiving a message which is similar to the IREP. When the UREQ trial fails, the node back-offs the path recovery trial exponentially. During the back-off time, other nodes in its one-hop area may attempt their path recovery, which may leads to the success of its next path recovery.

Figure 3 illustrates an example of upstream path recovery. Node S tries to send a packet to the sink node through node 2. However, node 2 does not have any upstream neighbor nodes since the link between nodes 2 and 3 has been broken. Thus, node 2 broadcasts a UREQ message and node S receives the UREQ message. Node S removes node 2 from its upstream neighbor table. Since node S can still reach the sink node through node 1, it replies to node 2 with a UREP message. Now, node 2 becomes capable of reaching the sink node through node S and it can continue sending packets.

Downstream path recovery. In downstream data transmission, a packet is forwarded along the path contained in the packet, i.e. source routing. Since nodes over the source route may be unreachable, a path recovery mechanism is inevitable. When an intermediate node detects a link breakage, it queues the

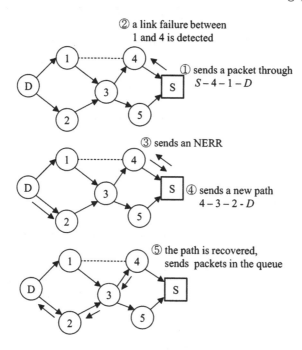

Fig. 4. An example of downstream path recovery

packet and unicasts an NERR message towards the sink node with a route request flag turned on. The sink node, upon receiving the NERR message, marks its routing table entry associated with the unreachable node as inactive, and then calculates a new path from the NERR originator to the original packet destination. This is done by simply executing the BFS algorithm which starts at the destination. This new path is transmitted to the NERR originator which resumes sending packets buffered in the queue. However, when the sink node cannot find a new path, it does not reply to the NERR message and an NERR timeout occurs at the NERR originator, instead. In this case, the NERR originator simply drops the packets buffered in the queue. Figure 4 shows an example of downstream path recovery.

4   Performance Evaluation

In this section, we present experimental results from both simulation and a real world test-bed. The performance was investigated by using ns-2 simulator [16] and the parameters used are summarized in Table 1. In our simulation, SMSR is compared with MDSR since they have the same goal, i.e. providing fault tolerance. In addition, they both belongs to source routing protocols and address centric routing protocols, unlike other data centric routing protocols such as [3]. However, in our real world test-bed, DYMO [13] (dynamic MANET on-demand routing) protocol was selected for comparisons, because its variants are widely used in real world sensor networks as a general purpose routing protocol.

Table 1. Simulation parameters

Parameter type	Value
Simulation area	50 m x 50 m
Propagation model	Two ray ground
Transmission/Carrier sensing range	10/20 meters
MAC protocol	IEEE 802.11
Number of nodes	50, 100, 150, 200, 250
Topologies	Random

4.1   Simulation Results

The number of shortest node-disjoint paths has a great impact on the efficiency of multipath routing protocols. Thus, we first investigated the average number of shortest node-disjoint paths with respect to network size. See Figure 5.

As mentioned before, the on-demand route discovery phase in MDSR cannot find the sufficient number of shortest node-disjoint paths. Furthermore, the network size does not help to find paths; even in dense networks, only 10% of nodes have two or more shortest node-disjoint paths. In contrast, the route construction mechanism in SMSR efficiently finds the shortest node-disjoint paths, as the network size increases. Note that this result does not mean that MDSR cannot

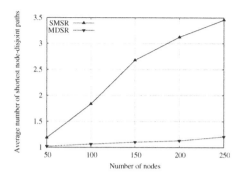

Fig. 5. Average number of shortest node-disjoint paths w. r. t. network size

find any multiple paths; instead, MDSR tends to find a longer or link-disjoint alternate path (not described in the figure).

Next, we measured the control message overhead and delivery ratio in two node failure scenarios; (a) an isolated failure scenario where each node fails individually with probability p, and (b) a scenario with a failure pattern where a certain node and its nearby nodes (with radius r) fail simultaneously with probability 0.01. See Figures 6 and 7. In the isolated failure scenario, most packet losses are caused by the creation of islands in sparse networks with 50 and 100 nodes. Thus, SMSR and MDSR show almost the same delivery ratio (especially, the result is exactly the same when $p=0.01$). However, the control message overhead in MDSR is about 12 times greater than that in SMSR. This is because the data flow from a sink node (say, node A) to a sensor node which forms an island requires a route discovery trial. In MDSR, when the sink node tries to send a packet to node A, it will initiate the route discovery process, which causes a lot of overhead. In SMSR, however, the sink node can easily find that node A does not have any upstream neighbors. This implies that there will be no overhead of flooding control message; there is only one-hop broadcasting of UREQ messages at node A.

In contrast, the delivery ratio in SMSR is a little better (0.1% higher on average) than that in MDSR in dense networks. The occurrence of temporal packet loss is possible in both SMSR and MDSR when no more alternate paths exist at an intermediate node. However, MDSR experiences additional packet losses due to flooded control messages. When there is no more alternate path at a source node, MDSR floods control messages to find other paths and they sometimes collide with other traffic. However, although SMSR sometimes cannot recover a downstream path at an intermediate node due to packet loss, it does not initiate a flooding of control message. Thus, packet losses caused by collisions are minimized.

In a patterned failure scenario, similar results to those of the isolated failure scenario are observed. The delivery ratio of SMSR is about 1% higher than that of MDSR, and the control message overhead of SMSR is 95% less than that of MDSR. Since the number of node failures increases as compared to

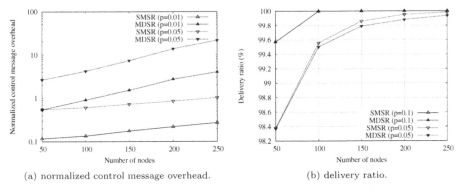

(a) normalized control message overhead.   (b) delivery ratio.

Fig. 6. Performance graph in the isolated failure scenario

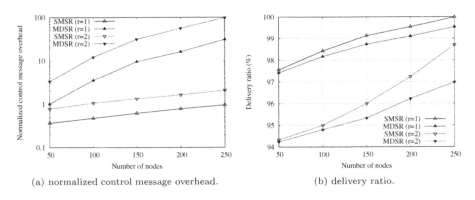

(a) normalized control message overhead.   (b) delivery ratio.

Fig. 7. Performance graph in the patterned failure scenario

the isolated failure scenario, the achieved delivery ratio and control message overhead become lower and higher than those of the isolated failure scenario, respectively. In MDSR, especially, as the number of node failures increases, the amount of control messages increases significantly. Accordingly, collisions occur more frequently and the delivery ratio does not increase significantly when the network size grows. In contrast, SMSR does not have the problems caused by the control message overhead. This enables SMSR to achieve a higher delivery ratio. In dense networks, the number of temporal packet losses caused by a path breakage at an intermediate node is minimized and almost all of packet losses occur due to the creation of islands.

4.2   Real World Test-Bed Results

To perform real world experiments, we implemented SMSR into NanoQplus [15], a multi-threaded operating system for sensor networks. The test-bed as shown in Figure 8 consisted of 25 sensor motes and they were all located in their transmission range with each other. However, using the MAC-layer filtering technique,

Fig. 8. Our real world test-bed

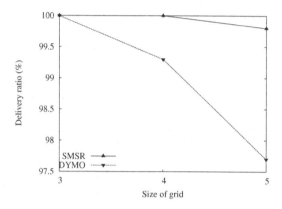

Fig. 9. Delivery ratio w. r. t. grid size

various logical grid topologies were formed (3 x 3, 4 x 4, and 5 x 5 grids). In those topologies, the top left corner node was set to be a sink node and the others were sensor nodes. Each sensor node periodically sent a report message to the sink node every 10 seconds. In response to the report message, the sink node replies with an application level acknowledge message. See Figure 9 and Table 2 for the results.

Due to the overhead of on-demand RREQ messages, the delivery ratio of the DYMO protocol significantly decreases as the size of grid increases. However, the SMSR protocol does not suffer from control message overhead; thus, it achieves higher delivery ratio than the DYMO protocol. The overhead of on-demand RREQ messages also affects a path construction. In the DYMO protocol, only 66% of nodes found shortest paths due to the collision of broadcasted RREQ

Table 2. The pecentage of nodes with the shortest path(s)

SMSR protocol	DYMO protocol
100%	66.3%

packets. However, SMSR succeeded in finding all shortest paths, because the control messages are flooded only once in the initialization phase. Furthermore, since SMSR constructs paths using nodes' upstream neighbor information and the hop-distance is only used to decide a priority of route information, the arrival time of IREQ and the temporal packet loss of IREQ usually do not affect the path length.

5   Conclusion

In WSNs, in order to cope with frequent changes of network topology due to the failure of nodes, multipath routing protocols have been proposed to provide fault tolerance. However, most of multipath routing protocols often depend on on-demand route discovery mechanism which invokes a large amount of flooding of control message. Furthermore, they cannot find a sufficient number of the shortest node-disjoint paths even though several ones exist. In this paper, we therefore proposed a scalable multipath source routing protocol to achieve the following goals: (a) reducing control message overhead, and (b) finding the shortest node-disjoint paths as many as possible with low computational complexity. In SMSR, intermediate nodes maintain only its upstream neighbor information and this information is gathered at the sink node. From the upstream neighbor information, the sink node calculates the shortest node-disjoint paths with a modified BFS algorithm and then packets are transmitted via the source routing technique along the selected paths.

Through ns-2 simulation, we observed that SMSR achieved 93.5% less control message overhead than a typical multipath routing protocol, MDSR on average. In addition, SMSR achieved a little better delivery ratio than MDSR. We also performed a real world experiment, and compared SMSR with DYMO, a well-known practical routing protocol. We observed that SMSR had higher delivery ratio and did not suffer from the control message overhead. Since this paper assumed static networks or networks with low mobility, an efficient algorithm is needed to deal with high mobility of nodes, which is our future work.

References

1. Akyildiz, I.F., Su, W., Sankarasubramaniam, Y., Cayirci, E.: A Survey on Sensor Networks. IEEE Communications Magazine 40(8), 102–114 (2002)
2. Al-Karaki, J.N., Kamal, A.E.: Routing Techniques in Wireless Sensor Networks: A Survey. IEEE Wireless Communications 11(6), 6–28 (2004)
3. Ganesan, D., Govindan, R., Shenker, S., Estrin, D.: Highly Resilient, Energy-Efficient Multipath Routing in Wireless Sensor Networks. ACM SIGMOBILE Mobile Comp. Commun. Rev. 5(4), 11–25 (2001)
4. Intanagonwiwat, C., Govindan, R., Estrin, D.: Directed Diffusion: A Scalable and Robust Communication Paradigm for Sensor Networks. In: Proc. of ACM Mobi-Com 2000 (August 2000)
5. Thulasiraman, P., Ramasubramanianand, S., Krunz, M.: Disjoint Multipath Routing to Two Distinct Drains in a Multi-Drain Sensor Network. In: Proc. of IEEE INFOCOM 2007 (May 2007)

6. Nasipuri, A., Castaneda, R., Das, S.R.: Performance of Multipath Routing for On-Demand Protocols in Mobile Ad Hoc Networks. ACM/Kluwer Mobile Networks and Applications (MONET) Journal 6(4), 339–349 (2001)
7. Wang, L., Zhang, L., Shu, Y., Dong, M.: Multipath Source Routing in Wireless Ad Hoc Networks. In: Proc. of IEEE CCECE 2000 (March 2000)
8. Marina, M.K., Das, S.R.: On-demand Multipath Distance Vector Routing in Ad Hoc Networks. In: Proc. of IEEE ICNP 2001 (November 2001)
9. Suurballe, J.W.: Disjoint Paths in a Network. Networks 4(2), 125–145 (1974)
10. Sidhu, D., Nair, R., Abdallah, S.: Finding Disjoint Paths in Networks. ACM SIG-COMM Computer communication Review 21(4), 43–51 (1991)
11. Ogier, R., Rutenburg, V., Shacham, N.: Distributed Algorithms for Computing Shortest Pairs of Disjoint Paths. IEEE Transactions on Information Theory, 443–455 (March 1993)
12. Johnson, D.B., Maltz, D.A., Hu, Y.-C.: The Dynamic Source Routing Protocol (DSR) for Mobile Ad Hoc Networks for IPv4. RFC4728 (February 2007)
13. Chakeres, I.D., Perkins, C.E.: Dynamic MANET On-demand (DYMO) Routing, draft-ietf-manet-dymo (work in progress), Internet Draft (November 2007)
14. Perkins, C.E., Belding-Royer, E.M., Das, S.R.: Ad hoc On-demand Distance Vector (AODV) routing. RFC 3561 (July 2003)
15. Embedded S/W research division web site, Electronics & Telecommunications Research Institute (ETRI), http://www.qplus.or.kr/
16. VINT Group, UCB/LBNL/VINT Network Simulator ns (version 2), http://www.isi.edu/nsnam/ns/

A Framework to Calibrate a MEMS Sensor Network

Kahina Boutoustous, Eugen Dedu, and Julien Bourgeois

Laboratoire d'Informatique de l'Université de Franche-Comté (LIFC)
1 cours Leprince-Ringuet, 25200 Montbéliard, France

Abstract. The Smart Surface[1] project aims at designing an integrated micro-manipulator based on an array of micromodules connected with a 2D array topology network. Each micromodule comprises a sensor, an actuator and a processing unit. One of the aims of the processing unit is to differentiate the shape of the part that is put on top of the Smart Surface. From a set of shapes this differentiation is done through a distributed algorithm that we call a criterion. The article presents Sensor Network Calibrator (SNC), a calibrator which allows to parametrize the Smart Surface and to determine the necessary number of sensors required by our Smart Surface. The tests will show that SNC is of great importance for choosing the number of sensors, and therefore to determine the size of the sensors grid.

Keywords: Sensor grid, shape differentiation, distributed computing, MEMS.

1 Introduction

During an assembly process, it is necessary to feed assembly line workstations with well-oriented and well-positioned parts. These parts are often jumbled and they need to be sorted and conveyed to the right workstation. To do so, the operations to be performed on parts are the following: identifying, sorting, orienting, positioning, feeding, and assembling. Among the most promising solutions to perform these tasks on microparts, is the combination of micro-electro mechanical systems (MEMS) in order to form an actuator arrays. However, if a single microactuator is not powerful enough to move a micropart, several microactuators working cooperatively might very well do it. A MEMS sensor/actuator array with embedded intelligence is referred as a Smart Surface.

The objective of the Smart Surface project is to design such an integrated MEMS system which will be able to identify, to sort, to orient and position microparts. This article deals only with the identification part of the process: A micropart is put on the Smart Surface which have to recognize the part shape among several models and give the proper orders to the control system to move

---

[1] This work is funded by the French National Agency for Research, by the Doubs departemental council and by the University of Franche-Comté.

D. Zhang et al. (Eds.): UIC 2009, LNCS 5585, pp. 136–149, 2009.
© Springer-Verlag Berlin Heidelberg 2009

it on the right place. In fact, recognition is not the proper term. Given a set of parts, the Smart Surface will have to *differentiate* all the parts within the set. As the processing power of the Smart Surface is embedded in very limited space, this differentiation process has to be optimized both in term of memory used and processing power needed. The differentiation is made by a distributed program loaded in the Smart Surface.

The aim of the Sensor Network Calibrator SNC which is presented in this article is to parametrize our Smart Surface, i.e. to find the size of the sensors grid necessary to differentiate our models. For that, a Smart Surface platform consisting of a Smart Surface prototype with a camera positioned above it is used. The rest of the paper is organized as follows. Section 2 details the Smart Surface project. Section 3 presents the SNC, while the tests are performed on section 4. Some related works to shape representation are presented in section 5 and they are followed by conclusions and presentation of future works.

2 The Smart Surface Project

There have been numerous projects of MEMS actuator arrays in the past and more precisely in the 1990's. These pioneer researches have developed different types of MEMS actuator arrays, based on actuators either pneumatic [1,2], servoed roller wheels [3,4], magnetic [5] or thermobimoph and electrostatic [6]. Some of these preliminary studies use a sensorless manipulation scheme based on Goldberg's algorithm [7] for parallel jaw grippers. The jaw grippers are obtained with MEMS actuator arrays by creating opposite field forces which then can orient and move the parts. Bohringer et al. [8] have proposed a concept called "programmable force field" which is an extension of Goldberg's algorithm. This manipulation scheme which is well-adapted for jaw grippers has shown some limitations when adapted to MEMS actuator arrays. For instance, the absence of a command law can lead to uncertain behaviours [9] or MEMS actuator arrays have to be programmed for each different kind of parts. More recent research has been conducted in order to include sensors and to add intelligence to MEMS actuator arrays but it either fails to develop it at a micro-scale [10] or to be fully integrated [11].

The objective of the Smart Surface project is to design a distributed and integrated micro-manipulator based on an array of micro-modules in order to realize an *automated positioning and conveying surface*. Each micro-module will be composed of a micro-actuator, a micro-sensor and a processing unit. The co-operation of these micro-modules thanks to an integrated network will allow to recognize the parts and to control micro-actuators in order to move and position accurately the parts on the Smart Surface. The parts are small, they cover a few numbers of micro-modules (e.g. 4 × 4).

Figure 1 shows the Smart Surface. The rectangular holes seen on the front-side are the air nozzles. Air-flow comes through a micro-valve in the back-side of the device and then passes through the nozzle. The advantage of this solution is that the micro-actuators, the most fragile part of the surface, are protected.

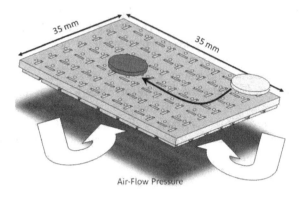

Fig. 1. An overview of our Smart Surface

The circle holes are used by the micro-sensors to detect the presence or not of the part on the surface.

The strength of our project is the multidisciplinary collaboration between six labs specialized in their field and more than twenty researchers. We are responsible for the information management inside the Smart Surface, i.e. distributed differentiation of the part and communication infrastructure.

3   The SNC Calibrator

One of the parameters of the Smart Surface is its number of sensors. Due to space restriction, this number has to be chosen as wisely as possible: if it is overestimated, the design of the SS will be impossible, if it is underestimated, the part differentiation will also be impossible. It is therefore a crucial parameter that has to be set.

3.1   Experimental Platform

The Smart Surface is still in design phase and it is noticeably easier to construct a Smart Surface Prototype (SSP) at a greater scale than the micro-scale SS. So, until its final fabrication, a Smart Surface platform has been built, which consists of Smart Surface Prototype (SSP), with a camera positioned above it (see fig. 2).

The Smart Surface Prototype (SSP) is a 30x30 cm square surface with a 15x15 actuators array. The air flow wich comes through actuators continuously moves the part on SSP. A camera positioned above the SSP allows free discretization of the part.

The Smart Surface platform allows us to perform real experiments.

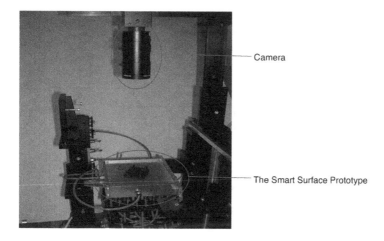

Fig. 2. Overview of the Smart Surface platform

3.2   SNC overview

This section presents the calibrator that has been implemented to define the number of the sensors to be embedded into the Smart Surface. The calibrator presented in fig. 3 receives as input:

- the video from the camera which is positioned above the SSP; this camera shoots the SSP, as well as the parts on top of it;
- the group of models which is recognized by the SSP. A model is a part which is passed as a parameter;
- the sizes of the sensors grid to test.

The calibrator provides as output the result of the differentiation that is an answer to the following question: For each given size of sensors grid, what is the differentiation rate?

For each model, a set of characteristics is defined: area, perimeter, etc. We will refer to them as criteria and their combination will be called the combination of criteria [12]. When a part is on the Smart Surface, the aim is to differentiate it among the various models given to the Smart Surface.

The differentiation consists of calculating the values of the criteria of the part on the Smart Surface, then these values will be compared with the values of the criteria of the models. The result of this comparison is the differentiation rate [12].

In our previous paper [12] we presented as future work the free rotation. In the current paper we present this free rotation. Another aspect of this paper is that it does not do exhaustive research, but only a few various models.

Fig. 4 presents the structure of our calibrator. The calibrator has two phases:

1. Offline: For each group of models of the SSP and each size of sensors grid, find the best combination of criteria (and their masks, see later) for the differentiation of the models between each other [12].

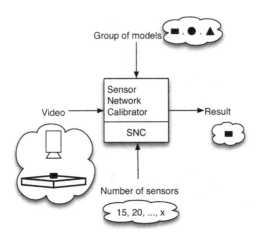

Fig. 3. Overview of the calibrator

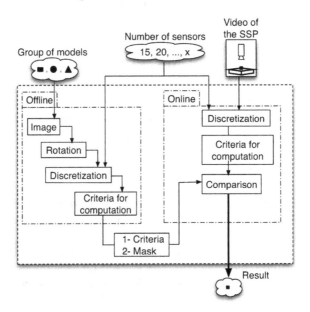

Fig. 4. Global structure of our calibrator

2. Online: An attempt to differentiate the part on the SSP is made using a differentiation algorithm, the various size sensors grid given as input and the results of the first offline phase.

3.3   Offline Phase

In this phase, for each group of models, to be differentiated among them, all combinations of criteria are determined. This phase is subdivided into five sub-phases:

1. all rotations[2] of $1°$ are generated, $MRot_i$, from the image of the model M_i, given as input, with respect to the centre of the image, and all translations of $width(MRot)/10$ pixels are generated from the image $MRot_i$;
2. a grid corresponding to the positions of the sensors (middle point of the cell) is drawn on the images;
3. the images are discretized in a matrix by affecting 1 if the sensor is covered by the part and 0 otherwise; in order to have negligible errors for the rotation, the resolution of the image should be much greater than the resolution of the SSP;
4. unique masks corresponding to the initial matrix without the rows and columns that contain only zeros are saved;
5. the values of each criterion are calculated for all masks of the model.

The following algorithm details these 5 sub-phases:

1: **for** each size of sensors grid (n, n), with
   $n \subset 15, 20, 25, 30, ..., 50$ **do**
2:     **for** each $M_i \subset M_1, M_2, M_3, ..., M_{nbr\_models}$ **do**
3:         Acquire the image Im of the model on the SSP
4:         **for** $d = 1°$ to $360°$ **do**
5:             Generate $ImRot$ by rotating the image Im by d degrees
6:             **for** each $y \subset 0, 10, 20, 30, ..., Size(ImRot)$ **do**
7:                 **for** each $x \subset 0, 10, 20, 30, ..., Size(ImRot)$ **do**
8:                     Generate $ImTrans$ by translating the image $ImRot$ by x steps on Ox and y steps on Oy
9:                     Discretize the image $ImTrans$
10:                    Generate and save the mask
11:                    Calculate and save the value for each criterion
12:                **end for**
13:            **end for**
14:        **end for**
15:    **end for**
16: **end for**

Among all the calculated criteria, the best criterion is chosen according to the differentiation rate, the memory cost and the execution time [12]. Finally, this criterion and its masks are given as input to the online phase.

3.4   Online Phase

This phase consists of differentiating the part on the SSP, which means determining to which model recognized by the SSP it is associated. This phase is divided into four sub-phases:

1. the camera positioned above the SSP takes a sequence of images of the SSP and the part on it;

---

[2] The OpenCV library was used for rotations and translations.

2. each image obtained is discretized (the image has only black and white pixels) to each grid size given as input to SNC, and the mask of the binary representation of this part is extracted;

3. the values of all combinations of the criteria of the masks are calculated;

4. the values of the criteria are compared with the values of the criteria of the models, to differentiate the part on the SSP.

The algorithm below describes this phase:

1: Film the part on the SSP
2: Generate the result tree of criteria values of the models recognized by the SSP
3: **for** each image of the part on the SSP **do**
4:     Discretize the image
5:     Generate the mask
6:     Compute the criteria values
7:     Compare with the values of criteria of each model
8:     Provide the results of the differentiation
9: **end for**

4   Tests

The aim of our work is to parametrize the Smart Surface, i.e. finding the right size of the sensors grid to be used for differentiating [12] groups of given models (fig. 5 shows one of these models on the SSP). For this, several tests have been performed on the SSP. The differentiation is made by computing the different criteria and by applying a differentiation algorithm [12].

A set of four basic models have been chosen (see fig. 6(a)). Starting from these models all group of three models have been generated (see fig. 6(b)–(e)). Several sizes of grid sensors are used see below.

Fig. 5. Picture of the SSP with a square on it

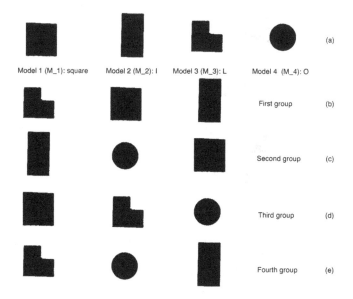

Fig. 6. (a) Definition of our models, (b)–(e) all groups of three models

4.1   Offline Phase

The offline algorithm is applied to each group of models as already described, using images of size 550x550, a rotation step of 1°, a translation step of 10 pixels and different grid sizes of the sensors $((15, 15)(20, 20), ..., (50, 50))$.

The offline phase consists of computing the values for differentiation criteria [12] calculated for the models M_1, M_2, M_3. Fig. 7(a) represents an example of results of the offline phase, for the models L, I, O, the last group in fig. 6(e) with D, C, A differentiation criteria:

- D: The sum of 1 located on both diagonals.
- C: The sum of the number of V shape angles.
- A: The number of 1 having at least three neighbors to 0 and forming a right angle.

Figure 7(b) shows a generated tree according to the results of figure 7(a). This tree is just a representation of results for the obtained criteria.

4.2   Online Phase

The aim of this phase is to determine for each group of models, the size of a grid of sensors that allows differentiating our models. For this, the differentiation rate for each part on the SS with each model must be calculated.

The algorithm of the online phase is applied to the group of models $\{L, I, O\}$ (see fig. 6(e)). The results are shown in fig. 8, representing the differentiation rate for the L, I and O belonging to group $\{L, I, O\}$.

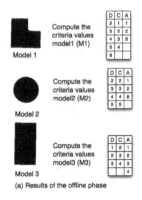

(a) Results of the offline phase

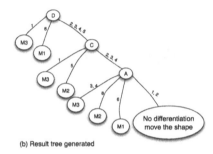

(b) Result tree generated

Fig. 7. An example of the result tree of criteria values according to a combination of criteria and a set of models

The size of the sensors grid of the SSP must be determined such that it allows a better differentiation rate for all groups of models. For that, the average[3] differentiation rate of our models has been computed. Fig. 8 shows also the average differentiation rate of group $\{L, I, O\}$. It can be easily observed that with 35 sensors a higher differentiation rate average is obtained. With the same number of sensors (35) the following results are obtained:

- For the L, the differentiation rate is 60%. It's not the highest value but it's a satisfactory result.
- For the I, the highest differentiation rate is 100%.
- For the O, the highest differentiation rate is 61.11%.

Fig. 9, fig. 10 and fig. 11 contain the differentiation rate of each model belonging to each group of models: $\{square, I, L\}$, $\{square, L, O\}$ and $\{square, I, O\}$ respectively (see fig. 6(b), fig. 6(c), fig. 6(d)) as well as the average differentiation rate for each of them.

---

[3] We consider that the models have the same probability (33%) to be put on the SSP, otherwise weights should be used to compute the average.

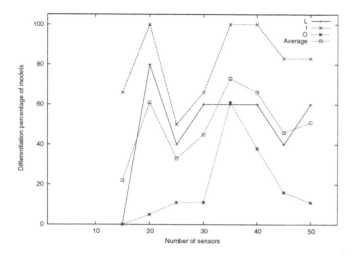

Fig. 8. Differentiation percentage of models L, I, O, and their average

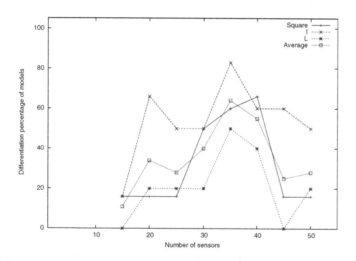

Fig. 9. Differentiation percentage of models $square, I, L$, and their average

Taking into account the values from fig. 9, fig. 10 and fig. 11 we can state that a sensors grid of $(35, 35)$ is an appropriate parameter for the SSP because a high differentiation rate average is obtained.

Logically, we thought that the differentiation rate would increase proportionally to the number of sensors but the results have shown that, starting from a threshold (35 sensors) the differentiation rate decreases. This is caused by the increasing number of information to manage which implies an increase of the binary representations.

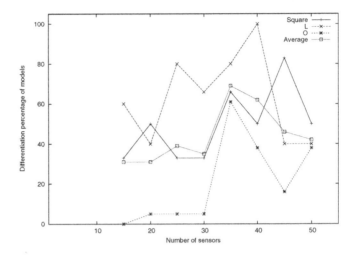

Fig. 10. Differentiation percentage of models *square*, *L*, *O*, and their average

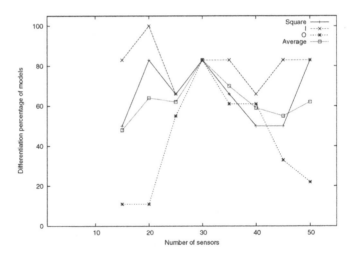

Fig. 11. Differentiation percentage of models *square*, *I*, *O*, and their average

5   Related Work

Several methods of shape representation exist in the literature. They are divided into two categories: *contour-based* methods and *region-based* methods. *Contour-based* methods are widely used. But generally, for complex images, the contour is not enough to describe the image content, therefore *region-based* methods are better.

5.1   Contour-Based Approaches

In the contour-based approach, the pixels of the contour are considered.

Fourier descriptors. This approach is divided into two steps:

1. The image is defined by a one-dimensional function called *shape signature*, which is nothing else than a compact representation of the image [13]. Many methods to calculate the signature have been developed. The most common shape signatures are: centroid distance [14], [15], chordLength signature [16] and area function.
2. Once the shape signature has been calculated, a Fourier transform is applied [17], [18]. It results in coefficients called Fourier descriptors of the shape. These descriptors represent the shape of the object in the frequency domain. The Fourier transform is invariant against translation, scale, rotation and their starting point.

Freeman code. Freeman coding consists in browsing the borders of the shape with elementary moves from a starting point and coding the movement [19], [20].

Freeman code is sensitive to rotation because Freeman code depends on the starting point. To reduce this dependence, the resulting number has to be the minimal. The Freeman code is invariant to translation. It is also invariant to a rotation of 90° for the 4-connectivity and 45° for the 8-connectivity [21], [22].

Fourier descriptors and Freeman code are widely used for big pictures where the outline of the image differs noticeably from the inside of the images (parts). In our study these methods are not very interesting given that we are working on tiny images where the contour is equal or nearly equal to the surface.

5.2   Region-Based Approaches

In region-based methods, all the pixels within a shape are taken into account to obtain the shape representation.

Grid based. In this method [23], a fixed-length grid of cells on the image is drawn. Going along our grid from top to bottom and from left to right, each cell that is wholly or partly covered by the form is affected with the value 1, and other cells with 0 [24]. This produces a binary number, which is the representation of our shape. The difference between two parts is given by an XOR between their binary representations. Such a binary representation is very sensitive to rotation, translation and dilatation, that is it requires a prestandardization.

Invariant moments. In this method [25], [26], [27] the invariant moments are used to represent the image. A set of seven descriptors exist, called Husont invariants, computed by normalizing central moments of order three. They are invariant to object scale, translation and orientation. They are used as input vectors for the classification method. There are several classification methods, among them neural networks are the most widely used because of their fault tolerance, their ability of classification and their generalizability. The invariant moments are widely used in three dimension models or large images that need to be compacted. It is not very useful to apply this method in our case because the images are very small.

6   Conclusions and Future Works

In this article we present the SNC calibrator which allows to parametrize our Smart Surface by determining the required number of sensors. Our tests performed on all groups of 3 out of 4 models show that a sensors grid of $(35, 35)$ is an appropriate parameter for the Smart Surface.

One of the ideas of our future work is to test more models with the SNC calibrator, and with a real Smart Surface when this will be operational. Also, to develop distributed algorithms for various criteria in order to implement them in the Smart Surface.

References

1. Pister, K., Fearing, R., Howe, R.: A planar air levitated electrostatic actuator system. In: IEEE Workshop on Micro Electro Mechanical Systems, pp. 61–71 (1990)
2. Fujita, H.: Group work of microactuators. In: International Advanced Robot Program Workshop on Micromachine Technologies and Systems, Tokyo, Japan, pp. 24–31 (October 1993)
3. Luntz, J.E., Messner, W.: A distributed control system for flexible materials handling. IEEE Control Systems 17(1) (February 1997)
4. Luntz, J.E., Messner, W., Choset, H.: Parcel manipulation and dynamics with a distributed actuator array: The virtual vehicle. In: IEEE Int. Conf. on Robotics and Automation (ICRA), pp. 1541–1546 (1997)
5. Liu, C., Tsao, T., Will, P., Tai, Y., Liu, W.: A micromachined permalloy magnetic actuator array for micro robotics assembly systems. In: The 8th International Conference on Solid-State Sensors and Actuators (1995)
6. Suh, J., Glander, S., Darling, R., Storment, C., Kovacs, G.: Combined organic thermal and electrostatic omnidirectional ciliary microactuator array for object positioning and inspection. In: Solid State Sensor and Actuator Workshop (1996)
7. Goldberg, K.Y.: Orienting polygonal parts without sensors. Algorithmica 10(2-4), 210–225 (1993)
8. Böhringer, K.F., Bhatt, V., Donald, B.R., Goldberg, K.Y.: Algorithms for sensorless manipulation using a vibrating surface. Algorithmica 26(3-4), 389–429 (2000)
9. Murilo, G.C., Peter, M.W.: A general theory for positioning and orienting 2d polygonal or curved parts using intelligent motion surfaces. In: ICRA, pp. 856–862 (1998)
10. Biegelsen, D., Berlin, A., Cheung, P., Fromherts, M., Goldberg, D., Jackson, W., Preas, B., Reich, J., Swartz, L.: Airjet paper mover. In: SPIE Int. Symposium on Micromachining and Microfabrication (2000)
11. Fukuta, Y., Chapuis, Y.A., Mita, Y., Fujita, H.: Design, fabrication and control of MEMS-based actuator arrays for air-flow distributed micromanipulation. IEEE Journal of Micro-Electro-Mechanical Systems 15(4), 912–926 (2006)
12. Boutoustous, K., Dedu, E., Bourgeois, J.: An exhaustive comparison framework for distributed shape differentiation in a MEMS sensor actuator array. In: International Symposium on Parallel and Distributed Computing (ISPDC), Krakow, Poland, July 2008, pp. 429–433. IEEE Computer Society Press, Los Alamitos (2008)
13. Loncaric, S.: A survey of shape analysis techniques. Pattern Recognition 31(8), 983–1001 (1998)
14. Zhang, D., Lu, G.: Content-based shape retrieval using different shape descriptors: A comparative study. In: ICME. IEEE Computer Society, Los Alamitos (2001)

15. Zhang, D., Lu, G.: Shape-based image retrieval using generic Fourier descriptor. SPIC 17(10), 825–848 (2002)
16. Zhang, D., Lu, G.: Study and evaluation of different Fourier methods for image retrieval. Image Vision Comput. 23(1), 33–49 (2005)
17. Diaz de León, R., Sucar, L.: Human silhouette recognition with Fourier descriptors. In: ICPR 2000, vol. III, pp. 709–712 (2000)
18. Derrode, S., Daoudi, M., Ghorbel, F.: Invariant content-based image retrieval using a complete set of Fourier-Mellin descriptors. In: ICMCS, vol. 2, pp. 877–881 (1999)
19. Lingrand, D.: Introduction au Traitement d'Images, 2nd edn. Vuibert, Paris (2008)
20. Bres, S., Jolion, J.M., Lebourgeois, F.: Traitement et analyse des images numériques. Hermès (2003)
21. Forssén, P.E., Moe, A.: Contour descriptors for view-based object recognition. Technical Report LiTH-ISY-R-2706, Dept. EE, Linköping University, SE-581 83 Linköping, Sweden (September 2005)
22. Sun, J., Wu, X.: Shape retrieval based on the relativity of chain codes. In: Sebe, N., Liu, Y., Zhuang, Y.-t., Huang, T.S. (eds.) MCAM 2007. LNCS, vol. 4577, pp. 76–84. Springer, Heidelberg (2007)
23. Sajjanhar, A., Lu, G.: A grid-based shape indexing and retrieval method. Australian Computer Journal 29(4), 131–140 (1997)
24. Shahabi, C., Safar, M.: An experimental study of alternative shape-based image retrieval techniques. Multimedia Tools Appl. 32(1), 29–48 (2007)
25. Prokop, R., Reeves, A.: A survey of moment-based techniques for unoccluded object representation and recognition. GMIP 54(5), 438–460 (1992)
26. Chen, C.: Improved moment invariants for shape discrimination. Pattern Recognition 26(5), 683–686 (1993)
27. Mercimek, M., Gulez, K., Velimumcu, T.: Real object recognition using moment invariants. Sadhana 30(6), 765–775 (2005)

Application Domain Driven Data Visualisation Framework for Wireless Sensor Networks

Mohammad Hammoudeh, Robert Newman, Christopher Dennett,
and Sarah Mount

School of Computing and IT
University of Wolverhampton
Wolverhampton, UK
{m.h.h,r.newman,c.dennett,s.mount}@wlv.ac.uk

Abstract. Wireless sensor networks (WSNs) have an intrinsic interdependency with the environments in which they operate. The part of the world with which an application is concerned is defined as that application's domain. This paper advocates that an application domain of a WSN application can serve as a supplement to analysis, interpretation, and visualisation methods and tools. We believe it is critical to elevate the capabilities of the visualisation service, the mapping service, proposed in [1] to make use of the special characteristics of an application domain. In this paper, we propose an adaptive Multi-Dimensional Application Domain-driven (M-DAD) visualisation framework that is suitable for visualising an arbitrary number of sense modalities and other parameters of the application domain to improve the visualisation performance. M-DAD starts with an initial user defined model that is maintained and updated throughout the network lifetime. The experimental results demonstrate that M-DAD visualisation framework performs as well or better than visualisation services without its extended capabilities.

1 Introduction

WSNs are being deployed for an increasingly diverse set of applications each with different characteristics and environmental constraints. As a consequence, scientists from different research fields have begun to realise the importance of identifying and understanding the characteristics and special deployment needs of different application domains. In many WSN deployments, the network owners have some knowledge about the monitored environment characteristics in which the target system operates. For example, in forest fire applications, information about the forest topography can be obtained from GIS systems or satellites maps.

A domain model carries knowledge of an application domain. It is a conceptual model of a system which describes the various real world entities involved in that system. The domain model provides a structural view of the system which we suggest using to complement the information gained from analysing data gathered by a WSN. The logical integration of a domain model and sensory data from multiple heterogeneous sensory sources can be effectively used

D. Zhang et al. (Eds.): UIC 2009, LNCS 5585, pp. 150–162, 2009.

to explain past observations as well as to predict future observations. It exploits the local semantics from the environment of each sensor. It also takes advantage of human guidance and information from other available sources, e.g. satellites. Furthermore, it maintains the overall coherence of reasoning about the gathered data and helps to estimate the degree of confidence using probabilistic domain models. The use of knowledge made available by the domain model can also be a key to meeting the energy and channel capacity constraints of a WSN system. The energy efficiency of the system can be improved by utilising a domain model in the process of converting data into increasingly distilled and high-level representations. Finally, domain models help early detection and reduction of the amount of ineffective data forwarding across the network, rather than sustaining the energy expense of transmitting ineffective messages further along the path to the destination.

2   Related Work

WSN applications that incorporate the special characteristics of the environment in which they operate are starting to appear on the horizon. The authors of the BBQ [2] focus on using probabilistic models of the real-world to provide approximate answers efficiently. In contrast to our work, efforts such as BBQ [2] have adopted an approach that assumes that intelligence is placed at the edge of the network, such as a sink, which is assumed to be less resource constrained than the sensor nodes. An interrogation-based approach can not guarantee that all anomalies will always be detected. Finally, this approach was found to be effective with stable network topologies. In highly dynamic network topologies the cost of checking whether the estimation is accurate becomes excessively high. Such a model will require collecting values of all attributes at one location at each time step, and the cost of doing so will most likely reduce any savings in source-sink communication that might result.

Motivated by BBQ, Ken [3] exploits the fact that physical environments frequently exhibit predictable stable and strong attribute correlations to improve compression of the data communicated to the sink node. This approach is subject to failure as basic suppression. It does not have any mechanism to distinguish between node failure and the case that the data is always within the error bound. They propose periodic updates to ensure models can not be incorrect indefinitely. This approach is not suitable for raw value reconstruction; for any time-step where the model has suffered from failures and is incorrect, the corresponding raw value samples will be wrong. Finally, as the approach presented in [2], Ken can only handle static network topologies and does not make use of redundancy.

The authors of [1] propose a distributed data visualisation service where groups of network nodes cooperate to produce local maps which are cached and merged at a sink node, producing a map of the global network. The sink node receives periodic map updates from each cluster head used to refine an up-to-date global map. Visual formats, such as maps, can be easily understood by people

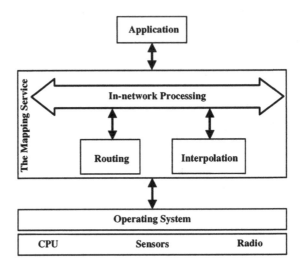

Fig. 1. Architecture of the distributed visualisation service taken from [1]

possibly from different communities, thus allow them to derive conclusions based on substantial understanding of the available data. This understanding gained from maps fulfils the ultimate goal of sensor network deployments which is not only to gather the data from the spatially distributed sensor nodes, but also convey and translate the data for scientists to analyse and study. The authors define map generation is essentially a problem of interpolation from sparse and irregular points. Given a set of known data points representing the nodes' perception of a given measurable parameter of the phenomenon, what is the most likely complete and continuous map of that parameter? In [1] the WSN is expected not only to produce map type visualisations but also to make use of the data supporting the maps for more effective routing, further intelligent data aggregation and information extraction, power scheduling and other network processes. Just as clustering, routing and aggregation allow for more sophisticated and efficient use of the network resources, a visualisation service would support other network services and make many more applications possible with little extra effort. There distributed visualisation service is made of four modules (see Figure 1): Application (contains the user defined applications, e.g. isopleth maps), Interpolation (a building block to generate maps), In-network Processing (process raw data received from various cluster heads) and Routing (responsible for data communication). This approach does not incorporate the characteristics of the application domain.

3   M-DAD Visualisation Framework Details

The proposed visualisation framework, M-DAD, utilises a blend of both inductive and deductive models to establish a successful mapping between sense data

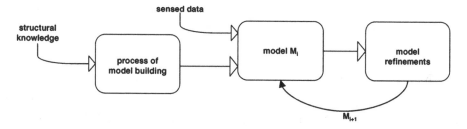

Fig. 2. Merging of inductive and deductive methods

and universal physical principles. Deductive methods rely on a precise application environment and the explicit knowledge, called structural knowledge, of the underlying domain using first principles to create a model of the problem typically yielding governing equations [4]. On the other hand, inductive methods utilises experimental data as the only source of available knowledge [4]. Some applications can only be treated using experimental data knowledge due to the lack of other application domain knowledge. Nevertheless, the use of inductive information helps in the generation of data consistency checks based on the structural knowledge abstractions given in the domain model. Finally, applications have been observed to perform significantly better if they use a combination of the two methods [5]. Figure 2 shows how the inductive and deductive methods can be merged to capture the advantages of both methods. After the structural knowledge is fed to the system model (deductive process), the sense data is used to refine and complement the basic structural model of the application domain. This refinement procedure can be done continuously throughout the network life to keep consistent mapping between the physical model and the sense data.

M-DAD makes use of knowledge given by the domain model in the map generation process. Knowledge from domain models provides guidance for map generation from high dimensional data set and has the potential to significantly speed up the map generation process and deliver more accurate maps. To the best of our knowledge, only few previous studies have considered the domain model. For instance, Hofierka et al. [6] incorporate the topographic characteristics to give better daily and annual mean precipitation predictions. The general lack of an appropriate data visualisation framework for exploiting these rich sense data resources motivates this work.

Moreover, M-DAD visualisation framework performs mapping from related multiple types of the sense data to overcome the limitations of generating a map from a single sense modality. Maps generated from a combination of different types of data are likely to lead to a more coherent map by consolidating information on various aspects of the monitored phenomena. Additionally, the effects of data noise on generated maps will be dramatically reduced, assuming that sensing errors across different data sets are largely independent and the probability an error is supported by more than one type of data is small. A natural approach is to make use of the relation between the multiple types of sense data to generate a map is to combine the maps generated from different types of data. We may combine the maps in different ways such as accepting a value at an observation point only when it is commensurate with all maps as defined in the given model.

3.1   Multivariate Spatial Interpolation in M-DAD

Most spatial data interpolation methods are based on the distance between the interpolation location P and the given set of data points. M-DAD defines a new metric for distance, suitable for higher dimensions, in which the concept of closeness is described in terms of relationships between sets rather than in terms of the Euclidean distance between points. Using this distance metric, a new generalised interpolation function f that is suitable for an arbitrary number of variables is defined. In multivariate interpolation every set S_i corresponds to an input variable i.e. a sense modality, called i, and referred to as a dimension. In M-DAD, the distance functions do not need to satisfy the formal mathematical requirements for the Euclidean distance definition. The power of such a generalisation can be seen when we include the time variable as one dimension. The spatial data interpolation problem can be stated as follows:

Given a set of randomly distributed data points

$$x_i \in \Omega, \; i \in [1, n], \; \Omega \subset \mathbb{R}^n \tag{1}$$

with function values $y_i \in \mathbb{R}$, and $i \in [1, N]$ we require a continuous function $f : \Omega \longrightarrow \mathbb{R}$ to interpolate unknown intermediate points such that

$$f(x_i) = y_i \text{ where } i \in [1, N]. \tag{2}$$

We refer to x_i as the observation points. The integer n is the number of dimensions and Ω is a suitable domain containing the observation points. When rewriting this definition in terms of relationships between sets we get the following:

Given N ordered pairs of *separated* sets $S_i \subset \Omega$ with continuous functions

$$f_i : S_i \longrightarrow \mathbb{R}, \; i \in [1, N] \tag{3}$$

we require a multivariate continuous function $f : \Omega \longrightarrow \mathbb{R}$, defined in the domain $\Omega = S_1 \cup S_2 \cup ... \cup S_{n-1} \cup S_n$ of the n-dimensional Euclidean space where

$$f(x_i) = f_i(x_i) \, \forall x_i \in S_i \text{ where } i \in [1, N] \tag{4}$$

The proof that f exists is omitted for brevity.

Using the point to set distance generalisation, the function f can be determined as a natural generalisation of methods developed for approximating univariate functions. Well-known univariate interpolation formulas are extended to the multivariate case by using *Geometric Algebra* (GA) in a special way while using a point to set distance metric. Burley et al. [7] discuss the usefulness of GA for adapting univariate numerical methods to multivariate data using no additional mathematical derivation. Their work was motivated by the fact that it is possible to define GAs over an arbitrary number of geometric dimensions and that it is therefore theoretically possible to work with any number of dimensions. This is done simply by replacing the algebra of the real numbers by that of the GA. We apply the ideas in [7] to find a multivariate analogues of univariate interpolation functions.

3.2 Scale-Based Local Distance Metric

In this section we modify the distance metric defined in Section 3.1 to include the knowledge given by the domain model. The domain model helps to significantly reduce the size of the support nodes set. The difference in the size of the support nodes set can be several orders of magnitude with increasing problem dimension. The increase in the support size can lead to an increase in the computation and processing times of the interpolation algorithm and lead to the same drawbacks of global interpolation methods. Therefore, the proposed metric attempts to balance the size of the support sets with the interpolation algorithm complexity as well as interpolation accuracy.

We define the term *scale* for determining the weight of every given dimension with respect to P based on a combined Euclidean distance criteria and the information already known about the application domain a prior network deployment. While the term *weight* is reserved for the relevance of a data site by calculating the Euclidean distance from that location to P. A special case is when f_i is identical for all S_i which means that all sets have the same scale.

For the purposes of M-DAD we define a new scale-based weighting metric, m_P, which uses the information given by domain model to alter the distance weighting function to improve the interpolation results when applied to an arbitrary number of dimensions. In M-DAD, the support set, C_i, for P is calculated using m_P. Symbolically, C_i is calculated as

$$C_i = L\left(d\left(P, E_j\right), \delta\left(S_i\right)\right) \forall E_j \in S_i \tag{5}$$

where S_i is a set of observation points, $i \in [1, N]$, L is a local model that selects the support set for calculating P, d is an Euclidean distance function, E_j is an observation point in the dimension S_i, and $\delta(S_i)$ a set of parameters for dimension S_i. Each dimension can have different set of parameters. These parameters are usually a set of relationships between different dimensions or other application domain characteristics such as obstacles. When predicting the value of a point in dimension S_i we refer to that dimension as S_P.

Uni-dimensional distance weighting functions can be extended to multi-dimensional distance weighting systems as follows

$$\omega = K\left(P, S_i\right), i \in [0, n] \tag{6}$$

where $K\left(P, S_i\right)$ is the distance from the interpolation position P to data set S_i and n is the number of dimensions in the system. Equation 6 can now be extended to include the domain model parameters of arbitrary dimensional system. Then the dimension-based scaling metric can be defined as

$$m_P = \sum_i L\left(K(P, S_i), \delta\left(S_i\right)\right) \ \ i \in [0, n] \tag{7}$$

where $S_i \neq C_P$ and C_P is the dimension containing P.

4   Distributed Self-adaptation in Visualisation Services

4.1   Benefits of Self-adaptation

In this section we extend the capabilities of M-DAD to overcome challenges imposed by the described external system changes, e.g. topographical changes, through applying self-adaptation intelligence to continuously adapt to erratic changes in the application domain conditions. At run time, M-DAD integrates the sensory data with contextual information to update the initial application domain model provided by network owners to maintain a coherent logical picture of the world over time. Self-adaptation is particularly useful in long-term WSNs deployments where the environmental conditions changes significantly over time which necessitate updating the domain model to reflect the changes in the contextual knowledge provided by the physical constraints imposed by the local environmental conditions where sensors are located. This allows visualisation service to evolve at run-time with less intervention of the user and leads to near-optimal and flexible design that is simple and inexpensive to deploy and maintain. This adaptation procedure will recover, over time, the effects of user domain modelling inaccuracies.

We realise that self-adaptation is a challenging problem and considerable work is being done by the research community in that area. However, in this work we aim to deal with a small set of adaptivity issues that have a significant effect on the visualisation service.

4.2   Adaptability Implementation in M-DAD

To implement adaptability in M-DAD we exploit the interpolation capability of the network to perform local training of the map generation service. Each node uses the readings of its surrounding nodes to predict its own reading value (y') using m_P (eq. 7). Then, y' is compared to the node measured value, y. It is desirable that the estimate of y' minimises the standard deviation (σ). Nodes modify the size of the support set to include the minimum number of nodes needed to predict y with a certain level of accuracy. Furthermore, in multi-dimensional applications, nodes will change the weight of each dimension to improve the prediction accuracy of y'. In fact, nodes will alter the relationships between different dimensions initially given in the domain model in order to recover the effect of inaccuracies in the given domain model or to adapt to emerging environmental changes. In that, these model updates influence the estimation results because y' is calculated using m_p. Finally, a prediction accuracy criterion, Δ, is defined as the average σ_j where $\sigma_j = \sum_i \sqrt{(y_i - y_i')^2}$ $j \in [1, n]$ and $i \in [1, N]$ where n is the number of dimensions and N is the number of readings in dimension j. Then Δ is written as $\Delta = \frac{\sum \sigma_j}{n}$ $j \in [1, n]$. Δ must always be minimised to achieve the best visualisation results.

However, when individual nodes alter their programmed domain model independently from the network, the mapping service may become unstable because of the inconsistency in the domain model defined on various nodes. Such inconsistencies may lead to inconsistent system states and conflicting differences in calculating mapping values. To ensure mapping stability we propose a *Virtual Congress Algorithm* to manage global model updates locally.

The Virtual Congress Algorithm (VCA) provides a high-level collaboration environment in which the system can achieve globally efficient behaviour under dynamic environmental conditions. The network is viewed as a virtual congress where nodes are *senators* who vote for *legislating* changes to the domain model in response to locally detected environmental conditions. This algorithm is an attractive solution as senators collaboratively decide upon their local knowledge on the behaviour and correctness of the system. Logically related nodes, *chambers*, are granted some power to impute the local changes, *federal laws*, that is not detected by all nodes in the network. A senator may introduce a proposal in the chamber as a *bill*. To prevent overloading the chamber with proposals, each senator must monitor the changes over time using equation Δ before putting them into a bill. Senators send their voting results to the proposing senator. The proposing senator, upon receiving the required number of votes v disseminate the bill to the chamber and all nodes implement the new changes that have been agreed on. The value of v was empirically estimated to be over 50% of chamber population because it helps to avoid false positives. Once a bill is approved by one chamber, it is sent to other chamber heads who may accept or reject it. In order for the bill to become a *state law*, all chamber heads must agree to identical version of the bill. When the bill is submitted to the *president*, the sink node, he may choose to sign the bill, thereby making it *a state law*.

5   Experimental Evaluation

Experiment 1: Incorporation of the Domain Model in the Visualisation Service

Aim. The aim of this experiment is to study the effect of integrating the knowledge given by the domain model into the visualisation service.

Procedure. The effective thermal diffusivity in a cargo ship is studied. Some aspects of a cargo ship fire were modelled, particularly, heat diffusion in the metal body of the ship. The chosen part of the ship deck is modelled by a brass sheet which contains a hole segment excavation to model an opened door. A simple domain model was defined to carry information about doors that when opened they impact the heat diffusion in the ship body. The hole segment that represents an opened door was excavated in the brass sheet with $10mm$ width and 2*cm* length. A FLIR ThermaCAM P65 Infrared (IR) camera [8] was used to take sharp thermal images and produce an accurate temperature analysis and results. The IR camera delivers 320×240 IR resolution (640×480 pixels, full colour) at $0.08C$ thermal sensitivity. Finally, a flame was placed on the middle of one edge of the brass sheet as a heat source. Brass (an alloy of copper and zinc) was chosen for this experiment because it is a good thermal conductor.

The first experiment was ran using the brass sheet before the hole segment excavation. After applying heat, thermal measurements from the Toradex Oak sensors were recorded in addition to a thermal image taken by the IR camera. The visualisation services were ran over a subset of the data collected from this experiment to observe how the heat will diffuse in the brass sheet in the absence of any obstacles. The same experiment was repeated on the sheet with the segment hole excavation and sensor thermal measurements as well as a IR camera image were taken after applying heat on the brass sheet. The visualisation service were ran using the same size of the thermal data-set used in the previous experiment. Three experimental runs were performed: (1) Run the visualisation services without any domain model knowledge. Particularly, the presence of the obstacle and its characteristics. (2) Run the visualisation service which integrates *some* of the domain model knowledge. Particularly, the presence of the obstacle, its position, and length. (3) Run the visualisation service which integrates all the knowledge given by the domain model. Particularly, the presence of the obstacle, its position, length, and strength.

Results and discussion. Figure 3 shows the heat diffusion map generated by the IR camera. Given that the heat is applied at the middle of the top edge of the brass sheet and the location of the obstacle, by comparing the left side and right side areas around the heat source, this figure shows that the existence of the obstacle has an effect on heat diffusion through the brass sheet. It its observed that the obstacle strongly reduced the temperature rise in the area on its right side. This map has been randomly down-sampled to 1000 points, that is 1.5% of the total 455×147 to be used by the visualisation service to generate the total heat map.

Figure 4 shows the map generated by the distributed mapping service described in [1]. Compared with Figure 3, the obtained map conserves perfectly the global appearance and many of the details of the original map with 98.5%

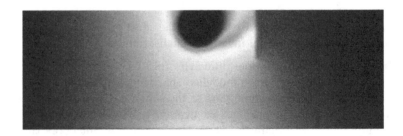

Fig. 3. Heat diffusion map taken by ThermaCAM P65 Infrared (IR) camera

Fig. 4. Heat map generated by the hierarchical mapping service defined in [1]

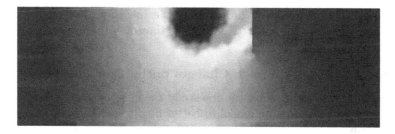

Fig. 5. Heat map generated by M-DAD given obstacle location and length

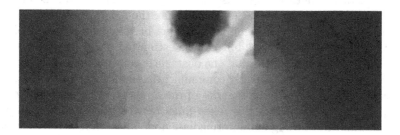

Fig. 6. Heat map generated by M-DAD given obstacle location, length, and width

less data. However, the area containing the obstacle has not been correctly re-
constructed and caused hard edges around the location of heat source. This is
due to attenuation between adjacent points and the fact that some interpolation
areas contain many sensor readings with almost the same elevation. That asserts
that modifications to map generation services are sometimes needed in order to
interactively correct the mapping parameters.

Figure 5 shows the map generated by the M-DAD visualisation framework.
M-DAD was given some information about the application domain including
the existence of the obstacle, its location and length. We observe that the map
obtained by M-DAD conserves perfectly the global appearance as the distributed
mapping service (Figure 3). However, using the given local semantics, M-DAD
reduced the prediction error and visually it accurately captured the effect of the

heat obstacle on heat diffusion through the brass sheet. The M-DAD generated map is smoother than that rendered with the distributed mapping service, only in some sub-regions containing the obstacle and around the heat source location.

Figure 6 shows the map generated by M-DAD with a more complex domain model than the previous M-DAD version (Figure 5). In this version we give M-DAD the obstacle width. We notice a better approximation to the real surface near the obstacle. The new details included in the domain model removed two artifacts from both ends of the obstacle. This is due to the inclusion of the obstacle width in weighting sensor readings when calculating P which further reduces the effect of geographically nearby sensors that are disconnected from P by an obstacle.

Conclusion. This experiment proves that the incorporation of the domain model in the visualisation service significantly improves the performance of the distributed mapping service.

Experiment 2: Adaptations to Changes in the Domain Model

Aim. The aim of this experiment is the study the effectiveness of the proposed VCA in modifying the domain model to better fit the current state of the application domain.

Procedure. The same experimental setup described in Experiment 1 is used here. The obstacle length was increased from $2cm$ to $3.6cm$. Then, the bill which contains the best detected obstacle length value, the federal laws, and the state laws were examined. Wireless communications breaks caused by an obstacle attenuation are hard to predict, but can be estimated using published metrics such that in [9]. It was assumed that the obstacle is continuous and the existence of this obstacle between two directly communicating nodes will break the wireless links between them. The local semantics of the application domain were defined to interpret the break of direct wireless links between two nodes while being able to communicate through an intermediate node(s) as *there exists an obstacle between the two communicating nodes.*

Results and discussion. Table 1 shows three M-DAD visualisation runs each with different node distributions. We test three different randomly distributed nodes topologies because obstacle detection according to the model described here is highly dependent on the nodes location and density around the obstacle. Table 1 shows the number of proposed bills, the best proposed bill and the agreed bill for each mapping run. We notice that the obstacle length was al-

Table 1. The obstacle length (in pixels) in the best proposed bill and the federal laws in three M-DAD visualisation runs at 1000 nodes density

Run	Num of bills	Best bill	Federal law
1	17	59.57	52.0
2	19	60.0	57.74
3	14	60.0	52.0

ways detected accurately and that the best proposed bill was not always agreed locally. This is partially due to the cluster formation process which is able to deal with obstacles (see [10]). Nonetheless, the average VCA agreed bills in the three mapping runs was 53.91 pixels which is close to the actual obstacle length (60 pixels). Adapting to the new obstacle length improves the produced map quality. Quantitatively, the RMS difference between the maps generated with 30 and 60 pixels obstacle length increased by 1.0.

We notice that in the three mapping runs, zero bills became federal laws. This is because all the changes in the application domain were local to part of the network and the majority of the clusters did not sense these changes. This illustrates the mutual benefit of localising the VCA and distributing it over two levels: the local/cluster level; and the global/network level.

Conclusion. This experiment shows that VCA helps to adapt to some changes in the domain model in a distributed manner.

6   Conclusion

In this paper we propose a new visualisation framework called M-DAD. M-DAD is capable of dealing with an arbitrary number of sense modalities, performs distributed self-adaptation and exploits the application domain model. M-DAD spontaneously responses to system changes. It starts with an initial model then it adapts and updates itself to give more precise image about the real world through a training procedure. Experimental results shows that M-DAD improves the visualisation quality in terms of maps predictive error and smoothness.

References

1. Hammoudeh, M., Shuttleworth, J., Newman, R., Mount, S.: Experimental applications of hierarchical mapping services in wireless sensor networks. In: SENSOR-COMM 2008: Proceedings of the 2008 Second International Conference on Sensor Technologies and Applications, pp. 36–43 (2008)
2. Deshpande, A., Guestrin, C., Madden, S., Hellerstein, J., Hong, W.: Model-driven data acquisition in sensor networks. In: VLDB 2004: Proceedings of the Thirtieth international conference on Very large data bases, VLDB Endowment, pp. 588–599 (2004)
3. Chu, D., Deshpande, A., Hellerstein, J., Hong, W.: Approximate data collection in sensor networks using probabilistic models. In: ICDE 2006: Proceedings of the 22nd International Conference on Data Engineering, p. 48 (2006)
4. Hertkorn, P., Rudolph, S.: From data to models: Synergies of a joint data mining and similarity theory approach. In: SPIE Aerosense 1999 Conference On Data Mining and Knowledge Discovery (1999)
5. Hertkorn, P., Rudolph, S.: Dimensional analysis in case-based reasoning. In: Statik, f., der Loft, D., Raumfahrtkonstruktionen, S.I. (eds.) International Workshop on Similarity Methods, pp. 163–178 (1998)
6. Hofierka, J., Parajka, J., Mitasova, H., Mitas, L.: Multivariate interpolation of precipitation using regularized spline with tension. Transactions in GIS 6, 135–150 (2002)

7. Burley, M., Bechkoum, K., Pearce, G.: A formative survey of geometric algebra for multivariate modelling. In: UK Society for Modelling and Simulation, pp. 37–40 (2006)
8. Systems, F.: Thermacam p.65 (2008), http://www.flir.com.hk/p65_print.htm (accessed November 6, 2008)
9. Extricom: Application Note - Wired and Wireless LAN Security. Juniper Networks (November 2007)
10. Hammoudeh, M., Kurtz, A., Gaura, E.: MuMHR: multi-path, multi-hop, hierarchical routing. In: International Conference on Sensor Technologies and Applications, SENSORCOMM 2007 (2007)

Hybrid Bluetooth Scatternet Routing

Karl E. Persson and D. Manivannan

Laboratory for Advanced Networking
Computer Science Department
University of Kentucky
Lexington, KY 40506
USA
{karl,mani}@cs.uky.edu
http://www.cs.uky.edu

Abstract. A Bluetooth® scatternet is a Wireless Personal Area Network (WPAN) formed by inter-connecting piconets using cross-over nodes called bridges. In order for arbitrary nodes to be able to communicate in a scatternet they must be able to discover each other, sometimes without knowing the peer device's identity, and establish routes. Traditionally, routing in wireless ad-hoc networks is done using either a proactive, reactive, or a hybrid approach. In this paper, we present a hybrid solution with a dual meaning. We use a hybrid zone routing approach, but also perform route discovery based on either a destination address or a service. The proactive part of the protocol establishes an *Extended Scatternet Neighborhood (ESN)* with a complete view of adjacent, directly connected, piconets. The reactive part utilizes a route discovery mechanism and establishes inter-piconet *modified source routes*. The route request dissemination, for both destination and service-based route discovery, is performed using a probabilistic gossiping strategy to reduce routing load.

Keywords: Bluetooth Networks, Scatternet, Hybrid, Zone Routing, Gossiping, Piconet, Personal Area Networks, Service Discovery.

1 Introduction

Due to lack of a standard for Bluetooth® scatternets and significant differences between proposed scatternet formation methods, communication between nodes in a scatternet requires a routing protocol that is directly compatible with the underlying formation approach. In addition, it is common that devices are not aware of the identities of their peers and then are not able to perform traditional, destination-address based, route discovery. Devices often need just a route to *some* peer device that offers the requested service rather than a specific peer.

As a basis for our approach we have identified the following important criteria for an efficient scatternet routing protocol:

– Minimizing topology induced bottlenecks and switching overhead.

D. Zhang et al. (Eds.): UIC 2009, LNCS 5585, pp. 163–177, 2009.
© Springer-Verlag Berlin Heidelberg 2009

- Route resilience by avoiding dependency on specific bridge nodes.
- Efficient topology utilization between neighboring piconet clusters and the direct bridge links between them.
- *Hybrid route discovery*: both destination- and service-based.
- Reduce reactive overhead due to inefficient route request flooding.
- Caching of routes during route discovery and periodic route invalidation to prevent cache poisoning.
- Logical placement of scatternet routing functionality in the Bluetooth® protocol stack.

A novel feature of our scatternet routing protocol is *hybrid route discovery*: the ability to either discover a scatternet peer directly based on its destination address or based on a service that it offers. The service-based route discovery can be viewed as an extension of the Service Discovery Protocol (SDP) [3], which by itself is used only within a piconet.

We base our approach on a 2-Slave/Slave mesh (SSM) [10] flat scatternet topology to *minimize bottlenecks and switching overhead*. We use only Slave/Slave bridge nodes of degree two, meaning that they participate in exactly two piconets.

Route resilience is important for fault tolerance and to prevent unnecessary route discovery operations due to the failure or unavailability of a specific bridge node. We also believe that an efficient scatternet routing protocol should be bridge link agnostic, and therefore propose using *modified source routes* that only contains intermediate piconet masters. This allows *any* available bridge node to be utilized when establishing a path between adjacent piconet masters.

We also observe that *efficient topology utilization* should take advantage of the bridge node overlap between adjacent piconets. While a single piconet is limited to one master and up to seven slaves, adjacent piconets provide a natural extension, or an *Extended Scatternet Neighborhood (ESN)*, between piconets that share common bridge nodes. A proactive table-driven approach is used within the ESN and a reactive modified source routing approach is employed elsewhere.

Route discovery must be performed for destinations or services that are not available within the ESN. However, to reduce routing load we do not just use flooding to propagate route requests. Instead we employ a two-tiered *probabilistic gossiping* strategy to determine whether a route request should be forwarded to a neighbor.

We also utilize route caching at piconet masters and periodically invalidate stale routes to prevent cache poisoning. Intermediate piconet masters that have lost connectivity to the next hop master can also attempt to repair the route locally if a different path to the destination or another, downstream, intermediate master along the route is available.

Perhaps the most important aspect of a functional scatternet routing protocol is logical placement in the protocol stack. None of the few existing scatternet routing approaches,[2, 11, 4], have taken this into consideration and merely discussed routing as a function of the Link Manager (LM). We believe that a scatternet routing protocol should be placed on top of the L2CAP layer, which allows application layer protocols to more easily incorporate scatternet routing.

By using our modified source routing approach we also eliminate routing loops, avoid having to use sequence numbers to determine route freshness at intermediate nodes, and reduce routing load. The tradeoff is larger overhead from the inclusion of the modified source route in the routing header.

This paper is organized as follows. In Section 2 we describe the background related to scatternet routing. Section 3 establishes some necessary preliminaries and concepts before we present our routing algorithm in Section 4. The basic idea behind our algorithm is discussed in Section 4.1. Thereafter, we present the complete algorithm in Section 4.2. In Section 5 we evaluate our approach and present simulation results. Finally, we conclude the paper in Section 6.

2   Background

In this section we summarize the main points of previous work on routing in Bluetooth® scatternets. Bhagwat *et. al* [2] present a Routing Vector Method (RVM), which is to the best of our knowledge one of the first attempts to address scatternet-specific routing issues; although it leaves out many issues such as mobility and route resilience. Sun *et. al* [7] present a tree-based scatternet topology, while Lin *et. al* [12] take a different approach and their solution forms a ring topology. Both of the previous two solutions require specific topology constraints, such as strict topology control and continuous maintenance, to operate. Instead of first forming a single monolithic scatternet Liu *et. al* [15] builds scatternets on-demand along requested routes, which is only beneficial for short-lived communication. Kapoor *et. al* [11] applies the Zone Routing Protocol (ZRP) to Bluetooth® scatternets, but does not consider topology formation and present their approach as a function of the Link Manager (LM).

3   Routing Preliminaries

In this section we describe some preliminaries and concepts that we use in our algorithm. We define and describe the ESN and the idea behind probabilistic gossiping. We base our routing approach on a 2-SSM flat scatternet topology, where bridge nodes are allowed to participate only as slaves in exactly two piconets and inefficient Master/Slave (MS) bridges are never used [9]. From here on we assume that such an underlying topology exists. We also assume that Inter-Piconet Scheduling (IPS) functionality exists, such as the MDRP [8] or the DRP [14] algorithm.

3.1   Extended Scatternet Neighborhood (ESN)

In this section we first clarify how a network *hop* is defined in the context of piconets and scatternets, and then define the ESN:

Definition 1. Piconet Hop
A physical link between any two Bluetooth® devices

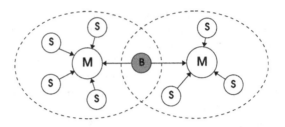

Fig. 1. Extended Scatternet Neighborhood (ESN)

Definition 2. 1-Scatternet Hop
A virtual hop (path) between any two piconet masters, which goes through a bridge node

Definition 3. ESN
The 1-scatternet hop region formed by the union of adjacent piconets

An ESN region is the union of any two piconets that are directly connected through a common bridge node, as illustrated in Figure 1. As we shall see later the ESN makes up our proactive routing zone. Within the ESN a local routing table at each piconet master is periodically updated with routes from adjacent masters. As is illustrated in Figure 2, this allows two slaves in adjacent piconets, four piconet-hops apart, to establish a route without querying the reactive part of the routing protocol. For example, a route can be established between slaves S_A and S_B, along the route $S_A \leftrightarrow M_1 \leftrightarrow B \leftrightarrow M_2 \leftrightarrow S_B$, using only proactive ESN routing information.

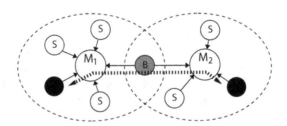

Fig. 2. A 4-piconet hop route within the ESN

3.2   Probabilistic Gossiping

Instead of flooding route requests throughout the scatternet, we employ an alternative strategy called probabilistic gossiping [5, 6]. The idea behind gossiping is to prevent excessive propagation of routing control messages throughout the network. For some threshold value p, where $p < 1$, a node forwards the route request with probability p and discards it with probability *(1 - p)*. However, a potential problem with this approach is that in a sparse network, where a piconet master has few neighbors (low out-degree), the master might not propagate the route request to *any* neighbors and therefore the request will never reach its intended destination. To remedy this situation we employ a 2-tier gossiping scheme similar to [5].

In the next section we first describe the basic idea behind our scatternet routing approach and then present the algorithm in detail.

4   A Hybrid Bluetooth Scatternet Routing Algorithm

4.1   Basic Idea

The word *hybrid* in our Hybrid Bluetooth Scatternet Routing (HBSR) algorithm has dual meaning. It signifies both destination versus service-based discovery as well as zone routing with a proactive approach within the ESN zone and reactive gossiping-based route discovery outside the zone. In this section we will describe the basic idea behind HBSR and summarize the main points of the algorithm.

In contrast to previous approaches, we do not incorporate scatternet routing as a function of the Link Manager (LM) but rather place routing functionality on top of the L2CAP layer in the Bluetooth® stack. By placing the HBSR routing header, which includes the modified source route, inside the L2CAP header, the overhead is significantly lower than for a similar approach at the link layer where the packet sizes are much smaller. However, L2CAP channels must be established on each master to bridge link.

In addition to providing destination and service-based route discovery, our hybrid strategy also uses zone routing to divide the routing protocol into proactive and reactive regions. We call the proactive region the ESN. From Definition 3 we have: *an ESN is the 1-scatternet hop region formed naturally by the union of any two adjacent piconets*. The simplest example of an ESN contains two piconets and is illustrated in Figure 1. Within an ESN adjacent piconet masters periodically exchange local piconet membership information through their common bridge nodes.

The reactive part of the protocol utilizes a route discovery mechanism to disseminate both destination- and service-based route requests for destinations outside the ESN zone. We employ a probabilistic gossiping strategy, when necessary, to control propagation of route requests throughout the scatternet, similar to [5, 6].

When an intermediate piconet master receives a route request packet it first checks whether it can provide a valid reply to the request. We assume that there are not any non-cooperative or malicious nodes in the scatternet.

If an intermediate master is unable to reply to a route request, it determines whether to forward the route request packet based on gossiping probability p_i, where $i \in \{1, 2\}$. By using two different gossiping probability values p_1 and p_2, where $p_1 < p_2$, we assign a higher forwarding probability (p_2) to sparsely connected piconets to provide better propagation and a lower value (p_1) to dense piconets with more forwarding bridge candidates. The threshold parameter $degree_{thres}$ determines if a piconet is sparsely or densely connected.

Even though our approach is based on source routing, each node along a scatternet route does *not* need to be included in the source route. We observe that it is only necessary to use a *modified source route* consisting of the piconet masters along a scatternet route.

For route replies from service-based route requests, intermediate nodes also cache a mapping between the service *UUID* and the destination address for the provider of the service in a table called *Service UUID_Table*. This allows the node to reply to future service-based requests if a valid route to a destination node with a mapping for the requested *UUID* exists in the ESN or in the route cache.

4.2   Algorithm

In this section we describe the details of the Hybrid Bluetooth Scatternet Routing (HBSR) algorithm. We first describe the behavior of the proactive portion of the algorithm using periodic exchanges of topology information. Thereafter we describe the reactive portion of the algorithm that performs route discovery.

Proactive ESN Maintenance. As mentioned in Section 3, we assume that a scatternet has been formed by a formation procedure such as BTDSP [9] and that efficient Inter-Piconet Scheduling (IPS) functionality exists, such as the MDRP algorithm [8] or the DRP algorithm [14]. Further, a local parameter t_{esn} is used to determine the frequency of the periodic ESN membership exchanges between neighboring masters.

Every t_{esn} seconds piconet masters periodically exchange connectivity information with adjacent piconet masters using the HBSR-ESN procedure (Figure 3). Each update includes the list of slaves within the piconet, as well as connectivity information for the slaves and identification of which of them are bridge nodes to other piconets. The bridge connectivity information is conveyed using an 8-digit bit mask. Each entry in the *esn_master* list corresponds to an adjacent piconet master and the *slaves* list contains each slave within the piconet.

The HBSR-ESN procedure works as follows. Upon expiration of the t_{esn} timer piconet masters execute the HBSR-ESN procedure (the *LT_ADDR* check prevents non-piconet masters from entering the procedure). For each adjacent piconet master in the *esn_master* list, a different bit mask is created to indicate bridge connections to piconets other than the destination piconet master. The bit mask is also used to determine bridge out-degree for the gossiping threshold values

```
HBSR-ESN(slaves, esn_masters, seq)
 1    if t_esn expired  and !LT_ADDR
 2      then seq ← seq + 1
 3        for  each  m_i  in esn_masters
 4        do for  each  s_k  in slaves
 5          do if slaves[s_k].bridge = 1 and
 6              slaves[s_k].piconet ≠ m_i
 7            then bit_mask[k] ← 1
 8            else  bit_mask[k] ← 0
 9          bit_mask[0] ← 0
10          HBSR-ESN-UPDATE(src = M_local, dst = m_i, slaves, bit_mask, seq)
11    return
```

Fig. 3. Pseudo code for HBSR ESN update procedure HBSR-ESN

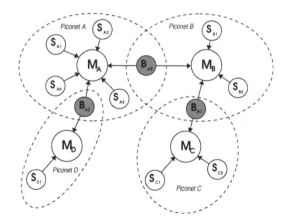

Fig. 4. Example ESN Routing Zone

Table 1. Piconet master M_A's ESN Routing Table

PicoID	BD_ADDR	SEQ	B	M	F
B	$<BD\_ADDR_{M_B}>$	seq_{M_B}	0	1	0
B	$<BD\_ADDR_{S_{B_1}}>$	seq_{M_B}	0	0	0
B	$<BD\_ADDR_{B_{AB}}>$	seq_{M_B}	1	0	0
B	$<BD\_ADDR_{S_{B_2}}>$	seq_{M_B}	0	0	0
B	$<BD\_ADDR_{B_{BC}}>$	seq_{M_B}	0	0	1
D	$<BD\_ADDR_{M_D}>$	seq_{M_D}	0	1	0
D	$<BD\_ADDR_{S_{D_1}}>$	seq_{M_D}	0	0	0
D	$<BD\_ADDR_{B_{AD}}>$	seq_{M_D}	1	0	0

in the HBSR-DISCOVERY procedure (described in Figure 5). Thereafter, the list of slaves and the bit mask are then scheduled for transmission to the adjacent piconet master across the next available bridge link on line 10 of the HBSR-ESN procedure.

The HBSR-ESN update process is done proactively by all piconet masters. Upon disconnect, restart, or other node failure resulting in loss of ESN information, a piconet master will simply re-advertise its membership information to neighbors with 0 as the sequence number. That requires neighboring masters to flush its current membership information for the failed peer master and prevents neighbors from discarding updated membership information from a peer when a failure results in loss of previous sequence number.

After each update the piconet master updates its ESN routing table with the new information. An example of an ESN routing table for a piconet master M_A is given in Table 1. For the purpose of illustration, let us consider the ESN routing table based on the topology in Figure 4.

Note that an ESN routing zone extends only 1-scatternet hop from any given piconet, so that nodes in piconet C (from Figure 4) are excluded from piconet master M_A's ESN. Table 1 contains six columns: *PicoID, BD_ADDR, SEQ, B,*

M, and F. *PicoID* is a local identifier given to each adjacent piconet. It is uniquely assigned to each entry that has the M flag set in an ESN exchange packet, which indicates that it is an adjacent piconet master. In addition, the B flag is set for table entries corresponding to nodes B_{AB} and B_{AD} to indicate that they have a bridge connection to the masters of the piconets with *PicoID* B and D respectively. The node B_{BC} also has the F flag set, which indicates that it is a bridge to a foreign piconet (meaning it has additional connectivity). Every new ESN update from an adjacent piconet master also includes an increasing sequence number, which invalidates previous entries for that *PicoID*. Note that due to our bridge link agnostic approach, specifically for the purposes of providing multiple inter-piconet routes, multiple entries with the same *PicoID* can have the bridge flag B set to indicate a bridge connection.

Route Discovery. Whenever a route request is initiated, or received from a neighboring piconet master, to either a destination or for a service, the HBSR-DISCOVERY procedure (illustrated in Figure 5) is executed by the piconet master. This procedure handles all route discovery operations, except route errors, and encompasses both destination and service-based route requests, as well as route reply generation.

We review the functionality of HBSR-DISCOVERY by refering to the line numbers shown in Figure 5. First, a check to determine that only piconet masters execute the procedure is performed on line 1. Then, lines 2-22 of HBSR-DISCOVERY determine whether a valid route is already available locally, either by way of the local master being the destination piconet master itself, the destination being a neighboring piconet master in the ESN, or a route being available in local route cache.

More specifically, on lines 5 or 6 the partial route from the source is set. When the master itself is the source of the discovery, the rte_to_src is empty (line 5). Otherwise, when the current master is an intermediate node the partial route from the source is set to $route_{partial}$ (line 6), which is the existing partial route gossiped in the HBSR-DISCOVERY procedure to the next *1-scatternet hop* piconet master nodes on lines 56-57. Next, if the target of the route discovery is a service (which is the case when a UUID is specified but a destination address is not), lines 7-10 determine whether there is already an existing mapping between the service UUID and a *BD_ADDR* in the local *ServiceUUID_Table*. This table caches UUID and *BD_ADDR* pairs from route request and reply packets. If a match is found, the *BD_ADDR* of a node that provides the service corresponding to the requested UUID is assigned to BD_ADDR_{DST} on line 8. If a match is not located, then the local SDP server is queried on line 9 for an intra-piconet service provider node. The reason that these calls are not reversed is that table lookups are a lot faster than the SDP queries and entries from previous SDP queries are cached in the *ServiceUUID_Table* for future use anyway.

Whether a BD_ADDR_{DST} is passed to the procedure (destination-based) or assigned on lines 7-10 (service-based request and cached mapping), line 11 performs a loop detection to ensure that BD_ADDR_{DST} and BD_ADDR_{local} do not appear in the partial route from the source node already, in which case the route discovery is marked *invalid* on line 22 to prevent propagation of routing

```
HBSR-DISCOVERY(p₁, p₂, degree_thres, BD_ADDR_local, BD_ADDR_SRC, BD_ADDR_DST, UUID ← NIL, route_partial ← NIL)
 1   if !LT_ADDR
 2     then if BD_ADDR_DST = NIL and UUID = NIL
 3        then return "No Destination BD_ADDR or Service UUID for Route Requests"
 4        if BD_ADDR_SRC = BD_ADDR_local or BD_ADDR_SRC ∈ LocalPiconet
 5           then rte_to_src ← NIL
 6           else rte_to_src ← REVERSE(route_partial)
 7        if BD_ADDR_DST = NIL and UUID in ServiceUUID_Table
 8           then BD_ADDR_DST ← LOOKUP-SERVICE-DEST(ServiceUUID_Table[UUID].list)
 9           else if BD_ADDR_DST = NIL and Local_SDP_Query(UUID)
10              then BD_ADDR_DST = BD_ADDR_local
11        if BD_ADDR_DST ≠ NIL and BD_ADDR_DST not in rte_to_src and BD_ADDR_local not in rte_to_src
12           then if BD_ADDR_DST = BD_ADDR_local or BD_ADDR_DST ∈ LocalPiconet
13              then route ← REVERSE(rte_to_src) + BD_ADDR_local
14              else if BD_ADDR_DST in ESN_Table
15                 then rte_to_dest ← ESN_Table[BD_ADDR_DST].route
16              else if BD_ADDR_DST in Route_Cache and Route_Cache[BD_ADDR_DST].fresh = 1
17                 then rte_to_dest ← Route_Cache[BD_ADDR_DST].route
18              if rte_to_dest
19                 then if BD_ADDR_local not in rte_to_dest and ( each hop_i in rte_to_src) not in rte_to_dest
20                    then route ← REVERSE(rte_to_src) + BD_ADDR_local + rte_to_dest
21                    else invalid ← TRUE
22              else invalid ← TRUE
23        if invalid ≠ TRUE and (route or UUID ≠ NIL)
24           then if rte_to_src = NIL and route
25              then return route
26              else if UUID ≠ NIL and route
27                 then SEND_SREP(BD_ADDR_local, rte_to_src[0].BD_ADDR, route, UUID)
28                    return "Service Reply Sent"
29                 else SEND_RREP(BD_ADDR_local, rte_to_src[0].BD_ADDR, route, BD_ADDR_DST)
30                    return "Route Reply Sent"
31           else if invalid ≠ TRUE
32              then non_sink ← ⟨⟩
33                 next_hops ← ⟨⟩
34                 for each e in ESN_Table
35                 do if e.F = 1
36                    then non_sink[e.PicoID] = TRUE
37                 for each e in ESN_Table
38                 do if e.M = 1 and non_sink[e.PicoID] = TRUE
39                    then next_hops[e.PicoID] = e.BD_ADDR
40                 if BD_ADDR_SRC ≠ BD_ADDR_local
41                    then for each hop_i in rte_to_src
42                    do if hop_i.BD_ADDR in next_hops
43                       then next_hops ← next_hops − ⟨hop_i⟩
44                 degree ← LENGTH[next_hops]
45                 if degree = 0
46                    then return "No Valid Next Hops for Route Requests"
47                    else if degree < degree_thres
48                       then p ← p₂
49                       else p ← p₁
50                 num_sent ← 0
51                 for each n_i.BD_ADDR in next_hops
52                 do r_n ← rand(0, 1)
53                    if r_n ≤ p and BD_ADDR_local not in rte_to_src
54                       then route_partial ← REVERSE(rte_to_src) + BD_ADDR_local
55                          if BD_ADDR_DST ≠ NIL
56                             then SEND_RREQ(BD_ADDR_local, n_i, route_partial, BD_ADDR_DST)
57                             else SEND_SREQ(BD_ADDR_local, n_i, route_partial, UUID)
58                          num_sent ← num_sent + 1
59                 if num_sent > 0
60                    then return "num_sent Route Requests Sent"
```

Fig. 5. Pseudo code for HBSR discovery procedure HBSR-DISCOVERY

loops. Unless the route discovery is invalid, lines 12-17 attempt to locate an existing route to the destination node's piconet master from either the local node, an ESN entry, or a route cache entry if available. First, the destination address is checked for a match against the local master, which does not add any *1-scatternet hops* to the modified source route other than the current piconet master itself as the destination. Then, the ESN table and the route cache are both checked for a route to BD_ADDR_{DST} on lines 14 and 16 respectively. If either of them contain a route to BD_ADDR_{DST}, denoted *(rte_to_dest)*, lines 18-21 perform additional loop detection to ensure that neither the existing node, BD_ADDR_{local}, nor any of the nodes already in the partial route from the source are in the route to the destination, which would cause a routing loop.

If no routing loops are detected, a complete modified source route, denoted *route*, is constructed by appending the reverse of the route to the source from the current node, denoted REVERSE*(rte_to_src)*; the current node's BD_ADDR, denoted BD_ADDR_{local}; and the route to the destination from the current node, denoted rte_to_dest, on line 20. It should be noted that by convention all routes are stored with the source as the first entry and the destination, or intermediate node if partial, as the last entry.

If a valid route to the destination is available on line 23, then lines 24-30 determine where the reply is sent. If the current piconet master or a node in the local piconet is the source of the route discovery, then the route is directly returned to the current piconet master on line 25. Otherwise, a reply packet must be sent toward the source of the discovery. Line 26 determines if the discovery is for a service UUID, in which case a reply, including the UUID and the modified source route to the destination piconet offering the service, is unicasted to the previous-hop piconet master and on along the modified source route back toward the source on line 27. Similarly, if the route discovery was initiated for a specific destination, a reply is unicasted back to the source on line 29. Note that the two procedures SEND_RREP and SEND_SREP, on lines 27 and 29 respectively, merely symbolize the generation of a route reply packet, for destination- and service-based requests respectively, and transmission to the previous hop ESN piconet master.

If a route reply can not be returned directly and the loop detection mechanism did not mark the discovery *invalid*, then additional route discovery operations are performed on lines 31-60 of HBSR-DISCOVERY to propagate the route request further. The first step in this process is to enumerate the piconets within the local ESN routing table that have at least one member with the F (*foreign*) flag set. This means that those neighboring ESN masters have at least one bridge connection to a piconet master that is not within the ESN; hence the connotation *foreign* piconet. This is done on lines 34-36 where each adjacent master entry is set to TRUE in the *non_sink* list when the F flag is set. Thereafter, on lines 37-39 the BD_ADDR for each entry found in the previous step is added to the *next_hop* list. Piconets that are in the *next_hop* list are next-hop candidates for finding a route to the destination, since line 14 established that the destination node is not within the ESN (in which case a route reply would have already been returned on lines 27 or 29).

If the route request packet was received from a neighbor (and not initiated), the master must also prune the previous hop neighbor as well as every other neighbor along the partial modified source route from consideration, so that the route request is not propagated back to the neighbor it was received from. This step is performed on lines 40-43.

The piconet master sets the *degree* on line 44. The degree is the number of forwarding nodes that are available after piconets with no foreign connections and nodes already in the modified source route have been pruned. It is used to determines the gossiping value, on lines 47-49, using the $degree_{thres}$ parameter as a threshold. The $degree_{thres}$ parameter is used for determining sparse or dense connectivity.

On lines 51-58, each of the remaining forwarding nodes are gossiped based on either p_1 or p_2 as the probabistic threshold, depending on the number (degree) of forwarding nodes and the $degree_{thres}$ threshold value. For successful gossips, either a service or a destination-based route request is propagated through the common bridge node to the next hop ESN piconet master. A loop detection is also performed on line 53 to ensure that is current piconet master is not already in the partial route from the source. Note that the two procedures SEND_RREQ and SEND_SREQ, on lines 56 and 57 respectively, merely illustrate the generation of a route request packet and transmission to the next hop ESN piconet master.

Route Reply. Route replies are generated by both destination nodes and intermediate nodes, on lines 27 or 29 of HBSR-DISCOVERY, depending on whether the request was for a service or destination respectively, and unicasted back along the reverse modified source route to the initiator. Due to the master-centric design of the algorithm, piconet masters reply to route requests on behalf of their piconet members. A piconet master is allowed to reply to a *destination-based* route request if:

- It is itself the target of the route request
- A node within its piconet is the target of the route request
- A node within its ESN is the target of the route request
- It has a valid route in its route cache to the target of the route request

For *service-based* route requests a piconet master is allowed to reply if:

- It provides the service sought in the route request itself
- Based on local SDP information, a node within its piconet provides the service sought in the route request
- An entry from the Service *UUID* cache matches the service sought in the route request and a valid route exists in its ESN or in the route cache

Route Maintenance. Each piconet master maintains a local route cache in which it stores routes that it receives from route request and route reply packets. The route cache is implemented as a node-centric path cache, and includes local timestamps and the *BD_ADDR* of the initiator of the route request/reply, and used to invalidate old routes and prevent duplicate route replies.

Each entry in the route cache consists of a route, a timestamp, and a source *BD_ADDR*. The route is always added relative to the master itself with the originator of the packet as the last hop. For example, if intermediate node C receives a route reply containing the modified source route $E \leftrightarrow D \leftrightarrow C \leftrightarrow B \leftrightarrow A$ from a node E, in response to a route request from node A, it adds the route $C \leftrightarrow D \leftrightarrow E$ to its route cache along with a current timestamp and the *BD_ADDR* of node E as well as the partial modified source route $C \leftrightarrow B \leftrightarrow A$ along with a timestamp and the *BD_ADDR* of node A. Periodic route cache maintenance is also performed to ensure that cached routes are fresh. To prevent cache pollution, a *stale* flag is set for routes old than t_{cache} seconds. After another t_{cache} seconds, stale entries are removed from the cache.

Route Error. When sending data packets along the *modified source routes*, the loss of an intermediate node along the route can cause abruption of the data flow, unless the intermediate node, at the point of next hop failure, has another route; either as its ESN neighbor or as another fresh route cache entry in which the destination is an intermediate node. When this occurs the intermediate piconet master, at the point of next hop failure, sends a route error reply packet back to the source node to trigger a new route discovery. As the route error passes through intermediate nodes it invalidates route cache entries for the destination.

5   Performance Evaluation

To evaluate the performance of the Hybrid Bluetooth Scatternet Routing (HBSR) algorithm we developed custom functionality for HBSR using the UCBT extension module [13] and the ns-2 [1] network simulator. We specifically evaluate the usefulness of the ESN zone routing approach and the route acquisition delay.

5.1   Extended Scatternet Neighborhood (ESN)

We evaluate the topology coverage of the ESN zone to determine the effectiveness of the proactive HBSR-ESN procedure in terms of how many destination nodes within the scatternet are reachable from any given source node by an ESN routing table lookup rather than invoking the reactive HBSR-DISCOVERY procedure.

We utilize BTDSP [9] and the ns-2 [1] network simulator to form random 2-Slave/Slave Mesh (SSM) scatternet topologies with 8, 16, 32, and 64 nodes respectively; each replicated 100 times. Thereafter we compute the all-pairs shortest paths (in terms of 1-scatternet hops) between any two nodes in the scatternet topology. As illustrated in Figure 2, any destination *within one 1-scatternet hops* is reachable within the ESN of the source node's piconet master. Therefore, any nodes within one 1-scatternet hops[1] of the source node can be reached without invoking the HBSR-DISCOVERY procedure. The results are illustrated in Figure 6.

From Figure 6 it should be noted that for scatternet topologies of 16 nodes or less, on average, about 50% of nodes within the scatternet are reachable without need for route discovery. For scatternet topologies with 32 nodes or less, on average, about 30% of nodes are directly accessible by way of ESN routing table lookups. As Bluetooth scatternets are most suitable for WPAN applications with around 30 nodes or less, as opposed to large-scale WPANs where IEEE 802.11 is more suitable, the hybrid HBSR approach eliminates the need for a third or more of the route discovery operations for such topologies.

5.2   Route Acquisition Delay

To evaluate the performance of the HBSR route discovery process and determine the most suitable IPS algorithm to use, we study the route acquisition delay, or in

---

[1] As illustrated in Figure 4, if both the source and the destination nodes are either pure slaves or bridges to piconets other than *between* the source and destination piconets, a *1-scatternet hop* could be 4 hops at the link level.

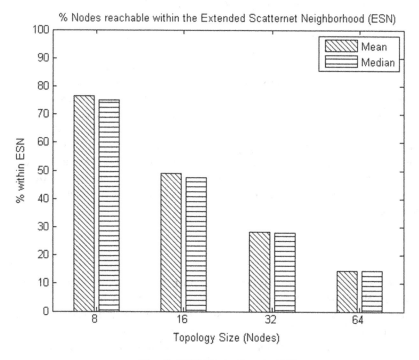

Fig. 6. ESN Node Reachability

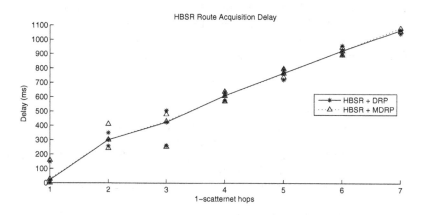

Fig. 7. HBSR Route Acquisition Delay

other words the amount of time before a route reply is returned to the HBSR-DISCOVERY initiator. We evaluate the performance of the HBSR-DISCOVERY process in conjunction with the Maximum Distance Rendezvous Point (MDRP) algorithm by Johansson *et al.* [8] as well as the Dichotomized Rendezvous Point (DRP) algorithm by Wang *et al.* [14].

To evelute route acquisition delay and scheduling delay we run the HBSR-DISCOVERY procedure from a fixed source node to random destination on connected 32-node 2-SSM topologies with between two and six bridge nodes.

From Figure 7 it can be seen that there is a significant delay incurred for destinations outside the ESN zone that require route discovery. The reason for this is two-fold: the need to buffering of packets at intermediate nodes due to specific rendezvous points where peer nodes have to be synchronized and the need to fragment L2CAP frames and transmit multiple packets as the modified source routes grow longer. It does show, however, that HBSR is more suitable for denser and more compact topologies than for long scatternet paths, in which case a specialized on-demand approach such as [15] might be more suitable. It should be noted that using the *modified source route* approach instead of hop-by-hop source routes requires only $\lfloor n \rfloor$ entries, where n is the number of piconet masters along the route.

6 Conclusion

In this paper we presented the Hybrid Bluetooth Scatternet Routing (HBSR) algorithm, which allowed scatternet nodes to discover peers by either destination address or by a service *UUID*. We also considered the underlying topology constraints and defined the ESN as the 1-scatternet-hop region formed by the union of adjacent piconets. Furthermore, our hybrid approach utilized a proactive approach within the ESN, provided loop-freedom, and used a reactive *modified* source-routing approach outside the ESN. The modified source-routes were bridge link agnostic and made up of only intermediate piconet masters, so that changes in individual bridge links did not affect the entire scatternet route. The routing protocol was placed above the L2CAP layer to allow easier access to routing functionality for application layer protocols.

References

1. ns2 - Network Simulator, http://www.isi.edu/nsnam/ns/
2. Bhagwat, P., Segall, A.: A routing vector method (rvm) for routing in bluetooth scatternets. In: IEEE International Workshop on Mobile Multimedia Communications (MoMuC 1999), pp. 375–379 (1999)
3. Bluetooth Special Interest Group. Bluetooth Specification (February 2001), http://www.bluetooth.com
4. Huang, C.-J., Lai, W.-K., Hsiao, S.-Y., Liu, H.-Y.: A self-adaptive zone routing protocol for bluetooth scatternets. Computer Communications 28(1), 37–50 (2005)
5. Li, L., Halpern, J., Haas, Z.: Gossip-based ad hoc routing. In: Proceedings of the 21st Annual Joint Conference of the IEEE Computer and Communications Societies (INFOCOM 2002) (June 2002)
6. Li, X.-Y., Moaveninejad, K., Frieder, O.: Regional gossip routing for wireless ad hoc networks. Mobile Networks and Applications 10(1-2), 61–77 (2005)
7. Sun, M., Chang, C., Lai, T.: A self-routing topology for bluetooth scatternets. In: Proceedings of I-SPAN 2002, Manila, Philippines (May 2002)

8. Johansson, P., Kapoor, R., Kazantzidis, M., Gerla, M.: Rendezvous scheduling in bluetooth scatternets. In: Proceedings of ICC 2002, New York City, New York, pp. 318–324 (April 2002)
9. Persson, K., Manivannan, D.: A fault-tolerant distributed formation protocol for bluetooth scatternets. International Journal of Pervasive Computing and Communications (JPCC) 2(2), 165–176 (2006)
10. Persson, K.E., Manivannan, D., Singhal, M.: Bluetooth scatternets: criteria, models and classification. Ad Hoc Networks 3(6), 777–794 (2005)
11. Kapoor, R., Gerla, M.: A zone routing protocol for bluetooth scatternets. IEEE Wireless Communications and Networking (WCNC 2003), 1459–1464 (March 2003)
12. Lin, T.Y., Tseng, Y., Chang, K., Tu, C.: Formation, routing, and maintenance protocols for the bluering scatternet of bluetooths. In: Proceedings of the 36th Hawaii International Conference of System Sciences, Big Island, Hawaii (January 2003)
13. University of Cincinnati, UCBT - Bluetooth extension for ns2, http://www.ececs.uc.edu/~cdmc/ucbt/
14. Wang, Q., Agrawal, D.P.: A dichotomized rendezvous algorithm for mesh bluetooth scatternets. Ad Hoc & Sensor Wireless Networks 1(1), 65–88 (2005)
15. Liu, Y., Lee, M.J., Saadawi, T.N.: A bluetooth scatternet-route structure for multihop ad hoc networks. IEEE Journal on Selected Areas in Communications 21(2), 229–239 (2003)

Self-estimation of Neighborhood Density for Mobile Wireless Nodes

Junji Hamada[1], Akira Uchiyama[1,2], Hirozumi Yamaguchi[1,2], Shinji Kusumoto[1], and Teruo Higashino[1,2]

[1] Graduate School of Information Science and Technology, Osaka University
[2] Japan Science Technology and Agency, CREST

Abstract. In this paper, we propose a method to estimate the density of nodes for pedestrians and/or vehicles with information terminals. The method enables us to provide intelligent services which are environment-aware with highly dynamic movement of nodes such as intellectual navigation that tells the user the best route to detour congested regions. In the proposed method, each node is supposed to know its location roughly (*i.e.* within some error range) and to maintain a density map covering its surroundings. This map is updated when a node receives a density map from a neighboring node. Also by estimating the change of the density, taking into account the movement characteristics of nodes, the density map is updated in a timely fashion. The simulation experiments have been conducted and the results have shown the accuracy of the estimated density maps.

1 Introduction

Recent innovation of wireless communication technology has brought us possibilities to deploy infrastructure-less wireless applications. For example, in Intelligent Transportation Systems (ITS), collision avoidance systems using Inter-Vehicle Communication (IVC) have been developed and are now being put on practical use [1]. IVCs have been investigated for other applications like traffic and environment information acquisition [2, 3, 4, 5].

A number of such studies commonly indicate that ad-hoc communication using short-range wireless devices improves the cost and efficiency of data fusion and diffusion, which have been done by infrastructure. In particular, if moving vehicles and pedestrians can estimate and obtain the information on their surroundings in real-time through ad-hoc communication, many services and applications can be provisioned without limitations due to deployment of infrastructures. For example, a human navigation system for emergency evacuation will be more intelligent if information on the density of people in its surroundings can be fed into the route decision engine of the system. However, real-time density estimation of mobile nodes by collaboration through ad-hoc networks has not been investigated yet.

In this paper, we propose a method for mobile wireless nodes, which may be pedestrians or vehicles with information terminals, to estimate the density

D. Zhang et al. (Eds.): UIC 2009, LNCS 5585, pp. 178–192, 2009.

of mobile nodes in their surroundings. In the proposed method, each node is assumed to know its location roughly (*i.e.* within some error range) and to maintain a density map covering its surroundings. This map is updated when a node receives a density map from a neighboring node. Also by estimating the change of the density, taking into account the movement characteristics of nodes, it is updated in a timely fashion.

The goal of our study is to propose an autonomous protocol to let mobile nodes have accurate density maps with reasonable amount of wireless ad-hoc communication traffic. To build a density map, with a certain interval, each node broadcasts its own density map where its *area of presence* (the area in which a true location is included) is merged. On receiving a density map from neighboring nodes, the node updates such a part of its own density map that the received cones density information seems more fresh. We note that there is a clear trade-off between the freshness of density information and the required amount of wireless capacity to exchange density information. To pursue this trade-off, we have two key ideas. First, we provide an *estimation function* that estimates the future density map based on its time-varying characteristics. As a simple example, if we know the maximum speed V_{max} of mobile nodes, an estimation function that estimates the density map after Δt time can be designed in such a way that each density value in the current map is spread over $V_{max} \cdot \Delta t$ region. Another function can be designed in such a way that the value is spread only to the directions toward which other nodes exist if mobile nodes are vehicles. This is based on the property that vehicles follow others. Second, we design an adaptive protocol that controls the transmission interval of messages depending on the density of surroundings, in order to avoid similar density maps to be emitted to the wireless channel.

The simulation experiments have been conducted and the correlation between the real and estimated density maps has been measured. The results in four different scenarios have shown that the proposed method could attain high accuracy of the estimated density maps.

2   Related Work

In Vehicular Ad-hoc NETworks (VANETs), there have been various approaches to aggregate and disseminate several types of contexts like road surface condition, temperature, traffic jam information [2, 3, 4, 5] Similar approaches have been considered in the field of Wireless Sensor Networks (WSNs) [6, 7, 8, 9]. Some of them consider aggregating data based on its similarity (*i.e.* elimination of data redundancy) and others consider in-network computing of given queries.

Our proposed method falls into these categories in the sense that it is aimed at aggregating (sensed) data with less amount of traffic. However, the proposed method is designed for mobile nodes to self-estimate their neighborhood density. Therefore, the data is time-varying in the scale of minutes while VANETs and WSNs target aggregation of data such as load surface condition and wide-area traffic condition information which are relatively stable in long-term. Hence,

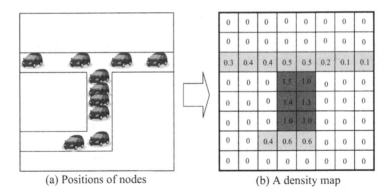

(a) Positions of nodes   (b) A density map

Fig. 1. Example of Density Map

we have to consider the trade-off between timeliness of data of mobile nodes' locations and traffic overhead. We note that object detection and tracking in WSNs have to deal with real-time motion of objects (thus the data must be time-varying in very short term). However, these applications are not aimed at aggregating data but detecting objects.

As we stated in the introduction, each node has estimation functions to estimate the dynamic change of the density map, and exchanges the estimated result with others to help increase the accuracy of density maps. Also depending on the neighborhood density, each node controls the transmission interval. Based on these two ideas, we have designed a protocol that deals with a unique problem, that is, self-estimation of density for mobile nodes. In this sense, our approach is original.

From the perspective of geographical information, our goal relates to localization algorithms [10,11,12,13], which aim to estimate positions of nodes. However, the goal of localization algorithms is to estimate each node's position by itself and does not much care about positions of other nodes. Hence, our goal is different from localization algorithms.

3   Self-estimation of Neighborhood Density

3.1   Overview

We assume that each node i is equipped with a wireless device and knows its (rough) location through GPS or other technologies. We also assume that the region is divided into square cells with s(m) edge. Based on this cell representation of geography, node i maintains a density map D_i, which represents locations of other nodes in its surroundings. Concretely, D_i has $X_i \times Y_i$ elements and each element $d_{x,y}(1 \leq x \leq X_i, 1 \leq y \leq Y_i)$ represents the node density in the cell (x,y). An example of a density map is shown in Fig. 1. We assume each node knows the maximum speed V_{max} of all the nodes. For example, this can be estimated based on the speed limits in the case of vehicles.

Each node i executes the following procedures every t seconds.

1. Node i updates its density map D_i by using a given estimation function f. We assume a typical moving pattern in the target environment is modeled into the estimation function. According to this model, $f(D_i)$ diffuses node density in each cell toward its surrounding cells that are supposed to be reachable within a message exchange interval denoted by t. This represents the estimated movement of other nodes. We note that in $f(D_i)$, if $d_{x,y}$ is less than a certain threshold denoted by TH_d after updating, $d_{x,y}$ is set to zero. For TH_d, we set the value which is too small or too old as density information, and is therefore not useful any longer.
2. Node i adds its location information to D_i. To do this, firstly, node i obtains its area of presence (denoted by R_i) from GPS or other measurement devices where R_i is the area which includes node i's true position. We represent R_i as a set of cells as follows;

$$R_i = \{(x_{i1}, y_{i1}), (x_{i2}, y_{i2}), \ldots, (x_{in}, y_{in})\}$$

where n is the number of cells included in the area of presence. Thus the expected density in each cell of R_i is $1/n$. Secondly, this value is added to the density value of each cell in the density map D_i. This procedure is executed only when the elapsed time since node i records R_i becomes longer than a certain Δt_i seconds. For Δt_i, we set the expected time for the density value $1/n$ added to each cell to be less than a certain threshold (denoted by ε) due to the estimation function. Hence, Δt_i should be set according to the estimation function.
3. Node i sends D_i to its neighbors.
4. Node i updates D_i when i receives D_j from neighboring node j.

We explain the details of these procedures in the following section.

3.2 Algorithm

Estimation Function. Density maps are updated by the estimation function f, which is given beforehand. Typical movement patterns in the target region and/or the target nodes are modeled in the estimation function. Here, we describe (i) the diffuse estimation function, (ii) the limited diffuse estimation function, and (iii) the hybrid estimation function as examples of typical movement patterns and their estimation functions.

Diffuse Estimation Function. When the maximum speed of nodes is the only known fact, there is a possibility that each node moves toward any directions in the region. Thus, the diffuse estimation function divides the value of density in each cell to its neighboring cells which have a shared edge with the cell. An weight $\alpha(0 < \alpha < 1)$ is considered when a value of density is divided so that aging of information can be regarded. Because the edge size of a cell is s(m) and updates are repeated every t seconds, the diffuse estimation function iterates

(a) Before updating   (b) After 1 iteration   (c) After 1 iteration
                       (Diffuse; α=0.9)   (Limited diffuse;α=0.9)

Fig. 2. Update by Estimation Function

```
for(step=0; step< ⌊t * Vmax/s⌋; step++){
    D'_i ← D_i;
    foreach (d_x,y ∈ D_i){
        d'_x,y      ← d_x,y + 0.2 * d_x,y * α;
        d'_x-1,y    ← d_x-1,y + 0.2 * d_x,y * α;
        d'_x,y-1    ← d_x,y-1 + 0.2 * d_x,y * α;
        d'_x+1,y    ← d_x-1,y-1 + 0.2 * d_x,y * α;
        d'_x,y+1    ← d_x-1,y-1 + 0.2 * d_x,y * α;
    }
    D_i ← D'_i;
}
return D_i;
```

Fig. 3. Diffuse Estimation Function

this procedure $\lfloor t * V_{max}/s \rfloor$ times. Fig. 2(b) and Fig. 3 show an example of the update by the diffuse estimation function and its pseudo-code, respectively.

In this function, Δt_i is determined based on k which satisfies the following condition:

$$\frac{\alpha^k}{2k^2 + 2k + 1} \leq \varepsilon \tag{1}$$

Here, k is the number of iteration by the diffuse estimation function. The left part in the above condition approximately denotes density in one cell after k steps, starting from a single cell of which density is 1. The denominator is the number of cells and the numerator means freshness of the latest recorded area of presence. Each iteration is executed once in s/V_{max} seconds. Therefore,

$$\Delta t_i = \frac{k * s}{V_{max}}. \tag{2}$$

Limited Diffuse Estimation Function. There are movable areas and unmovable areas if the target nodes are pedestrians or vehicles. Here, we consider an estimation function which distributes density in each cell to only movable areas in its neighboring cells. We do not assume any maps but exploit a density map to estimate movable areas in this function.

Fig. 2(c) and Fig. 4 show an example of an update by this limited diffuse estimation function and its pseudo-code, respectively. In this function, for each direction (*i.e.* up, bottom, left and right), we calculate the average density of cells to which distance from the diffused cell $d_{x,y}$ is less than m cells. Then, if the result is more than TH_{move}, $d_{x,y}$ is divided by the number of directions which satisfy the condition and diffused to them. In the same way as the diffuse estimation function, α is regarded for aging. This procedure is iterated $\lfloor t * V_{max}/s \rfloor$ times.

In the case of the limited diffuse estimation function, the number of cells which satisfy the condition varies every time it updates a density map. Thus, it is complicated to derive Δt_i precisely. For this reason, we use the same rule with the diffuse estimation function to determine Δt_i.

Hybrid Estimation Function. Because a density map is propagated among nodes step by step, the freshness of information in further areas is lower. Hence, it is sometimes hard to estimate movable areas in further regions based on the limited diffuse estimation function as we described before. We combine both the diffuse estimation function and the limited diffuse estimation function and propose the hybrid estimation function. In the hybrid estimation function, for the cells in the proximity of the current position, the limited diffuse estimation function is used and the diffuse estimation function is applied to distant areas from the current position.

We define the areas around the current position as the cells included in R_i, and use the limited diffuse estimation function for cells included in R_i and the diffuse estimation function for other cells. Δt_i is determined in the same way that the diffuse estimation function does for the simplicity.

Recording Area of Presence. Each element $d'_{x,y}$ after recording node i's area of presence is calculated as defined below.

$$d'_{x,y} = \begin{cases} d_{x,y} + \dfrac{1}{n}, & \text{if } (x,y) \in R_i; \\ d_{x,y}, & \text{otherwise.} \end{cases} \tag{3}$$

where n denotes the number of elements in R_i. In this formula, the larger the size of R_i, the smaller the value added to each cell in R_i becomes.

Merging Density Maps. When a node i receives a density map D_j from another node j, node i merges D_i with D_j. Because each density map does not include information which indicates freshness of density information in each cell, we regard higher density as more fresh (*i.e.* newer) information. This policy is based on the observation that density in each cell is diffused as time passes and hence higher density is likely to be fresh information. In merging of density maps, for each cell (x, y), the value $d'_{x,y}$ after the merging is computed as below.

$$d'_{x,y} = \max\{d^i_{x,y}, d^j_{x,y}\} \tag{4}$$

3.3   Reduction of Communication Overhead

Each node i sends its density map D_i every t seconds. The data size of D_i is inversely proportional to the size s^2 of a cell and proportional to the size of the

```
for(step=0; step< ⌊t * Vmax/s⌋; step++){
    D'i ← Di;
    foreach(dx,y ∈ Di){
        expand_num ← 1;
        sum ← 0;
        for(j ←1; j ≤ n; j++) sum += dx+j,y;
        avg ← sum/n; right ← false;
        if(avg ≥ THmove){
            right ← true; expand_num++;}
        sum ← 0;
        for(j ←1; j ≤ n; j++) sum += dx−j,y;
        avg ← sum/n; left ← false;
        if(avg ≥ THmove){
            left ← true; expand_num++;}
        sum ← 0;
        for(j ←1; j ≤ n; j++) sum += dx,y+j;
        avg ← sum/n; down = false;
        if(avg ≥ THmove){
            down ← true; expand_num++;}
        sum ← 0;
        for(j ←1; j ≤ n; j++) sum += dx,y−j;
        avg ← sum/n; up ← false;
        if(avg ≥ THmove){
            up ← true; expand_num++;}
        if(right)d'x+1,y ← dx+1,y + 1/expand_num * dx,y * α;
        if(left)d'x−1,y ← dx−1,y + 1/expand_num * dx,y * α;
        if(down)d'x,y+1 ← dx,y+1 + 1/expand_num * dx,y * α;
        if(up)d'x,y−1 ← dx,y−1 + 1/expand_num * dx,y * α;
        d'x,y ← dx,y + 1/expand_num * dx,y * α;
    }
    Di ← D'i;
}
return Di;
```

Fig. 4. Limited Diffuse Estimation Function

target region. We introduce a technique which adjusts the view of a density map sent to neighbors, depending on the number of neighbors, in order to pursue the trade-off between communication overhead and accuracy.

We denote a sub-density map of D_i as $\hat{D}_i$ hereafter. Ideally, it is better to send a density map D_i every t seconds in order to propagate density information to distant areas for higher accuracy. However, if the density around a node is high, it seems enough to send density maps from a few nodes in the surroundings because information in distant areas is likely to be very similar among those density maps.

Based on this idea, our technique uses a sub-density map $\hat{D}_i$, of which the size S_i is defined as below:

$$S_i = \frac{\beta}{N_i} (\beta \text{ is a certain constant}) \qquad (5)$$

where N_i is the number of neighbors for node i and β is a certain constant. Every t seconds, each node i sends either its density map D_i with the probability of $1/N_i$ or its sub-density map $\hat{D}_i$ otherwise. In addition, node i broadcasts D_i only if it has not sent D_i in the last T seconds in order to guarantee that a density map is sent in a certain period of time, node i broadcasts D_i only if it has not sent D_i in the last T seconds.

4   Experimental Results

4.1   Settings

We have evaluated the performance of the proposed method using a network simulator MobiREAL [14].

We have used two simulation areas of which the sizes are 100m × 100m and 1,000m × 1,000m. These areas have several roads of 10m or 20m width. For the 100m × 100m area, we have used three maps; *cross-road* in Fig. 5(a) which has

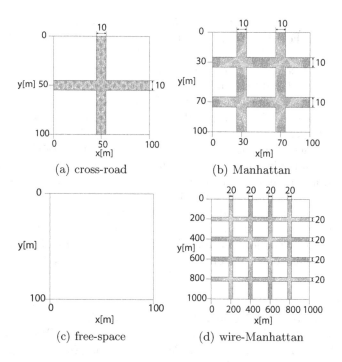

(a) cross-road   (b) Manhattan

(c) free-space   (d) wire-Manhattan

Fig. 5. Simulation Maps

Table 1. Simulation Settings

Parameters	cross-road	Manhattan	free-space	wire-Manhattan
area size (m×m)	100 × 100	100 × 100	100 × 100	1000 × 1000
road width (m)	10	10	10	20
length s of cell (m)	2	2	2	20
radio range R (m)	10	10	10	150
velocity of nodes (m/s)	[0.1, 1.0]	[0.1, 1.0]	[0.1, 1.0]	[36, 54](km/h)
bandwidth (Mbps)	1	1	1	1
number of nodes	200	200	200	453
estimation function $f(D)$; m=10 for hybrid	hybrid	hybrid	diffuse	hybrid
threshold TH_d of effective density in density map (node/cell)	0.015	0.01	0.015	0.055
threshold ε of effective density in area of presence (node/cell)	0.002	0.002	0.002	0.002
size of R_i (m)	49 × 49	49 × 49	49 × 49	60 × 60
transmission interval t of partial density map (s)	2	2	2	2
maximum transmission interval T of density map (s)	10	10	10	10

only one intersection, *Manhattan* in Fig. 5(b) which has 4 intersections, and *free-space* in Fig. 5(c). For the 1,000m × 1,000m area, we have used the map called *wire-Manhattan* in Fig. 5(d) which has 8 roads and 16 intersections. In these maps except the free-space map, nodes can only exist on roads, and in every map nodes were deployed uniformly before simulations. Each node moves along a road with a constant velocity which is randomly chosen from [0.1, 1.0](m/s) (in the cases of cross-road, Manhattan and free-space assuming pedestrians) or [36, 54](km/h) (in the case of wire-Manhattan assuming vehicles) at the beginning of simulations. Each node changes its direction to the opposite if it encounters a border, and randomly chooses one of the three directions except the backward direction if it enters an intersection. Simulation time is 600 seconds. The simulation settings are summarized in Table 1.

Through the analysis of simulation results, we have confirmed that the accuracy of density maps was very similar among the nodes of different initial locations and moving speeds. Therefore, in the following, we focus on the density map of a particular node (this node is denoted as p) if no explicit explanation is given.

4.2   Results

Accuracy of Number of Nodes. Fig. 6 shows the estimated number of nodes in the four maps, along the progress of simulation time. Also, Table 2 shows the average number of nodes in each case. We can see that these averaged values are very close to the original values. In all the cases except the wire-Manhattan,

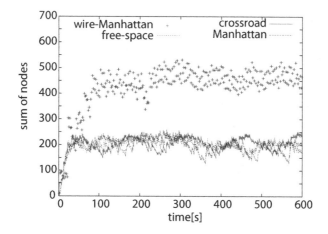

Fig. 6. Estimated Number of Nodes in Density Map of Node p

the large errors between the estimated and real node densities were measured before 30sec. because it is the initial phase of simulation where each node had started to collect information about the others and the density maps had not been constructed yet. Therefore, we focus on the state after 30sec., where the estimated number of nodes was stable with small errors from the real density. Since the size is quite larger than the others in the wire-Manhattan map, it took about 100sec. to obtain the density information in this case. Nevertheless, it also has the stable state after 100sec. where the estimated number of nodes was stable as well.

Fig. 7(a) and Fig. 7(b) show the real node distribution and its corresponding estimated density map of node p at time 450sec. in the case of the cross-road map. At this time, node p was at the point (50,50) (near the intersection). By comparing the estimated density map with the real node distribution, we can see some errors in the places away from the intersection. However, we can also observe that the estimated densities in the regions except roads were almost zero and those around the intersection were high. This result indicates the estimated density well captures the real node distribution. Similarly, Fig. 7(c) and Fig. 7(d) show the result in the case of the Manhattan map. Node p was at the point (80,30). Through comparison with the real distribution, we can see that

Table 2. Average Number of Nodes in Estimated Density Map

	Estimated # of nodes
cross-road (21s~600s)	206.098
Manhattan (21s~600s)	199.788
free-space (21s~600s)	202.720
wire-Manhattan (101s~600s)	455.595

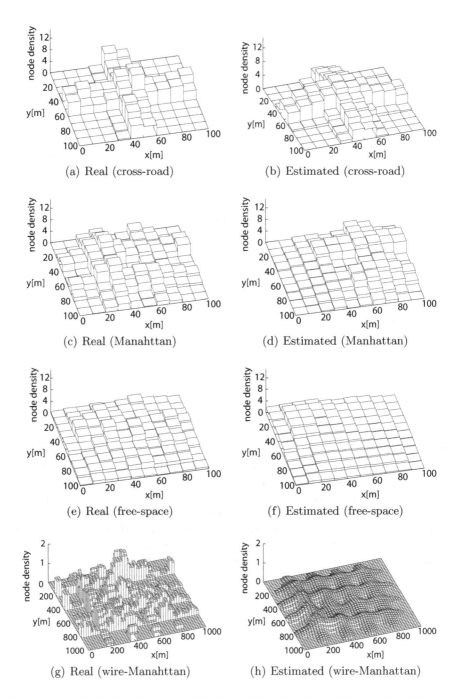

(a) Real (cross-road)

(b) Estimated (cross-road)

(c) Real (Manahttan)

(d) Estimated (Manhattan)

(e) Real (free-space)

(f) Estimated (free-space)

(g) Real (wire-Manahttan)

(h) Estimated (wire-Manhattan)

Fig. 7. Real Node Distribution and Estimated Density Map of Node p (at $450sec.$)

there are some errors around the points (30,30) and (30,80), while the density is well-represented in the area around node p. In the freespace map (Fig. 7(e) and Fig. 7(f)), node p was at the point (20,20). We can see the same characteristics with the case of the Manhattan map. Finally, Fig. 7(g) and Fig. 7(h) show the result in the wire-Manhattan map. The position of node p was (600,400). We can see that the estimated density is expanded out of roads though the shape of roads can be recognized from the density map. This is because the size of the region is larger compared to the other maps and hence the diffuse estimation function is applied to most of the region.

From these results, we confirmed that the accuracy of density estimation was higher around the node's location and the estimated density maps could represent the shape of the real density distribution.

Similarity of Density Distribution. To see the similarity between the estimated density distribution and the real density distribution, we used Kendall's τ [15]. Here, we introduce the concept of *granularity* to compare the two distributions. The granularity is represented by $g \times g$, which means that $g \times g$ cells are considered as one larger cell in computing the Kendall's τ. We have changed this granularity from 1×1 to 10×10. The results are shown in Table 3. The average Kendall's τ is increasing as the granularity becomes larger in most cases. This is

Table 3. Average Kendall's τ

	Granularity			
	1×1	2×2	5×5	10×10
cross-road (31s~600s)	0.751	0.761	0.755	0.718
Manhattan (31s~600s)	0.545	0.568	0.595	0.674
free-space (31s~600s)	0.538	0.571	0.607	0.635
wire-Manhattan (101s~600s)	0.463	0.523	0.646	0.670

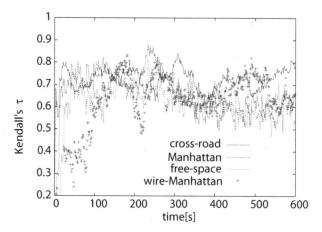

Fig. 8. Time vs. Kendall's τ ($g \times g = 10 \times 10$)

Table 4. Comparison of Communication Overhead

	cross-road	Manhattan	free-space	wire-Manhattan
Avg. bandwidth per node (kbps)	40	40	40	40
Avg. bandwidth with reduction per node (kbps)	11.28	16.16	20	10

Table 5. Effect of Communication Overhead Reduction on Kendall's τ

	reduction	no reduction
cross-road	0.718	0.722
Manhattan	0.674	0.738
free-space	0.635	0.689
wire-Manhattan	0.670	0.673

natural because the values of density are often expanded to wider regions (*i.e.* the outside) by the diffuse estimation function.

Also, Fig. 8 shows changes of Kendall's τ over time. At the beginning, Kendall's τ increases drastically because each node receives new density information from others. The Kendall's τ becomes stable in the steady phase after that. For the maps except for the free-space, the averages of Kendall's τ ranged from 0.67 to 0.718 and we can see the strong similarity. Even in the case of the free-space where it is difficult to predict the movements of nodes, the average Kendall's τ was 0.635. Therefore, the proposed technique represents the real node distribution well.

4.3   Reduction in Communication Overhead

Effect of Reduction in Communication Overhead. In our technique, the target region is divided into cells. The number of cells is 2500 in the default simulation setting, and we assume that each cell requires 4 bytes. Then, the data size of a density map is 10 Kbytes. Each node sends its density map periodically and hence the communication overhead may be large. To reduce this communication overhead, we use sub-density map as we mentioned in Sec.3.3.

In order to see the effect of this scheme, we evaluated the amount of traffic. The result is shown in Table 4. We could confirm that our scheme could reduce approximately 50%-75% of the original traffic.

Reduction in Communication Overhead vs. Accuracy. From the results shown in Table 5, we see Kendall's τ is lower when the communication overhead is reduced. Obviously, there is a trade-off between communication overhead and the accuracy of density maps. Therefore, it is important to determine parameters on communication appropriately.

5   Discussions

The proposed method uses a cell matrix to represent a density map. The cell matrix facilitates computation like merging and mobility estimation, while the data size may be large, depending on both the region and cell sizes. In WSNs, there is a method to build a contour map of the data sensed by wireless sensor nodes [6, 16]. Some other possibilities are using some encoding technique to compress the map. We are trying to clarify their advantages and disadvantages in terms of the trade-off between the computation overhead and data size.

We also discuss another important issue on position information. In the proposed method, each node may provide its position information with some error range. This has the following two advantages, (i) robustness to position errors caused by GPS or other measurements such as position estimation methods like Sextant [17] and UPL [12] due to their likelihood estimation in range-free localization, and (ii) privacy protection in which intentionally randomized positions obscures the true position.

6   Conclusion

In this paper, we have proposed a method for mobile nodes to self-estimate density in its proximity in real-time using ad-hoc wireless communications among these nodes. We have conducted simulation experiments in which correlation between the estimated map and the real density map had been measured.

The road traffic information can be collected and distributed through infrastructures like VICS, by which the covered regions are restricted to major highways and streets which are measured by base stations. On the other hand, the proposed method can utilize each vehicle's density map to build the map of wider areas, which cannot be covered by infrastructures only. This idea can also be applied to probe cars which collect information like traffic and weather. Also such density maps can be utilized by vehicles themselves for intelligent car navigation or other purposes. Consequently, the proposed method fit into many ITS applications.

Another potential application domain is personal navigation. In huge shopping centers and fireworks festivals (in the case of Japan) in which many people get around, observing their locations through their mobile terminals will be helpful not only for commercial use but also safe navigation toward exits.

Assuming these potential application examples, we are planning to conduct simulations in more realistic environments and to determine appropriate parameter settings and to validate usefulness of the method. Furthermore, autonomy of the protocol is our important goal where protocol parameters like message transmission intervals can be autonomously converged into appropriate values depending on its neighborhood density for zero-configuration.

References

1. Transport Ministry of Land, Infrastructure, and Tourism of Japan: Advanced safety vehicles (ASV) project, http://www.mlit.go.jp/jidosha/anzen/01asv/
2. Korkmaz, G., Ekici, E., Özgüner, F., Özgüner, U.: Urban multi-hop broadcast protocol for inter-vehicle communication systems. In: Proc. of ACM VANET, pp. 76–85 (2004)
3. Lochert, C., Scheuermann, B., Mauve, M.: Probabilistic aggregation for data dissemination in VANETs. In: Proc. of ACM VANET, pp. 1–8 (2007)
4. Yu, B., Gong, J., Xu, C.Z.: Catch-up: a data aggregation scheme for VANETs. In: Proc. of ACM VANET, pp. 49–57 (2008)
5. Zhao, J., Cao, G.: Vadd: Vehicle-assisted data delivery in vehicular ad hoc networks. IEEE Transactions on Vehicular Technology 57(3), 1910–1922 (2008)
6. Gupta, I., Renesse, R., Birman, K.: Scalable fault-tolerant aggregation in large process groups. In: Proc. of IEEE Int. Conf. on Dependable Systems and Networks (DSN), pp. 433–442 (2001)
7. Madden, S., Franklin, M.J., Hellerstein, J.M., Hong, W.: Tag: a tiny aggregation service for ad-hoc sensor networks. SIGOPS Oper. Syst. Rev. 36(SI), 131–146 (2002)
8. Boulis, A., Ganeriwal, S., Srivastava, M.: Aggregation in sensor networks: an energy accuracy trade-off. Ad Hoc Networks 1(2-3), 317–331 (2003)
9. Papadopouli, M., Schulzrinne, H.: Effects of power conservation, wireless coverage and cooperation on data dissemination among mobile devices. In: Proc. of ACM MobiHoc, pp. 117–127 (2001)
10. Goldenberg, D.K., Bihler, P., Cao, M., Fang, J., Anderson, B., Morse, A., Yang, Y.: Localization in sparse networks using sweeps. In: MobiCom, pp. 110–121 (2006)
11. Li, M., Liu, Y.: Rendered path: range-free localization in anisotropic sensor networks with holes. In: Proc. of MobiCom, pp. 51–62 (2007)
12. Uchiyama, A., Fujii, S., Maeda, K., Umedu, T., Yamaguchi, H., Higashino, T.: Ad-hoc localization in urban district. In: Proc. of IEEE INFOCOM, pp. 2306–2310 (2007)
13. He, T., Huang, C., Blum, B.M., Stankovic, J.A., Abdelzaher, T.: Range-free localization schemes for large scale sensor networks. In: Proc. of MobiCom, pp. 81–95 (2003)
14. Mobireal simulator, http://www.mobireal.net/
15. Press, W., Flannery, B., Teukolsky, S., Vetterling, W.: Numerical recipes in C: the art of scientific computing, 2nd edn. Cambridge University Press, Cambridge (1992)
16. Xu, Y., Lee, W.C., Mitchell, G.: CME: a contour mapping engine in wireless sensor networks. In: Proc. of IEEE ICDCS, pp. 133–140 (2008)
17. Guha, S., Murty, R., Sirer, E.: Sextant: a unified node and event localization framework using non-convex constraints. In: Proc. of ACM MobiHoc, pp. 205–216 (2005)

MeshVision: An Adaptive Wireless Mesh Network Video Surveillance System

Peizhao Hu[1,2], Ryan Wishart[2], Jimmy Ti[2], Marius Portmann[1,2], and Jadwiga Indulska[1,2]

[1] The University of Queensland,
School of Information Technology and Electrical Engineering
{marius,jaga}@itee.uq.edu.au
[2] National ICT Australia (NICTA)
{Peizhao.Hu,Ryan.Wishart,Jimmy.Ti}@nicta.com.au

Abstract. The major surveillance camera manufacturers have begun incorporating wireless networking functionality into their products to enable wireless access. However, the video feeds from such cameras can only be accessed within the transmission range of the cameras. These cameras must be connected to backbone infrastructure in order to access them from more than one hop away. This network infrastructure is both time-consuming and expensive to install, making it impractical in many rapid deployment situations (for example to provide temporary surveillance at a crime scene). To overcome this problem, we propose the MeshVision system that incorporates wireless mesh network functionality directly into the cameras. Video streams can be pulled from any camera within a network of MeshVision cameras, irrespective of how many hops away that camera is. To manage the trade-off between video stream quality and the number of video streams that could be concurrently accessed over the network, MeshVision uses a Bandwidth Adaptation Mechanism. This mechanism monitors the wireless network looking for drops in link quality or signs of congestion and adjusts the quality of existing video streams in order to reduce that congestion. A significant benefit of the approach is that it is low cost, requiring only a software upgrade of the cameras.

1 Introduction

The global market for digital surveillance cameras has increased drastically in recent years. This market has been driven by the widespread adoption of digital surveillance technologies by business owners as well as city councils seeking to reduce crime. The scale of this adoption is shown in London, England where it has been estimated that there are over 500,000 video cameras installed [5].

To simplify future camera deployments, as well as ongoing maintenance and video stream access, the major surveillance camera manufacturers have begun incorporating 802.11g wireless networking functionality into their camera product lines.

D. Zhang et al. (Eds.): UIC 2009, LNCS 5585, pp. 193–207, 2009.

At present the feeds from such wireless-enabled cameras can only be wirelessly accessed from one hop away. To view the video feed outside of the camera's wireless transmission range requires the camera and the viewer to be connected via backbone infrastructure. This infrastructure is time consuming and expensive to deploy. Consequently, it is not practical to quickly deploy a temporary surveillance network at a crime scene or public event.

When working with wireless networks, a significant problem arises: as the wireless medium is shared it is challenging to estimate the residual bandwidth in the network at any time. This makes it difficult to provide Quality of Service by reserving bandwidth for particular flows (such as a video stream). The wireless medium is also subject to high loss rates which necessitates the use of channel coding techniques that increase delays [2]. Additionally, wireless networks have large jitter and delay characteristics to which real-time streams are very sensitive [4].

To address these problems we propose the *MeshVision* system. The approach integrates a Wireless Mesh Network (WMN) routing protocol and a bandwidth adaptation mechanism into each of the wireless surveillance cameras.

WMN are multi-hop wireless networks consisting of resource-poor, mobile mesh clients and relatively static (and comparatively resource-rich) mesh routers. The mesh routers connect together to form a backhaul network over which traffic from the mesh clients is carried.

In our approach MeshVision surveillance cameras function as mesh clients that extend the coverage of an existing mesh network or form an independent network on their own. Importantly, such cameras can route traffic, enabling multi-hop wireless communication. This multi-hop network is self-configuring (the cameras automatically discover their neighbours and find routes through the mesh) and self-healing (in that they can recover from link or node failures).

An example of a WMN created by seven MeshVision surveillance cameras is shown in Figure 1. In the Figure, a user (shown as Viewer) is able to access a video stream from camera C1 four hops away. As no cabled infrastructure is required, such a network could be rapidly deployed by emergency services or police to monitor a disaster site or crime scene.

The MeshVision system also includes a dynamic Bandwidth Adaptation Mechanism. This mechanism runs on each MeshVision camera and monitors that camera's wireless interface send queue. Elongation of this send queue acts as an indicator of poor link quality or congestion on the wireless network. When the send queue length exceeds a predefined limit the bandwidth adaptation mechanism firstly attempts to reduce bandwidth usage on the network by reducing the bandwidth consumed by video streams. This reduction is achieved by adapting the video parameters (such as frame rate, compression rate, resolution, etc.) of video streams pulled from itself as well as upstream cameras. If further adaptation is not possible, the mechanism triggers rerouting of the video streams in an attempt to rebalance the load on the network.

The major contributions of our MeshVision approach include:

- MeshVision is a low-cost solution as it requires only a software upgrade of the surveillance cameras. Commercial products intending to fulfill a similar role

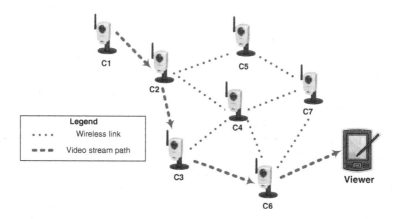

Fig. 1. An example of wireless mesh video surveillance network

(such as Motorola's MeshCam) bundle a camera with a dedicated wireless mesh router increasing the size, complexity and power requirements of the system.

- MeshVision includes an adaptation mechanism that intelligently adjusts the quality of video streams pulled from cameras on the network to ensure fair allocation of network bandwidth between cameras.
- The system includes a mesh network routing protocol that attempts to create high-capacity routes by routing around sections of the network experiencing interference and congestion.
- The bandwidth adaptation mechanism is integrated with the routing protocol so that when adaptation is not possible, rerouting of the video streams is attempted.

The remainder of this paper is structured as follows. In Section 2 we present background information relevant to our approach. An overview of related work in the field is then discussed in Section 3. We follow this in Section 4 with a discussion of MeshVision, our mesh networking and bandwidth adaptation approach for wireless surveillance cameras. An implementation is then presented in Section 5 and evaluated in Section 6. The paper is then concluded in Section 7.

2   Background

In this section of the paper we present information on the Ad hoc Distance Vector (AODV) routing protocol [7] and discuss our extended, congestion-aware version of AODV, which we refer to as AODV-CA [8]. It is this AODV-CA routing protocol that is used in our MeshVision implementation.

2.1   AODV

In the standard AODV routing protocol [7], route discovery is initiated when a node has a packet it wants to send but has no route to the packet's destination.

This results in the node broadcasting a Route Request message (RREQ) to all its one-hop neighbours.

Nodes that receive a RREQ that are (1) not the requested destination, or (2) do not have a fresh route to the destination forward the RREQ to all their one-hop neighbours. It should be noted that a node only forwards a RREQ if it has not received that RREQ before, or the metric associated with the RREQ is better than the metric it currently has for the route to the RREQ source. In this way the RREQ is flooded through the network with its spread controlled by a time to live field (decremented on each hop). Once this time to live value reaches zero, the RREQ is dropped.

When a RREQ is received by the requested destination node, or a node with a fresh route to the destination, a Route Reply (RREP) message is sent. This RREP travels back along the reverse path over which the corresponding RREQ was received. Each node that receives the RREP creates a route back to the sender of the RREP. When the RREP is received by the source of the RREQ, a bi-directional route exists between it and the requested destination.

2.2 AODV-CA

In our previous work we developed a congestion-aware variant of AODV referred to as AODV-CA [8]. Improvements over the standard AODV include a new routing metric to measure the "goodness" of routes as well as support for multi-radio nodes.

The new metric is known as the Channel Diverse Congestion Aware (CDCA) metric and has two components capturing the channel diversity and expected channel congestion along the route.

To acquire the link congestion information, the metric uses the IFQ (Interface Queue) length information from the node's wireless card driver. This queue contains all outbound layer-2 frames to be transmitted by the physical layer. A build up of frames in the IFQ indicates congestion, either due to traffic load or due to low link quality. Our routing metric incorporates the IFQ length as it also reflects a number of link parameters including: link quality, link capacity, interference, and background noise. Furthermore, the IFQ length is information that is locally available at the data link layer, and does not require communication with other nodes or any expensive operations such as active probing (an approach whereby probe packets are sent to all neighbours at regular intervals).

In order to make the IFQ lengths comparable between links with dissimilar data rates, we divide the IFQ length by the current data rate (BW) of a link to compute the estimated time required to empty the queue, which we refer to as the Queue Discharge Interval (QDI).

$$QDI = \frac{IFQ}{BW}$$

The QDI represents the minimum time a packet has to remain in the IFQ before being transmitted on to the physical medium. By normalizing the QDI we ensure that the QDI of different nodes with varying channel bandwidths are made comparable. The Cumulative QDI (CG) of a path consisting of n links is the sum of the QDIs of all links forming that particular path.

$$CG = \sum_{i=1}^{n} QDI_i = \sum_{i=1}^{n} \frac{IFQ_i}{BW_i}$$

The computed CG is included in the Route Request header of AODV-CA routing protocol and stored at each hop along the route. Subsequently received Route Request packets with a lower QDI value are updated to remain the lowest QDI possible. To select a route with the lowest QDI value, the CG value is also retained in the routing table as the cost of the Reverse Route to the source.

3   Related Work

In the literature a number of publications have examined the problem of flow control for multi-media streams as well as video streaming over wireless networks.

For example, Akyildiz et al. [1] developed the Rate Control Scheme (RCS) that works in a TCP-friendly way to control the transmission rate of video streams over lossy network links. Their approach uses *dummy* messages initially sent at the application's expected data, and then sent periodically, to gauge the remaining bandwidth and round trip time along a path. This information can be fed into an adaptive encoder to adjust video stream quality and thus the bandwidth consumed by the video stream. RCS is able to differentiate between link congestion and packet transmission errors, and apply different transmission control algorithms for each case. For example, packet losses due to link congestion cause the transmit rate at the sender to drop. Packet losses due to errors initially cause the transmission rate to be cut and a burst of probes to be sent to the receiver. Should these be acknowledged then the transmission rate resumes at its previous level. By treating congestion and packet errors separately, RCS is able to support higher bandwidths over lossy links than other TCP-style transmission control protocols can. A downside of this approach is that it is concerned with flow-control over a particular route and has no mechanisms to rebalance traffic in the network.

Zhu et al. also applied a similar rate allocation approach to minimize playback distortion while limiting the increase in network congestion [9]. In their work, each node has a MAC layer monitor, a congestion minimizing routing agent and an application layer video streaming agent. The MAC layer monitor records the time spent sending, the time spent waiting to send and the actual time receiving frames. This information is used to estimate link usage and residual bandwidth on the links. The routing agents distributively decide on routes through the multi-hop network for video streams while the streaming agent dynamically adapts the video feed (using information provided by the lower layers) in order to manage the handoff between playback distortion and network congestion.

A significant drawback of the approach is that it requires nodes to exchange a large amount of information about their existing video streams and current delay information whenever a new route needs to be discovered.

Licandro and Schembra presented a mechanism to support video feeds over a multi-hop wireless mesh network in [4] . In their approach, wireless surveillance cameras attach to an infrastructure mesh network. Each camera encodes its packets using MPEG-4 such that the quality (and hence packet size) does not cause the transmit buffer to grow more than a set length. The approach assumes a static backbone of mesh routers over which the surveillance traffic can be carried. Routing over the network is done using a proactive, multi-path approach in which multiple paths are proactively discovered between all nodes.

A significant issue with this approach is that it relies on a static mesh router backbone as the wireless cameras are not able themselves to form a mesh network. The use of multi-path routing also introduces unnecessary overheads in that it requires multiple independent routes to be discovered (and then maintained). Additionally a packet reordering and a packet jitter buffer are needed at the viewer side to remove the effects of the multi-path routing (whereby the same packet can arrive at different times at the receiver). A further problem lies in the use of a proactive routing protocol. Such protocols perform poorly when the network topology changes frequently (e.g., because of high node mobility).

Huang et al. [3], presented an approach to real-time media streaming designed for wireless networks. In their work they use the H.263 codec for video conferencing over the Internet. The video stream produced by the codec groups frames into a Group of Pictures (GOP). Within this GOP, there is one I-frame and a further 14 P-frames which reference the I-frame. One GOP is transmitted every second (i.e. the frame rate is 15 fps by default). In Huang et al.'s work P-frames are selectively dropped depending on the amount of congestion in the network (determined using packet Round Trip Time). Three levels of response are proposed with congested networks dropping all of the P-frames, lightly loaded networks dropping half the P-frames and unloaded networks dropping none. A significant problem with the approach is that with only 3 levels of adaptation available, it is very coarse-grained. Lastly, the approach was primarily developed for the MPEG family of codecs (as it depends on the use of P-frames) and cannot be widely applied to other encoding protocols, such as Motion JPEG.

4   MeshVision

The MeshVision system we introduce in this paper incorporates a wireless mesh network routing protocol as well as a dynamic bandwidth adaptation mechanism. This section covers each of these separately.

4.1   Wireless Mesh Network Routing Protocol

The mesh networking functionality that MeshVision brings to wireless surveillance cameras is enabled by a wireless mesh network routing protocol. While our approach is routing protocol independent, the protocol must meet certain requirements, particularly:

- The routing protocol must be low overhead.
- The routing protocol should discover routes on an as-needed basis.
- The routing protocol should consider congestion information when choosing a path between the source and the destination nodes in the mesh network.

The first two requirements are significant because the cameras typically come with a single wireless interface and have processors optimized for video processing. This limits the amount of network-related processing that can be done. Consequently, the routing protocol used on the camera must not require a high level of communication between nodes. This suggests that the protocol should use a reactive approach (like the AODV protocol) whereby routes are only discovered when needed.

The final requirement is for the protocol to be congestion-aware. As video streams are sensitive to network congestion it is important that a low-congestion route be discovered for each new video stream. MeshVision is then able to dynamically adapt the video stream quality to cope with changing network conditions and application requirements.

4.2   Dynamic Bandwidth Adaptation Mechanism

The second function of the MeshVision software is to balance video stream quality against network congestion. When the level of network congestion increases, the mechanism reduces the quality of video streams pulled from cameras on the network. Conversely, a drop in network congestion results in the mechanism attempting to increase the quality of video streams pulled from the surveillance cameras.

To facilitate this in MeshVision, each camera runs a bandwidth adaptation mechanism (BAM) daemon. The mechanism operates as follows.

Firstly, whenever an application pulls a video feed from a camera, it must register a Quality of Service window for the feed with that camera's BAM. This window contains maximum and minimum values for the video stream parameters (such as frame rate, resolution and compression ratio) and is stored by the BAM for the duration of the video feed.

Once video streams are being pulled from the camera, the BAM monitors the congestion on the wireless network surrounding the camera. This congestion is approximated by monitoring the length of the outgoing packet queue on the camera's wireless interface. In the Linux operating system this queue is referred to as the IFQ (Interface Queue), a term which we adopt in this paper. The IFQ length increases if packets cannot be sent fast enough, if the wireless medium is in use or if packets must be retransmitted.

The monitoring procedure and subsequent behaviour of the BAM is shown in the flowchart in Figure 2.

As shown in the flowchart, the BAM continuously monitors the IFQ value of the camera's wireless interface. When this value exceeds a set threshold, shown as IFQ_MAX, the BAM initiates the adaptation process. To distinguish this BAM from other BAMs we refer to it as the *adaptation initiator*.

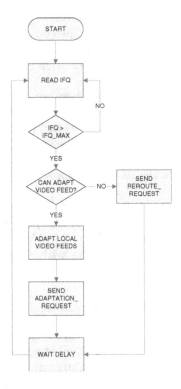

Fig. 2. Flowchart showing MeshVision bandwidth reduction process

If the adaptation initiator has video feeds that can be reduced in quality (i.e. the video feeds are not at their minimum quality specified in the Quality of Service window), the initiator firstly downgrades the quality of its own video feed and then sends an $ADAPTATION\_REQUEST$ message to all upstream cameras (i.e. cameras that route their video stream traffic through the adaptation initiator's camera).

If adaptation of the feeds is no longer possible (because video feeds drawn from the adaptation initiator are all at their lowest QoS level), rerouting of traffic is attempted. To do this the initiator sends out a $REROUTE\_REQUEST$ message. This message is sent to the furthest away camera (where distance is measured in hops). If, after a set delay period, the IFQ value on the initiator node has not reduced, a $REROUTE\_REQUEST$ is sent to the next furthest away camera. This process is repeated until all upstream cameras have been sent a $REROUTE\_REQUEST$.

When the BAM running on a camera receives a $REROUTE\_REQUEST$ it causes the routing protocol to relaunch the route discovery process. If a better path is discovered the video feed is switched over to the new path.

Here we have described how the BAM is able to reduce the quality of video feeds in order to balance quality against reducing network bandwidth. In situations where the available bandwidth increases, the above procedure can be run in reverse. That is, if the IFQ length on a camera remains higher than a set threshold, referred to as IFQ_MIN (where $IFQ\_MIN < IFQ\_MAX$), the BAM can adjust its own video feed quality in small increments. Each increment would be followed by a waiting period to see if any downstream cameras send an $ADAPTATION\_REQUEST$ indicating that video quality should be reduced again.

With such an approach it is possible that video quality reductions following an $ADAPTATION\_REQUEST$ free up too much bandwidth in the network which causes nodes to increase their video quality again. This may trigger another $ADAPTATION\_REQUEST$ from downstream cameras. This process could repeat itself indefinitely. To prevent this occurring, the video quality increase should include a hysteresis component so that increases following an $ADAPTION\_REQUEST$ become less aggressive.

We leave a full investigation of this bandwidth recovery process for future work and concentrate on the bandwidth reduction process in the rest of this paper.

5   Implementation

To evaluate the viability of the MeshVision system we created a proof-of-concept implementation. This implementation used the Axis 207W/WM and 211W wireless surveillance cameras from Axis Communications (shown in Figure 3). These camera models are equipped with an ARTPEC-A CPU, 32 MB (64 MB on the 211W) of RAM and a wireless interface with a 1.6 dBi antenna. The dimensions of the cameras are 85 x 55 x 34 mm and 44 x 88 x 200 mm respectively. The cameras use a custom build of Linux kernel 2.6.

The MeshVision system incorporates a routing protocol and also a Bandwidth Adaptation Mechanism.

To provide the routing functionality we employed our AODV-CA routing protocol (described in Section 2). The implementation of this protocol was based on the AODV-UU 0.9.5 open source code base from Uppsala University [6]. We used AODV-CA as it fulfills all the routing protocol requirements listed in Section 4.1.

The BAM component was implemented as a user-space daemon process written in C. For our proof-of-concept, the BAM applied adaptation to video streams by modifying the frame rate and MPEG-4 compression ratio only. These two

Fig. 3. The Axis 207W/MW and 211W cameras on which the prototype MeshVision implementation was constructed

parameters were used as they were the most easily changed on the camera platform, though in a full implementation other video parameters such as camera resolution could also be modified.

When performing an adaptation to reduce video quality, the BAM calculated the video stream's new compression $c_{i'}$ and frame rates $f_{i'}$ using the equations below. The term i is taken as the number of hops from the adaptation initiator:

$$c_{i'} = c_i + d \times (hc_i + 1) \times \alpha \times (c_{max} - c_{min}); \tag{1}$$

$$f_{i'} = f_i - d \times (hc_i + 1) \times (1 - \alpha) \times (f_{max} - f_{min}); \tag{2}$$

The terms in these two equations are to be interpreted as follows:

- c_i and f_i are the current values of compression ratio and frame rate before the adaptation;
- d is the percentage of the current video quality to which camera at each hop should be reduced; this should be set to a relatively small value (around 1-2%) to maintain the best video quality possible throughout the system;
- hc_i is the hop count from the initiator camera (e.g., hc to itself is 0);
- α is a weight parameter that biases the system toward either better image quality of individual frames (i.e., lower compression ratio) or better awareness of changes in a set of image frames (i.e., higher frame rate);
- c_{max} and c_{min} are the upper and lower bound of compression rate supported by the camera; and
- f_{max} and f_{min} are the upper and lower bound of frame rate supported by the camera.

6   Evaluation

To test the viability of our MeshVision scheme, we created an experimental testbed consisting of one 211W and five 207W/MW wireless surveillance cameras from Axis Communications. A chain topology was used for the network configuration as shown in Figure 4. The cameras were connected using 802.11g, wireless channel 1. As all cameras were within range of one another during the testing, layer-2 MAC filtering was used to enforce the network topology.

The roles of Client 1 and Client 2 within the testbed were performed by two Dell Latitude D610 laptops running Linux 2.6.24. The machines were equipped with one 802.11b/g interface each.

Three different experiments were performed as part of the evaluation which looked: at the maximum throughput the surveillance cameras could achieve over multiple hops, the maximum number of video streams that could be supported without the BAM running, and the number of video streams supported with the BAM active on each camera within the testbed.

6.1   Throughput Evaluation

In this first experiment, our goal was to measure the average maximum throughput that could be achieved using wireless mesh-enabled cameras arranged in a

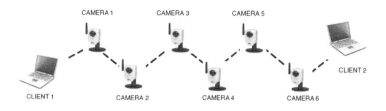

Fig. 4. Mesh network-enabled testbed topology

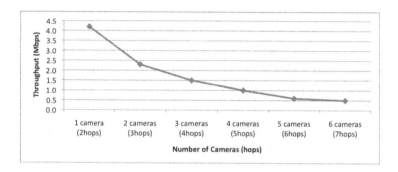

Fig. 5. Quantitative performance evaluation results

chain topology. The offered load for this experiment was produced using the *iperf* utility. Client 1 was set up to be an iperf client, while Client 2 functioned as an iperf server. It should be noted that the bandwidth adaptation approach was not used during this experiment.

We varied the number of cameras (i.e., hops) in the chain and measured the maximum throughput achieved between Client 1 and Client 2.

The results of the experiment are plotted in Figure 5. From the Figure it can be seen that the maximum throughput obtained for these experiments was 4.2 Mbps in the 2 hop scenario, dropping to approximately 500 Kbps in the 7 hop scenario. The drop in bandwidth as the number of hops increases can be explained by the shared nature of the wireless medium. Because of this characteristic, nodes can not send and receive at the same time; and each node is competing to send its own packets.

These results demonstrate that the MeshVision concept of loading routing software onto the wireless surveillance cameras is feasible. In particular, the resource-limited cameras can run the AODV-CA routing protocol, form a mesh network and are capable of sustaining hundreds of kilobits per second data rates over multiple hops.

6.2 Determination of Number of Supported Video Streams

In our initial testing we attempted to determine the number of video feeds that the network could support *without* the MeshVision adaptation mechanism. The

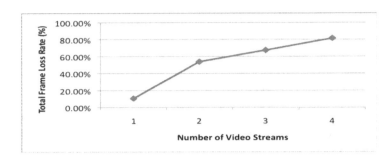

Fig. 6. Packet loss rates with no adaptation

tests were performed with the camera resolution set to 480x360. The MPEG-4 codec was used with 30% compression and a frame rate of 30 fps for transferring the video. The results of the test are shown in Figure 6 which plots the number of concurrent video streams against the number of lost layer-2 frames. The number of lost frames was determined using the Wireshark[1] packet sniffing utility. As can be seen in the Figure, the percentage of lost packet frames rises quickly as more video streams are added, reaching nearly 80% for 4 concurrent video streams. The network would not support any additional video streams beyond four.

These results suggest the need for video stream quality adaptation, particularly in dynamic networks where the video settings that give the best quality while supporting as many cameras as possible cannot be determined *a priori*.

6.3   Bandwidth Adaptation Mechanism Evaluation

To evaluate the performance of the bandwidth adaptation mechanism (BAM), the testbed was configured into the chain topology shown in Figure 7. This topology was enforced with MAC layer filtering.

As with the previous test, the cameras were set to use a resolution of 480x360 pixels with the MPEG-4 codec at 30% compression and 30 fps. The value of parameter d from equations 1 and 2 was set to be 1%.

In our testing, a video stream viewer application running on Client 1 was used to pull concurrent video feeds from each of the six cameras in the chain topology. The video streams were initiated starting with Camera 6, then in descending order to Camera 1. Arrows indicating the path taken by each of the video streams can be seen in Figure 7.

After a video feed was started, the BAM on Camera 1 evaluated its IFQ length. If this value was more than the IFQ_MAX, the bandwidth adaptation procedure described in Section 4 was run. Only when the IFQ value reduced below IFQ_MAX was a new video session started. The value of IFQ_MAX used for the experiments was particular to the wireless cameras driver implementation and determined based on prior experimentation.

---

[1] http://www.wireshark.org/

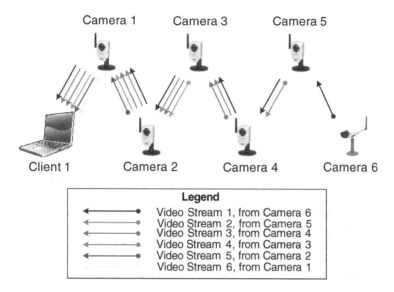

Fig. 7. Testbed topology showing direction of video flows from the cameras

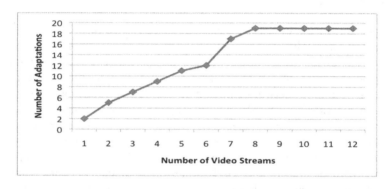

Fig. 8. Number of adaptations required to support the desired number of video streams

The number of network-wide adaptations required before the next video stream could be initiated is plotted in Figure 8.

As can be seen in the Figure, one video stream required two adaptations, while for 5 streams the adaptation processes needed to be run 12 times to reduce the IFQ value on Camera 1 to below IFQ_MAX. The corresponding frame loss rates are also given in Figure 9. As can be seen by comparing Figure 6 and Figure 9, the BAM was able to cut the layer-2 frame loss rate from nearly 80% to 5% (for four concurrent video streams).

Further tests were conducted with 7 to 12 video feeds. The 7th feed was pulled from Camera 6, the 8th from Camera 5 and so on. The number of adaptations required before the next stream could be initiated is shown in Figure 8, while the corresponding frame loss rates are shown in Figure 9.

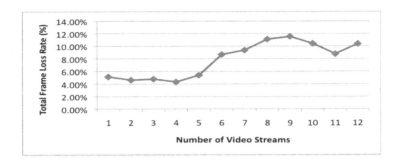

Fig. 9. Packet loss rates for video streams when using BAM

This experiment has shown that up to 12 concurrent video streams (2 pulled from each camera) can be supported with our adaptation approach. Running 12 concurrent video streams requires the adaptation procedure to be repeated 19 times. In comparison, when not using our adaptation approach a maximum of four video streams could be supported.

7   Conclusion

The current generation of wireless network cameras can only be wirelessly accessed one hop away. The cameras must be connected to backbone infrastructure before they can be accessed outside of the cameras wireless transmission range. To overcome this problem we introduced the MeshVision system. MeshVision combines wireless mesh network functionality with intelligent bandwidth adaptation. Cameras running MeshVision are able to route and forward traffic for one another. This means that video feeds can be accessed across multiple hops. The bandwidth adaptation mechanism running on every MeshVision camera seeks to balance video feed quality with available bandwidth in order to get the best performance out of the wireless mesh surveillance network. Testing of the MeshVision Bandwidth Adaptation Mechanism showed that it increased the number of concurrent video feeds pulled over a testbed network from 4 to 12.

Acknowledgement

NICTA is funded by the Australian Government as represented by the Department of Broadband, Communications and the Digital Economy and the Australian Research Council through the ICT Centre of Excellence program; and the Queensland Goverment.

References

1. Akyildiz, I.F., Akan, O.B., Morabito, G.: A Rate Control Scheme for Adaptive Real-Time Applications in IP Networks with Lossy Links and Long Round Trip Times. IEEE/ACM Transactions on Networking 13(3) (June 2005)

2. Feng, W., Walpole, J., Feng, W., Pu, C.: Moving towards massively scalable video-based sensor networks. In: Proceedings of the Workshop on New Visions for Large-Scale Networks: Research and Applications, pp. 12–14 (2001)
3. Huang, C.M., Yu, Y.T., Lin, Y.W.: An Adaptive control Scheme for Real-time Media Streaming over Wireless Networks. In: Proceedings of the 17th IEEE International Conference on Advanced Information Networking and Applications (AINA 2003), pp. 373–378 (2003)
4. Licandro, F., Schembra, G.: Wireless Mesh Networks to Support Video Surveillance: Architecture, Protocol, and Implementation Issues. EURASIP Journal on Wireless Communications and Networking 2007(1) (2007)
5. McCahill, M., Norris, C.: Cctv in london. Working paper No.6 for UrbanEye - the 5th Framework Programme of the European Commission, page 20 (2002)
6. Nordstrom, E.: University of Uppsala open source implementation of AODV
7. Perkins, C., Belding-Royer, E., Das, S.: Ad hoc On-Demand Distance Vector (AODV) Routing. RFC 3561 (2003)
8. Pirzada, A.A., Wishart, R., Portmann, M., Indulska, J.: A wireless mesh network routing protocol for incident area networks. Journal of Pervasive and Mobile Computing, Special Issue on Global Security (2009)
9. Zhu, X., Girod, B.: Media-aware multi-user rate allocation over wireless mesh network. In: Proceedings of the IEEE First Workshop on Operator-Assisted (Wireless Mesh) Community Networks (OpComm 2006) (September 2006)

SDEC: A P2P Semantic Distance Embedding Based on Virtual Coordinate System*

Yufeng Wang[1,3], Akihiro Nakao[2,3], and Jianhua Ma[4]

[1] Nanjing University of Posts and Telecommunication, 210003, China
[2] University of Tokyo, Japan
[3] National Institute of Information and Communications Technology (NICT), Japan
[4] Hosei University, Japan

Abstract. Large-scale P2P applications can benefit from the ability to predict semantic distances to other peers without having to contact them first. In this paper, we propose a novel semantic distance embedding approach, SDEC, in P2P network, which assigns synthetic coordinates to peers such that the distance between the coordinates of two peers approximately predicts the semantic distance between any two peers. Specifically, the semantic distance between peers is quantitatively characterized through vector space model based on peers' semantic profiles, and then, based on measured semantic distances from a peer to a handful of other peers and the current coordinates of those peers, we adopt the spring relaxation method, mimicking the physical mass-spring system, to simulate the semantic embedding procedure, which can find minimal energy configuration corresponding to relatively accurate semantic embedding. Simulation results show that a 3-dimensional Euclidean model can embed these peers with relatively high accuracy.

Keywords: Peer-to-Peer, semantic distance, similarity search.

1 Introduction

Knowledge of the semantic distances between all peers can significantly improve the search performance in P2P network. In general, there exist two ways to investigate the semantic-based cluster in P2P system, one way is: the implicit semantic patterns observed in successive searches can be used as the clustering criterion. For example, Ref. [1] proposed to create interest-based shortcut to locate content quickly. The basic idea is that if a peer has a particular piece of content that one is interested in, then it is likely that it will have other pieces of content that one is also interested in. Therefore, the peers with similar interest establish shortcut superposed on the P2P network to improve search performance; another way is: a peer explicitly represents its interest with keyword set summarized from its shared contents, then, through methods in Information Retrieval (IR), P2P systems infer peer's interest and guide it to appropriate semantic cluster. Specifically, Ref. [2] proposed a model in which peers advertise

---

* This research is partially support by the 973 Programs 2007CB310607 and 2009CB320504, 863 Project 2007AA01Z206, NSFC Grants 60802022 and 60772062.

D. Zhang et al. (Eds.): UIC 2009, LNCS 5585, pp. 208–220, 2009.

their expertise in the P2P network, and the knowledge about the expertise of other peers forms a semantic topology. Based on the semantic similarity between the subject of a query and the expertise of other peers, a peer can select appropriate peers to forward queries to, instead of broadcasting the query or sending it to a random set of peers. For a P2P system holding massive amount of data, efficient semantic based topology construction (that is, peers are enabled to actively influence network structure by choosing their neighbors) is a key determinant to its scalability. Several new algorithms are proposed to construct semantic small-world P2P networks, which consists of peers maintaining a number of short-range links which are semantically similar to the node, together with a small collection of long-range links that help increase recall rate of information retrieval as well as reduce network traffic [3~5].

In all the above approaches, it is imperative for each peer to know about the semantic distance to other peers. One basic method to learn semantic locality is to actively probe (or advertised by) all peers in the network, like approaches described above. But, in relatively small or middle-size P2P system, it is possible to perform extensive measurements and make decision based on global information. However, the cost associated with active monitoring to estimate distance is non-negligible (almost $O(N^2)$) for large-scale distributed applications.

In this paper, we develop an alternative way, SDEC (Semantic Distance Embedding based on virtual Coordinate System), to infer the semantic distance between any two peers in P2P system. SDEC assigns synthetic coordinates to peers such that the distance between the coordinates of two peers approximately predicts the semantic distances between any two peers. SDEC uses spring relaxation to find minimal energy configurations. Conceptually, this minimization places a spring between each pair of peers (i, j) with a rest length set to the known semantic distance (sd_{ij}). The current length of the spring is considered to be the distance between the peers in the coordinate space. The potential energy of such a spring is proportional to the square of the displacement from its rest length, and the sum of these energies over all springs is exactly the squared-error function in semantic distance estimation we want to minimize. Thus, we can minimize it by simulating the movements of peers under the spring forces. Specifically, a peer allows itself to be pushed for a short iterative step by the corresponding spring; each of these movements reduces the peer's error with respect to one other in the system. As peers continually communicate with other peers, they converge to coordinates that predict semantic distance well. The contribution of our paper lies in that we properly adapt ideas of spring relaxation to perform the semantic distance embedding in virtual coordinate system, which can approximate peers' real semantic distance well. Simulation results show that a 3-dimensional Euclidean model can embed peers' semantic distance with relatively high accuracy. Intuitively, our approach has great application in P2P system, for example, based on our approach, it is easy to cluster peer according to their content interests, which can greatly improve the search performance in P2P systems.

In general, in order to avoid the need for real-time measurement, virtual coordinate systems have been developed in Internet research field, to predict latencies between arbitrary hosts in a network. These systems allow a node to map itself to a virtual coordinate based on a small number of actual distance estimate from a subset of nodes, such that distance between two peers' synthetic coordinates predicts the RTT (Round-Trip-Time) between them in the Internet. Two main architectures for virtual coordinate systems have emerged: landmark-based and decentralized. Landmark-based systems rely on centralized components (such as a set of landmark servers) to predict distance between any two hosts. The set of landmarks can be pre-determined or randomly selected [6]. Decentralized virtual coordinate systems, do not rely on explicitly designated infrastructure nodes [7]. Those two kinds of systems share the similar querying mechanism used by each node to assign and maintain its own coordinates. That is, each node maintains a reference set of randomly (or intentionally) selected nodes from which to periodically query one node at random for an update. Each query response is used to recalculate the requester's coordinates, and coordinate updates are optimized based on system-dependent numerical error minimization techniques [8]. Specifically, based on spring relaxation method, Ref. [7] provided a simple, adaptive, decentralized algorithm, Vivaldi, for computing synthetic coordinates for Internet hosts. Ref. [9] deeply investigated the accuracy of those existing Internet latency embedding systems in terms of their proposed measurements, which also be used in our paper to illustrate the performance of our approach.

Our paper is greatly inspired by the related works above. To authors' knowledge, it is first work to apply the virtual coordinate system to infer the semantic distance in P2P network. The main benefit of our work lies in that, through measuring semantic distances from peers to a handful of other peers, SDEC can approximately predicts the semantic distances between any two peers.

The paper is organized as follows: section 2 offers the method to summarize peers' semantic profile based on documents shared in the peer. The semantic embedding algorithm, SDEC, is proposed in section 3, including the detailed procedure to perform semantic distance embedding in virtual coordinate space. In section 4, the simulation settings are given, and in terms of several measurements, the embedding accuracy of SDEC is evaluated in 2-dimension and 3-dimension Euclidean space. Finally, we briefly conclude our paper, and point out the future work.

2 Peer's Semantic Profile

Representation and extraction of semantic meanings from each peer is essential in our approach. In the paper, we assume that each peer is associated with a "profile", i.e., a summarization of its contents. Thus, our approach needs to compile user profiles containing information about users' preferences, and then measures the semantic distance between the profiles. From a real-world perspective, the documents held by a peer typically reflect the characteristics of that peer, since a peer has limited storage capability and may not keep documents that are not of interest. Therefore, users can be distinguished by the documents they hold. The goal of our paper was to investigate whether the algorithm, SDEC, can work and how it will perform in comparison with real semantic distance. This means that some simplifying assumptions had to be made in order to reduce the complexity of the problem, while, modeling the real word as realistically as possible. We chose not to work with real documents, for simplicity, we assume that document can be categorized based on the tagged semantic category. Preferences for different categories of documents can be used to distinguish the characteristics of each peer. Let p_i be the profile of user i. Profile p_i is defined as a vector of weights $p_i = \left(p_{i,C_1}, p_{i,C_2}, \cdots, p_{i,C_n}, \cdots \right)$, where the weight p_{i,C_n} denotes user i's preference for the documents described by the semantic category C_n, and p_{i,C_n} is de-

fined as follows: $p_{i,C_n} = \dfrac{|\Omega_{i,C_n}|}{|\Omega_i|}$ (1)

where Ω_i is the set of documents held by peer i and Ω_{i,C_n} is a subset of Ω_i including all documents pertaining to the semantic category C_n. Note that, in our algorithm,
file are not required to be text documents (for example, they may be music file as
well), but it is needed to have a textual description for those files, i.e., a number of
keywords summarizing their content.

Additionally, we assume that there exists a distance function which allows us to
calculate semantic distances between pairs of profiles. Specifically, we employ Vector Space Model (*VSM*) that has been widely used in previous information retrieval
literature. *VSM* measures semantic distance of two peers i and j, as follows:

$$d_{ij} = -\log sim(p_i, p_j) = -\log \frac{\sum_{k=1}^{K} P_{i,k} P_{j,k}}{\sqrt{\sum_{k=1}^{K} P_{i,k}^2} \sqrt{\sum_{k=1}^{K} P_{j,k}^2}}$$ (2)

Where K is the total number of semantic categories.

The above equation implies that, if peer i and j have similar tastes in certain style
of contents, then $sim(p_i, p_j)$ returns a large value, and the semantic distance between
peer i and j is relatively small. Intuitively, if two peers are semantically similar (that
is, small semantic distance between peers), they should not only have similar propor-
tions of topics, but also, the total number of documents should be close to each other
[4][5]. This assumption can be motivated by the following consideration: for example,
even though three peers A (with documents 500), B (with documents 400) and C
(with documents 10) possess similar semantic profile, intuitively, peers A and B
should be closer than other cases. Thus, we expand the above similarity-based semantic distance to measure weighted semantic distance between two peers. In brief, for
any two peers i and j, the semantic profile are represented as $\{N_i, p_i\}$ and $\{N_j, p_j\}$,
respectively, where N is the number of documents shared by corresponding peer, so
the final semantic distance sd_{ij} (weighted semantic distance with document number) is
given as:

$$sd_{ij} = \frac{1 + \log \max(N_i, N_j)}{1 + \log \min(N_i, N_j)} d_{ij} = -\frac{1 + \log \max(N_i, N_j)}{1 + \log \min(N_i, N_j)} \log sim(p_i, p_j)$$ (3)

Note that, for simplicity, our paper assumes that document can be categorized
based on the tagged semantic category and preferences for different categories of
documents can be used to distinguish the semantic profile of each peer. More general
approach to generate peers' semantic profile is to adapt TF×IDF weight (Term Fre-
quency×Inverse Document Frequency) often used in information retrieval and text
mining. Originally, TF×IDF weight is a statistical measure used to evaluate how important a word is to a document in a collection or corpus. The importance increases
proportionally to the number of times a word appears in the document but is offset by
the frequency of the word in the corpus [11]. We can sum the TF*IDF weights of

keywords in all documents shared by peer to represent the peer's semantic profile. But, our main motivation of this paper is to investigate the feasibility and applicability of virtual coordinate system in P2P semantic estimation, we simply use semantic category to represent each document. Ref. [12] also introduced several metrics, like Minkowski distance and Kullback-Leibler divergence etc., to represent the similarity (or dissimilarity) in semantic Web. One of our future works is to adopt other semantic distance measurements to verify our proposed approach.

3 SDEC Algorithm

In this section, we present a simple distributed algorithm, SDEC, which computes virtual coordinates for peers based on measurements of semantic distances from each peer to a few other peers. Then, we refine this distributed algorithm to converge quickly to relatively accurate coordinates. Let sd_{ij} be the actual semantic distance between peer i and j (calculated by the equation 3), and $coordinate(i)$ be the coordinate assigned to peer i. we can characterize the error in the coordinates using a squared-error function E, which measures how well our inferred coordinates match with the actual semantic distance:

$$E = \sum_i \sum_j \left(sd_{ij} - \|coordinate(i) - coordinate(j)\|\right)^2 \qquad (4)$$

Where $\|coordinate(i)\text{-}coordinate(j)\|$ is the distance between the coordinates of peer i and j in the chosen coordinate space. The reason to choose squared error function lies in that it has an analogue to the energy in a physical mass-spring system: minimizing the energy in a spring network is equivalent to minimizing the squared-error function in virtual coordinate system. Since the squared-error function is equivalent to spring energy, we can minimize it by simulating the movements of nodes under the spring forces. Specifically, define F_{ij} to be force vector that the spring between peer i and j exerts on peer i. From Hooke's law, we can show that F_{ij} is:

$$F_{ij} = \left(sd_{ij} - \|coordinate\ (i) - coordinate\ (j)\|\right) \times u(coordinate\ (i) - coordinate\ (j)) \qquad (5)$$

Where $\left(sd_{ij} - \|coordinate(i) - coordinate(j)\|\right)$ is the displacement of the spring from rest, which gives the magnitude of the force exerted by the spring on i and j (for the sake of simplicity, we set the spring constant as unity). The unit vector $u(coordinate(i)\text{-}coordinate(j))$ gives the direction of the force on i.

To simulate the spring network's evolution, SDEC considers iterative step δ_i (peer i's adaptive interval). At each interval, the algorithm moves peer i's position in virtual coordinate space a small distance in the direction of F_{ij} and then re-calculates all the forces. That is, when peer i with $coordinate(i)$ learns about peer j with $coordinate(j)$ and measures semantic distance between i and j, sd_{ij}, it updates its coordinates using the following rule:

$$coordinate(i) = coordinate(i) + \delta_i \times \left(sd_{ij} - \|coordinate(i) - coordiante(j)\|\right) \times u(cordinate(i) - coordinate(j)) \qquad (6)$$

In the procedure described above, we need deal with two challenges:

① Because, initially, all nodes start at the same location, SDEC must separate them somehow. Thus, we definite $u(0)$ to be a unit-length vector with a randomly chosen direction. Two peers occupying the same location will have a spring pushing them away from each other in some arbitrary direction.

② An additional challenge is handling peers that have a high error in their coordinates. If a peer i communicates with some peer that has coordinates predicting semantic distances badly, any update made by i based on those coordinates is likely to increase prediction error rather than decrease it. Intuitively, we hope the equation (6) achieve the following effects: an accurate node sampling an inaccurate node will not move much, and an inaccurate node sampling an accurate node will move a lot. Thus, SDEC adaptively varies the iterative step of peers i, δ_i, according to the following rule:

$$w_i = e_i / (e_i + e_j), \delta_i = c_1 \cdot w_i \qquad (7)$$

where e_i denote the local peer i's error estimate about its coordinate, and e_j represent the remote peer j's error estimate; c_1 is a constant, for experimental experience, $c_1=0.15$ causes little oscillation in simulations. The following problem is that the adaptive iterative step described above requires that peers have a running estimate of how accurate their coordinates are. Each peer compares the new measured semantic distance sample with the actual semantic distance, and maintains a moving average of recent relative errors (absolute error divided by actual semantic distance, denoted as e_s) to represent the peer's estimation error. That is, e_i is updated as follows:

$$e_s = \left\| \|coordinate\,(i) - coordinate\,(j)\| - sd_{ij} \right\| / sd_{ij}$$

$$e_i = e_s \times c_2 \times w_i + e_i \times (1 - c_2 \times w_i) \qquad (8)$$

Similarly, let $c_2=0.15$, in our simulation.

Based on the above procedures, the SDEC algorithm works as follows: each peer maintains its own current coordinates, starting with coordinates at the origin. Whenever a peer queries another peer, it measures the semantic distance to that peer and also learns that peer's current coordinates, then the following *ADJUST* function is invoked by the very peer. The above procedure is repeated, until the squared-error estimate, shown in Eq. (4), is less than certain threshold.

The outline of *ADJUST* function is given as follows:

// **INPUT:** Peer i measures node j to be sd_{ij} away, and node j said it has coordinate *coordinate*(j), and an error estimate of e_j.

// **OUTPUT:** peer i's estimated *coordinate*(i), and peer i's estimation error e_i

ADJUST(sd_{ij}, *coordinate*(j), e_j)

Compute the adaptive iterative interval δ_i, according to Eq. (7);

Update peer i's local coordinate *coordinate*(i), according to Eq. (6);
Update peer i's estimation error e_i, according to Eq. (8).

---

4 Simulation Settings and Results

4.1 Simulation Setting and Measurements

The following parameters are used in our simulations:

Number of Peers: 500~1000; Number of semantic categories: 10;

Number of documents on each peer: 5~100;

Document distribution to peers: the document distribution in P2P networks is rarely completely random, but often has certain properties. The finding of [13] suggest that the number of files per peer is significantly skewed in typical P2P networks: there are a few peers that hold a large number of documents whereas the majority of the peers share few files. We chose to model this by Zipf distribution with parameters $\alpha = 1.5$.

The distribution of semantic category to documents: we presume that each document can be classified according to the semantic category it covers, and, for our simulation, we assume this classification to be available for all documents, and furthermore, each document has exactly one semantic category.

Querying Patterns: obviously, querying patterns, that is, the way to select how much peers to query and who to query, will affect accuracy of our algorithm. In this paper, we experiment two query patterns: query peers with documents as much as possible, so-called regular querying, and query peers selected randomly, so-called random querying.

We adopt the following three measurements to evaluate the accuracy of our algorithm, SDEC. Note that, those measures are all introduced in related papers [9][14], and the former two metrics are typically used in virtual coordinate space to measure the relative embedding error, for comparison, we also use those two metrics to illustrate the embedding error of our algorithm.

As in [14], we define the average absolute relative error (*abr*) for all pairs of peers as follows:

$$
abr = \frac{\sum_{i \neq j \in X} \frac{\left| \|coordinate\ (i) - coordinate\ (j)\| - sd\,(i,\,j) \right|}{sd\,(i,\,j)}}{\left(|X| * (|X| - 1) \right)} \tag{9}
$$

Where X is the set including all peers in P2P system.

Similar error metric is Stress, defined as follows:

$$
stress = \frac{\sum_{i,\,j \in X} \left(\|coordinate\ (i) - coordinate\ (j)\| - sd\,(i,\,j) \right)^2}{\sum_{i,\,j \in X} sd\,(i,\,j)^2} \tag{10}
$$

The above measurements do not appropriately reflect the performance of our embedding procedure, for, generally, many applications need to know the relative semantic distance of other peers, thus, like [9], we define more appropriate measurement for semantic distance embedding system, that is, Relative Rank Loss (*rrl*).

Specifically, we say that peer j and k are swapped with relative to peer i, denoted as *swapped(i,j,k)*, if peer i's relative distance relationship to j and k is different in the original and embedded semantic space. We define $S(i)$, a subset of $(X-\{i\})\times(X-\{i\})$, to be $\{(j,k)|j\neq k$ and *swapped(i,j,k)*$\}$, and define the local relative rank loss at peer i to be $rrl(i)=|S(i)|/s$, where $s=(|X|-1)*(|X|-2)/2$. Then, the average local relative rank loss in our semantic distance embedding approach is defined as:
$$rrl = \frac{\sum_{i \in X} rrl(i)}{|X|} \quad (11)$$

4.2 Simulation Results

The simulation results include the following three parts: the comparison between embedding in 3-dimension and 2-dimension Euclidean space in terms of three measurements proposed above, the comparison among three different measurements and the preliminary comparison among different querying patterns.

① The comparison between embedding in 3-dimension and 2-dimension Euclidean space

The following three figures provide performance comparison between embedding in 3-dimension and 2-dimension Euclidean space in terms of three measures described above, *abr*, *stress* and *rrl*. The querying pattern used in those experiments is so-called one-fifth regular sampling, that is, each peer query one-fifth total peers with documents as much as possible, and all the following experimental results are the average of five runs.

From the below three figures (Fig. 1, Fig. 2 and Fig. 3), we can see that, in terms of all the measures, the performance of embedding in 3-dimension Euclidean space is better than in 2-dimension Euclidean. We also conducted many experiments for other querying patterns, and the similar results can be obtained.

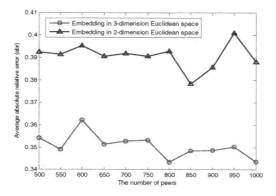

Fig. 1. Average absolute relative error (abr) vs. the number of peers

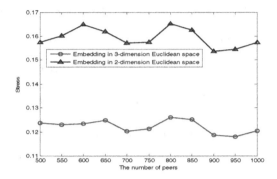

Fig. 2. Stress v.s. the number of peers

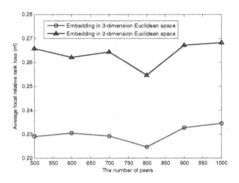

Fig. 3. Average local relative rank loss (rrl) v.s. the number of peers

② **The comparison among three different measurements**

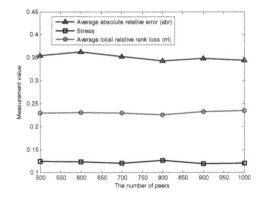

Fig. 4. The comparison of three measurement metrics

Fig. 4 compares three different measurement metrics, offered in this paper (the querying pattern is also one-fifth regular sampling). Interestingly, the measure of average local relative rank loss (*rrl*) is more appropriate metric for semantic embedding in virtual coordinate space, for it captures the intrinsic meanings of our semantic embedding. In [9], the authors also obtains similar conclusion for Internet latency embedding.

③ **The comparison among different querying patterns**
In this part of experiments, we firstly fix the number peers being queried (one-tenth of total number of peers), and compare the effect of sampling models (regular and random sampling) on the accuracy, average relative rank loss (*rrl*), in 2-dimension and 3-dimension Euclidean space. Fig. 5 shows that, in both spaces, regular sampling performs better than random sampling, and furthermore, as the number of peers increases, the oscillation in random sampling is greater than regular sampling. The similar trends also appear in other experiments with different sampling models.

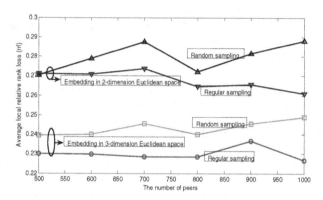

Fig. 5. The comparison between regular and random sampling in 2-dimension and 3-dimension Euclidean space

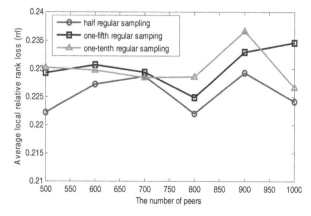

Fig. 6. The effect of the number of peers being queried on the accuracy

Secondly, fixing the sampling way as regular, we illustrate the effect of the number of peers being queried on the embedding accuracy, shown in Fig.6. Interestingly, the number of peers being queried almost has little influence on the embedding accuracy. The authors also conduct one-twentieths regular sampling, and obtain the similar result as Fig.6. The main reason is that, in our regular sampling model, a few peers with many documents actually act as the role of good "landmark" like Internet latency embedding system, so the number of peers being queried has little effect on the accuracy in our experiments. In future work, it is also deserved to investigate how to select landmarks to further reduce embedding error.

4.3 Discussion

Generally, the semantic properties in P2P system determine whether synthetic coordinate are likely to work well. In Euclidean space, a distance metric should satisfy the following axioms: non-negative, symmetry and triangle inequality. Obviously, the definition of semantic distance in our paper satisfies non-negative and symmetry, but does not always fulfill the triangle inequality, which means that, for any three peers i, j and k, the semantic distance from i to k must be less than or equal to the sum of the distances from i to j and j to k. Intuitively, these violations occurred in situations involving highly separable semantic dimension, in which peers i and j coincided on one dimension, and j and k, coincided on a second dimension. For example, the moon is similar to a gas jet (with respect to luminosity) and also similar to a football (with respect to roundness), but a gas jet and a football are not at all similar. The Fig. 7 shows the ratio of edges violating triangle inequality. Specifically, we randomly select three peers in the experiment, and calculate whether they violate triangle inequality or not, and get the ratio of violating triangle inequality by dividing all the violations with the number of probabilities to select three peer randomly. On average, in all the experiments, almost 10% of edges violate the triangle inequality, which is main reason to cause our embedding error (averagely, local relative rank loss in our semantic distance embedding system is almost twenty percent).

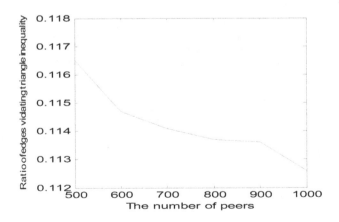

Fig. 7. Ratio of edges violating triangle inequality

Similarly, in real Internet, the latency relations among peers do not always satisfy the property of triangle inequality, largely because Internet is not well-enough connected (for routing policy, etc.), and no direct physical path between every pair of hosts exist. In order to accommodate the structural property of Internet, that is, a high-speed core in the middle and many dandrils connected to it, Ref. [7] proposed the 2-dimension Euclidean space plus the third dimension, "height", to simulate the situation that some hosts are behind the access link to the core, and Ref. [10] adopted hyperbolic space to embed Internet latency. Violation of triangle inequality is also main source of our embedding error. Thus, in future work, we should investigate deeply how to accommodate this feature in proper virtual coordinate space, and greatly improve the embedding accuracy.

In brief, from the above experiments, the SDEC algorithm can provide relatively accurate semantic embedding in P2P systems in 3-dimension Euclidean space. The main reason for the embedding error stems from some semantic edges (almost ten percent) violating the triangle inequality which should be satisfied in traditional Euclidean space.

5 Conclusion and Future Work

In P2P systems, the ability to predict semantic distance without prior communication allows systems to use semantic proximity information for better performance with less measurement overhead than probing. Inspired by significant research in Internet coordinate systems for estimating latency among nodes, in this paper, we propose a novel semantic distance embedding method in virtual coordinate system, SDEC, to approximate the semantic distance in virtual coordinate space. Specifically, in this paper, the weighted semantic distance is provided to characterize the actual semantic distance among peers, and then the detailed SDEC algorithmic procedure is proposed, which mimics the physical mass-spring system to minimize the energy in a spring network equivalent to minimizing the squared-error function in virtual semantic coordinate system. Finally, we introduce three metrics to measure the embedding error of our algorithm, and show SDEC can achieve relatively high accuracy.

Our main contribution lies in that, based on measured semantic distances from peers to a handful of other nodes and the current coordinates of those peers, SDEC assigns synthetic coordinates to each peer such that the distance between the coordinates of two peers approximately predicts the semantic distances between any two peers. Intuitively, our approach has great application in P2P system, for example, based on our approach, it is easy to cluster peer according to their content interest, which can greatly improve the search performance in P2P systems. However, our work in this paper is still preliminary, which can be greatly improved in the following aspects:

① Seek more appropriate embedding space to accommodate the intrinsic feature in semantic distance, violation of triangle inequality, which could significantly reduce the embedding errors, for our experiments show, averagely, twenty percentage of local relative rank loss emerges in our semantic distance embedding system, which is mainly caused by almost ten percentage of edges violating the triangle inequality.

② Work with real data, i.e., real documents, which imply that some specific technology is needed for automatically indexing documents with few but meaningful keywords, like TF*IDF etc.

③ Perform two-level embedding in P2P networks: based on our approach, it is easy to cluster peer to form virtual interest region. Intuitively, if peers in each interest region can be organized according to peer's proximity in underlying infrastructure, the performance can be improved further. So, our future work also includes, firstly, using SDEC to form semantic interest region, then, in each semantic interest region, using virtual coordinate system to embedding the geographical distance (then form geographical group).

④ Investigate how to simultaneously embed semantic distance and geographic distance in virtual coordinate system, which may reduce the embedding overhead.

References

[1] Sripanidkulchai, K., Maggs, B., Zhang, H.: Efficient content location using Interest-based locality in Peer-to-Peer systems. In: Proc. of IEEE INFOCOM (2003)

[2] Haase, P., Siebes, R.: Peer selection in Peer-to-Peer networks with semantic topologies. In: Proc. of WWW (2004)

[3] Lin, C.-J., Chang, Y.-T., Tsai, S.-C., Chou, C.-F.: Distributed social-based overlay adaptation for unstructured P2P networks. In: Proc. of the 10th IEEE Global Internet Symposium 2007 (2007)

[4] Jin, H., Ning, X.: Efficient search for Peer-to-Peer information retrieval using semantic small world. In: Proc. of the 15th EUROMICRO International Conference on Parallel, Distributed and Network-Based Processing (PDP) (2007)

[5] Witschel, H.F.: Content-oriented topology restructuring for search in P2P networks, Technical report (2005), http://wortschatz.unileipzig.de/~fwitschel/papers/simulation.pdf

[6] Ng, T., Zhang, H.: A network positioning system for the Internet. In: Proc. of the annual conference on USENIX Annual Technical Conference (2004)

[7] Dabek, F., Cox, R., Kaashoek, F., Morris, R.: Vivaldi: a decentralized network coordinate system. In: Proc. of SIGCOMM (2004)

[8] Zage, D.: Robust virtual coordinate systems with Byzantine participants. In: Proc. of the 37th Annual IEEE/IFIP International Conference on Dependable Systems and Networks (2007)

[9] Lua, E.K., Griffin, T.G., Pias, M., Zheng, H., Crowcroft, J.: On the accuracy of embeddings for Internet coordinate systems. In: Proc. of ACM SIGCOMM-Usenix Internet Measurement Conference, IMC (2005)

[10] Shavitt, Y., Tankel, T.: On the curvature of the internet and its usage for overlay construction and distance estimation. In: Proc. of the IEEE INFOCOM (2004)

[11] Salton, G., Buckley, C.: Term-weighting approaches in automatic text retrieval. Information Processing & Management 24(5), 513–523 (1988)

[12] Hu, B., Kalfoglou, Y., Alani, H., Dupplaw, D., Lewis, P.H., Shadbolt, N.: Semantic metrics. In: Proc. of 15th International Conference on Knowledge Engineering and Knowledge Management (2006)

[13] Saroiu, S., Gummadi, P., Gribble, S.: A measurement study of Peer-to-Peer file sharing systems. In: Proc. of Multimedia Computing and Networking (2002)

[14] Tang, L., Crovella, M.: Virtual landmarks for the internet. In: Proc. of the ACM SIGCOMM Internet Measurement Conference (IMC) (2003)

Dynamic Integration of Zigbee Devices into Residential Gateways for Ubiquitous Home Services

Young-Guk Ha[*]

Department of Computer Science and Engineering, Konkuk University,
1 Hwayang-dong, Gwangjin-gu, Seoul, Korea
ygha@konkuk.ac.kr

Abstract. In recent years, Zigbee becomes one of the most promising protocols for ubiquitous networking. So, it would be essential that residential gateways can effectively interoperate with Zigbee-enabled ubiquitous devices such as wireless sensors and digital appliances to provide ubiquitous home services. In this paper, I design and implement an effective architecture for dynamic integration of Zigbee devices into OSGi-based residential gateways, where ad hoc Zigbee devices are represented as device proxy services. And such proxy services can be automatically downloaded, installed and registered to the OSGi service registry by the dynamic device integration manager on the corresponding devices' joining the Zigbee network. Thus, ubiquitous home service applications can discover proxy services for the required Zigbee devices, and access the devices with the common proxy service interfaces without concerning the specific device access protocols and libraries.

Keywords: Ubiquitous service infrastructure, Zigbee device, ubiquitous sensor, residential gateway, OSGi service framework.

1 Introduction

The recent emergence of ubiquitous computing is rapidly changing information technologies and services area including smart home and automation. Nowadays, Zigbee [1] a de facto standard for WSNs (Wireless Sensor Networks) becomes one of the most promising protocols for smart home and automation due to its low-power consumption, low cost, and supports for various ad hoc network configurations [2, 3, 4]. In addition, Zigbee provides a light-weight software stack supporting multi-hop networking, device management, and security over the IEEE 802.15.4 WPAN (Wireless Personal Area Network) standard. So, it would be one of the most essential functionalities for residential gateway systems to support flexible interoperability between ubiquitous home service applications and various Zigbee-enabled devices such as Zigbee wireless sensors, digital and mobile appliances.

In this paper, I present design and implementation of an effective architecture for dynamic integration of Zigbee devices into residential gateways based on the OSGi (Open Service Gateway Initiative) service framework [5]. The main idea of the paper

---

[*] Corresponding author.

D. Zhang et al. (Eds.): UIC 2009, LNCS 5585, pp. 221–235, 2009.
© Springer-Verlag Berlin Heidelberg 2009

is that an ad hoc Zigbee device is represented as a *device proxy service* in the proposed architecture so that it can be dynamically registered, discovered, accessed and unregistered just like a common OSGi service [6]. Fig. 1 illustrates the overview of the proposed dynamic integration procedure for a Zigbee device. As illustrated, when a new device joins the Zigbee home network (e.g., newly deployed electric fan device in the figure), its corresponding device proxy service is downloaded from the device vendors' Web sites as an OSGi service bundle, installed to the residential gateway, and registered to the *service registry* automatically by the *DDIM* (*Dynamic Device Integration Manager*). Then, the ubiquitous home service application can be notified with or retrieve a proxy service for the electric fan using a service filter, and access the device with the common proxy service interface for electric fan devices without concerning the specific access protocol and library.

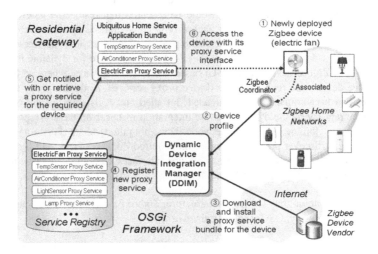

Fig. 1. Overview of the proposed dynamic integration procedure for Zigbee devices

This paper is organized as follows. Section 2 briefly explains related works and section 3 describes the detailed design of the proposed dynamic integration architecture and its major components. Section 4 explains implementation of the proposed architecture and experiments in our ubiquitous service test bed to prove the feasibility and effectiveness. Finally, as a conclusion, section 5 shortly reviews the paper and discusses some future works to extend the proposed architecture.

2 Related Works

In smart home and automation area, some tentative and proprietary researches on integrating sensor networks and ubiquitous devices were performed. Shunyang et al. [7] design and implement a home remote control network using Zigbee devices and a home gateway based on embedded Web server. They discussed the home wireless network technology based on Zigbee and its network topology, and demystified the hardware and software design of home gateway and device nodes. Baek et al. [8] present an intelligent home care system based on context-awareness, which consists of a sensor platform, a context-aware framework, and an intelligent service agent. Their sensor platform collects raw data for home environments and sends them to the context-aware framework to perceive contexts for home care services. In the Aware Home project [9], a living laboratory for research in ubiquitous computing for every-day activities is created using vision-based sensors, floor sensors, and other HCI (Human Computer Interaction) technologies.

The major difference of the proposed architecture from the related works is that the proposed architecture is based on the de facto standards actually used in the home network and automation industry such as Zigbee and OSGi. As a consequence, the proposed architecture can be immediately applied to and effectively facilitate the existing home network services and products. That is, the proposed DDIM-based dynamic integration architecture can enable home network service providers to pro-ductively develop various applications using Zigbee devices in the same way as using common OSGi services, home network device vendors to effectively deploy or up-grade software modules (bundles) for Zigbee devices, and consumers to be provided with more intelligent and flexible home network services using their Zigbee devices by just plugging in the devices.

3 The Proposed Architecture

As illustrated in Fig. 2, the proposed architecture is built on top of an OSGi-based residential gateway and consists of the DDIM, device proxy service bundles, home service application bundles, and a Zigbee network including a coordinator, device nodes, and its interfaces to the residential gateway. This section will describe each component in more detail.

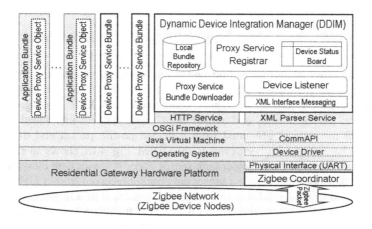

Fig. 2. Proposed dynamic integration architecture

3.1 Zigbee Home Networks

Generally, a Zigbee network consists of a coordinator and device nodes (i.e., sensor and appliance nodes) associated with the coordinator. The coordinator is a special node that manages the entire Zigbee network. And it also acts as a gateway or sink node of a WSN that collects data from deployed sensor nodes and transfers the data to a host system. In the proposed architecture, Zigbee home network nodes can either conform to the Zigbee Home Automation Application Profile [10] or have its own application protocol. Though, as shown in Fig. 3, each Zigbee device node needs to be designed to periodically send a packet containing its own profile (e.g., ID, class, address, and so on) to the coordinator to announce its existence. On receiving a device profile packet, the coordinator encodes the data stored in the packet into an XML (eXtensible Markup Language) message [11] and passes it to the DDIM for the further processing.

The proposed architecture provides two levels of interfaces to Zigbee home networks, that is, physical and logical interfaces. As shown in Fig. 2, a residential gateway can physically interfaces a Zigbee coordinator with an UART (Universal Asynchronous Receiver Transmitter) through a software stack consisting of a device driver and the Java CommAPI (Communications API). This physical interface can be replaced with another such as an USB (Universal Serial Bus) or IEEE1394.

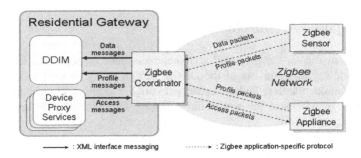

Fig. 3. Logical interface of residential gateways to Zigbee networks

To abstract physical interfaces and underlying application-specific protocols, as illustrated in Fig. 3, the proposed architecture allows the DDIM and device proxy services to logically interface the Zigbee coordinator with XML messages such as *device profile*, *device access*, and *sensor data messages*. As mentioned above, a device profile message is generated from a device profile packet and used to announce the existence of a Zigbee device to the DDIM. Fig. 4-(a) shows an example of a device profile message for a temperature sensor node. A sensor data message is also generated by the coordinator from a sensor data packet received from a Zigbee sensor node, and passed to the DDIM. Fig. 4-(b) shows an example of a sensor data message generated from a temperature sensor data packet. On the other hand, a device access message is generated by a proxy service for an application's invocation of the corresponding access method and passed to the coordinator to actually access the Zigbee device. Fig. 4-(c) shows an example of a device access message to turn on an electric fan. And Table 1 explains the XML tags used in the interface messages.

```
<devProfile>
  <devID>10:aa:03:00:00:fa:00:01<devID>
  <objectClass>ddim.sensor.TempSensor</objectClass>
  <netAddr>00:03</netAddr>
  <devPosition>LivingRoom</devPosition>
  <vendorURI>http://www.vendor.com</vendorURI>
  <bundleURL>ftp://vendor.com/down/temp_sens.zip</bundleURL>
</devProfile>
```

(a)

```
<sensorData>
  <devID>10:aa:03:00:00:fa:00:01<devID>
  <objectClass>ddim.sensor.TempSensor</objectClass>
  <netAddr>00:03</netAddr>
  <devPosition>LivingRoom</devPosition>
  <dataValue>25</dataValue>
  <dataUnit>Celsius</dataUnit>
</sensorData>
```

(b)

```
<devAccess>
  <devID>11:9a:05:00:00:fa:00:23<devID>
  <objectClass>ddim.appliance.ElectricFan</objectClass>
  <netAddr>00:1a</netAddr>
  <accessMethod>turnOn</accessMethod>
  <accessArgs>none</accessArgs>
</devAccess>
```

(c)

Fig. 4. XML interface message examples: (a) temperature sensor profile message, (b) temperature sensor data message, and (c) electric fan access message (for turnOn method)

3.2 Dynamic Device Integration Manager (DDIM)

DDIM the dynamic device integration manager is the core component of the proposed architecture, which consists of a proxy service registrar, a device status board, a local bundle repository, a device listener, and a proxy service bundle downloader. This subsection will explain how such internal modules of the DDIM work during the dynamic integration procedure that consists of *proxy service registration*, device *access*, and *proxy service unregistration* phases.

Proxy Service Registration and Device Accesses
Fig. 5 illustrates the procedure to register a proxy service for a newly deployed Zigbee device and to access the device with the proxy service.

Table 1. XML tags used in the interface messages

Tag name	Used in	Tag value
devID	All messages	Unique ID of the Zigbee device (e.g., 8-byte Zigbee MAC address)
objectClass	All messages	Java class name of the device proxy service.
netAddr	All messages	2-byte Zigbee network address of the device
devPosition	Device profile Sensor data	Position of the device in the service environment (need to be initialized manually or automatically before the deployment)
vendorURI	Device profile	URI (Uniform Resource Identifier) of the device vendor (e.g., URL of the vendor)
bundleURL	Device profile	URL (Uniform Resource Locator) of the downloadable device proxy service bundle
dataValue	Sensor data	Value of the sensor data
dataUnit	Sensor data	Unit of the sensor data
accessMethod	Device access	Name of a device access method defined in the proxy service interface
accessArgs	Device access	Values of arguments for the access method separated by ';' ("none" for no arguments)

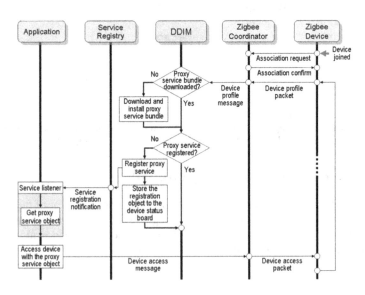

Fig. 5. Proxy service registration and device access procedure

When a new device is deployed and associated with the Zigbee coordinator, as mentioned above, the DDIM periodically receives an XML profile message of the device from the Zigbee coordinator. Internally, the device listener of the DDIM interprets the received device profile message and informs the proxy service registrar of the newly associated device. And if a proxy service bundle for the new device is not stored in the local bundle repository or out-of-date, the proxy service bundle downloader downloads the required proxy service bundle from the device vendor's download site, whose URL is described with the *bundleURL* tag in the profile message (refer to Fig. 4-(a)). In the download process, version information of the bundle manifest is referred to get the up-to-date proxy service bundle.

After downloading the proxy service bundle into the local bundle repository, the proxy service registrar installs the downloaded bundle and registers the proxy service to the OSGi service registry. When a proxy service is registered, some tag information from the profile messages is used as service properties (e.g., devID, objectClass, and devPosition). After the registration, the proxy service registrar stores the resulting *service registration object* for the proxy service into an entry of the device status board. The details of the device status board and service registration objects will be discussed later.

Then, a ubiquitous home service application interested in a newly deployed Zigbee device can retrieve or be notified with the registration of the device's proxy service using *service listeners* [9] and *service filter criteria* [12] (refer to the next subsection for more details on the service listeners and filers). After the registration of a device proxy service, the application can get the corresponding proxy service object and access the device by invoking appropriate methods of the proxy service object without concerning the details of the device access protocol. That is, as explained previously, generations and exchanges of Zigbee application-specific protocol packets for accessing devices are delegated to the Zigbee coordinator through the XML device access messages (refer to Fig. 4-(c)).

Accessing Sensor Data

After the registration of proxy services for Zigbee sensor nodes, ubiquitous home service applications can access data received from the sensor nodes through the corresponding sensor proxy service objects. Some kinds of sensor nodes, such as temperature sensor, humidity sensor, or illumination sensor nodes, send data packets to the coordinator periodically, whereas other kinds of sensor nodes, such as magnetic door sensor, CO gas sensor, or PIR (Pyroelectric Infrared) movement sensor nodes, send a data packet to the coordinator only when a designated event occurs.

In both cases, as illustrated in Fig. 6, the coordinator generates an XML-encoded sensor data message for each received sensor data packet and passes it to the DDIM. And the proxy service registrar of the DDIM gets the service registration object for the sensor node from the device status board and updates the "dataValue" property of the corresponding sensor proxy service with the value of the "dataValue" tag in the sensor data message (refer to Fig. 4-(b)) using the service registration object. Then a ubiquitous home service application is notified that a new data value is received from the Zigbee sensor node (i.e., the "dataValue" property of the sensor proxy service is modified) and can get the new data value by invoking an appropriate data read method of the corresponding sensor proxy service object.

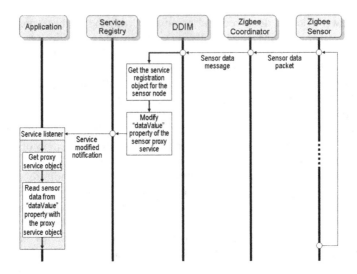

Fig. 6. Sensor data access procedure (with a data read method)

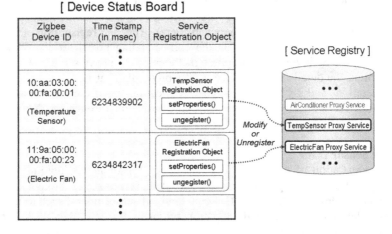

Fig. 7. An instance of the device status board

Fig. 7 shows an instance of the device status board storing entries for a Zigbee temperature sensor node and an electric fan device during the dynamic integration procedure. Each entry of the device status board maintains registration information for every registered proxy service, such as device IDs, registration objects and time stamps updated on receiving a periodic profile packet, so that the proxy service registrar can dynamically manage proxy services registered in the service registry (e.g., property modification or unregistration).

Unregistration of Device Proxy Services

As illustrated in Fig. 8, a device disconnected from the Zigbee home network (e.g., due to getting out of the radio range or being turned off) can not send periodic profile packets to the coordinator any more. To determine when the latest profile packet of each device is successfully received, the proxy service registrar of the DDIM continuously checks time stamp values of the device status board, each of which is updated on receiving a periodic profile packet from Zigbee devices. And if there are no updates of a device's time stamp for some specific period of time, the proxy service registrar unregisters the proxy service of the device from the service registry using its registration object and then removes the corresponding entry from the device status board.

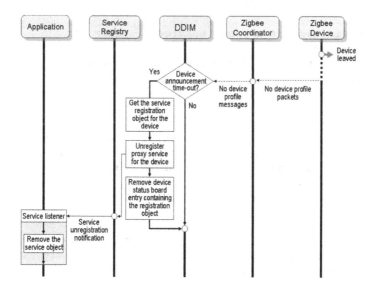

Fig. 8. Proxy service unregistration procedure

3.3 Device Proxy Services and Applications

As explained previously, device proxy services can be downloaded from the device vendors' download sites, installed and registered to a residential gateway on demand by the DDIM. As shown in the code fragments in Fig. 9, a residential gateway application can be notified with the registration of proxy services for the required Zigbee devices using OSGi service listeners [9] together with service filter criteria (code fragment <a>) that are based on the LDAP (Lightweight Directory Access Protocol) search filter specification [12]. Note that service properties (e.g., devID, objectClass, devPosition, dataVaue, and dataUnit) can be used as service attributes to describe the search filter criteria. After being notified with the registration of a proxy service for the required device, the application can get the proxy service object (code fragment <b>) and access the device through the corresponding *common proxy service interface* (code fragment <c>).

```
// OSGi application for accessing Zigbee electric fans
public class Activator implements BundleActivator {
// Proxy service object for an electric fan
  ElectricFan elecFan = null;
  ServiceReference sr = null

  public void start(BundleContext bc) throws Exception {
    // Definition of a proxy service filter for
    //   Zigbee electric fans positioned in the living room
    String filter =
           "(&(objectClass=ddim.appliance.ElectricFan)
             (devPosition=LivingRoom))";

    // Definition of a proxy service listener for
    //   electric fans
    ServiceListener sl = new ServiceListener() {
      public void ServiceChanged(ServiceEvent ev) {
        sr = ev.getServiceReference();

        // Gets  a  service  object  when  notified  with  the
        //   registration of an electric fan proxy service
        if (ev.getType() == ServiceEvent.REGISTERED)
            elecFan = (ElectricFan)bc.getService(sr);
        }
    }; // end of the service listener

    try {
      // Registers the electric fan service listener
      //   with the filter
      bc.addServiceListener(sl, filter);
         ...
      // Accesses the newly deployed Zigbee electric fan
      if (elecFan != null) elecFan.turnOn(sr);
         ...
    } catch (Exception e) {
         ...
    }
  } // end of the start
     ...
} // end of the application bundle
```

Fig. 9. Residential gateway application code example for Zigbee devices

Fig. 10 shows examples of the common proxy service interfaces for some Zigbee sensors and appliances, such as temperature sensors, magnetic sensors, electric fans, and air conditioners, which are actually used to implement the ubiquitous home service applications explained in the next section.

```
// Common service interface: ddim.sensor.TempSensor
public interface TempSensor {
  // Polls the sensor node to get temperature value
  abstract public int getTempCelsius(ServiceReference ref);
  // Reads temperature value received from the sensor node
  abstract public int readTempCelsius(ServiceReference ref);
}


// Common service interface: ddim.sensor.MagnetSensor
public interface MagnetSensor {
  // Polls the sensor node to get door/window status
  //     (true: open, false: closed)
  abstract public boolean getStatus(ServiceReference ref);
  // Reads door/window status received from the sensor node
  abstract public boolean readStatus(ServiceReference ref);
}


// Common service interface: ddim.appliance.ElectricFan
public interface ElectricFan {
  // Turns on the electric fan
  abstract public void turnOn(ServiceReference ref);
  // Turns off the electric fan
  abstract public void turnOff(ServiceReference ref);
  // Sets the speed level of the electric fan
  //     (speed level: 1, 2, 3, and so on)
  abstract public void setSpeedLevel(ServiceReference ref,
                                            int speed);
}


// Common service interface: ddim.appliance.AirConditioner
public interface AirConditioner {
  // Turns on the air conditioner
  abstract public void turnOn(ServiceReference ref);
  // Turns off the air conditioner
  abstract public void turnOff(ServiceReference ref);
  // Sets the desired temperature of the air conditioner
  abstract public void setTempCelsius(ServiceReference ref,
                                            int temp);
}
```

Fig. 10. Common proxy service interfaces for Zigbee devices

4   Implementation and Experiments

4.1   System Implementation

As illustrated in Fig. 11-(a), a prototype residential gateway system is built on a laptop PC equipped with a Zigbee coordinator module using an open source OSGi framework Knopflerfish [13] and Java SDK (Software Development Kit) [14]. And the core software modules of the proposed architecture are implemented including the DDIM, proxy service bundles for Zigbee devices, and experimental ubiquitous home service applications for climate control and home security.

For the climate control application, a Zigbee temperature sensor node, an air conditioner, and an electric fan are used. As shown in the Fig. 11-(b), a Zigbee sensor node used in the experiments are composed of a main communication module and an additional sensor module that is stackable on the main module. Especially, the main module can act as a temperature sensor node by itself or as a magnetic door sensor node when connected with an external magnetic sensor. To control the non-Zigbee air conditioner and electric fan through the Zigbee home network, Zigbee-enabled wireless power sockets are used (refer to Fig. 11-(c)). Note that only the "turnOn" and "turnoff" methods for those devices are implemented at this time because the Zigbee power sockets used for the experiments only support simple power control functionality.

Prototype residential gateway
(laptop PC with OSGi framework)

Zigbee communication module
with a temperature sensor
(connected with an external magnetic sensor)

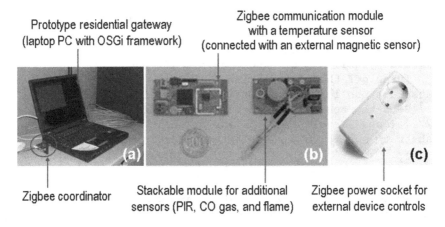

Zigbee coordinator

Stackable module for additional
sensors (PIR, CO gas, and flame)

Zigbee power socket for
external device controls

Fig. 11. Residential gateway and Zigbee home network components for experiments

And for the home security application, two Zigbee magnetic sensor nodes are used, each of which is composed of a main Zigbee communication module and an external magnetic sensor. During the experiments, one magnetic sensor node is attached to the door and the other is attached to the window of the test bed. Fig. 12 shows the overall home network configuration for the experiments. As shown in the figure, the residential gateway system is connected to the proxy service bundle download server through the Internet to download the proxy service bundles for the Zigbee devices used in the experiments (i.e., temperature sensor node, magnetic sensor node, air conditioner, and electric fan). And it also connected to the cell phone message server to send an intrusion alarm message to the user for the home security experiment.

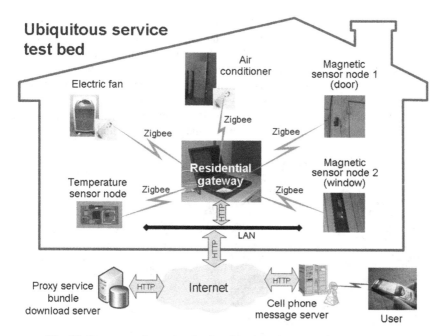

Fig. 12. System configuration for the ubiquitous home service experiments

4.2 Experiments and Results

Fig. 13-(a) shows the floor plan of the ubiquitous service test bed for the experiments. In the first experiment, the climate control application monitors the current temperature of the test bed with the retrieved "TempSensor" proxy service for the temperature sensor node on the ceiling. Specifically, the application monitors the current temperature by invoking the "readTempCelsius" method of the "TempSensor" proxy service every time a periodic data packet from the temperature sensor node is received. And if the temperature of the test bed exceeds the predefined limit, the application tries to retrieve an "ElectricFan" or "AirConditioner" proxy service from the service registry. When the application finds the "AirConditioner" proxy service for the air conditioner in the test bed, it turns on the air conditioner by invoking the "turnOn" method of the "AirConditioner" proxy service as shown in Fig. 13-(b). When a Zigbee-enabled electric fan is newly deployed to the test bed, an "ElectricFan" proxy service is downloaded from the proxy service bundle download server and registered to the service registry. Then, the application is automatically notified with the registration of the "ElectricFan" proxy service and turns on the electric fan by invoking the "turnOn" method of the "ElectricFan" proxy service.

In the second experiment, the home security application monitors the security status of the test bed with the "MagnetSensor" proxy service for the magnetic door sensor node deployed before the experiment as shown in Fig. 13-(c). When the door is open, the magnetic door sensor node sends a data packet to the coordinator. Then the application is notified that the "dataValue" property of the "MagnetSensor" proxy service is modified and gets the status of the door by invoking the "readStatus" method of the

"MagnetSensor" proxy service. After knowing that the door is open, the application sends an alarm message to the user through the cell phone message server. When an additional magnetic sensor node is newly deployed to the window of the test bed as shown in Fig. 13-(c), the home security application is notified with the registration of another "MagnetSensor" proxy service. Then the application reads the "devPosition" property value (i.e., initialized as "Window" before the deployment) of the proxy service and automatically gets ready to detect intrusions through the window of the test bed by using the "MagnetSensor" service for the new magnetic sensor node.

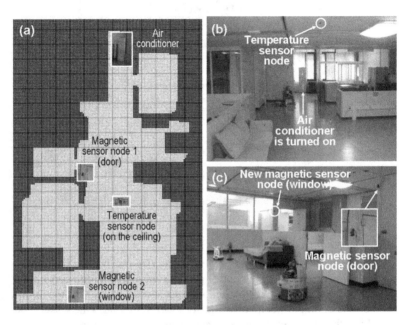

Fig. 13. Snapshots from the ubiquitous home service experiments

5 Conclusion

In this paper, I proposed an effective architecture for dynamic integration of ad hoc Zigbee devices into OSGi-based residential gateways for ubiquitous home services. And I implemented the proposed architecture and made some experiments in our ubiquitous service test bed to prove its feasibility and effectiveness. I expect that the proposed architecture will contribute to the development of ubiquitous service systems not only for home network service domains but for a variety of service domains including u-automotive, u-office, and u-hospital services.

The current issue of the proposed architecture is to enhance the security. For instance, if a Zigbee device node that contains an URL to its proxy service bundle with malicious codes is deployed, the residential gateway and the entire service system may be in danger. Thus, it is essential to authenticate Zigbee device nodes and their proxy service bundles for the security of ubiquitous service systems that are based on the proposed architecture. Basically, I am planning to resolve such security problem by using digitally signed proxy service bundles combined with MANET (Mobile Ad hoc Network) security technologies [15] for authenticating deployed ad hoc Zigbee device nodes.

References

1. Kinney, P.: ZigBee Technology: Wireless Control that Simply Works. In: Communications Design Conference, San Jose (2003)
2. Callaway, E., Gordy, P., Hester, L., Gutierrez, J.A., Naeve, M., Heile, B., Bahl, V.: Home networking with IEEE 802.15.4: a developing standard for low-rate wireless personal area networks. IEEE Commun. Mag. 40, 70–77 (2002)
3. Zigbee Alliance: Zigbee Vision for the Home: Zigbee Wireless Home Automation. Zigbee Whitepaper (2006)
4. Zigbee Alliance: Zigbee Enables Smart Buildings of the Future Today. Zigbee Whitepaper (2007)
5. OSGi Technology, http://www.osgi.org/About/Technology
6. OSGi Alliance: OSGi Service Platform Core Specification Release 4, Version 4.1. OSGi Specification (2007)
7. Shunyang, Z., Du, X., Yongping, J., Riming, W.: Realization of Home Remote Control Network Based on ZigBee. In: International Conference on Electronic Measurement and Instruments (ICEMI 2007), Xi'An, China (2007)
8. Baek, S., Lee, H., Lim, S., Huh, J.: Managing Mechanism for Service Compatibility and Interaction Issues in Context-aware Ubiquitous Home. IEEE Trans. Consumer Electron. 51(2), 524–528 (2005)
9. Kidd, C.D., Orr, R., Abowd, G.D., Atkeson, C.G., Essa, I.A., MacIntyre, B., Mynatt, E., Starner, T.E., Newstetter, W.: The Aware Home: A Living Laboratory for Ubiquitous Computing Research. In: International Workshop on Cooperative Buildings (CoBuild 1999), Position paper, Pittsburgh (1999)
10. Zigbee Alliance: Zigbee Home Automation Public Application Profile Version 1.0. Zigbee Specification (2007)
11. W3C: Extensible Markup Language (XML) 1.0 4th edn. W3C Recommendation (2006)
12. Howes, T.: RFC1960 - A String Representation of LDAP Search Filters. IETF Network WG Specification (1996)
13. Knopflerfish - Open Source OSGi, http://www.knopflerfish.org
14. Java SDK, http://java.sun.com/javase
15. Zouridaki, C.: Security in Mobile Ad Hoc Networks. VDM Verlag, Saarbrücken (2008)

Fine-Grained Evaluation of Local Positioning Systems for Specific Target Applications

Erwin Aitenbichler[1], Fernando Lyardet[2], Aristotelis Hadjakos[1], and Max Mühlhäuser[1]

[1] Technische Universität Darmstadt, Hochschulstrasse 10, 64289 Darmstadt, Germany
[2] SAP Research CEC Darmstadt, 64283 Darmstadt, Germany

Abstract. Location-aware software has become widespread outdoors. Indoor applications are now on the rise. However, careful selection of the appropriate local positioning system (LPS) and application fine-tuning are required in order to guarantee acceptable user experience. We present a simulation-based approach that includes application characteristics, LPS characteristics, and building characteristics to this complex task and illustrate how the appropriate LPS can be chosen and how applications can be fine-tuned. A sophisticated indoor navigation system is used as sample application. The paper also provides insights into subtle details and caveats of different LPS technologies from an application and building viewpoint.

1   Introduction

While the Global Positioning System (GPS) is the de-facto standard for outdoor positioning, there is currently no single standard for indoor positioning. Here, developers can choose from several different Local Positioning System (LPS) technologies which all have their specific advantages and disadvantages [1,2]. The most important question for a developer when choosing an LPS is if it suits the needs of a specific application.

A first hurdle for the comparison is that depending on the underlying technology, the accuracy of an LPS is specified in different ways. For RF-based systems it is common to specify the radius of a circle containing 95% of all measurements for a given location or the RMS error as accuracy. In contrast, for an Infrared Badge system the maximum range could be specified as a property.

Beside *accuracy*, the *resolution* of an LPS is an important property. These two properties are often only loosely connected. For example, the system with the highest resolution may often not be the best choice. Consider an application that needs to determine in which room a user currently is. WLAN-based systems provide 3D coordinates with centimeter resolution and are known to have an accuracy of about 2-3 meters, but if the user is standing close to a wall, a system accuracy of 2-3 meters does not allow to distinguish between rooms reliably. An Infrared Badge system has only room resolution, but because light does not pass through walls, it also has room accuracy. Thus, the latter system is a better match for the given application.

A more fundamental problem is that these diverse LPS properties cannot be directly matched with the diverse requirements of an application. For example, the following application requirement could be specified: "Explain object X to the user as soon as she

D. Zhang et al. (Eds.): UIC 2009, LNCS 5585, pp. 236–250, 2009.
© Springer-Verlag Berlin Heidelberg 2009

can see it, but never if she cannot see it." To match application requirements with the characteristics of currently available LPSes, a general approach is needed. In this paper, we present a simulation framework allowing a detailed analysis of the impact of LPS properties on an application.

This paper is structured as follows. After a discussion of related work in Section 1.1, we present the architecture of our simulation framework in Section 2. The general properties of LPS are evaluated in Section 3. As an example for a reasonably complex application we present the Context-aware Indoor Navigation System (CoINS) in Section 4. Then we present the results of a simulation-based evaluation of CoINS with four different LPSes currently useable with modern mobile phones in Section 5. We then derive the *application success rate* from the experimental data. This measure denotes the probability that the user can be guided correctly, i.e., the system will provide the user with the correct directions at the correct time. Finally, the paper is concluded in Section 6.

1.1   Related Work

General descriptions of LPS properties and system comparisons are subject of book chapters in [2] and [1]. Over the past few years, a notable progress in the field of LPS research was the fusion of data from multiple LPS systems with very different characteristics. Hightower et al. describe the use of particle filters to combine the data from WLAN and Infrared, which is a symbolic location source [3]. Woodman et al. describe the combination of WLAN with a Pedometer, which is a relative location source [4].

However, to the knowledge of the authors, there are currently no existing approaches for the generic matching of LPS properties with application requirements.

2   Simulation Framework

Figure 1 shows the architecture of the simulation framework. The **Application Description** is an XML file specifying the requirements of an application in an LPS-independent way. The most important elements for pedestrian applications are *location tests* and *walk tests*:

- **Point(P):** Expresses that the application needs to determine that a user is at a location P. The permitted tolerance can be specified as a simulation parameter.
- **Rect(P,Q):** Expresses that the application needs to determine that a user is in the spatial area defined by a cuboid ranging from P to Q.
- **Walk(P,Q):** Expresses that a user is expected to walk from P to Q and the application needs to determine that the user has reached Q.

Such elementary tests can be combined to describe more complex requirements:

- **Test** is a structuring element that surrounds the tags described above. The simulator determines the probabilities of true positives (TP), false positives (FP), true negatives (TN), and false negatives (FN) for each test. Tests can be nested and previously executed tests can be referenced and included as subtests.

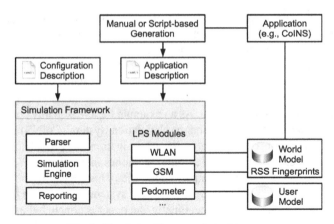

Fig. 1. Simulation Framework Architecture

- **Testunit** serves as a structuring element to group tests of the same kind. The difference to nested tests is that nesting expresses a is-subtest-of relationship, while test units express an is-kind-of relationship.

The **Application Description** can either be written manually or generated automatically using a script. For complex applications like CoINS the latter approach is beneficial. Here, the script directly interacts with the route planning component of CoINS to generate test cases.

The **LPS Modules** simulate the behavior of specific LPS systems. These modules may need additional information from the World Model, such as Received Signal Strength (RSS) fingerprints or user body dimension data to simulate a pedometer-based LPS. The LPS modules and their associated data are application-independent.

The **Configuration Description** controls the whole simulation. It defines which tests of the application description should be executed using which LPS systems and what kind of reports should be generated.

2.1 LPS Modules

This section gives a brief overview of the indoor positioning systems that are supported by the LPS Modules of the simulator.

Wireless LAN. Devices with WLAN interfaces can be tracked within a WLAN infrastructure. The simplest form of WLAN tracking determines in which cell the user currently is. This way, it is possible to locate users with an accuracy of about 25-50m. By using location fingerprinting, the accuracy of WLAN systems can be improved to about 3m [5,6]. However, fingerprinting requires the creation and maintenance of radio signal propagation maps, which is considerable effort if not done by robots [3]. WLAN tracking can be completely done in the infrastructure without requiring any special software on the client or it can be done on the client. There are several software products for WLAN positioning available, e.g., PlaceLab [7] or Ekahau [8]. The big advantage of this approach is that it does not require any specialized hardware and thus can be used in conjunction with off-the-shelf smartphones and portable computing devices.

GSM. The location of a mobile phone can be either determined network-based or client-based. Unfortunately, there is only little standardization of APIs beside the E911 requirement and cellphone locations can often only be obtained by purchasing operator-specific APIs. These are often limited to single operators and countries, and each location fix costs a fee. However, similar to WLAN, it is also possible to perform client-based positioning with GSM [9]. Furthermore, it is also possible to apply fingerprinting techniques.

Ultra-WideBand. UWB systems utilize a much larger RF spectrum for their measurement signals. This allows them to handle multipath effects adequately, resulting in an order of magnitude better accuracy compared to systems based on a single frequency. One of the most advanced UWB location systems is available from Ubisense [10]. The Ubisense system comprises UbiTags carried by people or objects and several stationary UbiSensors. UWB systems employ the so-called inverse-GPS (IGPS) principle, which is similar to GPS, but with reversed roles: UbiTags emit short UWB pulses, which are received by at least three UbiSensors. The sensors measure the time differences of arrival of the UWB pulse and use trilateration to calculate the tag's position. In addition, Ubisense measures the angles of arrival to improve the reliability of the position information. UWB systems provide an accuracy down to about 15cm. However, they require specialized hardware at the user and in the infrastructure.

Pedometer. Pedometers are usually based on an acceleration sensor and count steps by analyzing its signal data. This principle works most reliable when wearing the sensor on the foot or in the shoe [11]. The accuracy decreases when the sensor is worn on a helmet [12], in the pocket [13], or in the hand [14], but users can still be located with a reasonable accuracy. Such a positioning system is typically constructed out of a pedometer and an electronic compass to get orientation information. However, because the positioning error continuously increases in such a system, sensor fusion with an absolute positioning system, e.g., WLAN, can considerably improve its accuracy [4].

QR Codes. Quick Response (QR)-Codes [15] are two-dimensional barcodes that were standardized by ISO in the year 2000 (ISO/IEC 18004). To date, QR reading software is available for almost any smartphone. QR codes can be used to create "physical world hyperlinks". A user having a camera phone can scan the image of a QR Code causing the phone's browser to launch and redirect to the programmed URL. QR codes can be used to determine physical location by encoding locations into URLs.

Infrared Badge Systems. detect if a badge worn by a user is within line-of-sight distance of a stationary receiver. Elpas [16] is a badge-based system that combines Infrared, low frequency RF proximity sensing, and high frequency RF. It can cover entire buildings and depending on the amount of infrastructure deployed, its accuracy varies between 25m and 2m. Elpas provides only symbolic location. The number of supported distinct positions is equal to the number of sensors deployed.

It is also interesting to investigate the use of GPS indoors. GPS [17] is basically not suitable for indoor positioning, because the system requires a direct line of sight from the receiver to multiple satellites. GPS Repeaters can be installed into the infrastructure of buildings to make GPS available indoors. A repeater consists of a receiving antenna mounted with a clear view to the sky and a sending antenna mounted indoors. The sender has a range of about 3-10 meters and forwards the combined signals of all visible satellites observed at the location of the outdoor antenna. Consequently, the number of supported distinct positions is equal to the number of repeaters.

3   Evaluation of Positioning Systems

Because WLAN, GSM, acceleration sensors, and cameras are available in modern cell-phones, we selected positioning based on WLAN, GSM, pedometer, and QR codes for a detailed evaluation. As a first prerequisite for a simulation, the LPS properties are determined at the application site. WLAN and GSM positioning require the creation of RSS fingerprint maps. To simulate pedometer input, the movement characteristics of several people using body-worn sensors are collected.

Figure 2 shows the Piloty Building at the University of Darmstadt. It is a four-story building that accommodates most of the computer science groups. The floors are

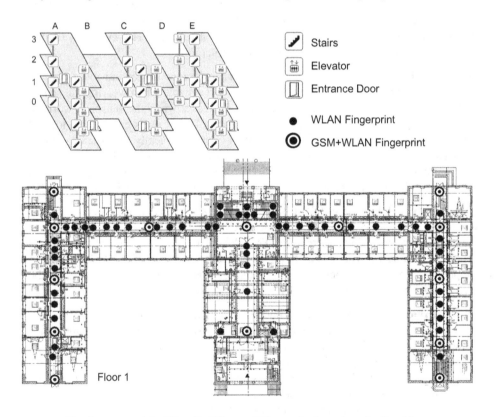

Fig. 2. Layout of the Piloty Building and Fingerprint Locations for One Floor

connected through six different stairs and four elevators. The footprint of the building is approximately 110m x 55m.

The small dots show the locations where the WLAN fingerprints were measured. A fingerprint was typically taken in front of each office door. The big dots show the locations where WLAN and GSM fingerprints where measured. In total we took WLAN fingerprints at 225 different locations and GSM fingerprints at 43 different locations.

3.1 WLAN Fingerprinting

A single RSS measurement of the access point i is denoted as s_i. When all visible access points are measured at a certain location, then the result is a vector $S = (s_1, ..., s_m)$. To reduce the effect of noise, S is measured multiple times, resulting in a data set $T = (S_1, ..., S_n)$. A fingerprint for a defined position $p = (x, y, z)$ is a tuple of location and average RSS vector: $f = (p, \frac{1}{n} \sum_{i=1}^{n} S_i)$. Fingerprints are measured at all locations important to an application. The result is the set $F = \{f_1, ..., f_n\}$ containing all fingerprints.

A mobile terminal that wants to determine its position first measures an RSS vector S_x. Because of the structure of this environment, the position is estimated by calculating the weighted average of the two closest fingerprints in signal space. These are

$(p_1, S_1) = \arg \min_{(p,S) \in F} |S - S_x|$ and
$(p_2, S_2) = \arg \min_{(p,S) \in F \wedge p \neq p_1} |S - S_x|.$

The estimated position p_x is

$$p_x = \frac{|S_1 - S_x|}{|S_1 - S_x| + |S_2 - S_x|} p_2 + \frac{|S_2 - S_x|}{|S_1 - S_x| + |S_2 - S_x|} p_1$$

The WLAN fingerprints were recorded with an UMPC at 225 different locations in the building, typically in front of each office door and at other spots that could be important for navigation. Each fingerprint was calculated by averaging at least 20 samples. In a separate measurement, a total of 8692 test samples were recorded at the same locations and the positioning algorithm was applied to that data. The result indicates an RMS error of 1.81m. Figure 3(a) shows the Cumulative Distribution Function (CDF).

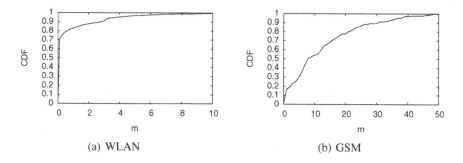

(a) WLAN   (b) GSM

Fig. 3. General Accuracy of Fingerprinting

3.2 GSM Fingerprinting

GSM positioning uses the same algorithm as described before for WLAN. The GSM fingerprints were recorded with an iPhone at 43 different locations in the building. In a separate measurement, a total of 430 test samples were recorded at the same locations. The result indicates an RMS error of 16.82m and the CDF is shown in Figure 3(b). The results of WLAN and GSM fingerprinting are summarized in Table 1.

Table 1. Collected Fingerprints

Property	WLAN	GSM
Number of fingerprint locations	225	43
Number of test point samples	8692	430
Minimum number base stations per location	2	3
Maximum number base stations per location	13	9
Average number of base stations per location	6.16	6.72
RMS error	1.81m	16.82m

3.3 Pedometer

To collect the necessary sample data for the Pedometer LPS simulation module we used our MotionNet [18] sensor system and recorded data from six different users. One sensor was worn on the foot, one on the head (on a headset) and one attached to an UMPC in the hand. Figure 4 shows the sensor signals and the derived step signals acquired during a 28m walk.

Steps can be detected very reliably from the foot signal using the following signal processing steps. First, a highpass filter (IIR, Butterworth, 10 Hz, 10th order) is applied to remove static and low-frequency components from the signal. Next, the signal is rectified. A moving average filter (window size 0.1s) is then used to smoothen the signal. Finally, a hysteresis threshold filter obtains the binary step signal.

The signals from hand and head are significantly weaker and therefore more difficult to process. To detect steps, we first apply a bandpass filter (IIR, Butterworth, 1-3 Hz, 10th order) to obtain a sine-like signal. Steps are counted if the maximum value between zero crossings exceeds a threshold value.

From the calculated step signals we can derive the average step length, its standard deviation, and the recognition rates at the foot, head, and hand of each user. Table 2 summarizes the results.

Table 2. Step Detection Recognition Rates

User	$E(l_{step})$	$\sigma(l_{step})$	Foot	Head	Hand
1	75.3 cm	1.98 cm	100%	98%	94%
2	83.1 cm	3.66 cm	100%	94%	94%
3	83.2 cm	3.39 cm	100%	96%	97%
4	70.1 cm	4.33 cm	100%	95%	96%
5	85.3 cm	2.33 cm	100%	99%	99%
6	72.2 cm	1.82 cm	100%	99%	98%
Avg	78,2 cm	2.92 cm	100%	97%	96%

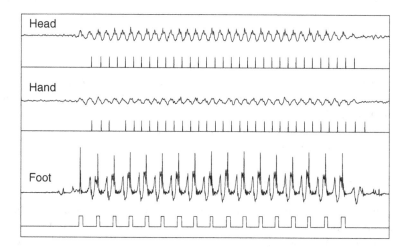

Fig. 4. Sensor Data and Derived Step Signals for Pedometer LPS

4   The CoINS Application

After the general analysis of the positioning systems, the next step is to create the application description. In this work we use the Context-aware Indoor Navigation System (CoINS) [19] as reference application that should be simulated. First, the following section provides a brief overview of CoINS.

The aim of the Context-aware Indoor Navigation System (CoINS) is to provide efficient user navigation in buildings with a strong emphasis on the "human factor". When considering the human as part of the system, the term *efficient* does not longer simply correspond to the shortest path calculated by some mathematical method. To efficiently navigate users to their destinations, it is also vital that they can quickly comprehend and execute the navigation instructions they receive from the navigation system. For example, a good route description would consist of a low number of turns, turns would be at "landmarks" the user can easily identify, and would always clearly indicate the directions in which the user is supposed to walk.

4.1   World Model

The CoINS world model is a hybrid model that combines symbolic graph-based models with geometric models. A symbolic model is required for indoor navigation, because *room numbers, corridor names, floor numbers*, etc. have an intuitive semantics to users. Using geometric coordinates for end-user interaction would not be suitable. The geometric model is needed for determining the shortest paths and to obtain orientation information for guiding users into the correct directions. The world model serves two main purposes.

First, it supports transformations between geometric coordinates and symbolic locations and vice versa. When a 3D tracking system is used that provides geometric coordinates to locate users, the model must be able to transform this coordinate into a symbolic location, such as a room number. The pathfinding algorithm of CoINS starts with the symbolic models to create a coarse plan of the route. After that, the geometric models are used for fine-planning.

Second, the model enables efficient pathfinding. The design of the CoINS world model has been refined over several iterations to ensure that the search sets are as small as possible and that the basic relations needed by the pathfinding algorithm can be checked efficiently. In most cases, users will mostly move in two dimensions. Movements in the height dimension usually only occur when changing floors, which is modeled by using separate maps for each floor.

4.2 User Centric Adaptation

The user model we have developed and applied in our indoor navigation technology combines three aspects besides user identification data: physical capabilities, user preferences, and location access rights. This model presents a Multiattribute Utility Theory-based architecture that enables decision making according to user interests.

To select the most suitable path for a specific user we use the Simple Multi-Attribute Rating Technique [20]. Under this technique, every path can be described by individual preference attributes and through the value functions of each single attribute, the preference strength can be measured.

4.3 CoINS Architecture

CoINS is based on the open-source communication middleware MundoCore [21]. For the implementation of CoINS, we adopted a service-oriented architecture, because it allows deploying application components according to different scenarios and improve their reuse by other applications. E.g., if a client only supports a web browser, all components of CoINS can run on a server in the Internet. A more powerful client such as an UMPC could already run the whole CoINS system locally.

CoINS uses the Mundo Context Server [22] to track the locations of users. Because this software provides an abstraction layer above the physical sensors, CoINS can use standardized queries and does not have to be aware of the underlying sensor technology.

The Presentation Component of CoINS can be either accessed as web interface through a web server or from rich clients. The web-based solution has the advantage that no software deployment is necessary on clients, but location tracking is limited to QR codes or purely infrastructure-based solutions. In contrast, rich clients can provide more customized user interfaces and support additional local positioning systems.

5   Evaluation of CoINS

We performed our experiments in the Piloty building of TU Darmstadt. Despite room numbers being systematically constructed of building wing letter, floor number, and room number, e.g., A121 stands for wing A, floor 1, room 21, navigation in the building is not always straightforward. For example, one computer pool in level 0 is accessible to

Directions = { IntermediateSegment Connector } EndSeg-
ment End;
IntermediateSegment = [Turn] "walk" ("to end of corridor" |
Straight);
EndSegment = [Turn] [Straight];
Connector = Door | Elevator | Stairs | ε;
End = "destination is on your" ("left" | "right");
Straight = "straight for" number "meters";
Door = "go through door";
Elevator = "take elevator" [Side] Floor;
Stairs = "take stairs" [Side] Floor;
Side = "on your" ("left" | "right");
Floor = "to floor" Number;

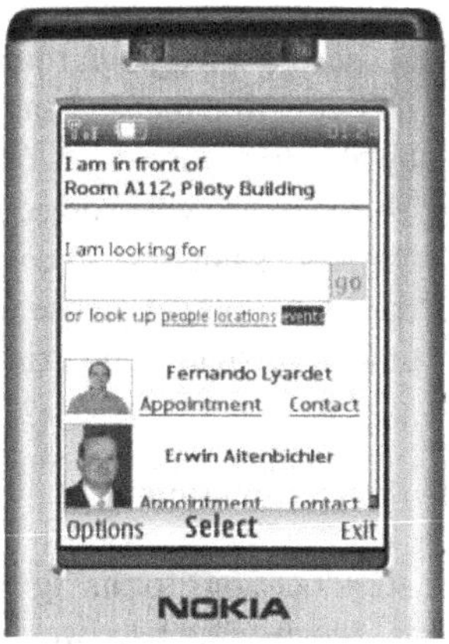

Fig. 5. CoINS: EBNF Grammar for Directions and Screenshot

students 24 hours a day. The connecting doors around this area are locked for security reasons. Also, several connecting doors on other levels cannot be passed by students or visitors. Not all elevators can reach all levels and the three wings of level 3 are not directly interconnected on level 3. Consequently, the building structure is complex enough to pose some challenges to an indoor navigation system.

To start the guiding process, a user opens the CoINS application on her mobile terminal and selects the desired destination. The application allows to search the database for people, room numbers, events, etc. Alternatively, a user could read a QR code from the business card of an employee to select the destination. CoINS then determines the user's current location and calculates the navigation route.

CoINS gives the user textual directions how to proceed to finally get to the desired destination location. Figure 5 shows the grammar describing the directions CoINS could possibly generate. It is somewhat simplified but in principle covers all possible directions CoINS would generate for the Piloty building.

The locations that must be recognized by an LPS can be derived from this grammar. The whole navigation route can be decomposed into multiple segments. An LPS is expected to provide the information if the user has reached the end of a segment, i.e., *Connector* or *End*. This way, CoINS is able to verify whether the user has successfully followed the instructions and it can proceed with explaining the next segment to user.

A route consists of a *start location*, an arbitrary number of *intermediary segments*, and one *end segment*. In case of the Piloty building, an intermediary segment always ends with the end of a corridor, a connecting or exit door, stairs, an elevator, or in open space. When the end of such a segment is reached, the user receives the next direction. Finally, the end segment ends with the desired destination, e.g., an office room. Hence, a location system suitable for CoINS must fulfill the following requirements:

– When starting the navigation, the system must be able to determine the absolute position of the user with a high accuracy. At least floor and section of the building must be correct.

– The ends of intermediary segments must be detected with a very high accuracy, because a navigation route will typically consist of multiple segments. Especially it is vital that the system does not report any false positives, because the user must be able to see the stairs or an elevator when the system tells her to use it.
– The accuracy when detecting the end of the end segment should be reasonably high, but it does not have to be as high as for the ends of intermediary segments, because the user is already close to the destination. It is not so important that the system is able to recognize the exact door when navigating to a specific office.

5.1 Start Locations

The start locations for navigation are often identical with the ends of intermediary segments, because the user would often start at an entrance door or elevator. However, in general it is necessary to detect the correct floor and wing anywhere in the building. Table 3 shows the results for WLAN and GSM fingerprinting. The user can also take a picture of a QR code to determine her location. QR codes are printed on the doorplates in the Piloty building. The column TP contains the percentage of true positives and the column FP contains the percentage of false positives.

Table 3. Start Locations

Test	GSM TP	GSM FP	WLAN TP	WLAN FP	QR TP	QR FP
Correct floor	26%	8.75%	99.8%	0%	100%	0%
Correct floor and wing	13.1%	2.21%	99.1%	0%	100%	0%
Correct entrance	100%	1.14%	100%	0%	100%	0%

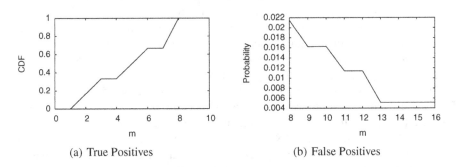

(a) True Positives   (b) False Positives

Fig. 6. Accuracy of Locating Entrance Doors with GSM

The results show that GSM is not accurate enough to distinguish between the floors of the building. For that reason, we introduce a new test that tries to distinguish between the six entrance doors of the building in one level. The results are shown in Figure 6 and indicate that this is possible. We choose the radius r_s=8m for the small circle and the radius r_l=12m for the large circle. r_l must not exceed 13m, because the minimum distance between any two test points in this set is 26m. The meaning of these two circles is explained below.

5.2   Intermediary Segments

There are 33 areas in the building which are ends of intermediary segments. To verify that we can reliably detect these areas, the following experiment was performed. From the center of each area we draw two concentric circles and then distinguish the following cases.

- If a user stands in the small circle, i.e., very close to the location of a *Connector*, we absolutely expect the system to react. We chose *3 meters* as diameter for this circle. It is mandatory that an LPS detects this occurance with a probability close to 100%. The test is counted as a *true positive* if 50% of the test point samples fulfill this criteria.
- If a user stands in the large circle, i.e., close enough to the location of a *Connector* to physically see it, then it is acceptable when the system reports that the user has reached the segment end. From empirical tests we have determined that about *4 meters* are the upper bound for this feature.
- If the user stands anywhere outside these two circles, the system must never report that the user has reached the end of the segment. This would result in the user receiving an instruction that would be useless to her. Hence, such *false positives* must be avoided and the probability of this occurance must be close to 0%.

5.3   End Segments

The end segment extends from the last intermediary segment to the destination location of the navigation. This is typically the location of an office. Hence, the simulator simulates a user walking from the location of the last connector to the destination location. The error calculation is the same as for intermediary segments.

5.4   Routes

A route consists of a start point, zero or more intermediary segments, and an end segment. The application description comprises 2282 different combinations of intermediary segments. Figure 7 shows an example route and how the individual errors are accumulated to give the TP and FP values for the whole route. The test method is very strict: If some segment of the route fails with a probability P, then the whole route also fails at least with probability P.

Segment Type	Segment Name	TP	FP
start	E120	0.98	0.05
intermediate	EC1	1.00	0.00
intermediate	CA2	1.00	0.40
end	A210	1.00	0.00
route	E120-A210	0.98	0.43

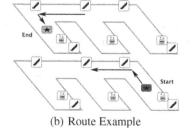

(a) Error Calculation   (b) Route Example

Fig. 7. Accumulation of Errors when Testing Routes

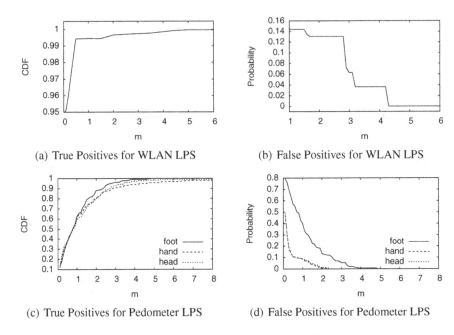

(a) True Positives for WLAN LPS

(b) False Positives for WLAN LPS

(c) True Positives for Pedometer LPS

(d) False Positives for Pedometer LPS

Fig. 8. Success and Failure Rates for Entire Routes

Figure 8 shows the results of the WLAN test. Based on the TP curve, we can select r_s=1m, which meets the defined requirement. However, the false positives are still considerable at r_l=4m. We can either stay with this requirement and accept a FP probability of 3.6% or change r_l to 4.3m.

Figure 8 shows the results from the Pedometer test. The sensor worn on the foot provides the best results. Steps can be detected reliably from this sensor, while not all steps can be detected based on the data from the head and hand sensors.

5.5   Application Success Rates

Finally, from the simulation output, the overall application success rates can be calculated. The results are summarized in Table 4. The results indicate that WLAN positioning with the initial requirements r_s=150cm, r_l=400cm cannot be satisfied well, because the application success rate would only be 95.5%. If we allow r_l=430cm then the application success rate becomes 99.1% and is only limited by the accuracy of the start position fix. An application success rate of 99.1% means that about 110 of 111 users will not encounter a single glitch when interacting with the CoINS system.

The test case GSM+Pedometer is constrained, because GSM is only able to distinguish between the six building entrances. Hence, guidance can only start at the entrances in this case.

Reading a QR code is a reliable way to determine one's start position. However, this method requires manual user interaction. Once the position is known, CoINS can perform quite accurately using compass and pedometer. If the step sensor is mounted

Table 4. CoINS Application Success Rates

System(s)	Start Location	Route	Total
WLAN (4.3m)	99.1%	100.0%	99.1%
WLAN (3.2m)	99.1%	96.4%	95.5%
GSM+Pedometer (foot, 5m)	98.8%	100.0%	98.8%
QR+Pedometer (foot, 5m)	100.0%	100.0%	100.0%
QR+Pedometer (foot, 4m)	100.0%	98.3%	98.3%
QR+Pedometer (head, 4m)	100.0%	97.2%	97.2%
QR+Pedometer (hand, 4m)	100.0%	94.0%	94.0%

on the foot or in the shoe, the results are significantly better compared to sensor on head or in the hand. The case *sensor in the hand* is quite interesting, because a mobile phone with an acceleration sensor could be directly used to implement a pedometer.

6 Conclusion

We have described an application-oriented method for evaluating LPS systems in an application and building context. The system uses a clear separation between the descriptions of application requirements and LPS properties to make both parts interchangeable. Building characteristics are considered where appropriate. The system provides the following three key benefits:

- Most importantly, with the calculation of the application success rate it is possible to directly get an estimate for the end user experience from the LPS characteristics. This result can be used as a basis for LPS selection.
- The simulator helps to determine the optimal values for application parameters, such as tolerance values.
- The reporting function can be used to identify the subtests responsible for the highest errors. A user could then selectively improve the LPS system in those areas, e.g., by measuring additional fingerprints or deploying additional sensors.

The presented evaluation method was applied to our CoINS system together with LPS technologies that are available in modern mobile phones. With the help of the simulator, we could confirm that CoINS can perform well with the given LPS systems if the application parameters are configured properly.

Acknowledgements. This work was supported by the SmartProducts project, funded as part of the Seventh Framework Programme of the EU under grant number 231204.

References

1. Aitenbichler, E.: A Focus on Location Context. In: Max Mühlhäuser, I.G. (ed.) Ubiquitous Computing Technology for Real Time Enterprises, ISR, pp. 257–281 (2008)
2. Kolodziej, K.: Local Positioning Systems: LBS applications and services. CRC Press, Boca Raton (2006)

3. Hightower, J., Borriello, G.: Particle Filters for Location Estimation in Ubiquitous Computing: A Case Study. In: Davies, N., Mynatt, E.D., Siio, I. (eds.) UbiComp 2004. LNCS, vol. 3205, pp. 88–106. Springer, Heidelberg (2004)
4. Woodman, O., Harle, R.: Pedestrian Localisation for Indoor Environments. In: UbiComp 2008: Ubiquitous Computing. (2008)
5. Song, Y.: In-House Location Tracking. Master's thesis, Darmstadt University of Technology (2002)
6. Bahl, P., Padmanabhan, V.N.: A Software System for Locating Mobile Users: Design, Evaluation, and Lessons. Technical report, Microsoft Research (2001)
7. LaMarca, A., Chawathe, Y., Consolvo, S., Hightower, J., Smith, I., Scott, J., Sohn, T., Howard, J., Hughes, J., Potter, F., Tabert, J., Powledge, P., Borriello, G., Schilit, B.: Place Lab: Device Positioning Using Radio Beacons in the Wild. In: Gellersen, H.-W., Want, R., Schmidt, A. (eds.) PERVASIVE 2005. LNCS, vol. 3468, pp. 116–133. Springer, Heidelberg (2005)
8. Ekahau: WiFi-based Real-time Tracking and Site Survey Solutions (2009), http://www.ekahau.com/ (last visited January 16, 2009)
9. Hartl, A.: A Provider-Independent, Proactive Service for Location Sensing in Cellular Networks. In: GTGKVS Fachgespräch (Online Proceedings) (2005)
10. Ubisense: Homepage. The Smart Space Company (2009), http://www.ubisense.net/ (last visited January 16, 2009)
11. Nike: Nike Plus (2009), http://nikeplus.nike.com/ (last visited January 19, 2009)
12. Beauregard, S.: A Helmet-Mounted Pedestrian Dead Reckoning System. In: 3rd International Forum on Applied Wearable Computing, IFAWC (2006)
13. Blanke, U., Schiele, B.: Sensing Location in the Pocket. In: UbiComp 2008 Adjunct Proceedings (2008)
14. Randell, C., Djiallis, C., Muller, H.: Personal Position Measurement Using Dead Reckoning. In: Proceedings of the Seventh IEEE International Symposium on Wearable Computers (2003)
15. Denso Wave Inc.: QR Code Homepage (2009), http://www.denso-wave.com/qrcode/ (last visited January 19, 2009)
16. Visonic Technologies: Elpas (2009), http://www.visonictech.com (last visited January 16, 2009)
17. Kaplan, E.: Understanding GPS Principles and Applications. Artech House Publishers (1996)
18. Hadjakos, A., Aitenbichler, E., Mühlhäuser, M.: Syssomo: A Pedagogical Tool for Analyzing Movement Variants Between Different Pianists. In: Ruffaldi, E., Fontana, M. (eds.) Enactive 2008 Proceedings, Pisa, Edizioni ETS, pp. 75–80 (2008)
19. Lyardet, F., Szeto, D.W., Aitenbichler, E.: Context Aware Indoor Navigation. In: Aarts, E., Crowley, J.L., de Ruyter, B., Gerhäuser, H., Pflaum, A., Schmidt, J., Wichert, R. (eds.) AmI 2008. LNCS, vol. 5355, pp. 290–307. Springer, Heidelberg (2008)
20. von Winterfeldt, D., Edwards, W.: Decision Analysis and Behavorial Research. Cambridge University Press, Cambridge (1986)
21. Aitenbichler, E., Kangasharju, J., Mühlhäuser, M.: MundoCore: A Light-weight Infrastructure for Pervasive Computing. Pervasive and Mobile Computing 3(4), 332–361 (2007)
22. Aitenbichler, E., Lyardet, F., Mühlhäuser, M.: Designing and Implementing Smart Spaces. Cepis Upgrade, 31–37 (August 2007)

Indoor Positioning System Using Beacon Devices for Practical Pedestrian Navigation on Mobile Phone

Yutaka Inoue[1,2], Akio Sashima[1,2], and Koichi Kurumatani[1,2]

[1] ITRI, National Institute of Advanced Industrial Science and Technology (AIST)
[2] CREST, Japan Science and Technology Agency (JST),
2-41-6, Aomi, Koto-ku, Tokyo, 135-0064, Japan
{yutaka.inoue,sashima-akio,k.kurumatani}@aist.go.jp

Abstract. In this paper, we propose a positioning system for indoor pedestrian navigation services using mobile phones. Position information services with a Global Positioning System (GPS) are widely used for car navigation and portable navigation. Their navigation systems facilitate development of industry and increase the convenience of civil life. However, such systems and services are available only for locations in which satellite signals can be received because users' self-positions are computed using GPS. Therefore, we developed a system for indoor environments, operating with a user's mobile terminal and battery-driven beacon devices in a server-less environment. Moreover, to provide convenient services using position information indoors, we developed an indoor navigation system that is useful in commercial facilities and office buildings. The system consists of smart phone and license-free radio beacon devices that can be driven with little electric power. In our proposed method, probabilistic estimation algorithms are applied to estimate self-positions in indoor locations, such as those where it is impossible to receive GPS signals. Feature of the system is that 2.5-dimensional indoor positioning is possible to calculate with low computational power device such as mobile phone. The system works autonomously, i.e., the user's device receives wireless beacon signals from the surrounding environment and can thereby detect a user's position independently from the mobile terminal, thereby obviating server-side computation.

Keywords: Indoor positioning, Localization, Particle filter, Navigation, Smartphone, Mobile phone, Beacon, License-free radio wave.

1 Introduction

In navigation systems, an important function estimates self-positions of users to determine a route from a current position to a destination. For position information services, Global Positioning Systems (GPSs) have been widely used in outdoor environments. Generally, a GPS is applied to fulfill that position-estimation function for navigation systems used in open-field areas. In addition to in-car systems, navigation systems for pedestrians using position-estimation functions with application of GPS have received increasing attention as a cellular telephone service [1]. Positioning services using mobile phones can provide evacuation functions [2] that can navigate a

D. Zhang et al. (Eds.): UIC 2009, LNCS 5585, pp. 251–265, 2009.
© Springer-Verlag Berlin Heidelberg 2009

user to emergency evacuation areas during and after disasters such as earthquakes and typhoons. Such services are fundamentally intended to provide users with route information when moving in an automobile or on foot from a location to a destination, or to provide a map of the actual location's surrounding areas.

Although GPS systems were originally designed for military use, civilians now use such systems with the many consumer GPS receivers now available. Consequently, navigation service providers using GPS need no extra devices for infrastructure or system development. Providers can therefore offer the product or service easily. However, because GPS cannot be used indoors, respective users' positions cannot be known precisely using GPS receivers. It is necessary to consider methods to estimate positioning in indoors for comfort and safety in everyday life. To provide an indoor positioning service, research into indoor self-position estimation has so far been carried out using various devices [3,4,5,6]. Although such approaches are effective for self-position estimation indoors, the studies neglect the discussion of practicality. In fact, their positioning systems have not been considered that indoor positioning estimation and practical application software, such as positioning for indoor pedestrian navigation, need simultaneously to operate in low computational power device. Therefore, previous methods are difficult to consider their provision as practical services for pedestrians using a mobile phone.

An important factor for widening the use of systems and services is consideration of the ease of infrastructure preparation and system operation. Therefore, to realize the function of self-position estimation required for an indoor navigation system, we use an ultra-slim network node [7,8]: it is small, low-powered, and wireless. Moreover, the device can be manufactured inexpensively because it is manufactured with the minimum parts necessary for providing the system's required functions. The installation is simple: ultra-slim network node devices can be attached every several tens of meters in an environment (e.g., wall, ceiling, window). A user's receiver receives data sent from the ultra-slim network nodes installed in an environment. The received data are then used for self-positioning analyses.

As described herein, we propose an indoor autonomous positioning system to provide practical pedestrian navigation services indoors. The system can operate on a mobile terminal such as a smart phone by receiving radio beacon signals from beacon devices in the environment. The system operates autonomously without server access; the installed beacon devices can be driven using batteries. Therefore, our system can preserve user privacy.

2   Architecture

In this section, we describe the architecture of indoor positioning system using wireless beacon devices. Our positioning system is intended to offer practical service using indoor position information. Therefore, we designed a positioning system that can operate autonomously using only users' terminals without server communication. Installation and management of the equipment are necessary costs if the positioning system requires communication servers. The system also preserves user privacy because the self-position of users can be computed in a mobile terminal by analyzing the beacon signal data sent from the receiver via Bluetooth.

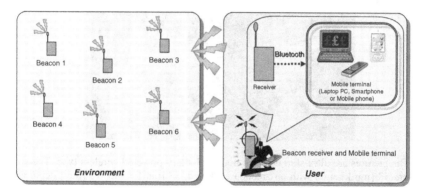

Fig. 1. System overview

2.1 System Design

To provide practical use service, we must design a system that addresses realistic problems occurring in each process, such as design for application software, installation to facilities, operation and maintenance. For example, we must consider whether the system can function correctly when many users simultaneously used positioning services in indoor facilities. We defined the following requirements to produce a practical indoor positioning system.

- Responsiveness: robust positioning system for noisy real-world environments.
- Autonomy: operation using only mobile terminals without server communication.
- Reliability: system performance in a crowded environment.
- Maintainability: installation and management of devices in facilities.

Responsiveness is an important factor to satisfy general users by mobile navigation service. If the users can not utilize comfortably the system in real environment, the localization system is regarded as useless study for the general public. Advantages of autonomous system are possible to respond quickly to localization and access to the service during the power outage, such as in emergency. Their benefits will contribute to build practical system in terms of computing decentralization and portability. Reliability and maintainability have an impact on system management and operating cost. Our system can be worked easily in temporary indoor facility also, such as exhibition hall at World Expos, because the system adopts license-free radio beacon of VHF and low-power battery-driven devices.

As shown in Fig. 1, the position is estimated on a mobile terminal with a beacon receiver that receives signal data transmitted from radio beacon devices installed in indoor environments. The radio beacon device can be attached easily to a ceiling or wall because it is small and lightweight without connecting cables such as a power supply cable or a LAN connection cable. It is also possible to supply a power supply by the cable. Via the receiver, users can receive beacon signals transmitted from radio beacon devices in the environment. The beacon receiver receives the beacon signals. Thereafter, the signals are sent via Bluetooth to a user with a mobile terminal.

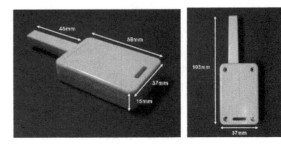

Fig. 2. The pictures are ultra-slim network node of battery-powered wireless type. The specifications are 58 [mm] height with an antenna excluded, 37 [mm] width, 15 [mm] depth and 21 [g] weights with battery excluded.

Localization methods using radio wave can be classified to two types of approaches. One is Time Differential of Arrival (TDOA) as typified by GPS and the other is Received Signal Strength (RSS) such as RADAR [9] and PlaceLab [10]. TDOA based approach is hard to apply to localize in a narrow space, because it can use for estimating in open locations such as differential time of arrival signals is significant. Therefore, RSS is often applied to indoor localization system. We also designed positioning engine based on RSS for indoor environment.

2.2 Beacon Device

We applied an ultra-slim network node (Fig. 2) as the beacon device for an indoor positioning system. The ultra-slim network node is small (58 [mm] × 37 [mm] × 15 [mm], with an antenna excluded) and light (21 [g], with battery excluded). The device operates with a single button-type battery. These devices have transmitted signal data that are assigned to each node. The device consumes less power than other typical radio devices because the beacon signals are transmitted using license-free radio with low electric power. The frequency band that is used is of very high frequency (VHF).

We designed the embedded communication software so that the device can function also as a receiver by rewriting the device's EPROM in its Micro Processing Unit (MPU). This device is useful as an installed beacon transmitter and a receiver. Therefore, the cost of manufacturing the device is expected to be low.

2.3 RSS Fingerprinting

We measured the RSS of the wireless beacon devices attached in our laboratory to investigate location fingerprinting in a noisy real environment. The office installation (e.g., partition, desk, and chair) layout of our laboratory is shown in Fig. 3. The room dimensions are 13.4 [m] × 11.4 [m]. Each area is divided by partitions of about 1.5 [m] height. The six beacon devices are installed in the place. Points shown in Fig. 3 represent positions of beacon devices installed for the experiment.

The beacon devices are set on positions higher than the partitions instituted in the room, i.e., on positions higher than 1.5 [m]. The beacon signal receivers were set on the position lower than the partitions, i.e., on positions lower than 1.5 [m]. Moreover, in the room, office automation equipment (e.g., printer, PC, and display) and wireless applications (e.g., wireless LAN and Bluetooth devices) are set up.

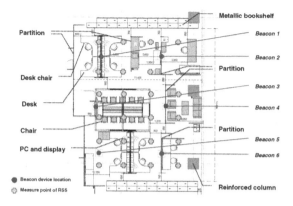

Fig. 3. Experimental environment in our laboratory

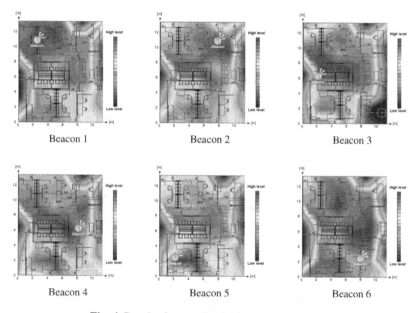

Fig. 4. Result of measuring RSS in our laboratory

Figure 4 shows averaged RSS data of samples measured at each position in our laboratory. The data were measurements on 24 points for every installed beacon device in the laboratory. The RSS fingerprinting is a result that is approximated by planar interpolation based on the measurement data of beacon signals. The beacon in the figure signifies the position of a device installed for the experiment. Color variations of Fig. 4 show the signal strength of the beacon devices installed in the environment.

The environmental result shows the following characteristics of the beacon devices available by license-free radio with VHF.

- The RSS undergo a change with distance of a measured point from a beacon.
- The beacon signal can be diffracted obstructions, such as partitions and desks.
- The RSS of a beacon signal diffracted and reflected by obstructions becomes remarkably weaker than the signal before obstruction.
- Wireless applications in an office, such as wireless LAN and Bluetooth, exhibit no mutual interference.

The RSS can be computed when it receives beacon data if the device is used as a receiver. The self-position estimation function will be realized by application of a learning algorithm or statistical analysis using the RSS data as training data. The function estimates the user's present position when the user's receiver inputs the RSS data acquired in real time.

3 Positioning System

This section presents methods for implementing indoor positioning using beacon signals. We developed a compact positioning engine tuned up for practical indoor pedestrian navigation service on a mobile phone. Localization in the positioning engine is estimated through analysis using stochastic reasoning algorithms using one or more received beacon signal data. The computing power of MPU in the mobile phone is sufficient for processing to localize the user if our localization algorithm is appropriated for positioning users in indoor buildings. The software programs for localization can be operated in a smart phone or mobile phone. Therefore, a user's terminal need not communicate with any server.

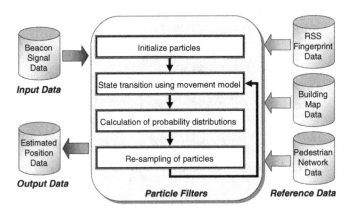

Fig. 5. Positioning engine using particle filters

3.1 System Configuration

As shown in Fig. 5, the input data of this positioning system are real-time data sent from a mobile terminal to a beacon receiver and the preliminarily prepared data stored in the terminal. These preparation data, such as RSS fingerprint data, building map data and pedestrian network data, are saved in the external memories of the mobile terminal. The data sets are also used for robust estimation. These reference data are used for probability calculation in the positioning engine to filter the generated candidates of estimated current position and past trajectory of a user.

The system's pinpointing engine has applied particle filters [11,12]. Even if only a few beacon signals can be received, positioning estimation can be performed using an approximation method for the probability distribution of the whole space such as the particle filter. Moreover, because the method can seek a user's position locally, calculation costs are also reducible.

Based on the inputted signal data, this positioning system estimates a user's self-position sequentially. The storage data referred to with the particle filter were implemented by a data format, which is designed to be suitable for the positioning system. Because of such purpose-designed system architecture, we created a positioning engine that can compute a mobile phone user's position rapidly.

3.2 Storage Data

The data necessary to operate the software that is used practically on mobile phones must be much smaller than that for operation on a PC. Furthermore, mobile phones might download the necessary data by server communications to update software in the latest state. In such a case, if the download data size is small, communication times and fees can be saved.

In a navigation system, data needing the biggest capacity are data to draw the building map. Therefore, we designed the vector data format optimized for an indoor pedestrian navigation aimed at practically used mobile phones.

The data format can express, geometrically, the movement topology information of pedestrian and RSS fingerprint map as well as map information. It can be reduced data size than expression with image data such as a raster map. Complicated processing, such as turning the map, zooming in, and zooming out can be conducted easily in a CPU with little computation power.

Table 1 presents comparative data for comparison of some image formats with the vector format developed by us. The data used for comparison are map information of the same three floors in a commercial building. The building's floor area is about 10,000 m^2; total floor area for the map data is 30,000 m^2. Fewer vector map data were used by this system than map data compressed by the general picture format, as shown in the table. The purpose-designed data format is a useful means to offer a practical application.

Table 1. Comparison of vector data size and raster image size

Format	Conversion Software	Option	Size [kB]
Vector	Developed in-house	-	21.4
Bitmap	Windows Paint	640 × 240 [pix], 24 bit full color.	1350.2
JPEG	Windows Paint	640 × 240 [pix].	67.5
TIFF	Windows Paint	640 × 240 [pix].	218.5
PING	Windows Paint	640 × 240 [pix].	127.0

3.3 Particle Filters

The particle filter is a method to approximate the probability distribution in the state by the distribution of the many particles with the weight in state space. The state in time t is set to s_t, and the observation value is set to z_t, where the observation value to time t is expressed with $Z_t = \{z_1, \ldots, z_t\}$. From the posterior probability $P(s_{t-1}|Z_{t-1})$ and state transition probability $P(s_t|s_{t-1})$ of $t-1$ by assuming the Markov property of the state transition, the prior probability $P(s_t|Z_{t-1})$ of time t is expressed as follows:

$$P\left(s_t|Z_{t-1}\right) = \int P\left(s_t|s_{t-1}\right)P\left(s_{t-1}|Z_{t-1}\right)dx_{t-1} \tag{1}$$

where if $P(z_t|Z_{t-1})$ is set constant, from likelihood $P(z_t|s_t)$ and prior probability $P(s_t|Z_{t-1})$ in time t, posterior probability $P(s_t|Z_t)$ in time t can be expressed as follows using Bayes' theorem.

$$P\left(s_t|Z_t\right) \propto P\left(z_t|s_t\right)P\left(s_t|Z_{t-1}\right) \tag{2}$$

A user's position is estimated by calculating the expectation of the posterior probability $P(s_t|Z_t)$. The posterior probability $P(s_t|Z_t)$ of time t is approximated by particles $\{c_t^{(1)}, \ldots, c_t^{(N)}\}$ and weights $\{w_t^{(1)}, \ldots, w_t^{(N)}\}$ expressing in state s_t, and is updated consecutively as follows.

1. Sampling: Selection of particles based on weight
   By following weights $\{w_{t-1}^{(1)}, \ldots, w_{t-1}^{(N)}\}$ of N-particles $\{c_{t-1}^{(1)}, \ldots, c_{t-1}^{(N)}\}$ approximated posterior probability $P(s_{t-1}|Z_{t-1})$ of time $t-1$ discretely, and new particles $\{c_{t-1}^{(1)'}, \ldots, c_{t-1}^{(N)'}\}$ are chosen.
2. Propagation: State transition based on probability
   Chosen particles $\{c_{t-1}^{(1)'}, \ldots, c_{t-1}^{(N)'}\}$ are propagated following to state transition probability $P(s_t|s_{t-1})$, and N-particles $\{c_t^{(1)}, \ldots, c_t^{(N)}\}$ in time t is generated.
3. Estimation: Approximate calculation of user's position
   The user position is estimated by evaluating weights $\{w_t^{(1)}, \ldots, w_t^{(N)}\}$ of particles $\{c_t^{(1)}, \ldots, c_t^{(N)}\}$ based on a likelihood function using RSS fingerprinting.

4 Experiments

This section explains an experiment to verify the positioning system's practicality; it shows the experimental result. The positioning system was investigated using some experiments.

The first experiment estimates a standing user's position by searching for a plane space in the map using a particle filter. This experiment was conducted in the office room. The other experiment estimates a position of the standing user which is limited in the topological space defined on the map of the particle moving space in the environment. The topological information used by this experiment was inputted by what was set virtually of a human line of flow into map space. This experiment was performed in passages in the building for conduct in the viewpoint of more practical navigation. The experiment was also conducted localization a walking user. In this case, we examined positioning in the movement state of the walker, which is one important factor for practical navigation services.

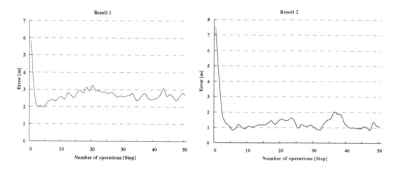

Fig. 6. Positioning prediction vs. trial number. Data are averages of 30 runs.

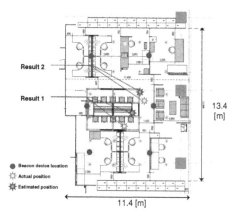

Fig. 7. Positioning result in the room

4.1 Positioning in a Room

In the office room, we experimented with the positioning system using license-free radio beacon devices. This investigation revealed the positioning accuracy in indoor space. We estimated a user's position without using pedestrian network data. In the experiment, the positioning accuracy was inspected for two arbitrary places.

As pre-measured data for RSS fingerprint map, the RSS interpolation data presented in section 2.3 are used for positioning by the particle filter. The particle filter parameters are assumed as the following: the re-sampling frequency is every operation; the particles are 500 in all. Experiments were performed as input with the beacon signal data of each position measured in a real environment.

The position average errors for all calculations in each place are shown in Fig. 6. These results are average values of 30 trials. The average error is about 1.0–3.0 [m], and the estimated position using the particle filter converges at 5–10 [step]. Figure 7 shows positions estimated by this system, real positions of the user, and beacon device locations.

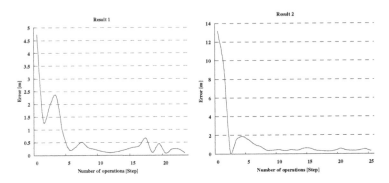

Fig. 8. Positioning prediction vs. trial number. Data represent the averages of 30 runs.

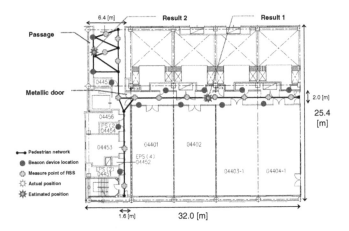

Fig. 9. Positioning result on passages

4.2 Positioning on Passages

The experiment was conducted to estimate the position of a standing user on the passage in a building. In this experiment, the moving space of particles was restricted using pedestrian network data. Inspection of the positioning accuracy is performed for two locations.

Beacon data acquired for 14 places were used for the sample RSS fingerprint map. The particle filter parameters are assumed as re-sampling every operation, the particles are 50 in all. The experiment was performed as input of the measured data for each position in a real environment.

The average positioning errors of all operations are shown in Fig. 8. The results are averages of 30 trials. The mean of the positioning error is understood as about 0.5–1.0 [m], the estimated positions by particles converge at 10 [step]. Figure 9 shows the estimated positions, user's real positions, the pedestrian network, and the location of beacon devices.

Furthermore, we measured a trajectory on the passage in a building to estimate the position of a moving walker. In this experiment, a pedestrian's moving trajectory was estimated using beacon data obtained while moving on the passage in the building. The walker position tracking is performed by particles moving in a pedestrian network space. The sampling data of the RSS and the particle filter parameters are identical to previous described for this section.

The experimental result is shown in Fig. 10. In the initial stage of positioning estimation, the positioning error is likely to result from non-convergence of the localization. However, an approximate position was estimated after a pedestrian moved several meters. In consideration of the time lag to a user position display screen, the positioning accuracy was almost able to detect the position with precision of 0.5–2.0 [m].

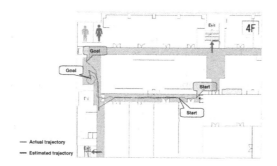

Fig. 10. Moving trajectory of a pedestrian

4.3 Discussion

We conducted experiments in a building to localize standing-still and state of movement. The user's position in the office room was desirable for planar detection. Therefore, the experiment was performed by extension onto a two-dimensional space of moving area for particles. On the other hand, in the experiment examining the passage, the movement space of the particles was limited on the pedestrian network to use practical services such as the navigation with the mobile phone.

Calculation costs of computer increase, although the resolution ability of the positioning might be increased by enlarging movement space of the particles. As with the experiment in the passage, calculation costs can be reduced by limiting the movement space of the particles. Generally, normal method using particle filter needs high calculation cost compared to the proposed method to estimate indoor positioning by pedestrian network, since the number of particle in the algorithm changes according to search space size for positioning. The system can also recognize a floor inhabiting the user. The floor estimation algorithm is necessary to cost computation power, because the process must always work to estimate user's floor for practical use in commercial buildings. Therefore, calculation cost had better be as low cost as possible with low computational power device such mobile phones.

The positioning experiment for a pedestrian in a passage examined the pedestrian network. The reported position is shifted from the actual position before arrival to the vicinity of the central door. Probably this occurs because the door of the center is steel and the arrival area is near an elevator. Those factors cause instability of electric waves. Because this positioning system has a small search cost, low computing power terminals, such as cellular phones, are useful to estimate the user's position completely during movement. This study is intended to produce a system that offers indoor navigation service for pedestrian on mobile phones, the method using pedestrian network data is more effective for guidance to stores and other everyday destinations. Using guidance within some divisions, such as the inside store and exhibition hall, applying the method of using lattice-shaped pedestrian network data is also considered.

5   Related Works

In recent years, position information services, such as navigation services, have become indispensable for civil life, home life, industry, etc. In outdoor situations, GPS-based positioning systems, such as car navigation systems, have already been realized on a commercial basis. The system serves as a substitute for a human navigator because it is able to locate users' self-positions and provide directions to a destination.

The near current position is computable using data received from the satellite in areas where a signal from positioning satellites is not intercepted, e.g. nearly enclosed outdoor areas. On the other hand, regarding indoor environments, it is difficult to receive GPS signals. Approaches of transmitting GPS signals to indoor environments have been proposed and tested, such as Pseudolite-GPS [3] and the GPS Re-radiation System [4].

Pseudolite-GPS is a system using a transmitter that emits a pseudo-GPS signal generated by simulations. The system renders it difficult to receive near and distant signals from the transmitting antenna to alleviate the phenomenon known as the Near-Far Problem. Furthermore, because GPS signals require extraordinary temporal precision for time synchronization among real and pseudo-GPS satellites, it is difficult to maintain accurate time synchronization on the system. It becomes difficult for users to acquire self-positioning when a time prediction error arises between the system and GPS. Furthermore, it requires greater effort to match the time of Pseudolite-GPS to GPS' time and to attach equipment to use the system.

The GPS Re-radiation System receives real GPS-signals in open field areas, forwards them with a cable, and transmits them to the indoor environment. The system is impossible to use in areas where it cannot also receive GPS signals outdoors. Moreover, this system renders it impossible to specify a user's precise position because it only reradiates GPS signals received by antennas installed in an outdoor location. Additionally, it is necessary to install many GPS receiving antennas outdoors to raise the position-tracking precision.

If indoor positioning and navigation systems without GPS were realized, they would become key technologies for use in many position information services. Various non-GPS methods have already been applied to indoor positioning systems. For instance, Active Bats [5] and Cricket [6] are techniques that can offer position information by receiving information sent from transmitter devices. Using these methods, a user can detect a position in the mode of only whether the user is in a certain area specified by the transmitter position. Therefore, the number of transmitters must be increased to improve the position detection accuracy, which raises the cost for installation of devices and equipment maintenance.

In fact, RADAR [7], PlaceLab [8], and AirLocationII [15] are methods to estimate the position in indoor using radio electric field strength of Wi-Fi signals. These methods have an advantage in that they require no special devices except Wireless LAN units. However, it is difficult to achieve high positioning accuracy because Wi-Fi changes the transmission mechanism and power according to radio situations. Consequently, the electric field strength becomes unstable. Furthermore, wireless LAN units require large amounts of electric power, which requires electric power cable installation for environmental devices; alternatively, it shortens battery life for end-users' portable devices. Moreover, the system cannot operate in case of a power failure.

Ubisense [16] use Ultra Wideband (UWB) technology for positioning. The system uses tags and UWB base stations. The base stations can pinpoint the tag location. However, the system cannot recognize self-positions of users on their own portable devices because each user's position is managed with servers.

Some positioning methods [17,18] have been proposed to estimate user locations using probabilistic estimation algorithms, such as Bayesian filters. The pedestrian localization system [17] estimates the user's position with particle filters using Wi-Fi signal strength and a foot-mounted inertial sensor. However, the localization system does not presuppose that the computations for positioning operate on a mobile terminal: smart phones or mobile phones are not the target terminal of such systems. A localization system using Zone-Based RSS Reporting [18] uses Location Fingerprinting. The system is based on the premise that the user's terminal communicates with servers.

In contrast, we designed a system that improves the weaknesses of an indoor positioning system, as described above. Our indoor autonomous positioning system using battery-driven beacon devices can estimate the user's position only on a mobile terminal. The positioning algorithms using the system can be operated not only on a Laptop PC but also on a low computing power terminal, such as a mobile phone. The system is highly decentralized and can operate in server-less environments; it has no central repository of the user's position. Therefore, the system preserves a user's privacy and reduces the management cost.

6 Conclusion and Future Works

We presented a positioning system that can operate mobile terminal using wireless beacon devices. We designed the system with the intention of building a practical indoor positioning system incorporating Responsiveness, Autonomy, Reliability, and Maintainability. Especially, a feature of our system is a software engine that is able to operate on a smart phone or mobile phone, i.e., the user also has access to self-positioning in server-less environments.

The positioning system is able to estimate the user's location by receiving radio beacon signals from beacon devices installed in an indoor environment. The user's privacy might not be preserved if the positioning system must communicate with servers. However, our positioning system can preserve user privacy and reduce management costs because the system operates autonomously, thereby obviating server communications. This server-less system presents advantages not only of privacy protection, but fewer relay times and operable architecture during power outages.

The beacon device is suitable for indoor buildings with equipment that inhibits radio waves because VHF, which is adopted as a frequency band for the devices, has characteristically easy diffraction of radio waves in comparison with UHF, such as Wi-Fi. The battery-driven beacon device and receiver communicate with license-free radios, which require little electric power.

We have conducted a field experiment [13] on an indoor pedestrian navigation service to investigate the positioning system's practicality. In the experiment, we installed wireless beacon devices [14] in indoor facilities. The experiment was conducted to investigate the availability and usability of the indoor navigation system applied in our positioning system. License-free radio beacon devices enhanced by us to raise performance. An autonomic navigation system is realized by compact system design, such as positioning algorithms for low calculation costs, a human flow network format optimized for pedestrian path searching in indoor building and vector map format designed for downsizing of the total data.

We obtained opinions by brief multiple choice questionnaire and group discussion to obtain direct users' opinion in this experiment. Most opinion is that map screen would be better to rotate automatically; because the users are unsure whether waking direction matched the map aspect on the screen. We have been improving the system to provide practical service based on user feedbacks of a field experiment.

Our navigation system using the positioning system is applicable for services of other navigation for shopping and sightseeing, for instance, as an emergency evacuation system [19] that functions in server-less environments using only mobile phones. Moreover, the navigation system is applicable for operation for indoor locomotion of robots that require complex control, such as cooperative humanoid robots [20]. Possible applications of this system are sightseeing navigation system, emergency evacuation system, building management system and robot navigation system.

We plan to improve the system by including an interface and navigation screen. Moreover, we are planning to study the device using various electric sensors, such as an acceleration sensor and a geomagnetic sensor, for enhancement of the positioning precision.

References

1. Arikawa, M., Konomi, S., Ohnishi, K.: Navitime: Supporting Pedestrian Navigation in the Real World. IEEE Pervasive Computing 6(3), 21–29 (2007)
2. Saigaiji-Navi (2007),
   http://www.kddi.com/english/corporate/news_release/2007/0522/
3. Stone, J., LeMaster, E.A., Powell, J.D., Rock, S.M.: GPS Pseudolite Transceivers and their Applications, Institute of Navigation National Technical Meeting, San Diego, California, USA (1999)
4. HNRRKIT.: Hanger Network GPS Re-Radiating Kit,
   http://gpsnetworking.com/

5. Addlesee, M., Curwen, R., Hodges, S., Newman, J., Steggles, P., Ward, A., Hopper, A.: Implementing a Sentient Computing System. IEEE Computer Magazine 34(8), 50–56 (2001)
6. Priyantha, N.B., Chakraborty, A., Balakrishnan, H.: The Cricket Location-Support System. In: Proc. the 6th ACM International Conference on Mobile Computing and Networking (ACM MOBICOM 2000), Boston, MA, pp. 32–43 (2000)
7. Ultra-Slim Network Node Development for Ubiquitous Community – General Purpose Network Node for Sensor Network or IC Tag – (2004),
   http://www.aist.go.jp/aist_e/latest_research/2004/20041220/20041220.html
8. Ohba, K.: Ultra-Slim Network Node Development – Aiming to the ubiquitous and the ubiquitous-robot society. AIST Today 5(4), 20–21 (2005)
9. Bahl, P., Padmanabhan, V.N.: RADAR: an in-building RF-based user location and tracking system. In: IEEE Infocom 2000, vol. 2, pp. 775–784 (2000)
10. LaMarca, A., Chawathe, Y., Consolvo, S., Hightower, J., Smith, I., Scott, J., Sohn, T., Howard, J., Hughes, J., Potter, F., Tabert, J., Powledge, P., Borriello, G., Schilit, B.: Place Lab: Device Positioning Using Radio Beacons in the Wild. In: Gellersen, H.-W., Want, R., Schmidt, A. (eds.) PERVASIVE 2005. LNCS, vol. 3468, pp. 116–133. Springer, Heidelberg (2005)
11. Doucet, A., Freitas, N., Gordon, N. (eds.): Sequential Monte Carlo Methods in Practice. Springer, Heidelberg (2001)
12. Ristic, B., Arulampalam, S., Gordon, N.: Beyond the Kalman Filter: Particle Filters for Tracking Applications, Artec House (2004)
13. Inoue, Y., Ikeda, T., Yamamoto, K., Yamashita, T., Sashima, A., Kurumatani, K.: Usability Study of Indoor Mobile Navigation System in Commercial Facilities. In: Proc. of the 2nd International Workshop on Ubiquitous Systems Evaluation (USE 2008) in UbiComp 2008, Seoul, South Korea, pp. 45–50 (2008)
14. Ikeda, T., Inoue, Y., Yamamoto, K., Yamashita, T., Sashima, A., Kurumatani, K.: CompPass System: A Low power Wireless Sensor Network System and its Application to Indoor Positioning. In: First International Workshop on Automated and Autonomous Sensor Networks (AASN) in CSTST 2008, Paris, France (2008)
15. AirLocation II (2006),
   http://www.hitachi.co.jp/New/cnews/month/2006/07/0713.html
16. UbiSense.: Local position system and sentient computing (2004),
   http://www.ubisense.net/
17. Woodman, O., Harle, R.: Pedestrian Localisation for Indoor Environments. In: Proc. of the 10th International Conference on Ubiquitous Computing (UbiComp 2008), Seoul, South Korea, pp. 114–123 (2008)
18. Kjærgaard, M.B., Treu, G., Linnhof-Popien, C.: Zone-Based RSS Reporting for Location Fingerprinting. In: LaMarca, A., Langheinrich, M., Truong, K.N. (eds.) Pervasive 2007. LNCS, vol. Pervasive 2007, pp. 316–333. Springer, Heidelberg (2007)
19. Inoue, Y., Sashima, A., Ikeda, T., Kurumatani, K.: Indoor Emergency Evacuation Service on Autonomous Navigation System using Mobile Phone. In: Proc. the 2nd International Symposium on Universal Communication, Osaka, Japan (2008)
20. Inoue, Y., Tohge, T., Iba, H.: Cooperative Transportation System for Humanoid Robots using Simulation-Based Learning. Applied Soft. Computing 7(1), 115–125 (2007)

NavTag: An Inter-Working Framework Based on Tags for Symbolic Location Coordinates for Smart Spaces

Vlad Stirbu

Nokia Research Center
vlad.stirbu@nokia.com

Abstract. Location information and sensor networks are key ingredients in realizing smart spaces by customizing the behavior of the application according to users' locations and by being able to sense and act upon the physical space. This paper presents a flexible interworking model for complex smart space environments, in which points of interest are represented as tags, while spatial representations are achieved by representing the physical space as a tag space encoding a quadtree. The mechanism is beneficial for reducing the modeling and maintenance costs of location in smart spaces, as well as providing a low entry barrier for integration with other information systems.

1 Introduction

Modern office buildings have a set of support functions, such as air conditioning system, heating system, wired network cables, electricity cables and access control systems, that supports the activity that takes place inside. Typically these facilities are added or upgraded during the normal maintenance cycles that can be years apart. Each system is installed and maintained by different specialized teams. Although, these systems are installed in the same physical space, several aspects like tradition, current accepted best practices in an industry sector or regulation, lead to different perspectives of the shared space. For example, the space management team sees the space as a set of rooms, the air conditioning team sees the space as a network of tubes with certain locations for vents, the IT support team sees the wired network as an array of network ports. The common pattern observed here is that each support team assigns symbolic names to their location of interest. An important aspect to highlight is that the symbolic names do not overlap.

Up to now, the sensor and actuator have generally been investigated as dedicated systems tight to particular environments, such as the facilities mentioned in office buildings. The design decisions, although efficient for the target environment, have led to vertical solutions that are difficult to integrate into a single unified environment. While the heterogeneous aspects of sensor and actuator networks have been extensively investigated in research literature [1, 2, 3], we are particularly concerned with the symbolic location model used by the different infrastructure systems. We investigate different location systems suitable for ubiquitous computing, how they can be used in this context and propose a framework that harmonizes the individual symbolic location models to allow the sensing and actuation capabilities of the different SANs to be mashed across the various application domains enabled by the building smart space.

D. Zhang et al. (Eds.): UIC 2009, LNCS 5585, pp. 266–280, 2009.

The objective of this paper is to present NavTag, a flexible interworking framework that represents the smart space points of interest as tags in a symbolic location coordinates system. Tags metadata can be represented in a lattice model and a graph model that enable comprehensive location aware queries, such as position, range, path, distance and closest neighbor. The elementary queries can be piped together or linked to other information systems in the smart space.

This paper is structured as follows. Section 2 provides an overview of work already done on location and context modeling in pervasive environments. Section 3 describes two scenarios that motivated this work. Section 4 describes the challenges of using symbolic location coordinates. Section 5 presents the concepts, relations and the interworking model of the NavTag framework. Section 6 contains the validation of applicably of the proposed framework in a smart space environment. Concluding remarks and areas that need further investigation are provided in Section 7.

2   Related Work

This section presents existing work on modeling location information and context in ubiquitous and pervasive environments.

2.1   Location Information in Smart Spaces

Becker and Dürr [4] have investigated several location based models in the context of ubiquitous computing. Basically, applications interact with the location system to request position of objects, find the nearest neighbor of an object, navigate between two objects, find all the objects within a certain boundary or visualizing the objects on a map. In order to support such interactions, a location model has to provide object positions, distance functions, topological relations (e.g. spatial containment and spatial connectedness) or orientation.

Geometric location models describe locations in the space using geometric figures. These figures can be described using coordinates in a local cartesian reference system or a global system (e.g. GPS). One advantage of such a system is that it has built-in ability to describe containment. Explicit modeling is needed to capture connectedness.

Symbolic location models are defining the position in the space with the help of abstract symbols (e.g. human-friendly label such as room or street names). Explicit modeling is needed in order to describe the containment and connectedness relations between the objects. Set-based and hierarchical models are able to model well containment while graph based models are better at modeling the connectedness.

The common understanding is that each model alone are not able to fulfill all the requirements of the applications. Limitations can be addressed by hybrid models that combine several symbolic models with geographic models at the expense of high modeling cost.

The modeling and operational costs, and the expertise required are a major challenge for the wide adoption of location aware systems.

2.2   Context Models

Strang and Linnhoff-Popien [5] have investigated the most relevant context model-ing approaches. Six categories have been identified based on the data structures used for representing and exchanging contextual information. *Key-Value* models represent the simplest approach in representing context and are used to describe capabilities. *Markup Schemes* models use hierarchical data structures consisting in markup tags with attributes and content (e.g microformats [6]). *Graphical* models use UML. *Ob-ject Oriented* models use object-oriented techniques (e.g. encapsulation, reusability, in-heritance) to capture context. *Logic Based* models use facts, expressions and rules to define context with a high degree of formalism. *Ontology Based* models use ontologies to represent concepts and relationships.

Graphical, object oriented, logic based and ontology based models are feature rich tools providing high and formal expressiveness for context modeling. However, the use of this tools requires a high level of expertise that is not widely available among the ordinary users. Previous research (e.g. Place Lab [7]) has shown that the use of these tools are not a prerequisite when dealing with context aware systems. Naive tools like key-value and markup schemes models become powerful tools in the hands of the users.

The success of the Web 2.0 phenomena has shown that lightweight approaches based on collaborative tagging [8] provide the tools that will allow the end user to interact and manage complex machinery without expert knowledge or supervision.

3   Motivating Scenarios

The following section describes two sample scenarios that emphasize the heterogene-ity and dynamics of the semantic location models, and integration with management systems in a typical smart building.

3.1   Maintenance of Broken Vending Machine

A smart power meter detects that there is an unusual consumption pattern with a ma-chine connected to an *electrical socket* and notifies a management application. The management application identifies that the appliance in question is vending machine located in the *Demo Lab*. The management application places an order with the vend-ing machine maintenance company. The maintenance company acknowledges the ticket and performs a remote check of the vending machine. The problem cannot be detected remotely and a on-site maintenance is scheduled. The request is sent to the building management application to give access rights on the premises for the maintenance per-sonnel. Access rights are assigned to the maintenance technician mobile device. When the technician arrives at the location he is using the indoor navigation to find the path to the vending machine. He can open the *front door*, activate *elevator control*, arrives to the *Demo Lab* and performs maintenance to the machine.

3.2   Personalization of Very Dynamic Smart Space Environments

Trade shows and industry fairs are typically held in specialized buildings that feature a very large open space that can be easily partitioned, depending on the characteris-tics of each event, into smaller parts, called boots. Each event preparations involves complex teams that work months before, starting with planning, then with modifying and extending the existing facilities (e.g. installing temporary electricity circuits, access control systems) prior to the event, and ending with the activities that take place during the event. Typically, these tasks are happening between other events and when required expert teams are available.

For example, a specialized team is performing testing operations for a new audio video equipment that is going to be used in an event that will happen in six weeks. To complete the operation they will need access to the smart space layout and the available infrastructure (e.g. ventilation system, electricity) as on the day of the event. Based on test findings, the team members change the layout in the area for maximizing the performance, add precise instructions where to position the equipment, as well as program the ventilation and sensor systems to handle the additional heat load.

4 Symbolic Location Coordinates: Characteristics and Challenges

The scenarios presented in Section 3 emphasize that a single physical space may have multiple perspectives, each with its own symbolic location model that depends on the various users performing their activities there. We can easily identify some perspectives that are building infrastructure specific (e.g. the ventilation, electrical wiring or security and access control) and some that are specific to the humans using the space (e.g. the room naming scheme, the demo lab). The humans perspective of the space is a very important topic as each person may have its own perspective, leading in some open environments to an explosion of perspectives of the space.

The dynamics of the perspectives of the space is another important aspect. The building infrastructure perspectives are typically long living while the ones related to the humans activity in the space tend to be more dynamic. Regardless, an important characteristic is that each perspective can change independently of the other perspectives.

The set of challenges that can be encountered in a smart place environment, characterized by the heterogeneity of the different perspectives the users have of the physical space, can be split in two categories: operational and programming related. From the operational perspective, a provider of a smart space has to determine which is the most appropriate location model that fulfills the requirements of its users and what is the modeling cost. From a programming perspective, developers have to create applications that are able to engage in smart spaces without prior knowledge on what particular location model is deployed in a particular smart space. In practical terms, the smart space applications have to be tolerant when handling location related information, so that it can accommodate from simplest location model to the most sophisticated one.

A mapping mechanism is needed to expose in a lightweight fashion a unified view of the perspectives of the space and, at the same time, to preserve the ability of each party to maintain and extend its own perspective.

5 The NavTag Framework

This section presents the components of the NavTag framework. We start from the basic concepts of representing points of interest in the smart space as tags and how they relate to each other. Then, perspectives are collections of tags that belong to different users and groups of users, and depending on their functional role in the smart space we assign them to one of the following categories: user - for user related tags, infrastructure - for building infrastructure or support functions related tags, and system - for internal use of the framework. Among these, the system perspective sits at the core of the framework, being responsible with maintaining the containment relationships between tags as well as possible spatial relations between the physical smart space and global map systems. Connectors are user generated structures that capture connectedness relations between tags. Finally, we describe the interworking model enabled by the tags, the connectors and the system perspective. The model is based on few query primitives that, when pipelined, allow complex location-aware operations across multiple perspectives and different information systems that, by themselves, are not aware of each other.

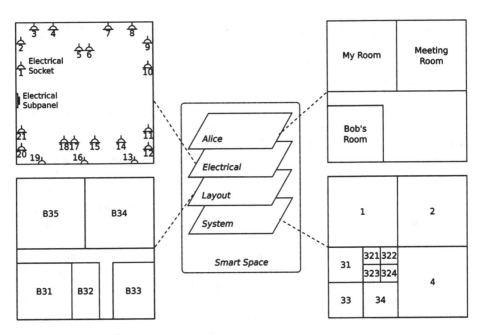

Fig. 1. Perspectives and tags in the smart space

5.1 Tags

Definition 1. *All **points of interest** in the smart space belong to a partially ordered set* $S = \{p_1, \ldots, p_n\}$ *with the association relation* $\leq$, *where* $p_i \leq p_j$ *means that the point of interest* p_i *is associated with the point of interest* p_j. *For all* $p_i, p_j, p_k \in S$, *we have:*

1. *Reflexivity:* $p \leq p$;
2. *Antisymmetry:* $p_i \leq p_j \wedge p_j \leq p_i \Rightarrow p_i = p_j$;
3. *Transitivity:* $p_i \leq p_j \wedge p_j \leq p_k \Rightarrow p_i \leq p_k$.

Direct association or *tagging* $\preceq$ is a particular association relation used as the atomic operation for establishing association relations $\leq$.

Definition 2. *For any points of interest p_i and p_j in S, we say that p_i is **tagging** p_j if:*

1. *$p_i \preceq p_j$ and $p_i \leq p_k \leq p_j$, then $p_i = p_k$ or $p_k = p_j$*
2. *$p_i \leq p_j$ is valid if and only if there is a finite sequence $p_{k1}, \ldots, p_{km}$ such that $p_i \preceq p_{k1} \preceq \cdots \preceq p_{km} \preceq p_j$.*

Definition 3. *For any point of interest in the smart space there is a corresponding **tag** $t = (l, T_t, B_t, u)$, where:*

1. *l is a non-hierarchical keyword that uniquely identifies the point of interest in the smart space;*
2. *$T_t = \{t_i \mid t_i \preceq t\}$, called **tags collection**;*
3. *$B_t = \{t_j \mid t \preceq t_j\}$, called **bookmarks collection**;*
4. *u is the unique identifier for the tag owner.*

A graphical representation of a tag structure is provided in Fig. 2.

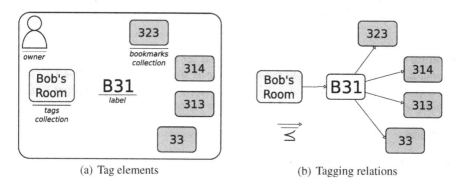

(a) Tag elements   (b) Tagging relations

Fig. 2. Tag structure

5.2 Perspectives

Depending on the entities that are responsible with the management of the tags we can distinguish that there are three types of perspectives: system, infrastructure and user.

User Perspectives. Smart space users create tags that are assigned to corresponding user perspectives. Tags belonging to the user perspective are chosen *informally* and *personally* by their owner.

Infrastructure perspective. Infrastructure perspectives are collections of tags associated with the infrastructure of the building hosting the smart space. Each perspective presents a specific infrastructure function or support system (see Fig. 1), such as room layout, electrical circuits, ventilation system, network ports, etc.

Tags belonging to the infrastructure perspective are chosen *formally* by the maintainer, and corresponding labels belong to a well-known domain specific language. These tags have the bookmark collection tags in the system perspective.

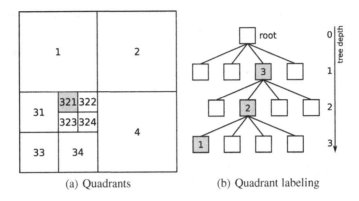

(a) Quadrants   (b) Quadrant labeling

Fig. 3. System tags labeling

System perspective. *Spatial containment* and *spatial positioning* in the smart space is achieved by decomposing the physical space using a quadtree data structure, e.g. Fig. 3(a). The system manages the data structure and the quadrants are points of interest for the system.

Definition 4. *Let Q be the set of quadrants, and let L_{sys} be a language having the alphabet $\Sigma_{sys} = \{1,2,3,4\}$. A **quadrant labeling** is a mapping label $: Q \rightarrow L_{sys}$ that maps a quadrant $q \in Q$ to a word $l_{sys} = l_1 \ldots l_n \in L_{sys}$, where l_i is the quadrant symbol at depth i, e.g. 1 for NW, 2 for NE, 3 for SW and 4 for SE.*

A graphical representation of a system tag labeling is provided in Fig. 3.

Definition 5. *Let u_{sys} be the system user. A **system perspective** is a partially ordered set $P_{sys} = \{t_{sys} \mid t_{sys} = (l_{sys}, T_t, B_t = \emptyset, u_{sys})\}$ with **spatial containment** relation $\sqsubset$, where $t_{sys} \sqsubset t'_{sys}$ means that system tag t_{sys} contains t'_{sys} if l_{sys} is a prefix for l'_{sys}. For all $t_{sys}, t'_{sys}, t''_{sys} \in P_{sys}$, we have:*

1. *Reflexivity: $t_{sys} \sqsubset t_{sys}$;*
2. *Antisymmetry: $t_{sys} \sqsubset t'_{sys} \wedge t'_{sys} \sqsubset t_{sys} \Rightarrow t_{sys} = t'_{sys}$;*
3. *Transitivity: $t_{sys} \sqsubset t'_{sys} \wedge t'_{sys} \sqsubset t''_{sys} \Rightarrow t_{sys} \sqsubset t''_{sys}$.*

Spatial positioning of a system tag is done by converting the tag label to an internal Cartesian coordinate system.

Definition 6. *Let $C = [0,1]^2$ be a Cartesian coordinate system. A system tag **position** is a mapping $p_{quad} : P_{sys} \rightarrow C$ that maps a system tag $t_{sys} = (l_{sys}, T, \emptyset, u_{sys})$ to a point having coordinates (x,y) in C, which corresponds to the top-left corner of the quadrant:*

$$p_{quad}(t_{sys}) = (\sum_{i=1}^{n} \left(\frac{1}{2}\right)^i x(l_i), \sum_{i=1}^{n} \left(\frac{1}{2}\right)^i y(l_i)), \text{ where}$$

$$x(l_i) = \begin{cases} 0 & \text{if } l_i \in \{1,3\} \\ 1 & \text{if } l_i \in \{2,4\} \end{cases} \text{ and } y(l_i) = \begin{cases} 0 & \text{if } l_i \in \{1,2\} \\ 1 & \text{if } l_i \in \{3,4\} \end{cases}$$

Definition 7. *A system tag **edge size** is a mapping function* $e_{quad} : P_{sys} \rightarrow [0,1]$ *that maps a system tag to the length of the quadrant edge:*

$$e_{quad}(t_{sys}) = \frac{1}{2^n}$$

A graphical representation of spatial positioning and edge size example for an arbitrary system tag is provided in Fig. 4.

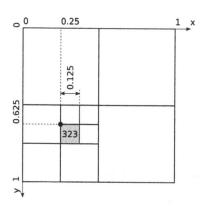

Fig. 4. Spatial positioning and edge size of system tags

Additional metadata (e.g. GPS coordinates of the smart space bounding box, length, height, deviation from north-south orientation, etc.) that can facilitate the conversion between the internal Cartesian coordinate system to a global geometric coordinate system, can be associated with the system perspective.

5.3 Connectors

Connectedness relations between tags in the smart space are represented by *connectors*.

Definition 8. *A **connector** $c = (t_{source}, t_{target}, B_c, u)$ is a unidirectional relation where:*

1. *t_{source} is the relation source;*
2. *t_{target} is the relation target;*
3. *$B_c = \{t_{sys} \mid t_{sys} \in P_{sys}\}$ indicates the spatial positioning of the connector;*
4. *u is a unique identifier for the connector owner.*

Bi-directional connectedness relations are represented by two symmetric *connectors* between the respective tags.

Definition 9. *For any $t_i, t_j \in \bigcup P \setminus P_{sys}$, there is a **connectedness** relation $\mapsto$, such that $t_i \mapsto t_j$ if there is a connector c, such that $c = (t_i, t_j, B_c, u)$.*

The default behavior when creating a new *connector* is to bookmark the root tag in the quadtree perspective corresponding to the t_{source} tag. This type of connector is called *implicit* connector, e.g. Fig. 5. A smart space user can change the default behavior when

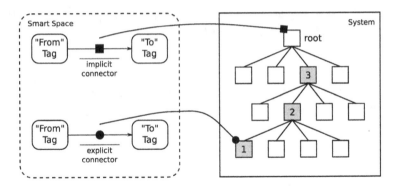

Fig. 5. Implicit and explicit connectors

a connector is created or at any later time, by bookmarking specific tags in the system perspective. With this operation the connector becomes an *explicit* connector.

5.4 Interworking Model and Query Operations

Lattice model. In the smart space S, there are two special points of interest: first is the *smart space* tag that represents the smart space, another is the *root* tag that represents the root of the quadtree in the system perspective.

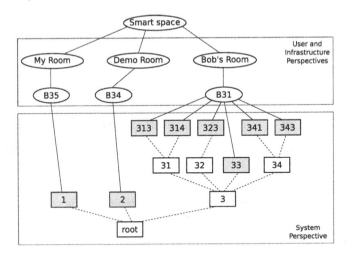

Fig. 6. Lattice model

Following the *association* relation $\leq$, we can arrange the tags belonging to the user and infrastructure perspectives in a lattice. For placing the system tags in the lattice, the NavTag system performs an operation in which the *containment* relations $\sqsubseteq$ between system tags are projected as a special internal *association* relations. In this lattice, the *smart space* tag is the *supremum* and the *root* tag is the *infimum* (see Fig. 6).

Definition 10. *A **position query** is a mapping $q_{position} : \bigcup P \setminus P_{sys} \to P_{sys}$ that maps a requested tag $t = (l, T_t, B_t, u) \notin P_{sys}$ to a set of tags in the system perspective:*

$$q_{position}(t) = \bigcup_{t' \in B_t \setminus P_{sys}} q_{position}(t') \cup (B_t \cap P_{sys})$$

Following recursively the association relations, the first tag encountered in the system perspective determines the *accuracy* of spatial positioning.

Definition 11. *A **range query** is a mapping $q_{range} : P_{sys} \to \bigcup P \setminus P_{sys}$ that maps a set of system tags R to a set of tags in infrastructure and user perspectives:*

$$q_{range}(Q) = \begin{cases} \displaystyle\bigcup_{t \in R'} q_{range}(T_t) \cup T_t & \text{if } Q = R, \text{ where } R' = \bigcup_{t_{sys} \in R} \{t'_{sys} \mid t_{sys} \sqsubset t'_{sys}\} \\[2ex] \emptyset & \text{if } Q = \emptyset \\[2ex] \displaystyle\bigcup_{t \in Q} q_{range}(T_t) \cup T_t & \text{otherwise} \end{cases}$$

Containment relations exist only between system tags and containment decisions can be made in the system perspective. Containment related decisions in other perspectives must be resolved to tags in the system perspective.

Definition 12. *Let $t_i, t_j \in \bigcup P \setminus P_{sys}$. Then:*

1. *t_i is contained in the physical area of t_j, if:*

$$\bigcup_{t_{sys} \in q_{position}(t_i)} \{t'_{sys} \mid t_{sys} \sqsubset t'_{sys}\} \subset \bigcup_{t_{sys} \in q_{position}(t_j)} \{t'_{sys} \mid t_{sys} \sqsubset t'_{sys}\};$$

2. *t_i and t_j overlap in the physical area A, if:*

$$A = \bigcup_{t_{sys} \in q_{position}(t_i)} \{t'_{sys} \mid t_{sys} \sqsubset t'_{sys}\} \cap \bigcup_{t_{sys} \in q_{position}(t_j)} \{t'_{sys} \mid t_{sys} \sqsubset t'_{sys}\} \notin \emptyset.$$

Graph model. Connectors defined in infrastructure perspectives allows the system to construct graphs that encode the connectedness relations between tags. The graph model and the lattice model can be used together to perform connectedness related operations.

Definition 13. *A **path query** in the layout perspective P_{layout} is a mapping $q_{path} : P_{layout}^2 \to (t_n)$ that maps a start tag t_{start} and a destination tag t_{dest} to a sequence of paths, each path being represented by a sequence of tags $(t_n) \in P_{layout}$:*

$$q_{path}(t_{start}, t_{dest}) = \begin{cases} ((t_1, \ldots, t_n)_k) & \text{if } t_{start} \mapsto t_1 \mapsto \ldots \mapsto t_n \mapsto t_{dest} \text{ and } n \geq 1 \\ () & \text{otherwise} \end{cases},$$

where k is the number of paths.

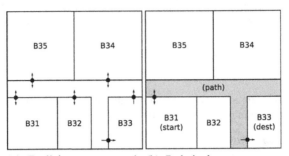

(a) Explicit connectors in layout perspective

(b) Path in layout perspective

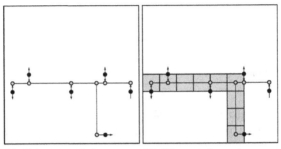

(c) Helper graph in system perspective

(d) Distance in system perspective

Fig. 7. Graph model

A graphical representation of path function is provided in Fig. 7(b).

Definition 14. *A **distance query** in layout perspective P_{layout} is a mapping $q_{distance}$: $P^2_{layout} \to \mathbb{R}$ that maps a start tag t_{start} and a destination tag t_{dest} to a real number:*

$$q_{distance}(t_{start}, t_{dest}) = \sum_{t_{sys} \in (t_{sys})} e_{quad}(t_{sys}), \text{ where}$$

$$(t_{sys}) = (B_{c_1}, t_{sys_1}, \dots, t_{sys_n}, B_{c_2}) \subset \bigcup_{t \in q_{path}(t_{start}, t_{dest})} q_{position}(t), \text{ and}$$

$$c_1 = (t_{start}, t_1, B_{c_1}, u), c_2 = (t_n, t_{dest}, B_{c_2}, u), \text{ where } t_1, t_n \in q_{path}(t_{start}, t_{dest})$$

A graphical representation of distance function is provided in Fig. 7(d).

Definition 15. *Let L be a language and $w \in L$ a word. A **closest neighbor query** is a mapping $q_{neighbor} : \bigcup P \setminus P_{sys} \times L \to \bigcup P \setminus P_{sys}$ that maps a reference tag t_{ref} and a word w to a tag $t = (l, T_t, B_t, u)$:*
$q_{neighbor}(t_{ref}, w) = t$, *where w is a prefix of l*

if

$$q_{distance}(t_{ref}, t) = \min_{\{t_i | t_i \notin P_{sys} \text{ and } w \text{ prefix of } l_i\}} (q_{distance}(t_{ref}, t_i)).$$

Path and closest neighbor queries can be defined only for infrastructure perspectives that have explicit connectors. Additional path and distance queries can be defined for other infrastructure perspectives.

6 Case Study

The environment selected to validate the applicability of the NavTag framework consist of a smart space associated with an office building, where we attempt to replicate the motivating scenarios presented in Section 3. We have used the conventions used in Finland for naming rooms (e.g. B32 represents room *2* on floor *III* in *B* wing), and electric circuits (e.g. Electrical socket 1.4 represents the *4*th socket on circuit *1*). For improved readability, the physical smart space is considered square and spacial positioning of points of interest is coarse.

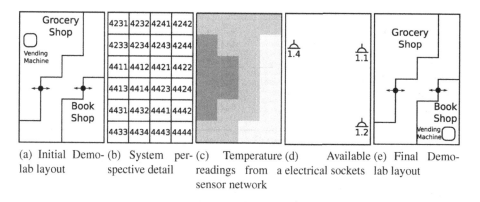

(a) Initial Demo-lab layout (b) System perspective detail (c) Temperature readings from a sensor network (d) Available electrical sockets (e) Final Demo-lab layout

Fig. 8. Demolab - validation environment

The tags relevant for validating the scenarios are listed in Table 1, and the connectors are listed in Table 2.

We consider that the *Demolab* is located in room *B33*. When the smart power meter detects the unusual consumption pattern on *Electrical socket 1.4* it performs a position query to detect the spatial positioning, e.g. $q_{position}(Electrical socket 1.4) = \{4233\}$. Then it performs a range query to find the points of interest in the corresponding physical area, e.g. $q_{range}(4233) = \{B33, GroceryShop, Electrical socket 1.4, VendingMachine\}$. Taking this result, the management application detects that the malfunction is caused by *Vending Machine*. A maintenance personnel is assigned a ticket that contains access right to the Demolab and directions to reach the vending machine, e.g. $q_{path}(Corridor, VendingMachine) = (4433, 4434, 4432, 4414, 4413, 4411, 4233)$.

Table 1. Selected tags in validation environment

l	T_t	B_t	u
B31	Bob's Room	33, 313, 314, 323, 342, 342	Layout Manager
B32	-	324, 342, 344, 413, 431, 433	"
B33	Demo Room	423, 424, 44	"
B34	Meeting Room	2	"
B35	My Room	1	"
Corridor	-		"
Electrical socket 1.1	-	4244	Electrical Maintenance
Electrical socket 1.2	-	4442	"
Electrical socket 1.3	-	4434	"
Electrical socket 1.4	-	4233	"
My Room	-	B35	Alice
Meeting Rom	-	B34	"
Bob's Room	-	B31	"
Demo Room	Grocery Shop, Book Shop	B33	"
Grocery Shop	-	423, 4241, 4243, 4411, 4412, 4413, 4431	Research Team
Book Shop	-	444, 4424	"
Vending Machine (initial)	-	4233	"
Vending Machine (final)	-	4444	"

Table 2. Selected connectors in validation environment

t_{source}	t_{target}	B_c	u
Corridor	B33	4344, 4433	Layout Manager
B33	Corridor	4242, 4224	"
Alley	Grocery Shop	4432, 4431	Research Team
Grocery Shop	Alley	"	"
Alley	Book Shop	4423, 4424	"
Book Shop	Alley	"	"

Once in place, the maintenance personnel diagnose the machine and detects that the malfunction is caused by operating at high temperature. He gets instructions to move the machine in the *Book Shop*. The *Vending Machine* needs to be in proximity of an available electrical socket, in an area with temperature in a certain range. A batch query is built that first determines the spatial positioning of *Book Shop* (e.g. $q_{position}(BookShop) =$ $\{4424, 444\}$), next the result is passed to the building monitoring system to find the temperature in respective quadrants $\{4443, 4444, 4442, 4424\}$ (see Fig. 8(c)), and to an electricity management system to find out which electrical sockets are available in the requested quadrants $\{Electrical socket 1.2\}$, see Fig. 8(d). The results are compared and the *Vending Machine* is moved to the matching quadrant $\{4444\}$, see Fig. 8(e).

7   Conclusion and Future Work

In this paper we have proposed a lightweight interworking framework that uses tags to represent smart space points of interest in symbolic location coordinates. The framework is intuitive and non-intrusive, location information modeling being done by the smart space users following the established methodologies in each particular application domain. This collaborative effort, conducted without expert supervision, reduces the modeling and operational cost of deploying smart spaces.

The interworking framework takes advantage of both lattice theory and graph theory, by combining them in a novel way. The lattice model captures containment and adjacency relations between the tags by using a set of special tags, managed by the system, that correspond to quadrants in a quadtree. The graph model captures connectedness relations between tags. The lattice and the graph models are internal structures of the framework, and are generated by the system from metadata information that is associated with the tags.

Furthermore, the model can be extended by using other data structures than quadtrees for encoding containment relations in the system perspective. An additional direction, will be to expand the NavTag concept beyond a single smartspace.

Acknowledgements

The author would like to thank Prof. Tommi Mikkonen from Tampere University of Technology for valuable guidance while preparing this manuscript, and reviewers for their comments and suggestions.

References

[1] Akyildiz, I., Su, W., Sankarasubramaniam, Y., Cayirci, E.: A survey on sensor networks. Communications Magazine, IEEE 40(8), 102–114 (2002)
[2] Sugihara, R., Gupta, R.K.: Programming models for sensor networks: A survey. ACM Trans. Sen. Netw. 4(2), 1–29 (2008)
[3] Frank, C., Römer, K.: Algorithms for generic role assignment in wireless sensor networks. In: SenSys 2005: Proceedings of the 3rd international conference on Embedded networked sensor systems, pp. 230–242. ACM Press, New York (2005)
[4] Becker, C., Dürr, F.: On location models for ubiquitous computing. Personal Ubiquitous Comput. 9(1), 20–31 (2005)
[5] Strang, T., Linnhoff-popien, C.: A context modeling survey. In: Workshop on Advanced Context Modelling, Reasoning and Management, UbiComp 2004 - The Sixth International Conference on Ubiquitous Computing, Nottingham/England (2004)

[6] Microformats.org, http://www.microformats.org/
[7] Hightower, J., LaMarca, A., Smith, I.E.: Practical lessons from place lab. IEEE Pervasive Computing 5(3), 32–39 (2006)
[8] Halpin, H., Robu, V., Shepherd, H.: The complex dynamics of collaborative tagging. In: WWW 2007: Proceedings of the 16th international conference on World Wide Web, pp. 211–220. ACM Press, New York (2007)
[9] Ye, J., Coyle, L., Dobson, S., Nixon, P.: A unified semantics space model. In: Hightower, J., Schiele, B., Strang, T. (eds.) LoCA 2007. LNCS, vol. 4718, pp. 103–120. Springer, Heidelberg (2007)

Mobile Web 2.0-Oriented Five Senses Multimedia Technology with LBS-Based Intelligent Agent

Jung-Hyun Kim, Hyeong-Joon Kwon, Hyo-Haeng Lee, and Kwang-Seok Hong

School of Information and Communication Engineering, Sungkyunkwan University,
300, Chunchun-dong, Jangan-gu, Suwon, KyungKi-do, 440-746, Korea
{kjh0328,katsyuki,hyohaeng}@skku.edu, kshong@skku.ac.kr
http://hci.skku.ac.kr

Abstract. Ubiquitous-oriented realistic next generation mobile multimedia technology requires new approaches that sufficiently reflect human's sensory information and mobile Web 2.0-oriented collective intelligence and social networking concepts. Hence, we suggest and implement enhanced user location-based five senses multimedia technology that realizes a collective intelligence and mobile social networking between multi-mobile users. This includes 1) mobile station-based mixed-web map module via mobile mash-up, 2) authoring module of location-based five senses multimedia contents using ubiquitous-oriented sensor network and WiBro(Mobile Wi-Max), and 3) LBS-oriented intelligent agent module that includes ontology-based five senses multimedia retrieval module, social network-based user detection interface and user-centric automatic five senses multimedia recommender interface.

1 Introduction

Multimedia and Location Based Services (LBS) are applied in areas including advertisements, education, entertainment, scientific research and spatial temporal applications. Ubiquitous-oriented realistic next generation mobile multimedia technology will require completely new approaches. These will sufficiently reflect individual sensory traits and emotional information. A highly optimized design will be able to be quickly scanned by users who are verified by sensory or biometric information.

However, LBS and media convergence-based conventional studies [1-5] have focused generally on mobile MCP (Multimedia Content Provider)-centered monolithic personalized mobile multimedia services. These include DMB (Digital Multimedia Broadcasting) service, location-sensitive pedestrian navigation, generic tourist guide and multimedia cartography. They referred to the organizational application side such as framework, compression, communication and security technology to play, edit, link, and embed a variety of structural information in a multimedia form. We have not searched related studies [6-7] on mobile station-based realistic multimedia technology that sufficiently reflect the five senses or emotional information. Also lacking is acceptance of collective intelligence-oriented Web 2.0's core concepts, such as participation and sharing of arbitrary multimedia or knowledge. In summary, ubiquitous-oriented realistic next generation multimedia technology will require new approaches. These must sufficiently reflect individual sensory information with the progress of the

D. Zhang et al. (Eds.): UIC 2009, LNCS 5585, pp. 281–295, 2009.

next generation mobile stations and wireless Internet/communication technologies. These technologies include Wireless Broadband (WiBro) system, and feature Web 2.0-based user-centric media, individual message exchanging function between users, information without spatiotemporal-dependency, participational and active media.

In this paper, we suggest and implement enhanced user location-based five senses multimedia technology that realizes a collective intelligence and mobile social networking between multi-mobile users, toward a mobile Web 2.0. A collective intelligence is a shared or group intelligence that emerges from the collaboration and competition of many individuals. Our application includes 1) mobile station with a GPS (Global Positioning System) unit-based mixed-web map module via mobile mash-up, 2) authoring module of location-based five senses multimedia contents using ubiquitous-oriented sensor network and WiBro (Mobile Wi-Max), and 3) LBS-oriented intelligent agent module that includes ontology-based five senses multimedia retrieval module, social network-based user detection interface and user-centric automatic five senses multimedia recommender interface.

2   Related Work

2.1   Geographic Information System (GIS) and LBS Application Technology

GIS is an information system to capture, store, analyze, manage and present data that are spatially referenced to location. GIS technology can include scientific investigations, resource management, asset management, environmental impact assessment, urban planning, cartography, criminology, geographic history, marketing, and logistics. As examples, GIS might allow emergency planners to calculate easily emergency response times in the event of a natural disaster; GIS might be used to find wetlands that need protection from pollution; GIS can be used by a company to site a new business to take advantage of a previously under-serviced market. LBS are an information and entertainment service, accessible with mobile stations through the mobile network. It utilizes the ability to make use of the geographical position of the mobile station [8~10]. This concept of location-based systems is not compliant with the standardized concept of real-time location systems and related local services (RTLS), as noted in ISO/IEC 19762-5 and ISO/IEC 24730-1. With control plane locating, the service provider obtains the location based on the radio signal delay of the closest cell-phone towers (for phones without GPS features). This can be slow as it uses the 'voice control' channel [10]. In the UK, networks do not use triangulation; LBS services use a single base station, with a 'radius' of inaccuracy, to determine a phone's location. This technique was the basis of the E-911 mandate and is still used to locate cell phones as a safety measure. Mobile messaging plays an essential role in LBS. Messaging, especially SMS, has been used in combination with various LBS applications, such as location-based mobile advertising. SMS is still the main technology carrying mobile advertising / marketing campaigns to mobile phones.

A classic example of LBS applications using SMS (Short Message Service) is the delivery of mobile coupons or discounts to mobile subscribers who are near advertising restaurants, cafes, or movie theatres. The Singaporean mobile operator, MobileOne, carried out such an initiative in 2007. It involved many local marketers and was reported to be a huge success in terms of subscriber acceptance. The mobile generation does not restrict users to a fixed desktop location but allows mobile computing, anywhere anytime. Tourist guides are the most common application scenario for location-based services. The mobile city guide GUIDE for the city of Lancaster (UK) was one of the first systems to integrate "personalized" information to the user. Nevertheless, at the time the project started, real personalized multimedia on mobile devices was out of the question. More recent projects, such as LoL@ presenting a city guide for the city of Vienna (Austria), integrated multimedia in mobile city guides. However, these systems do not address the dynamic creation of personalized multimedia.

2.2 Mobile Multimedia Application and Convergence Technology

Convergence of media occurs when multiple products come together to form one product with the advantages of all of them. For example, Mobile phones increasingly incorporate digital cameras, mp3 players, camcorders, voice recorders, and other devices. This type of convergence is very popular. Multimedia Messaging Services (MMS) are another good example. They are a standard for telephone messaging systems that allows sending messages that include multimedia objects (images, audio, video, rich text) and not just text as in Short Message Service (SMS).

Mobile phones with built-in or attached cameras or with built-in MP3 players are very likely to have MMS messaging client - software that interacts with the mobile subscriber to compose, address, send, receive, and view MMS messages. MMS Technology is tapped by various companies to suit different solutions. CNN-IBN, India's biggest English news channel, has Mobile Citizen Journalism where citizens can send MMS photos directly to the studio. It is mainly deployed in cellular networks along with other messaging systems such as SMS, Mobile Instant Messaging and Mobile E-mail. Its standardization effort is mainly done by 3GPP, 3GPP2 and Open Mobile Alliance (OMA). Incidentally, the "mobile service provisions" aspect refers to more than the ability of subscribers to be able to purchase mobile phone like services, as is often seen in co-marketing efforts between providers of land-line services. Rather it is one major ambition of wireless - the ability to access all of the above including speech, Internet, and content/video while on the go and requiring no tethering to the network via cables. Given advancements in WiBro/WiMAX and other leading edge technologies, the ability to transfer information over a wireless link at combinations of speeds, distances and non line of sight conditions is rapidly improving. We find interesting research approaches with the Cuypers system [11] and the OPERA project [12]. Mobile devices are not in their research focus, even though they deal with personalization. Mobile multimedia content can be created dynamically. For example, research approaches [13-14] use constraints and transformation rules to generate the personalized multimedia content, amongst other things. However, our observation is, that these approaches depended on limited media elements (limited sensory modalities) and restricted wireless network regions, such as AP (Access Point) wireless LAN-based only audio, video, text, and image selected according to the user profile information and composed in time and space using an internal multimedia model. They are not a collective intelligence-oriented content with participation and sharing-based Web 2.0's core concepts [15].

2.3 Web 2.0 and Collective Intelligence

Web 2.0 encapsulates the concept of the proliferation of interconnectivity and interactivity of web-delivered content. Web 2.0 describes trends in the use of World Wide Web (WWW) technology and web design that aim to enhance creativity, communications, secure information sharing, collaboration and functionality of the Web. Its concepts have led to the development and evolution of web culture communities and hosted services. Such an example is social-networking sites that focus on building online communities of people who share interests and activities, or who are interested in exploring the interests and activities of others. Other examples include blogs, and video sharing sites that allows individuals to upload video clips to an Internet website, wikis that are a page or collection of web pages designed to enable anyone who accesses them to contribute or modify content, using a simplified markup language [16~17]. Folksonomy is the practice and method of collaboratively creating and managing tags to annotate and categorize content. Collective intelligence is a shared or group intelligence that emerges from the collaboration and competition of many individuals. It can also be defined as a form of networking enabled by the rise of communications technology, namely the Internet.

Web 2.0 has enabled interactivity and thus, users are able to generate their own content. Collective Intelligence draws on this to enhance the social pool of existing knowledge. Henry Jenkins, a key theorist of new media and media convergence draws on the theory that collective intelligence can be attributed to media convergence and participatory culture [18]. In this field, knowledge focused by different voting methods has the potential for many unique perspectives to converge through the assumption that uninformed voting is to some degree random and can be filtered from the decision process leaving only a residue of informed consensus. Critics point out that often bad ideas, misunderstandings, and misconceptions are widely held, and that structuring of the decision process must favor experts who are presumably less prone to random or misinformed voting in a given context.

New media is often associated with the promotion and enhancement of collective intelligence. The ability of new media to easily store and retrieve information, predominantly through databases and the Internet, allows information to be shared without difficulty. Thus, through interaction with new media, knowledge easily passes between sources [19], resulting in a form of collective intelligence. The use of interactive new media, particularly the Internet, promotes online interaction and this distribution of knowledge between users. In this context, collective intelligence is often confused with shared knowledge. The former is knowledge that is generally available to all members of a community, whilst the latter is information known by all members of a community [20].

3 Location-Based Five Senses Multimedia Technology

3.1 Overview

The system architecture of location-based five senses multimedia technology for mobile Web 2.0 is given Fig. 1. It consists of two major modules; 1) A distributed processing-based convergence and representation module of multimedia contents fusing ubiquitous-oriented the five senses information and GPS-based location information; and 2) Interactive LBS-based intelligent agent that including mobile social network-based user detection interface, user-centric automatic five senses multimedia recommender interface and semantic- and keyword-based five senses multimedia retrieval module, to realize mobile Web 2.0-oriented collective intelligence.

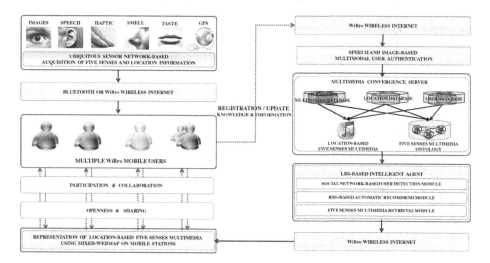

Fig. 1. System architecture for Location-Based Five Senses Multimedia Technology

In Fig. 1, the acquired individual five senses information via embedded camera, microphone, mobile-sensor network and GPS unit-based location information are transmitted into the 'five senses multimedia database' and 'location database' on the convergence server by the WiBro network. Then, the convergence module creates and stores new-multimedia content that is fused by user selected-various media effects, with contents in the 'multimedia database'. Since, LBS-based intelligent agent automatically displays and recommends new-create five senses multimedia contents, they correspond to the present user location or pre-populated location of user-interest or semantic- and keyword-based five senses multimedia retrieval results, on the mobile station-based web-map. This application is designed to enable anyone who accesses it to contribute or modify or re-build five senses multimedia contents. The ability of new media to easily store and retrieve information, predominantly through databases and the Internet, allows information to be shared without difficulty. Thus, through interaction with new media, knowledge easily passes between sources, resulting in a form of collective intelligence. In live situations, the inclusion of a user together with sound, images, and motion video multimedia can arguably be distinguished from conventional motion pictures or movies both by the scale of the production and by the possibility of audience interactivity or involvement. Interactive elements can include speech commands, mouse manipulation, text entry, touch screen, video capture of the user, or live participation in live presentations.

3.2 Mobile Station-Based Mixed-Web Map Interface

In case mixed-web map consists of two or more geographic maps are produced with the same geographic parameters and output size, the results can be accurately overlaid to produce a composite map. This study designed and implemented the mobile station with a GPS unit-based mixed-web map interface using a location-based mobile mash-up with Google and Yahoo maps. This application is an essential component technology that enables to design and realize the LBS-based intelligent agent including user-centric automatic five senses multimedia recommender interface, mobile social networking-based user detection interface, and LBS-based five senses multimedia contents retrieval and representation module in section 4.

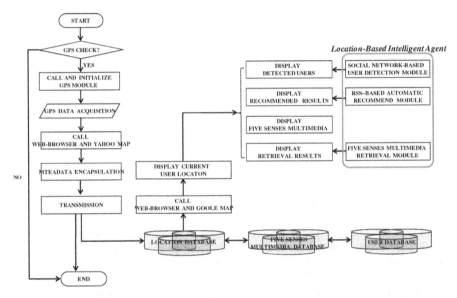

Fig. 2. The block-diagram in the location server side for mixed-web map module

The proposed mobile station-based mixed-map interface is designed using 2- and 3-dimensional geographical position information provided by Google and Yahoo maps, and then controls the map data independently in the location server side. The entire system architecture and integrated block-diagram in the location server side for the proposed mobile station with a GPS unit-based the mixed-web map interface are depicted in Fig. 2. This module is systematized by 4 major steps: 1) it obtains user-centric location information that includes current user location and user-interested location via mobile station with a GPS unit by multi-mobile station user that try to access the LBS-based various services. Then, 2) the obtained large-scale and continuous user-centric location information is transmitted and stored to location database in server side via WiBro wireless Internet. In the next step, 3) the mixed-web map interface accomplishes mobile mash-up and mapping process with commercial web-map service such as Google and Yahoo maps API, using the transmitted geographic parameters that are transformed into longitude and latitude coordinates. Finally, 4) it provides the mixed- web map based various application technologies such as real-time location and tracking and user-centric automatic five senses multimedia recommender to multi-mobile station user, by LBS-based intelligent agent.

3.3 Ubiquitous-Oriented Five Senses Multimedia Contents

In this paper we designed and implemented five senses information processing-based cross multimedia convergence/creation technology that is more advanced core multimedia-conversion technology over multiple mobile platforms. It includes XML-based encoding, GPS unit-based location information, and ubiquitous-oriented five senses - image, speech, haptic, smell, and taste - recognition technology. This paper created a Wibro mobile-server network-based five senses multimedia content, fusing and synthesizing between the five natural senses with GPS unit-based location information. The block-diagram for the five senses-based multimedia convergence module proposed is shown in Fig. 3.

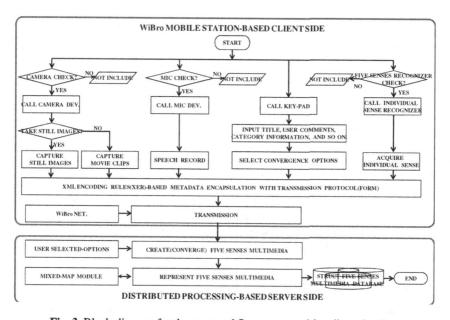

Fig. 3. Block-diagram for the proposed five senses multimedia technology

▪ *Acquisition and Processing of Five Senses Multimedia Contents*: It has currently constructed 512 'Five Senses Multimedia Databases' and 1,382 'location databases' depending on numerous users and various locations. The multi-mobile station (including PDAs or mobile phones) acquire the image, movie-clip, speech, touch, smell and taste information. They are captured from mobile stations with built-in cameras and microphone. They are obtained automatically by ubiquitous sensor network-oriented haptic devices, smell and taste recognition interfaces that are realized already in pattern recognition-based our preliminary studies using [20-22]. Then, they are transmitted to the 'five senses multimedia database' using the WiBro Network. The sensitivity or insensitivity of a human, often considered with regard to a particular kind of stimulus, is the strength of the feeling in which it results, in comparison with the strength of the stimulus. Simple examples - WiBro station's screen dumps on sequential acquisition steps (from (A) initial menu state to (J) transmission step) of five senses information via embedded camera, microphone, keypad on touch-screen, and individual recognition interface are captured in Fig. 4.

Fig. 4. WiBro station screen dumps on sequential acquisition steps of five senses information; (A) Initial menu state; (B) Ready state for five senses acquisition; (C) Capture step of images and movie clips; (D) and (E) Selection step of recorded speech message and background music; (F) Automatic acquisition step of haptic, smell and taste information from sensor network-oriented recognition interfaces; (G) Entrance step of user's recommendation, title and categorizing information for XML-based metadata encapsulation including five senses and location information; (H) and (I) User-centric selection step of special effects options and background image for multimedia convergence; (J) Transmission step of encapsulated XML-based metadata.

▪ *Transmission of Five Senses Multimedia Contents*: We designed and implemented XML metadata- and WiBro-based content encoding and transmission interface, including XML Encoding Rules (XER) and transmission protocol. The acquired five senses and location information are encapsulated by XML-based metadata with user's recommendation, title and categorizing information, and so on. WiBro-based wireless transfer protocol allows the transfer of encapsulated XML-based metadata to distributed computing-based multimedia convergence server that converges into five senses and location-based new multimedia content.

▪ *Convergence and Representation of Five Senses Multimedia Contents*: This paper accepted convergence or synthesis methods for five senses multimedia convergence interface include with six essential functions: 1) photo slide-show function using time interval between multi-images, with accompanying audio; 2) chroma-key and edge detection-based image convergence function between background image and object image; 3) speech synthesis function between background music and original message speech; 4) image-based short message function with image and text message; 5) movie clip including speech and image information; and 6) sound-image synthesis function in which is a still image with synchronized sound, or sound technologically is coupled to a captured image, as opposed to a recorded speech. Since then, the multimedia representation module in the client-side displays the newly created location-based five senses movie clip and still image using MPEG-4 and JPEG-based cross display module that is able to represent five senses multimedia under multi-mobile platform.

3.4 LBS-Oriented Intelligent Agent

3.4.1 User-Centric Automatic Five Senses Multimedia Recommender Interface

This agent allows two agent functions. 1) Automatic five senses multimedia indication module guides and draws five senses multimedia's position information that is registered in the user settings-customized distance that is estimated by the radial distance between the user's current location and the location of user-interest using coordinate transformation and trigonometrical function, and 2) RSS (Really Simple Syndication)-based automatic five senses multimedia recommender module notifies and displays automatically the updated or the best five senses multimedia content using the user's annotation and evaluation-based ranking scores in the location of user-interest, on the mobile station-based mixed-web map. RSS is web feed formats used to publish frequently updated work. It benefits publishers by letting them syndicate content automatically, and readers who wish to subscribe to timely updates from favored websites. In summary, according as the recommended five senses

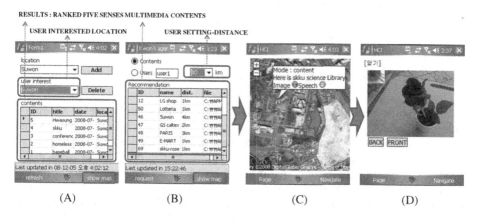

Fig. 5. Simple examples for user-centric automatic five senses multimedia recommender interfaces; (A) RSS (Really Simple Syndication)-based automatic five senses multimedia recommender module, (B) Automatic five senses multimedia indication module, (C) Mixed mobile map-based display step on WiBro mobile station, (D) Representation step of the selected LBS-based five senses multimedia contents

multimedia content is updated or edited by multi-user and they can create new five senses multimedia using LBS-based intelligent agent, a collective intelligent five senses multimedia technology for enhanced creativity, information sharing, and collaboration works is completed. Simple examples for the user-centric automatic five senses multimedia recommender interface are depicted in Fig. 5.

3.4.2 Social Network-Based User Detection Interface

Mobile social networking is social networking where one or more individuals with similar interests or commonalities, it converse and connect with one another using mobile stations. However, most of these are extensions of PC-based services, whilst others are pure mobile-focused offerings. Consequently, we designed and implemented a social network-based user detection interface, to communicate and share LBS-based five senses multimedia contents between multiple users in user-interest groups or user-interest locations to which they belong, and register as friends a group of members they selected from their work group. This function will reduce the cumbersome chores of adding a new individual one friend at a time. In our mobile communities, mobile phone users can now create their own profiles, make friends, hold private conversations, share photos and videos. It provides innovative features that extend the social networking experience into the real world. Fig.6 shows the WiBro mobile station-based user interface for social network-based user detection.

Fig. 6. Simple examples for social network-based user detection interface

3.4.3 Keyword- and Semantic-Based Five Senses Multimedia Retrieval Module

Multimedia search and retrieval has become an active research field thanks to the increasing demand that accompanies many new practical applications. The applications include large-scale multimedia search engines on the Web, media asset management systems in corporations, audio-visual broadcast servers, and personal media servers for consumers. Diverse requirements derived from these applications impose great challenges and incentives for research in this field. In this paper, we designed and implemented LBS-based five senses multimedia retrieval module including Java-based keyword retrieval interface and semantic-based retrieval interface using five senses multimedia ontology. These retrieval modules are called by a LBS-based intelligent agent. Fig. 7 shows integrated block-diagram of the Java-based keyword retrieval interface and semantic-based retrieval interface.

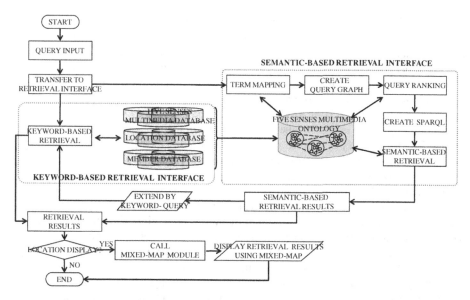

Fig. 7. Integrated block-diagram of keyword- and semantic-based retrieval interface

▪ *Java-Based Keyword Retrieval Interface*: Keywords are used generally in retrieving items from a vast information source, for instance a catalog or a search engine. An index term or descriptor in information retrieval is a term that captures the essence of the topic of a document, and can consist of a word, phrase, or alphanumerical term. They are created by analyzing the document either manually with subject indexing or automatically with automatic indexing or more sophisticated methods of keyword extraction. Keywords are stored in a search index. In this paper, we adopt Apache Lucene library that is a high-performance, full-featured text search engine library written entirely in Java. Lucene has a very flexible and powerful search capability that supports a wide array of possible searches including AND, OR and NOT, fuzzy logic searches, proximity searches, wildcard searches, and range searches to locate indexed items, and it is a technology suitable for nearly any application that requires full-text search, especially cross-platform. The first thing it does is create an *IndexSearcher* object pointing to the directory where the contents have been indexed by title, location, user's annotation and tags, and then create a *StandardAnalyzer* object. The *StandardAnalyzer* is passed to the constructor of a *QueryParser* along with the name of the default field to use for the search. This will be the field that is used if the user does not specify a field in their search criteria. It then parses the actual search criterion that was specified giving us a *Query* object. We can run the *Query* against the *IndexSearcher* object. This returns a *Hits* object which is a collection of all the contents that met the specified criteria [23].

▪ *Semantic-Based Retrieval Interface Using Five Senses Multimedia Ontology*: The semantic-based retrieval interface allows two semantic query scopes: 1) Multimedia title and 2) administrative district name from user-centric multimedia domain ontology such as five senses-based multimedia, user annotations and location information, for semantic-based five senses multimedia retrieval module. This paper accepted the semantic annotation and phase-based five senses multimedia retrieval method using a semantic relationship query with multimedia title and administrative district name. The implemented semantic-based retrieval interface includes three major steps; 1) *Term mapping step* that maps between ontology resource and the input query language; 2) *Query graph construction step* using relations between mapped ontology resources in step 1; and 3) *SPARQL(SPARQL Protocol and RDF Query Language) query conversion step* using the query graph created in step 2. After 3 steps, the constructed SPARQL query is used to search the knowledge in the five senses ontology, and form the XML document from the search result. Term mapping is the process of connection between the input query and the ontology resource. The query is split by the space, and each token is mapped when the token is the same as the name or label of the class or instance in the ontology. The mapped ontology resource constructs all possible query graphs using the 'Minimum Spanning Tree' algorithm, then a spanning tree with weight less than or equal to the weight of every other spanning tree [24]. The relation between the constructed query graphs is checked to expand the query graph using the ontology's schema. Schema define the relation between classes, then if the query user input is a instance, the class that belongs to the instance and the higher classes are used to check the relations. After checking the relation, both graphs in the relation link to the relation's direction for expansion.

4 Experiments and Results

This paper designed and implemented a prototype with WiBro-based collective intelligent five senses multimedia. It included the convergence module of five senses and location-based multimedia contents using the WiBro-based mobile stations with a GPS unit, LBS-based intelligent agent module, LBS-based five senses multimedia retrieval module, and speech and tooth image-based intuitive multimodal user authentication module using user-centric multimedia ontology. The application is implemented in Microsoft Visual Studio 2005-supported c# and c++ using the Microsoft.Net Compact Framework 2.0 and Windows Mobile 5.0 Pocket PC SDK. Experimental environments consisted of a blue-tooth module for data communication between the mobile station and GPS unit, and WiBro-based mobile stations and individual sense recognizers for the ubiquitous-oriented mobile-sensor network. Three WiBro mobile stations with GPS units are used during the experiments, they are MSM 6500(EVDO) and 520MHz CPU-based SAMSUNG SPH-M8200. It is a PDA type WiBro station that runs Window Mobile 6.0 OS and supports WiBro and CDMA EV-DO connectivity. The bar type device is 16.6mm thick and has enhanced usability with a full touch screen (2.8"). It supports Terrestrial DMB, Bluetooth, file viewer, and enhanced User Created Content (UCC) related functions such as video editor and background music. We accepted the KT (Korea Telecom) WiBro service. It is able to use a broadband Internet service while moving at a speed of up to 120km/h and has a faster speed than HSDPA (High Speed Downlink Packet Access). Fig. 8 shows the WiBro mobile station's screen captures for the convergence experiments (acquisition→transmission→display) of LBS-based five senses multimedia.

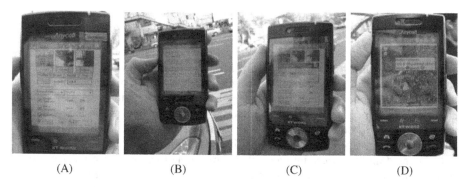

(A)   (B)   (C)   (D)

Fig. 8. WiBro mobile station's screen captures for the convergence (creation) experiment of five senses multimedia; (A) Acquisition step of contents that include five senses information, user's message (annotation), and title, and user-selected category information and convergence options, (B) Acquisition step of location information using GPS unit, (C) Transmission step of acquired five senses and location information into multimedia convergence server, (D) Mixed mobile map-based display step on WiBro mobile station of concentrated LBS-based five senses multimedia contents

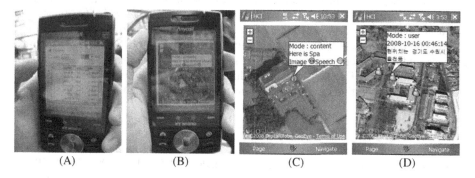

(A)   (B)   (C)   (D)

Fig. 9. The screen dumps and captures on the WiBro mobile station for LBS-based intelligent agent; (A) distance settings for user-interest locations and initial detection results depending on distance settings, (B) The result on mixed mobile map of automatic multimedia recommender agent user entered by user setting; in this case the user settings for user-interest locations have radius 5km, (C) and (D) are screen dumps on mixed mobile map for the result of user-centric automatic five senses multimedia recommend interface and social network-based user(who is registered friend) detection interface using the WiBro mobile station

The field tests for the LBS-based intelligent agent module, which includes user-centric automatic five senses multimedia recommender interface and social network-based users (registered friends) detection interface, are performed in the Seoul and Suwon Areas of South Korea, since the KT WiBro services are available in Seoul (including the subway) and 19 cities in the metropolitan area. The screen dumps from the WiBro mobile station for LBS-based intelligent agent module in shown Fig. 9, and they include the user-centric automatic five senses multimedia recommender interface and social network-based user detection interface.

5 Conclusions

In this study, we propose an enhanced WiBro-based collective intelligent five senses multimedia technology. It includes five senses and location-based multimedia convergence module, LBS-based intelligent agent module with five senses multimedia retrieval module, and speech and tooth image-based intuitive multimodal user authentication module. In contrast to other proposed static or active media-based mobile multimedia studies, our approach is unique in four aspects: 1) This study, which represents the convergence technology of five sense information acquired from ubiquitous-oriented multi-devices into a single form, is able to expand into more personal and realistic multimedia service, to reflect individual sensory information, 2) this issue may satisfy and reflect the Web 2.0's core concepts such as mobile-based indirect experiences, enhanced creativity, information sharing, and collaboration works. In addition, 3) user-specific MMS (Multimedia Messaging Service) is possible in the relatively low memory and storage capacity available on mobile stations, since our approach orients user-centric multimedia technology with the LBS-based intelligent agent. Finally, 4) according as this study used the WiBro system for high speed broadband wireless Internet access, it is able to provide more seamlessly / quickly a variety of location information and five senses multimedia contents to various user terminals, compared with WIFI-based conventional wireless LAN. In the future, we will try to accomplish personalization of realistic five senses multimedia via location-based context-awareness. This will be extended to various application fields, such as enhanced education, entertainment, and realistic MMS service using location-based collective intelligent five senses multimedia technology with an implementation of five senses representation devices such as portable olfactory exhaling apparatus.

Acknowledgement

This research was supported by MIC, Korea under ITRC IITA-2009-(C1090-0902-0046), and the Korea Science and Engineering Foundation (KOSEF) grant funded by the Korea government (MEST) (No. 20090058909).

References

1. Boll, S., et al.: Personalized Mobile Multimedia meets Location-Based Services. In: Proc. Multimedia Inf. Syst. Workshop at 34th Annual Convention of the German Informatics Society, pp. 64–69 (2004)
2. Choi, Y.B., et al.: Applications of human factors in wireless telecommunications service delivery. International Journal of Services and Standards 1(3) (2005)
3. Moreno, R.: Learning in High-Tech and Multimedia Environments. Current Directions in Psychological Science 15(2) (2005)
4. Naphade, M., et al.: Large-Scale Concept Ontology for Multimedia. IEEE Multimedia 13(3) (2006)
5. Avrithis., Y., et al.: Introduction to the special issue on Semantic Multimedia. Web Semantics: Science, Services and Agents on the World Wide Web 6(2), 137–138 (2008)

6. Hiroshi, N., et al.: Development of the delivery environmental improvement system applying multimedia and the senses of a human being, Tokyo Denki Daigaku Furonthia Kyodo Kenkyu Senta 2004, Nendo Kenkyu Seika Hokokusho (2005)
7. Kim, S.-Y., et al.: Realistic Broadcasting Using Multi-modal Immersive Media. In: Ho, Y.-S., Kim, H.-J. (eds.) PCM 2005. LNCS, vol. 3768, pp. 164–175. Springer, Heidelberg (2005)
8. Steiniger, S., Neun, M., Edwardes, A.: Foundations of Location Based Services. University of Zurich (2006)
9. GSM Association, Permanent Reference Document SE. 23: Location Based Services (2002)
10. Wang, S., et al.: Location Based Services for Mobiles: Technologies and Standards. In: Proc. IEEE International Conference on Communication. IEEE, Los Alamitos (2008)
11. van Ossenbruggen, J.R., et al.: Cuypers: a semi-automatic hypermedia presentation system, Technical Report INS-R0025, CWI, Netherlands (2000)
12. Lemlouma, T., Layäida, N.: Adapted Content Delivery for Different Contexts. In: Conf. on SAINT 2003 (2003)
13. Lemlouma, T., Layäida, N.: Context-Aware Adaptation for Mobile Devices. In: IEEE Int. Conf. on Mobile Data Management (2004)
14. Metso, M., et al.: Mobile Multimedia Services Content Adaptation. In: 3rd Intl. Conf. on Information, Comm. and Signal Processing (2001)
15. Scherp, A., et al.: Generic support for personalized mobile multimedia tourist applications. In: Int. Multimedia Conference proceedings of the 12th annual ACM international conference on Multimedia table of contents, pp. 178–179 (2004)
16. Oxford University Press.: Oxford English Dictionary (2007)
17. Encyclopædia Britannica.: Inc., Encyclopædia Britannica (2007)
18. Flew, T.: New Media: an introduction. Oxford University Press, Melbourne (2008)
19. Jenkins, H.: Fans, Bloggers and Gamers: Exploring Participatory Culture. New York University Press, New York (2006)
20. Kim, J.H., et al.: Distributed-computing-based multimodal fusion interface using VoiceXML and KSSL for wearable PC. Electronics Letters, IET 44(1), 58–60 (2008)
21. Kim, J.H., et al.: MMSDS: ubiquitous Computing and WWW-based Multi-Modal Sentential Dialog System. In: Sha, E., Han, S.-K., Xu, C.-Z., Kim, M.-H., Yang, L.T., Xiao, B. (eds.) EUC 2006. LNCS, vol. 4096, pp. 539–548. Springer, Heidelberg (2006)
22. Cheon, B., et al.: Implementation of Floral Scent Recognition System Using Correlation Coefficients. In: Proc. APIC-IST 2008 (2008)
23. Paul, T.: The Lucene Search Engine: Adding search to your applications, http://www.javaranch.com/journal/2004/04/Lucene.html
24. Pettie, S., Ramachandran, V.: An Optimal Minimum Spanning Tree Algorithm. JACM 49(1), 16–34 (2002)

Conflicting-Set-Based Wormhole Attack Resistant Localization in Wireless Sensor Networks[*]

Honglong Chen[1], Wei Lou[1], and Zhi Wang[2]

[1] Department of Computing,
The Hong Kong Polytechnic University, Kowloon, Hong Kong
{cshlchen,csweilou}@comp.polyu.edu.hk
[2] State Key Laboratory of Industry Control Technology,
Zhejiang University, Hangzhou, P. R. China
wangzhi@iipc.zju.edu.cn

Abstract. The wormhole attack sniffs packets in one point in the network, tunnels them through a wired or wireless link to another point to cause severe influence on the localization process or routing process in the network. In this paper, we analyze the impact of the wormhole attack on the localization in wireless sensor networks and we propose a wormhole attack resistant secure localization scheme. The main idea of our proposed scheme is to build a so-called conflicting set for each locator based on the abnormalities of message exchanges among neighboring locators, and then to identify all dubious locators which are filtered out during localization. Our proposed scheme can identify the dubious locators with a very high probability to achieve secure localization. The simulation results show that it outperforms the existed schemes under different network parameters.

Keywords: Conflicting Set, Secure Localization, Wireless Sensor Networks, Wormhole Attack.

1 Introduction

Wireless sensor networks (WSNs) have been well studied in the past few years and numerous related applications have been developed. Particularly, sensor networks are usually deployed in a hostile environment, where the sensor nodes are vulnerable to various types of attacks in the network. In this paper, we concentrate on the localization against the *wormhole attack* [1], which can be mounted by two colluding external attackers. In such network, there are three types of nodes deployed including sensors, locators and attackers, which all have the same transmission range R. The locators have fixed locations and have known their own locations in advance. The sensors are location-unknown and they can estimate their locations by measuring the distances to the locators. Two colluding attackers disrupt the localization procedure of the sensors by relaying the received packets through a *wormhole link*, which provides a direct low-latency transmission channel between them. Being as external attackers that cannot compromise legitimate nodes or their cryptographic keys, the wormhole attackers cannot acquire the

---

[*] This work is supported in part by grants PolyU 5236/06E, PolyU 5232/07E, PolyU 5243/08E, and NSFC No. 60873223 and No. 90818010.

D. Zhang et al. (Eds.): UIC 2009, LNCS 5585, pp. 296–309, 2009.

content, e.g., the type, of the sniffed packets. In this paper, we assume that there is no region in the network attacked by more than one wormhole attack. Fig. 1 illustrates the impact of the wormhole attack on the localization when the Time Difference of Arrival (TDoA) method is applied to estimate the distances between the locators and the sensor. Without the wormhole attack, the sensor S will conduct the self-localization based on d_1, d_2, d_3 and d'_4 using the maximum likelihood estimation (MLE) approach [2]. However, as the packets transmitted by the locators L_4, L_5 and L_6 can be relayed to S through the wormhole link. When S measures the distances with the packets from L_4, L_5 and L_6 using TDoA method, take L_6 for example, the packet from L_6 goes through the path $L_6 \rightarrow A_1 \rightarrow A_2 \rightarrow S$ to reach S. As the transmission time in the wormhole link can be ignored, the time difference of arrival is introduced only in two segments of the transmission path, from L_6 to A_1 and from A_2 to S. Thus, the measured distance between S and L_6 is $d_6 + d_0$, instead of the actual distance d'_6. Similarly, S will measure the distances to L_4 and L_5 as $d_4 + d_0$ and $d_5 + d_0$, respectively. As A_2 relays the packets from A_1 with the maximum transmitting power level, the upper limit of d_0 is R, thus the measured distances introduced by the wormhole attack may be larger than R. Consequently, S will adopt false distance measurements into localization, leading to an incorrect estimation of the location. Therefore, an ordinary localization scheme without considering the adversarial attacks cannot fulfil the positioning task in the scenario under the wormhole attack.

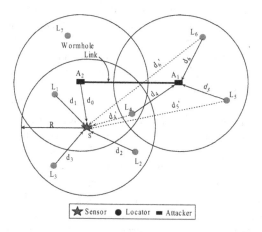

Fig. 1. Wormhole attack in the TDoA-based localization

To overcome the impact of the wormhole attack on the localization, we propose an attack-resistant localization scheme in this paper. The main idea of our proposed scheme is to build a so-called *conflicting set* for each locator based on the abnormalities of message exchanges among neighboring locators, and then identify all the *dubious* locators (such as L_4, L_5 and L_6 in Fig. 1) which can be filtered out during localization. The main contributions of this paper are summarized as follows: 1) We propose a mechanism to build conflicting set for each locator according to the the abnormalities of message exchanges among neighboring locators; 2) We propose a novel secure localization scheme which is wormhole attack resistant including wormhole attack detection and dubious lo-cators identification; 3) We present simulations to demonstrate the effectiveness of our proposed scheme.

The remainder of this paper is organized as follows. In Section 2, we provide the related work on secure localization. In Section 3, we propose the secure localization scheme which is wormhole attack resistant. Section 4 presents the performance evalua-tion. Section 5 gives the concluding remarks on this work.

2   Related Work

Many localization mechanisms [3,4] in WSNs have been developed recently. However, these systems can not obtain satisfied performance when adversarial attacks exist in the network. Thus, researchers have proposed several secure localization systems [5] for the hostile environment.

Liu et al. [6] propose two secure localization schemes against the compromise attack, range-based and range-free respectively. SPINE [7] applies the verifiable multilatera-tion and verification of positions of mobile devices into the secure localization in the hostile network. The mechanism in [8] introduces a set of covert base stations (CBS), whose positions are not known to the attackers, to check the validity of the nodes. Lazos et al. ROPE [9] is a robust positioning system with a location verification mechanism that verifies the location claims of the sensors before data collection. DRBTS [10] is a distributed reputation-based beacon trust security protocol aimed at providing secure localization in sensor networks. Based on a quorum voting approach, DRBTS drives beacons to monitor each other and therefore enables them to decide which should be trusted. A suit of techniques in [11] are introduced to detect malicious beacons which supply incorrect information to the sensor nodes.

Khabbazian et al. [12] formulate the influence of wormhole attack on building the shortest path in routing protocols. In [1] a new, general mechanism called *packet leashes* based on the notions of geographical and temporal leashes is proposed to detect the wormhole attack. Wang et al. [13] detect the wormhole attack by visualizing the anoma-lies introduced by the attack based on all the distance messages between each two nodes. [14] further improves [13] to make it more suitable for large scale network by selecting some feature points to reduce the overlapping issue and preserving the major topology features. Xu at el. [15] propose a wormhole attack detection algorithm which uses a hop counting technique as a probe procedure, reconstructs local maps for each node and uses a feature called "diameter" to detect abnormalities caused by wormholes. In [16], a wormhole attack detection scheme is proposed using the maximum number of independent neighbors of two non-neighbor nodes. However, all the above worm-hole detection schemes emphasize the detection without considering the localization scenario.

The above schemes only consider the detection of wormhole attack without the secure localization. SeRLoc [17] detects the wormhole attack based on the *sector uniqueness* property and *communication range violation* property using the directional antennas, then filters out the attacked locators to obtain secure localization. HiRLoc [18] further utilizes antenna rotations and multiple transmit power levels to provide higher localization resolution. The schemes in [6] can also be applied in localization against wormhole attacks. However, all these schemes have drawbacks: SeRLoc and HiRLoc cannot obtain satisfied localization performance as some attacked locators may still be undetected, and [6] can not be competent in the scenario with many attacked locators. Our proposed scheme in this paper can overcome the above drawbacks without using extra hardware such as directional antennae required in SeRLoc and HiRLoc.

3   Wormhole Attacks Resistent Secure Localization Scheme

In this section, we first give several definitions about the network, after which we propose the wormhole attack resistant localization scheme.

The localization of the sensor is attacked by the wormhole only if the sensor enters the transmission area of either attacker and exchange messages with the locators through the wormhole link. Two different types of wormhole attacks, named *duplex wormhole attack* (Fig. 2(a)) and *simplex wormhole attack* (Fig. 2(b)), are defined as follows:

Definition 1. *Duplex wormhole attack:* The sensor is under a duplex wormhole attack when it lies in the common transmission area of the two attackers. That is, messages transmitted from either attacker can arrive at the sensor.

Definition 2. *Simplex wormhole attack:* The sensor is under a simplex wormhole attack when it lies in the transmission range of either one attacker but not in the common transmission area of the two attackers. That is, messages transmitted from only one attacker can arrive at the sensor.

Definition 3. *Neighboring locator:* The neighboring locators of a sensor refer to the locators that can exchange messages with the sensor, either via the wormhole link or not.

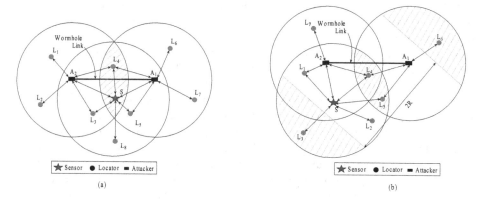

Fig. 2. Illustrations of wormhole attack: (a) Duplex wormhole attack; (b) Simplex wormhole attack

Definition 4. *Valid locator:* The neighboring locators, which are in the transmission range of the sensor, are called valid locators (V-locators) because their messages can be directly received by the sensor to obtain correct distance measurements.

Definition 5. *Dubious locator:* The locators, which are inside the transmission range of the attacker and can exchange messages with the sensor via the wormhole link, are called dubious locators (D-locators) since their distance measurements may negatively affect the localization process. In the following of this paper, we denote the set of V-locators, D-locators, and neighboring locators of the sensor as $\mathcal{L}_V$, $\mathcal{L}_D$ and $\mathcal{L}_N$. We also denote $\mathcal{D}_R(u)$ as a disk centered at u with radius R. As shown in Fig 1, for the sensor S,

$$\mathcal{L}_V = \{L_1, L_2, L_3, L_4\}, \ \mathcal{L}_D = \{L_4, L_5, L_6\}, \text{ and } \mathcal{L}_N = \{L_1, L_2, L_3, L_4, L_5, L_6\}.$$

When the sensor is under a wormhole attack, the localization process would be disrupted as the existence of dubious locators. As shown in Fig. 3, our proposed scheme firstly detects the wormhole attack. If the wormhole attack is detected, dubious locators identification scheme will be triggered, after which the localization based on the correct distance measurements is conducted.

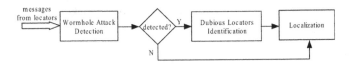

Fig. 3. Flow chart of the proposed secure localization scheme

3.1 Wormhole Attack Detection

Before conducting self-localization, the sensor first detects the existence of wormhole attack. The sensor broadcasts a *Loc_req* message and waits for the *Loc_ack* messages from its neighboring locators. When receiving the *Loc_req* message, each locator responds a *Loc_ack* message. The sensor will use the received *Loc_ack* messages to build the set of its neighboring locators as well as measure the distance to each neighboring locator using the received *Loc_ack* message. To counteract the random queueing delay introduced on the locators and sensor, the sensor measures the response time of each locator using the mechanism described in [19]: When broadcasting the *Loc_req* packet, the sensor records the local time T_0. Every locator gets the local time T_1 by time-stamping the packet at the MAC layer (i.e. the time when the packet is built at the MAC layer) instead of time-stamping the packet at the application layer. Similarly, when responding the *Loc_ack* packet, the locator puts the local time T_2 at the MAC layer, both T_1 and T_2 are attached in the *Loc_ack* packet. When receiving the *Loc_ack* packet, the sensor gets its local time T_3, and calculates the response time of the locator as $(T_3 - T_0) - (T_2 - T_1)$. It is noted that this mechanism only only eliminates the random delay at the MAC layer of the locators from the response time.

The following four detection schemes can detect the wormhole attack independently.

Detection scheme D1 based on node's self-exclusion property. The node's self-exclusion states that a node cannot receive packets transmitted by itself in a loop-free path. Therefore, if the sensor receives packets transmitted by itself, it can simply determine that it is under a wormhole attack.

Detection scheme D2 based on packet unduplication property. The packet unduplication property states that a node can receive at most one copy of the same message from one neighboring node. As L_4 in Fig. 2(b), when locator L_4 responses S's Loc_req message, the Loc_ack messages can be received by S twice, one directly from L_4 and the other from A_2 which is replayed from A_1 to A_2 through the wormhole link. Therefore, if S receives more than one message from the same neighboring locator for each request, it determines that it is under a wormhole attack.

Detection scheme D3 based on node's spatial constraint property. The node's spatial constraint property states that the measured distance between two neighboring nodes cannot be larger than R. As we mentioned in the introduction, the measured distance between the sensor and its neighboring locator may be larger than R due to the wormhole attack. Therefore, the sensor can check whether any measured distance is larger than R to detect a wormhole attack.

Detection scheme D3 based on neighboring nodes' spatial constraint property. The neighboring nodes' spatial constraint property suggests that a node cannot receive messages from two neighboring nodes simultaneously if the distance between these two nodes is larger than $2R$. As shown in Fig. 2(b), after receiving the Loc_req message from neighboring locators, S checks whether the distance between any two locators is larger than $2R$. If S detects that the distance of two locators (e.g., L_3 and L_6) is larger than $2R$, it derives that it is under a wormhole attack.

The procedure of the wormhole attack detection uses the above four detection schemes: The sensor first builds the set of its neighboring locators with the received Loc_ack messages from the neighboring locators. It then uses detection scheme D1 to detect the duplex wormhole attack and uses detection schemes D2, D3 or D4 to detect the simplex wormhole attack. The algorithm of the wormhole attack detection process lists in Algorithm 1:

Algorithm 1. Wormhole attack detection

1: Broadcast a Loc_req message.
2: Wait for the Loc_ack messages to measure the distance and calculate the response time of each locator.
3: **if** detect the wormhole attack based on scheme D1 **then**
4:     A duplex wormhole attack is detected.
5: **else if** detect the wormhole attack based on schemes D2, D3 or D4 **then**
6:     A simplex wormhole attack is detected.
7: **else**
8:     No wormhole attack is detected.
9: **end if**

3.2 Dubious Locators Identification

The main idea of the dubious locators identification algorithm is to build a so-called conflicting set for each locator based on the abnormalities of message exchanges among neighboring locators. The conflicting set is defined as below:

Definition 6. *Conflicting set:* The conflicting set of a locator L_i, denoted as $C(L_i)$, contains all the abnormal neighboring locators of the locator L_i, including (1) L_i itself if it can receive the message sent by itself, (2) neighboring locators that are within the transmission range of L_i but receive the same message from different paths for more than once, and (3) neighboring locators that are outside the transmission range of L_i but can exchange messages with L_i.

Each locator can build its conflicting set based on the periodical *Beacon* message exchanges with its neighboring locators. When a locator detects the *Beacon* message abnormality, it will consider the sender locator of this *Beacon* message as the abnormal neighboring locator and put this sender locater into its conflicting set. When such a locator receives a *Loc_req* message from the sensor, it will response a *Loc_ack* message including its conflicting set to the sensor.

The relation between the locator and its conflicting set is elaborated as the following theorem.

Theorem 1. Given a network under a wormhole attack, (1) if L_i lies in $\mathcal{D}_R(A_2) \backslash \mathcal{D}_R(A_1)$, $C(L_i)$ contains all the locators in $\mathcal{D}_R(A_1)$; (2) if L_i lies in $\mathcal{D}_R(A_1) \backslash \mathcal{D}_R(A_2)$, $C(L_i)$ contains all the locators in $\mathcal{D}_R(A_2)$; (3) if L_i lies in $\mathcal{D}_R(A_1) \cap \mathcal{D}_R(A_2)$, $C(L_i)$ contains all the locators in $\mathcal{D}_R(A_1) \cup \mathcal{D}_R(A_2)$.

Proof: (1) For a locator L_j in $\mathcal{D}_R(A_1)$, it can exchange the *Beacon* message with its neighboring locators. As L_i lies in $\mathcal{D}_R(A_2) \setminus \mathcal{D}_R(A_1)$, it can calculate the distance between L_j and L_i. If L_i lies out of $\mathcal{D}_R(L_j)$, it derives that it receives a packet from a locator outside $\mathcal{D}_R(L_i)$, hence, $L_j \in C(L_i)$; otherwise, if L_i lies in $\mathcal{D}_R(L_j)$, a direct transmission path between L_i and L_j exists in addition to the transmission path through the wormhole link. Consequently, L_i can receive the same message from L_j for more than once. Therefore, $L_j \in C(L_i)$. Moreover, since any other locators $L_k \notin \mathcal{D}_R(A_1)$ cannot exchange message with L_i through the wormhole link, there is no abnormality in the communication between L_i and L_k. Therefore, $C(L_i)$ contains all the locators in $\mathcal{D}_R(A_1)$.

(2) Similar to case (1), if L_i lies in $\mathcal{D}_R(A_1) \setminus \mathcal{D}_R(A_2)$, $C(L_i)$ contains all the locators in $\mathcal{D}_R(A_2)$.

(3) If L_i lies in $\mathcal{D}_R(A_1) \cap \mathcal{D}_R(A_2)$, it can exchange the *Beacon* message with all the locators in $\mathcal{D}_R(A_1) \cup \mathcal{D}_R(A_2)$. For each locator $L_j \in \mathcal{D}_R(A_1) \cup \mathcal{D}_R(A_2)$, L_i will add it into $C(L_i)$. As L_i can also receive the message transmitted by itself, $L_i \in C(L_i)$. Meanwhile, locator $L_k \notin \mathcal{D}_R(A_1) \cup \mathcal{D}_R(A_2)$ cannot be in $C(L_i)$ as the message exchange between L_i and L_k is not interfered by the wormhole link. Therefore, $C(L_i)$ contains all the locators in $\mathcal{D}_R(A_1) \cup \mathcal{D}_R(A_2)$. ∎

Corollary 1. A locator is in its conflicting set if and only it lies in $\mathcal{D}_R(A_1) \cap \mathcal{D}_R(A_2)$.

As shown in Fig 2(a), L_1, L_2, L_3 lie in $\mathcal{D}_R(A_2) \setminus \mathcal{D}_R(A_1)$, L_4 lies in $\mathcal{D}_R(A_1) \cap \mathcal{D}_R(A_2)$, and L_5, L_6, L_7 lie in $\mathcal{D}_R(A_1) \setminus \mathcal{D}_R(A_2)$. For L_3, it will build its conflicting set as $C(L_3) = \{L_4, L_5, L_6, L_7\}$. For L_4, its conflicting set is $C(L_4) = \{L_1, L_2, L_3, L_4, L_5, L_6, L_7\}$. for L_8, its conflicting set is empty.

Duplex Wormhole Attack. When the sensor is under a duplex wormhole attack as shown in Fig. 2(a), all the locators in $\mathcal{D}_R(A_1) \cup \mathcal{D}_R(A_2)$ are D-locators. The sensor needs to check the conflicting sets of its neighboring locators to identify the V-locators and D-locators.

Theorem 2. When the sensor is under a duplex wormhole attack, $\forall L_i$ such that $C(L_i) \neq \emptyset$, $L_i \in \mathcal{L}_D$.

Proof: When the sensor is under a duplex wormhole attack as shown in Fig. 2(a), all locators in $\mathcal{D}_R(A_1) \cup \mathcal{D}_R(A_2)$ are neighboring locators of the sensor. According to Theorem 1, $\forall L_i \in \mathcal{D}_R(A_1) \cup \mathcal{D}_R(A_2)$, $C(L_i) \in \mathcal{D}_R(A_1) \cup \mathcal{D}_R(A_2)$. For each $L_j \notin \mathcal{D}_R(A_1) \cup \mathcal{D}_R(A_2)$, as its message cannot travel through the wormhole link, there will be no abnormality of the message exchange between L_j and other locators, thus $C(L_j) = \emptyset$. Therefore, $\forall L_i$ such that $C(L_i) \neq \emptyset$, $L_i \in \mathcal{L}_D$. ∎

Identification scheme I1: When the sensor detects that it is under a duplex wormhole, it can obtain the conflicting sets of the neighboring locators from the received *Loc_ack* messages. The sensor consider the ones with non-empty conflicting set as D-locators.

Simplex Wormhole Attack. As shown in Fig. 2(b), when the sensor is under a simplex wormhole attack, only the locators in $\mathcal{D}_R(A_1)$ are D-locators. We propose the following three identification schemes to identify all D-locators in this scenario.

Theorem 3. When the sensor is under a simplex wormhole attack, $\forall L_i$ such that if $\exists L_j \in C(L_i)$ but $L_j \notin \mathcal{L}_N$, $L_i \in \mathcal{L}_D$.

Proof. When the sensor is under a simplex wormhole attack, as shown in Fig. 2(b), according to Theorem 1, if $\exists L_j \in C(L_i)$, L_j must lie in $\mathcal{D}_R(A_1) \cup \mathcal{D}_R(A_2)$. If $L_j \notin \mathcal{L}_N$, $L_j \in \mathcal{D}_R(A_2) \setminus (\mathcal{D}_R(A_1) \cup \mathcal{D}_R(S))$. Therefore, $L_j \in \mathcal{D}_R(A_2) \setminus \mathcal{D}_R(A_1)$. Considering $L_j \in C(L_i)$, which leads to the conclusion that $L_i \in \mathcal{L}_D$. ∎

When the sensor detects that it is under a duplex wormhole, it can obtain the conflicting sets of the neighboring locators from the received *Loc_ack* messages.

Identification scheme I2. When the sensor is under a simplex wormhole attack, it obtains the conflicting sets of the neighboring locators from the received *Loc_ack* messages. By detecting the existence of non-neighboring locators in the conflicting set of one locator, the sensor can determine that this locator is a D-locator. In the scenario of Fig. 2(b), L_4, L_5 and L_6 will add L_7 into their conflicting sets, so the sensor can identify them as D-locators.

Theorem 4. When the sensor is under a simplex wormhole attack, $\forall L_i$ such that $C(L_i) = C(L_j)$ where $L_j \in \mathcal{L}_D$ and $L_j \notin C(L_j)$, $L_i \in \mathcal{L}_D$.

Proof. When the sensor is under a simplex wormhole attack, if $L_j \in \mathcal{L}_D$ and $L_j \notin C(L_j)$, according to Corollary 1, $L_j \notin \mathcal{D}_R(A_1) \cap \mathcal{D}_R(A_2)$. As $L_j \in \mathcal{L}_D$, L_j lies in $\mathcal{D}_R(A_1) \setminus \mathcal{D}_R(A_2)$, and $C(L_j)$ contains all the locators in $\mathcal{D}_R(A_2) \setminus \mathcal{D}_R(A_1)$. Therefor, $\forall L_i$ such that $C(L_i) = C(L_j)$, L_i must also lies in $\mathcal{D}_R(A_1) \setminus \mathcal{D}_R(A_2)$, which means $L_i \in \mathcal{L}_D$. ∎

Identification scheme I3. When the sensor is under a simplex wormhole attack, if it detects a dubious locator whose conflicting set does not include itself, then any locator whose conflicting set equals to this locator's is considered as a D-locator. For example, in Fig. 2(b), if the sensor S detects L_5 is a D-locator who lies in $\mathcal{D}_R(A_1) \setminus \mathcal{D}_R(A_2)$, then L_6 with the same conflicting set will be considered as a D-locator.

Theorem 5. When the sensor is under a simplex wormhole attack, if the distance between two neighboring locators of the sensor, L_j and L_k, is larger than $2R$, and $C(L_j) = \emptyset$, $C(L_k) \neq \emptyset$ and $L_k \notin C(L_k)$, $\forall L_i$ such that $C(L_i) = C(L_k)$, $L_i \in \mathcal{L}_D$.

Proof. When the sensor is under a simplex wormhole attack as shown in Fig. 2(b), if $C(L_k) \neq \emptyset$ and $L_k \notin C(L_k)$, then L_k cannot lie in $\mathcal{D}_R(A_1) \cap \mathcal{D}_R(A_2)$, therefore, L_k can only lie in $\mathcal{D}_R(A_1) \setminus \mathcal{D}_R(A_2)$ or $\mathcal{D}_R(A_2) \setminus \mathcal{D}_R(A_1)$. As $C(L_j) = \emptyset$, $L_j \in \mathcal{D}_R(S) \setminus (\mathcal{D}_R(A_1) \cup \mathcal{D}_R(A_2))$. Since the distance between two neighboring locators L_j and L_k is larger than $2R$, L_k does not lie in $\mathcal{D}_R(S)$. Since L_k is a neighboring locator of S, which meas L_k lies in $\mathcal{D}_R(S) \cup \mathcal{D}_R(A_1)$, L_k must lie in $\mathcal{D}_R(A_1) \setminus \mathcal{D}_R(A_2)$. According to Theorem 4, $\forall L_i$ such that $C(L_i) = C(L_k)$, $L_i \in \mathcal{L}_D$. ∎

Identification scheme I4. When the sensor is under a simplex wormhole attack, if it detects that the distance of two neighboring locators L_j and L_k are larger than $2R$, L_j's conflicting set is empty, L_k's conflicting set is not empty and does not contain L_k itself, then, all the locators having the same conflicting set with L_k are considered as D-locators. Take L_3 and L_6 in Fig. 2(b) for example, the distance between them is larger than $2R$, so the sensor can determine that $L_6 \in \mathcal{D}_R(A_1) \setminus \mathcal{D}_R(A_2)$. As $C(L_5) = C(L_6)$, L_5 will be considered as a D-locator.

The procedure to identify the dubious locators works as follows: After the locators build their conflicting sets, if the sensor detects that it is under a duplex wormhole attack, it identifies the D-locators using the identification scheme I1. Otherwise, if the sensor detects that it is under a simplex wormhole attack, it identifies the D-locators using the identification scheme I2, I3, and I4. At the end, all other neighboring locators which are not included into the D-locators are considered as V-locators. The algorithm of the dubious locators identification process lists in Algorithm 2:

3.3   Localization

After wormhole attack detection and dubious locators identification, the sensor can identify some valid locators. However, among the dubious locators, there may exist some locators which are also valid locators, such as L_3, L_4 and L_5 in Fig. 2(a) and L_3, L_4 in Fig. 2(b). Therefore, their distance measurements can be used into localization. As the sensor may receive multiple copies of the same message from these locators, it will consider the one with the shortest response time as the correct distance measurement. For the distance measurements which are larger than R due to the wormhole attack or

---

Algorithm 2. Dubious locators identification process

1: Each locator Periodically exchanges the *Beacon* messages with all its neighboring locators and builds its conflicting set based on the received *Beacon* messages.
2: When receiving the *Loc_req* message from the sensor S, each locator replies the *Loc_ack* message including its conflicting set to S.
3: **if** S detects a duplex wormhole attack **then**
4:     Conduct scheme I1 to build $\mathcal{L}_D$.
5: **end if**
6: **if** S detects a simplex wormhole attack **then**
7:     Conduct schemes I2, I3, and I4 to build $\mathcal{L}_D$.
8: **end if**
9: **for** each neighboring locator $L_i \notin \mathcal{L}_D$ **do**
10:     $L_i \rightarrow \mathcal{L}_V$
11: **end for**

---

measurement error, the sensor filters them out before localization. At the end, the valid distance measurements of the valid locators are used in the MLE localization.

4 Simulation Results

In this section, we present the simulation results to demonstrate the effectiveness of our proposed secure localization scheme. The network setting are as following: the transmission range R is equal and is set to $15m$; the locators are deployed with the Poisson distribution, and their density is set as $\rho_l = 0.006/m^2$; the measurement error of the distance follows a normal distribution $N(\mu, \sigma^2)$, where $\mu = 0$ and $\sigma = 0.5$; we assume the length of the wormhole link $L > R$ to avoid the endless packet transmission loop of the attackers, the label L/R of the x axis denotes the ratio of the length of the wormhole link to the transmission range.

Fig. 4 shows the performance comparison of SeRLoc scheme [17] and our proposed scheme in terms of the probability of successful wormhole attack detection. It shows

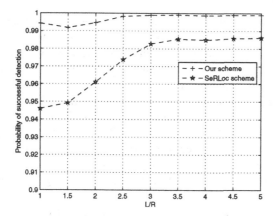

Fig. 4. Probability of successful wormhole detection in WSNs

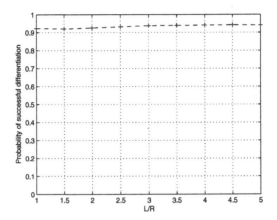

Fig. 5. Probability of dubious locators identification

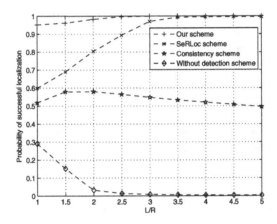

Fig. 6. Probability of successful secure localization

that our proposed scheme outperforms SeRLoc scheme under different values of the length of the wormhole link. As our proposed scheme takes the duplex wormhole attack and the distance measurement bound into consideration, which SeRLoc does not investigate, our proposed scheme can obtain higher performance. It is demonstrated in Fig. 4 that our proposed scheme provides successful wormhole attack detection probability at least 99%, and it gets very close to 100% when $L/R \geq 2.5$.

Fig. 5 shows the probability that the sensor successfully identifies all the dubious locators. In the dubious locators identification schemes, if the required condition for any identification scheme is satisfied, the sensor can trigger the corresponding identification scheme to identify all the dubious locators without failure. It shows that our proposed scheme provides perfect performance on identifying dubious locators (with the probability at least 92%).

Fig. 6 shows the performance comparison of our proposed scheme, SeRLoc scheme, the consistency scheme [6] and the scheme without any detection process when the

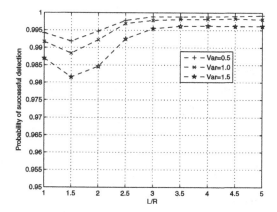

Fig. 7. Effects of distance measurement error on secure localization performance

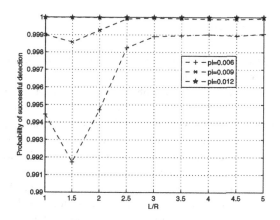

Fig. 8. Effects of locator density on secure localization performance

sensor is under the wormhole attack in terms of the probability of successful secure localization. The SeRLoc scheme identifies some D-locators using the sector uniqueness property and communication range violation property, then conducts self-localization based on the rest locators. However, SeRLoc scheme does not distinguish the duplex wormhole attack and simplex wormhole attack, and the communication range violation property may be invalid under the duplex wormhole attack. The consistency scheme identifies the D-locators based on the consistency check of the estimation result, the most inconsistent locator will be considered as a D-locator. We define the secure localization as successful when $d_{err1} \leq d_{err2} + f_{tol} * R$, where d_{err1} (and d_{err2}) denotes the localization error with (and without) using the secure localization scheme, f_{tol} is the factor of localization error tolerance (0.1 in our simulations). The performance of the scheme without any detection process shows the impact of the wormhole attack on the localization process. It is obvious that our proposed scheme provides much better performance than the other schemes. The simulation shows that our proposed scheme obtains the performance with a probability higher than 95% when $L/R < 2.5$ and a probability very close to 100% when $L/R \geq 2.5$.

Fig. 7 demonstrates the effects of distance measurement error on the performance of our proposed scheme. It shows that when the standard deviation $\sigma = 0.5$ of the distance measurement error (that is, the error ranges in $[-1.5, 1.5]m$ with a probability larger than 99%), the proposed scheme obtains the best performance. As the standard deviation σ gets larger, the performance becomes worse. However, even when $\sigma = 1.5$, the probability of successful localization is also not smaller than 98%, indicating that our proposed scheme works well even when great distance measurement error exists.

In Fig. 8, the effects of locator density on the performance of our proposed scheme is illustrated. Evidently, the improvement of locator density conduces to better secure localization performance. When the locator density $\rho_l = 0.012$ (with average degree around 6), our proposed scheme achieves a performance with the probability equals to 100%.

5   Concluding Remarks

In this paper, we analyze the impact of the wormhole attack on the range-based localization. Based on the analysis, we propose a secure localization mechanism which is wormhole attack resistant by using the wormhole attack detection and dubious locators identification. We also present the simulation results to demonstrate that our proposed scheme outperforms other existing schemes. In this paper, we only consider the scenario where the network has no packet loss when two nodes exchange messages with each other. This requirement can be supported by using acknowledgements for the successful packets and retransmission for the lost packets. Moreover, the proposed scheme is described based on the TDoA ranging method, but it can be easily applied to the localization approach with the radio signal strength indicator (RSSI) method as well. In the future, our work will focus on the secure localization when the sensor is under multiple wormholes' attack simultaneously.

References

1. Hu, Y.C., Perrig, A., Johnson, D.B.: Packet Leashes: A Defense Against Wormhole Attacks in Wireless Networks. In: Proc. of IEEE INFOCOM (2003)
2. Zhao, M., Servetto, S.D.: An Analysis of the Maximum Likelihood Estimator for Localization Problems. In: Proc. of the 2nd Int'l Conf. on Broadband Networks (2005)
3. Savvides, A., Han, C., Srivastava, M.: Dynamic Fine-Grained Localization in Ad-hoc Networks of Sensors. In: Proc. of ACM MOBICOM (2001)
4. Mao, G., Fidan, B., Anderson, B.D.O.: Wireless Sensor Network Localization Techniques. Computer and Telecommunications Networking, 2529–2553 (2007)
5. Boukerche, A., Oliveira, H.A.B.F., Nakamura, E.F., Loureiro, A.A.F.: Secure Localization Algorithms for Wireless Sensor Networks. IEEE Communications Magazine (2008)
6. Liu, D., Ning, P., Du, W.: Attack-Resistant Location Estimation in Sensor Networks. In: Proc. of IEEE IPSN (2005)

7. Capkun, S., Hubaux, J.P.: Secure Positioning of Wireless Devices with Application to Sensor Networks. In: Proc. of IEEE INFOCOM (2005)
8. Capkun, S., Cagalj, M., Srivastava, M.: Secure Localization With Hidden and Mobile Base Stations. In: Proc. of IEEE INFOCOM (2006)
9. Lazos, L., Poovendran, R., Capkun, S.: ROPE: Robust Position Estimation in Wireless Sensor Networks. In: Proc. of IEEE IPSN (2005)
10. Srinivasan, A., Teitelbaum, J., Wu, J.: DRBTS: Distributed Reputation-based Beacon Trust System. In: Proc. of the 2nd IEEE Int'l Symposium on Dependable, Autonomic and Secure Computing (2006)
11. Liu, D., Ning, P., Du, W.: Detecting Malicious Beacon Nodes for Secure Localization Discovery in Wireless Sensor Networks. In: Proc. of IEEE ICDCS (2005)
12. Khabbazian, M., Mercier, H., Bhargava, V.K.: Wormhole Attack in Wireless Ad Hoc Networks: Analysis and Countermeasure. In: Proc. of IEEE GLOBECOM (2006)
13. Wang, W., Bhargava, B.: Visualization of Wormholes in Sensor Networks. In: Proc. of ACM WiSe (2004)
14. Wang, W., Lu, A.: Interactive wormhole detection and evaluation. Information Visualization 6, 3–17 (2007)
15. Xu, Y., Chen, G., Ford, J., Makedon, F.: Detecting Wormhole Attacks in Wireless Sensor Networks. In: Proc. of IFIP (2008)
16. Maheshwari, R., Gao, J., Das, S.R.: Detecting Wormhole Attacks in Wireless Networks Using Connectivity Information. In: Proc. of IEEE INFOCOM (2007)
17. Lazos, L., Poovendran, R.: SeRLoc: Robust Localization for Wireless Sensor Networks. ACM Transactions on Sensor Networks, 73–100 (2005)
18. Lazos, L., Poovendran, R.: HiRLoc: High-Resolution Robust Localization for Wireless Sensor Networks. IEEE Journal on Selected Areas in Communications 24, 233–246 (2006)
19. Chen, H., Lou, W., Ma, J., Wang, Z.: TSCD: A Novel Secure Localization Approach for Wireless Sensor Networks. In: Proc. of The Second Int'l Conf. on Sensor Technologies and Applications (2008)

Novel and Efficient Identity-Based Authenticated Key Agreement Protocols from Weil Pairings

Hua Guo[1,2], Yi Mu[1], Xiyong Zhang[3], and Zhoujun Li[2]

[1] School of Computer Science Software Engineering, University of Wollongong,
NSW 2522, Australia
[2] School of Computer Science & Engineering, Beihang University,
Beijing 100083, PRC
[3] Zhengzhou Information Science and Technology Institute,
Zhengzhou, 450002, PRC
{hg999,ymu}@uow.edu.au, xyzhxy3711@sina.com

Abstract. It is often a challenging task to make a system satisfy desirable security properties and maintain a low computational overhead. In this paper, we attempt to minimize the gap for two identity-based key agreement protocols, in the sense that we allow our key agreement protocols to satisfy all general desirable security properties including master-key forward security and in the meanwhile achieve a good computational efficiency. Our protocols are novel, since we are able to make use of several nice algebraic properties of the Weil Pairing to outperform other state-of-the-art key agreement protocols. To our knowledge, our second protocol is the first identity-based protocol that provides master key forward security and satisfies all basic desirable security properties based on the key extraction algorithm due to Sakai and Kasahara.

Keywords: Authenticated key agreement, Master key forward secrecy, Weil pairing, Provable security.

1   Introduction

Key agreement is a cryptographic primitive, which plays an important role in secure communications. Using a key agreement protocol, two or more parties can generate a shared session key by making use of their long-term keys and ephemeral messages exchanged over an open network. The shared secret session key is then used for secure communication. In a PKI based key exchange setting, each party needs to obtain a certificate, extract the public key, check certificate chains and finally apply a key agreement protocol to generate a shared secret. The process is tedious and requires the involvement of a trusted third party who issues public key certificates. In 1984, Shamir [1] introduced the notion of identity-based cryptography, where end users can choose an arbitrary string as their public key, and the corresponding private key is created by binding the

D. Zhang et al. (Eds.): UIC 2009, LNCS 5585, pp. 310–324, 2009.
© Springer-Verlag Berlin Heidelberg 2009

identity string with the master secret of a trusted authority called Key Generation Centre (KGC). After Shamir's seminal work, Sakai et al. [2] invented an identity-based key agreement scheme based on bilinear pairings over eliptic curves, which was further streamlined by Boneh and Franklin [3] in their well-known security-provable identity-based encryption scheme and Sakai and Kasahara [4] in their new identity-based key construction using pairing. The reader is referred to [5] for a survey.

Many identity-based key agreement protocols were based on Shamir's identity-based notion. The introduction of parings to identity-based cryptography opened up an entirely new field for identity based key agreement. Many novel identity-based key agrement protocols from pairings were introduced (e.g., [6,7,8,9,10,11]). As outlined in [5], these protocols are based on two types of key extraction algorithms: one was introduced by Sakai et al. [2], and the other was introduced by Sakai and Kasahara [4], which can be tracked back to the work by Mitsunari [12]. In the first key extraction algorithm, the private key of the user is a product of the master key and a point, associated with the user identity, in a group of an elliptic curve; while in the second key extraction algorithm, the corresponding private key is obtained by first computing an inverse of the sum of the master key and a random value of the cyclic group $\mathbb{Z}_q^*$ associated with the user identity, and then multiplying a point of the elliptic curve with the inverse. It is clear that the second type of private key generation algorithm is more efficient than the first one since the identity string can be mapped to an element of the cyclic group instead of a point on an elliptic curve directly. However, most of the known identity-based key agreement protocols are based on the first type key extraction algorithm.

In 2005, McCullagh and Barreto [9] (MB) presented the first identity-based authenticated key agreement protocol based on the second kind of key extraction algorithm, which is more efficient in terms of computation complexity compared to those based on the first type of key extraction algorithm. We notice that several identity-based authenticated key agreement protocols were proposed with the same key extraction algorithm ([9,10,11]). However, they have some security weakness and none of these protocols possesses the master key forward security except the one presented by McCullagh and Barreto. Unfortunately, the McCullagh and Barreto protocol is vulnerable to the key compromise impersonation. The reason these protocols do not capture the master key forward security is that the session tokens from the second type of key extraction algorithm is based on the different bases so that Diffie-Hellman key can not be computed.

Session key escrow is one of the inherent properties of the identity-based key exchange, where the private key generator can also obtain the final shared session key since it knows the master key. This property is useful to enforce control where confidentiality and audit are subject to the law. However, key escrow is not desirable when the KGC is not fully trusted. We found that an identity-based key agreement protocol without key escrow implies the master key forward security.

In this paper, we first propose a new two-party authenticated identity-based key agreement protocol with key escrow. Although we select two random values to construct the key token, we use the special properties of the Weil pairing to achieve the computation and communication efficiency. Our protocol only needs one pairing computation and one point of the elliptic curve for communication. We prove the security of our protocol under a gap assumption in the random oracle by adopting Blake-Wilson *et al.*'s security model [13] and demonstrate that our protocol achieves implicit mutual key authentication with the security properties such as known session key security, key-compromise impersonation resilience and unknown key-share resilience according to Blake-Wilson *et al.* [13] and Cheng [14].

We then present an improved protocol which can turn the key escrow off. By using a trace map, we allow each user to obtain a point from the receiving message. This point is essentially a product of a random value chosen by the other user and the generator of a group; therefore it can be used to construct a Diffie Hellman key to prevent KGC (or the adversary) from computing the final session secret key. Another attractive feature of our protocol is that we prove the master key forward security based on a computational assumption. Our second scheme inherits security features from the first one and also captures the master-key forward security. Forward secrecy is one of the most important properties. In the identity-based key agreement scheme, forward secrecy can be further specified as perfect forward secrecy and the master key forward secrecy (we will explain later). To our best knowledge, none of other existing protocols constructed from the second type of key extraction algorithm holds this security property.

The rest of this paper is organized as follows. In Section 2, we describe the preliminaries including Weil pairing and security definitions. In Section 3, we present our first protocol with key escrow, which meets the security requirements defined in Section 2. In Section 4, we introduce the improved protocol with escrow freeness. In Section 5, we compare our protocols with other existing schemes, in order to justify our claims. In Section 6, we present a security analysis to demonstrate that our schemes are semantically secure and possess master key forward security. In Section 7, we conclude the paper.

2   Preliminaries

Before proposing our new identity-based key agreement schemes, we review some basic concepts, including the pairing primitives, assumptions and the security model of the authenticated key exchange.

2.1   Weil Pairing and Security Assumptions

Most of the known authenticated key exchange protocols are based on bilinear pairings, and the most popular bilinear pairings are Weil pairing and Tate pairing. In this paper, we choose Weil pairing due to some of its nice properties, which are useful for our schemes. The notations defined will be used in other sections in this paper.

Before giving the notation of Weil pairing, we first recall the definition of the set of n-torsion points.

Definition 1. *Let q be prime, $E(\mathbb{F}_q)$ be an elliptic curve over the prime finite field $\mathbb{F}_q$, and n be a prime divisor of the order of $E(\mathbb{F}_q)$ with $\gcd(n,q) = 1$. Then, there exists a finite field $E(\mathbb{F}_{q^k})$ which is the least finite field containing all the points of order n in $E(\overline{\mathbb{F}_q})$, where $\overline{\mathbb{F}_q} = \bigcup_{i \geq 1} \mathbb{F}_{q^i}$. The set of points on $E(\mathbb{F}_{q^k})$ with orders divisible by n is usually denoted by*

$$E[n] = \{P \in E(\mathbb{F}_{q^k}) \mid nP = \mathcal{O}\}$$

and is called the set of n-torsion points.

Note that the group of n-torsion points has the structure $E[n] \simeq \mathbb{G}_1 \oplus \mathbb{G}_2$, where $\mathbb{G}_1 (\subset E(\mathbb{F}_q))$ and $\mathbb{G}_2$ are generated from two primitive elements, say P_1 and P_2, respectively. One of the most important operations is the trace map which means that a point in the extension field can be reduced to a point in the base field. We denote by $\text{Tr}: E(\mathbb{F}_{q^k}) \longrightarrow E(\mathbb{F}_q)$ the trace function, induced from the finite field trace map from $\mathbb{F}_{q^k}$ to $\mathbb{F}_q$. For simplicity we denote by $\text{Tr}_i(P)$ the mapping of a point in $E[n]$ to a point in $\mathbb{G}_i$, where $i \in \{1,2\}$, in fact $\text{Tr}_1(\cdot) = \frac{1}{k}\text{Tr}(\cdot), \text{Tr}_2(\cdot) = \text{Tr}(\cdot) - \text{Tr}_1(\cdot)$. We will use this map in the security proof and present the improved protocol without key escrow. Now, we define the Weil pairing.

Definition 2. *Let $\mathbb{G}_1, \mathbb{G}_2(\mathbb{G}_1 \oplus \mathbb{G}_2 \simeq E[n])$ and $\mathbb{G}_T$ be cyclic groups of prime order n, P_1 is a generator of $\mathbb{G}_1$, P_2 is a generator of $\mathbb{G}_2$. ψ is an isomorphism from $\mathbb{G}_2$ to $\mathbb{G}_1$ with $\psi(P_2) = P_1$. The Weil pairing is a mapping of the following type:*

$$e_n : E[n] \times E[n] \to \mathbb{G}_T.$$

e_n *maps to the group $\mathbb{G}_T$ of n-th roots of unity.*

The Weil pairing holds the following useful properties:

1. Identity: For all $P \in E[n]$, $e_n(P,P) = 1$.
2. Alternation: For all $P, Q \in E[n]$, $e_n(P,Q) = e_n(Q,P)^{-1}$.
3. Bilinearity: For all $P, Q, R \in E[n]$, $e_n(P+Q,R) = e_n(P,R) \cdot e_n(Q,R)$, and $e_n(P,Q+R) = e_n(P,Q) \cdot e_n(P,R)$.
4. Non-degeneracy: For all $P \in \mathbb{G}_1$ and $Q \in \mathbb{G}_2$, $e_n(P,Q) \neq 1$.
5. Computability: For all $P, Q \in E[n]$, $e_n(P,Q)$ is computable in polynomial time.

The security of our schemes can be reduced to the Computational Diffie-Hellman problem and the k-Gap-BCAA1 assumption, which are used to prove the master key forward security and the semantic security, respectively.

Computational Diffie-Hellman (CDH) Assumption

For $a, b \in_R \mathbb{Z}_q^*$ and some values of $i, j, k \in \{1, 2\}$, given (aP_i, bP_j), computing abP_k is hard.

Bilinear Collision Attack Assumption (k-BCAA1 [8])

For an integer k, and $x \in_R \mathbb{Z}_q^*$, $P_2 \in \mathbb{G}_2$, $P_1 = \psi(P_2)$, $\hat{e} : \mathbb{G}_1 \times \mathbb{G}_2 \to \mathbb{G}_T$, given

$$(P_1, P_2, xP_2, h_0, (h_1, \frac{1}{h_1 + x} P_2), \cdots, (h_k, \frac{1}{h_k + x} P_2)),$$

where $h_i \in_R \mathbb{Z}_q^*$ and different from each other for $0 \leq i \leq k$, computing $\hat{e}(P_1, P_2)^{\frac{1}{x+h_0}}$ is hard.

Gap Bilinear Collision Attack Assumption (k-Gap-BCAA1 [8])

For an integer k, and $x \in_R \mathbb{Z}_q^*$, $P_2 \in \mathbb{G}_2$, $P_1 = \psi(P_2) \in \mathbb{G}_1$, $\hat{e} : \mathbb{G}_1 \times \mathbb{G}_2 \to \mathbb{G}_T$, given

$$(P_1, P_2, xP_2, h_0, (h_1, \frac{1}{h_1 + x} P_2), \cdots, (h_k, \frac{1}{h_k + x} P_2)),$$

where $h_i \in_R \mathbb{Z}_q^*$ and are different from each other for $0 \leq i \leq k$, and the access to a decision Bilinear Inverse Diffie Hellman oracle (DBIDH) where given $(P_1, P_2, aP_1, bP_2, \hat{e}(P_1, P_2)^r)$, it returns 1 if $\hat{e}(P_1, P_2)^r = \hat{e}(P_1, P_2)^{\frac{a}{b}}$, else returns 0, computing $\hat{e}(P_1, P_2)^{\frac{1}{x+h_0}}$ is hard.

2.2 Desirable Security Attributes

Let A and B be two legitimate entities that execute the protocol correctly. The following are some basic desirable properties of authentication key exchange protocols, as outlined by Chen [8].

Known-key secrecy (K-KS). Each run of the protocol between A and B should produce unique and independent secret session key. The compromise of one session key should not affect the secrecy of keys established in other sessions.

Forward secrecy (FS). Long-term private keys's disclosure of one or more of the entities should not affect the secrecy of previous session keys established by honest entities. It can be considered as three cases from different levels of this property:

- Partial forward secrecy (s): Compromising some but not all of the entities' long-term keys can not disclose previously established session keys;
- Perfect forward secrecy (d): Compromising all of the entities' long-term keys can not disclose previously established session keys;
- Master key forward security (m): Compromising long-term key of the key generation center can not affect the secrecy of the previously session keys. This is a particular property in the identity-based systems and it implies perfect forward secrecy.

Key-compromise impersonation (K-CI) resilience. Suppose A's private key is compromised. It is obvious that an adversary who knows this key can impersonate A to other entities (e.g. B). However, compromising A's private key should not enable the adversary to impersonate any other entity (e.g. B) to A.

Unknown key-share (UK-S) resilience. Entity A cannot be coerced into sharing a key with any entity C while A believes that she is sharing the key with another entity B.

No key control. Neither entity should be able to forge the session key with a preselected value.

2.3   Security Models

In this paper, we adopt the security model proposed by Bellare and Rogaway [15] and extended to public key construction by Blake-Wilson *et al.* [13] to prove the security of our protocols.

The model includes a set of parties and each party involved in a session is modeled by an oracle. An oracle $\Pi_{i,j}^s$ denotes an instance of a party i involved with a partner party j in a session s where the instance of the party j is $\Pi_{j,i}^t$ for some t. These parties can not communicate directly; instead they only communicate with each other via an adversary. An adversary can access the oracle by issuing some specified queries as follows.

Send($\Pi_{i,j}^s, m$): This query models an active attack. $\Pi_{i,j}^s$ executes the protocol and responds with an outgoing message x or a decision to indicate accepting or rejecting the session. If the oracle $\Pi_{i,j}^s$ does not exist, it will be created. Note that if $m = \lambda$, then the oracle is generated as an initiator; otherwise as a responder.

Reveal($\Pi_{i,j}^s$): $\Pi_{i,j}^s$ returns the session key as its response if the oracle accepts. Otherwise, it returns $\bot$. Such an oracle is called *opened*.

Corrupt(i): The party i responds with its private key.

Test($\Pi_{i,j}^s$): At some point, the adversary can make a Test query to a fresh oracle $\Pi_{i,j}^s$. $\Pi_{i,j}^s$, as a challenger, randomly chooses $b \in \{0,1\}$ and responds with the real agreed session key, if $b = 0$; otherwise it returns a random sample generated according to the distribution of the session key.

The security of a protocol is defined using the two-phases game $\mathcal{G}$ played between a malicious adversary $\mathcal{A}$ and a collection of oracles. At the first stage, $\mathcal{A}$ is able to send the above first three oracle queries at will. Then, at some point, $\mathcal{A}$ will choose a fresh session $\Pi_{i,j}^s$ on which to be tested and send a Test query to the fresh oracle associated with the test session. After this point, the adversary can continue querying the oracles but can not reveal the test oracle or its partner, and cannot corrupt the entity j. Eventually, $\mathcal{A}$ terminates the game simulation and outputs a bit b' for b. we say $\mathcal{A}$ wins if the adversary guesses the correct b. Define the advantage of $\mathcal{A}$ as:

$$\mathsf{Adv}^{\mathcal{A}}(k) = \mid 2\Pr[b' = b] - 1 \mid,$$

where k is a security parameter. The fresh oracle in the game is defined as follows.

Definition 3. (Fresh oracle [14]) *An oracle $\Pi_{i,j}^s$ is called fresh if (1) $\Pi_{i,j}^s$ has accepted; (2) $\Pi_{i,j}^s$ is unopened; (3) j has not been corrupted; (4) there is no opened oracle $\Pi_{j,i}^t$, which has had a matching conversation to $\Pi_{i,j}^s$.*

Remark 1. The above definition of fresh oracle is especially defined to address the key-compromise impersonate resilience since the Corrupt query could have been sent to entity i by the adversary [5].

In this work, we use the concatenation of the messages in a session to define the session ID, thus to define the matching conversation, i.e., two oracles $\Pi_{i,j}^s$ and $\Pi_{j,i}^t$ have a matching conversation to each other if both of them have the same session ID.

Now we are ready to give the definition of a secure authenticated key agreement protocol.

Definition 4. *[13] Protocol Π is a secure authenticated key agreement protocol, if:*

1. *In the presence of the benign adversary (who faithfully relays messages between parties), on $\Pi_{i,j}^s$ and $\Pi_{j,i}^t$, both oracles always accept holding the same session key and this key is distributed uniformly at random on session key space;*
   and if for every probability polynomial time(PPT) adversary $\mathcal{A}$:
2. *If two oracles $\Pi_{i,j}^s$ and $\Pi_{j,i}^t$ have matching conversations and both i and j are uncorrupted, then both accept and hold the same session key;*
3. $\mathsf{Adv}^{\mathcal{A}}(k)$ *is negligible.*

As mentioned by Chen [5], if a protocol is proved to be secure with respect to the above definition 4, then it achieves implicit mutual key authentication and the basic security properties, i.e., known session key security, key-compromise impersonation resilience and unknown key-share resilience. However, this security model does not cover forward secrecy property. Here, we modify the definition from Chen [5] to define the master key forward secrecy as follows:

Definition 5. *A protocol is said to have master key forward secrecy if any PPT adversary wins the game with negligible advantage when it chooses an unopened challenger $\Pi_{i,j}^s$ which has a matching conversation to another unopened $\Pi_{j,i}^t$ and both oracles accepted and the master key is disclosed.*

Remark 2. Since the master key forward secrecy implies perfect forward secrecy, we can say a protocol also has perfect forward secrecy if we can prove that the protocol has master key forward secrecy.

3   A New Authenticated Key Agreement Using Weil Pairing with Key Escrow

As all other identity-based cryptsystems, we assume the existence of a trusted Key Generation Center (KGC) that is responsible for the creation and secure distribution of users' private keys.

3.1   The Scheme

Our new scheme is specified by three randomized algorithms: Setup, Extract and Key Agrement.

Setup. This algorithm takes a security parameter k as input and follows the following steps:

1. Select a prime q and generate a Weil pairing $\hat{e} : E[q] \times E[q] \rightarrow \mathbb{G}_T$, where $E[q] = \mathbb{G}_1 \oplus \mathbb{G}_2$. $\mathbb{G}_1, \mathbb{G}_2$ are two cycle subgroups of order q of $E[q]$, and $\mathbb{G}_T$ is a cycle group of order q, ψ is a map from $\mathbb{G}_2$ to $\mathbb{G}_1$. Then choose a generator $P_2 \in \mathbb{G}_2^*$ of $\mathbb{G}_2$ randomly and set $P_1 = \psi(P_2)$.
2. Choose a value $s \in \mathbb{Z}_q^*$ and compute $P_{pub} = sP_1$.
3. Choose two cryptographic hash functions $H_1 : \{0,1\}^* \rightarrow \mathbb{Z}_q^*$, $H_2 : \{0,1\}^* \rightarrow \{0,1\}^n$ for some n.

The KGC publishes params $= \langle q, E[q], \mathbb{G}_1, \mathbb{G}_2, \mathbb{G}_T, \hat{e}, P_1, P_2, \psi, P_{pub}, H_1, H_2 \rangle$ as the system parameters and keeps s as its own secret master key. The parameters are distributed to the users of the system through a secure and authenticated channel.

Extract. The KGC takes as input params, master key, and an arbitrary $ID_{Ident} \in \{0,1\}^*$, and generates the private key

$$d_{Ident} = \frac{1}{s + H_1(ID_{Ident})} P_2$$

and sends it to the user.

Suppose two parties A and B want to establish a session key. Let $Q_{Ident} = (s + H_1(ID_{Ident}))P_1$ where $Ident = \{A, B\}$. The Key Agreement phase is conducted as follows.

Key Agreement. To establish a shared session key, A and B randomly choose their private ephemeral keys, respectively, (x_A, y_A) for A and (x_B, y_B) for B, from $\mathbb{Z}_q^*$, and compute the corresponding ephemeral public keys $T_1 = x_A Q_B + y_A P_2$ for A and $T_2 = x_B Q_A + y_B P_2$ for B. They then exchange T_1 and T_2 as described in Figure 1.

After the message exchange, A checks if $Tr_2(T_2) = \mathcal{O}$ or not. If so, A aborts the protocol; otherwise computes the shared secret $K_{AB} = \hat{e}(T_2, y_A d_A - x_A P_1)$ as his session secret. Similarly, B checks $Tr_2(T_1)$ and computes $K_{BA} = \hat{e}(T_1, y_B d_B - x_B P_1)$ as his session secret.

3.2   The Correctness of the Scheme and the Key Escrow Property

Protocol Correctness. By the properties of the Weil pairing, i.e., $\hat{e}(P_1, P_1) = 1$, $\hat{e}(P_2, P_2) = 1$, and $\hat{e}(P_1, P_2) = \hat{e}(P_2, P_1)^{-1}$, we can easily get the following equation:

$$K_{AB} = \hat{e}(T_2, y_A d_A - x_A P_1)$$

$$
\begin{array}{|ll|}
\hline
A & B \\
 & \\
x_A, y_A \in_R \mathbb{Z}_q^* & x_B, y_B \in_R \mathbb{Z}_q^* \\
T_1 = x_A Q_B + y_A P_2 & T_2 = x_B Q_A + y_B P_2 \\
\hline
\end{array}
$$

$$\xrightarrow{\quad T_1 \quad}$$

$$\xleftarrow{\quad T_2 \quad}$$

if $\mathrm{Tr}_2(T_2) \neq \mathcal{O}$, do $\qquad\qquad$ if $\mathrm{Tr}_2(T_1) \neq \mathcal{O}$, do

$K_{AB} = \hat{e}(T_2, y_A d_A - x_A P_1) \qquad K_{BA} = \hat{e}(T_1, y_B d_B - x_B P_1)$

$sk_A = H_2(A\|B\|T_1\|T_2\|K_{AB}) \qquad sk_B = H_2(A\|B\|T_1\|T_2\|K_{BA})$

Fig. 1. The first scheme with key escrow

$$
= \hat{e}(x_B Q_A + y_B P_2, \ \frac{y_A}{s + H_1(ID_A)} P_2 - x_A P_1)
$$

$$
= \hat{e}((s + H_1(ID_A)) x_B P_1 + y_B P_2, \ \frac{y_A}{s + H_1(ID_A)} P_2 - x_A P_1)
$$

$$
= \hat{e}((s + H_1(ID_A)) x_B P_1, \ \frac{y_A}{s + H_1(ID_A)} P_2) \cdot \hat{e}(y_B P_2, \ \frac{y_A}{s + H_1(ID_A)} P_2)
$$

$$
\cdot \hat{e}((s + H_1(ID_A)) x_B P_1, -x_A P_1) \cdot \hat{e}(y_B P_2, -x_A P_1)
$$

$$
= \hat{e}(P_1, P_2)^{y_A x_B} \cdot \hat{e}(P_1, P_2)^{x_A y_B}
$$

$$
= \hat{e}(P_1, P_2)^{y_A x_B + x_A y_B}.
$$

Similarly, we can get $K_{BA} = \hat{e}(P_1, P_2)^{y_A x_B + x_A y_B}$. Thus, the secret keys computed by A and B are equal, namely, they successfully established the shared secret $K = K_{AB} = K_{BA}$ after running an instance of the protocol. The final shared secret session key is then $sk = H_2(A\|B\|T_1\|T_2\|K)$, where $H_2 : \{0,1\}^* \to \{0,1\}^n$.

Key Escrow. After the execution of the protocol, KGC can also compute the session secret using the master secret key s. KGC proceeds as follows:

1. Compute $x_A Q_B = \mathrm{Tr}_1(T_1)$, $y_A P_2 = \mathrm{Tr}_2(T_1)$ and $x_B Q_A = \mathrm{Tr}_1(T_2)$, $y_B P_2 = \mathrm{Tr}_2(T_2)$.
2. Compute $x_A P_1 = x_A Q_B \cdot (s + H_1(ID_B))^{-1}$ and $x_B P_1 = x_B Q_A \cdot (s + H_1(ID_A))^{-1}$.
3. Compute the shared secret

$$
K = \hat{e}(x_A P_1, y_B P_2) \cdot \hat{e}(x_B P_1, y_A P_2),
$$

$$
= \hat{e}(P_1, P_2)^{x_A y_B} \cdot \hat{e}(P_1, P_2)^{x_B y_A}
$$

$$
= \hat{e}(P_1, P_2)^{y_A x_B + x_A y_B},
$$

which is the session secret shared between A and B, and can be used to compute the final session secret key.

3.3 Discussion

Using the properties of the Weil pairing, our scheme is efficient in terms of the cost of the computation and the communication bandwidth. Each party only needs to transmit one point on the elliptic curve and compute one Weil pairing. Moreover, Our scheme does not need any pre-computation.

In identity-based key agreement protocols, one of the most important properties is the master-key forward security. Unfortunately, it is not hard to prove that key escrow implies impossibility of master key forward security. More precisely, if the KGC can obtain the final session key between two users, then an adversary who has the master key can also compute this session key since the adversary has the same power as the KGC. Therefore, our scheme cannot achieve the master key forward security since it has the property of key escrow: if the master key s has revealed to an adversary $\mathcal{B}$, then $\mathcal{B}$ can compute $x_A P_1$ and $x_B P_1$ as well from the message flows in the session, i.e., T_1 and T_2, and obtain the final secret key easily.

4   Authenticated Key Agreement without Key Escrow

In the above scheme with key escrow, we introduce two random values for each user to establish the final shared session secret key. Using the trace map Tr, we allow each user to obtain a point in $\mathbb{G}_2$ from the receiving message which is a point in $E[q]$. This point is essentially a product of a random value chosen by the other user and the generator of the group $\mathbb{G}_2$ which is a public parameter; therefore it can be used to construct a Diffie Hellman key in order to prevent KGC from computing the final session secret key. Thus, the master key forward security can be achieved.

The algorithms of Setup and Extract are the same as the first protocol. The only difference is that we compute the second part of the session key by using trace map Tr to construct a Diffie-Hellman key that can prevent the KGC (or an adversary), who obtains the master key, from computing the final session secret key.

Key Agreement. As in the basic scheme, A and B randomly choose their private ephemeral keys, respectively, (x_A, y_A) for A and (x_B, y_B) for B, from $\mathbb{Z}_q^*$, and compute the corresponding ephemeral public keys $T_1 = x_A Q_B + y_A P_2$ for A and $T_2 = x_B Q_A + y_B P_2$ for B. They then exchange T_1 and T_2 as described in Figure 2.

After the message exchange, A does the follows:

1. Compute $y_B P_2 = \text{Tr}_2(T_2)$.
2. Compute the shared secrets $K_{AB,1} = \hat{e}(T_2, \ y_A d_A - x_A P_1)$ and $K_{AB,2} = y_A \cdot (y_B P_2)$.

Similarly, B computes $K_{BA,1} = \hat{e}(T_1, \ y_B d_B - x_B P_1)$ and $K_{BA,2} = y_B \cdot (y_A P_2)$ as his session secrets.

Protocol Correctness. Similar to the scheme with key escrow, we can easily verify its correctness:

$$K_{AB,1} = \hat{e}(T_2, \ y_A d_A - x_A P_1)$$
$$= \hat{e}(x_B Q_A + y_B P_2, \ \frac{y_A}{s + H_1(ID_A)} P_2 - x_A P_1)$$

$$\begin{array}{|ll|}
\hline
A & B \\
& \\
x_A, y_A \in_R \mathbb{Z}_q^* & x_B, y_B \in_R \mathbb{Z}_q^* \\
T_1 = x_A Q_B + y_A P_2 & T_2 = x_B Q_A + y_B P_2 \\
& \xrightarrow{\ T_1\ } \\
& \xleftarrow{\ T_2\ } \\
y_B P_2 = \mathrm{Tr}_2(T_2) & y_A P_2 = \mathrm{Tr}_2(T_1)) \\
K_{AB,1} = \hat{e}(T_2,\ y_A d_A - x_A P_1) & K_{BA,1} = \hat{e}(T_1,\ y_B d_B - x_B P_1) \\
K_{AB,2} = y_A \cdot (y_B P_2) & K_{BA,2} = y_B \cdot (y_A P_2) \\
sk_A = H_2(A\|B\|T_1\|T_2\|K_{AB,1}\|K_{AB,2}) & sk_B = H_2(A\|B\|T_1\|T_2\|K_{BA,1}\|K_{BA,2}) \\
\hline
\end{array}$$

Fig. 2. The second scheme without key escrow

$$= \hat{e}((s + H_1(ID_A))x_B P_1 + y_B P_2,\ \frac{y_A}{s + H_1(ID_A)}P_2 - x_A P_1)$$

$$= \hat{e}((s + H_1(ID_A))x_B P_1,\ \frac{y_A}{s + H_1(ID_A)}P_2) \cdot \hat{e}(y_B P_2,\ \frac{y_A}{s + H_1(ID_A)}P_2)$$

$$\cdot \hat{e}((s + H_1(ID_A))x_B P_1,\ -x_A P_1) \cdot \hat{e}(y_B P_2, -x_A P_1)$$

$$= \hat{e}(P_1, P_2)^{y_A x_B} \cdot \hat{e}(P_1, P_2)^{x_A y_B}$$

$$= \hat{e}(P_1, P_2)^{y_A x_B + x_A y_B},$$

and

$$K_{AB,2} = y_A \cdot (y_B P_2) = y_A y_B P_2.$$

Similarly, we can obtain $K_{BA,1} = \hat{e}(P_1, P_2)^{y_A x_B + x_A y_B}$ and $K_{BA,2} = y_B \cdot (y_A P_2) = y_A y_B P_2$. Thus, the secret keys computed by A and B are equal; namely, they successfully established the shared secrets $K_1 = K_{AB,1} = K_{BA,1}$ and $K_2 = K_{AB,2} = K_{BA,2}$ after running an instance of the protocol. The final shared secret session key is then $sk = H_2(A\|B\|T_1\|T_2\|K_1\|K_2)$, where $H_2 : \{0,1\}^* \rightarrow \{0,1\}^n$.

Key Escrow freeness. After the execution of the protocol, KGC can not compute the session secret using the master secret key s. More precisely, KGC can compute K_1 as in the first scheme, but it can not compute $K_2 = y_A y_B P_2$ even if it owns $y_A P_2$ and $y_B P_2$, because of the hardness of the Computation Diffie-Hellman problem. As the same reason, an adversary who holds the master key can not compute K_2 and the final secret session key; therefore, the improved protocol possesses the master key forward security.

5   Efficiency Analysis and Comparison

We compare our schemes with those schemes outlined by Chen [5], in terms of the security properties, the known security reduction and computation cost. We adopt the following notations to explain the computational performance of each scheme and omit addition operations as they are trivial compared to other operations.

P: Pairing.
M: Multiplication in $\mathbb{G}_i$, $i = 1, 2$.
E: Exponentiation in $\mathbb{G}_T$.

The comparison is outlined in Table 1 where the second column lists all the basic security attributes: known-key secrecy (k-ks), forward security (fs), key compromise impersonate (kci), and unknown-key share (uks). Forward security can be classified as partial forward security (s), perfect forward security (d) and master key forward security (m). Note that we use ✓ to indicate that the property is proved to be satisfied and × otherwise, and use - to denote that there is no an acceptable proof.

Table 1. Comparison of the identity-based key agreement schemes in the literature. Ours$_1$ and Ours$_2$ denote our first scheme and second scheme respectively.

Schemes	Security Properties					Reduction	Performance
	k-ks	fs s d m			kci uks		
MB-1 [9]	-	✓ ✓ ✓	×	×	-	-	$P + 3M$
MB-2 [9]	✓	✓ × ×		✓	✓	k-GBCAA1	$P + E + 2M$
Xie [10]	b	r o k	e		n	-	$P + E + 3M$
LYL-1 [11]	-	- - -	×		- -	-	$P + 2E + 2M$
LYL-2 [11]	-	- - -	×		- -	-	$P + 2E + 2M$
MB-1+2	✓	✓ ✓ ✓	×	✓	✓	k-GBCAA1	$P + 2E + 2M$
e-MB [5]	✓	✓ × ×		✓	✓	k-BCAA1	$3P + 2M + E$
Ours$_1$	✓	✓ ✓ ✓	×	✓	✓	k-GBCAA1	$P + 5M$
Ours$_2$	✓	✓ ✓ ✓	✓	✓	✓	k-GBCAA1+CDH	$P + 6M$

According to Table 1, every scheme has some weakness, except our second scheme which satisfies all basic security properties. In security reduction, only MB-2, MB-1+2, e-MB, and our two schemes provided a security reduction. The first three are due to McCullagh and Barreto [9](MB) and their variants. The security of MB-2, MB-1+2 and both of our schemes are reduced to gap assumption, and the security of e-MB is reduced to a computational assumption.

Considering the computational cost, since bilinear pairing is the most expensive computation compared to other operations, we pay more attention to this operation. In e-MB, they add an equation to check the key token and reduce the security to a computational assumption, thus the scheme needs three pairing computations. Moreover, it also needs a pre-computation operation. Although other schemes need only one pairing computation, the schemes of MB-2, Xie, LYL-2 and MB-1+2 all need pre-commutation of the pairing. Only MB-1, LYL-1 and our schemes need only one pairing computation without any pre-computation. Therefore, our schemes are more efficient in the cost of computation. All schemes need only one point for communication except e-MB which needs two points for communication.

According to the comparisons given above, the security of our two schemes can be reduced to the gap assumption. However, our second scheme is the only one which satisfies all basic security properties and especially possesses the perfect forward security and the master key forward security. Compared with other schemes, it requires a user to compute only one bilinear pairing and transmit one message.

6 Security Analysis

6.1 Security of the First Scheme with Key Escrow

In this section, we will give a rigorous proof of the security of the first protocol using Blake-Wilson et al. security model in the random oracle model.

As pointed out by Cheng [16], we should first check if the receiving message T is in the specified message space prior to accepting the session. Otherwise, there may exist potential attacks, for example, little sub-group attack.

Theorem 1. *If H_1, H_2 are random oracles and the $(q_1\text{-}1)$-Gap-BCAA1 assumption holds, then the first scheme is a secure key agreement scheme. In particular, suppose $\mathcal{A}$ is an adversary that attacks the scheme in the random oracle model with non-negligible probability $n(k)$ (for security parameter k), makes at most q_1 H_1 queries, and creates at most q_o oracles. Then, there exists an algorithm $\mathcal{B}$ that solves the $(q_1\text{-}1)$-Gap-BCAA1 problem with advantage*

$$\mathsf{Adv}_{\mathcal{B}}^{(q_1-1)-\mathsf{Gap-BCAA1}}(k) \geq \frac{1}{2 \cdot q_1 \cdot q_0} \cdot n(k).$$

Due to the limited space, the full proof of the above theorems is omitted here.

Remark 3. Since the protocol is proved to be secure in the security model defined by [13] and [14], it achieves implicit mutual key authentication and the basic security properties, i.e., known session key security, key-compromise impersonation resilience and unknown key-share resilience.

6.2 Master Key Forward Security

In this section, we consider the security of the scheme without key escrow. As we mentioned before, if KGC cannot compute the final session key, then an adversary who steals the master key can't compute the final session key either, which means the master key forward security. Therefore, we will provide the proof of semantic security and the master key forward security.

Firstly let us check the semantic security of the scheme. As mentioned before, in this scheme, we add a Diffie-Hellman key to prevent the KGC from computing the final security. Since the security of the first scheme is reduced to $(q_1\text{-}1)$-Gap-BCAA1 assumption, and the additional part of the session secret K_2 is essentially a Diffie-Hellman key, thus it doesn't affect the reduction. Therefore, the proof of the scheme without key escrow is similar to the proof of the scheme with key escrow. The only thing we need to do is to compute the extra Diffie-Hellman key in the Reveal query, regardless of the use's secret key and the $(q_1\text{-}1)$-Gap-BCAA1 assumption. We omit the details. We will focus on the proof of master key forward security, which is one of the most contributions in this paper.

Theorem 2. *The second scheme has master key forward secrecy provided the Computational Diffie-Hellman (CDH) assumption is sound and H_2 is modelled as random oracle. Specifically, suppose $\mathcal{A}$ wins the game with non-negligible advantage $n(k)$, then there exists a polynomial-time algorithm $\mathcal{B}$ to solve the Computational Diffie-Hellman problem with advantage:*

$$\mathsf{Adv}_A^{CDH,R} \geq \frac{1}{2}n(k).$$

Due to the limited space, the full proof of the above theorems is omitted here.

According to the definition of the forward security, if a protocol satisfies with master key forward security, then it must hold perfect forward security. So we can claim that our protocol without key escrow satisfies with perfect forward security and master key forward security.

7 Conclusion

We have presented two novel ID-based authenticated key agreement protocols inspired from the Sakai-Kasahara key generation algorithm from Weil pairing [4]. Our first protocol was designed under the key escrow model and the second one eliminates the key escrow. The security of the two protocols can be reduced to the gap assumption and the master key forward security of the second protocol without key escrow is reduced to a computational assumption in the random oracle model. To our knowledge, our second protocol is the first identity-based authenticated key exchange protocol based on the Sakai-Kasahara key generation algorithm and possesses the master key forward security, and is efficient in terms of the computational and communication bandwidth.

References

1. Shamir, A.: Identity-based cryptosystems and signature schemes. In: Blakely, G.R., Chaum, D. (eds.) CRYPTO 1984. LNCS, vol. 196, pp. 47–53. Springer, Heidelberg (1985)
2. Sakai, R., Ohgishi, K., Kasahara, M.: Cryptosystems based on pairing. In: Proceedings of Symposium on Cryptography and Information Security, Okinawa, Japan (2000)
3. Boneh, D., Franklin, M.: Identity-Based Encryption from the Weil Pairing. In: Kilian, J. (ed.) CRYPTO 2001, vol. 2139, pp. 213–229. Springer, Heidelberg (2001)
4. Sakai, R., Kasahara, M.: ID based cryptosystems with pairing on elliptic curve, Cryptology ePrint Archive, Report 2003/054 2003
5. Chen, L., et al: Identity-based Key Agreement Protocols From Pairings. International Journal Information Security 6, 213–241 (2007)
6. Smart, N.P.: An identity based authenticated key agreement protocol based on the Weil pairing. Electronics Letters 38, 630–632 (2002)
7. Shim, K.: Efficient ID-based authenticated key agreement protocol based on the Weil pairing. Electronics Letters 39, 653–654 (2003)

8. Chen, L., Kudla, C.: Identity based authenticated key agreement from pairings. In: Proceedings of the 16th IEEE Computer Security Foundations Workshop, pp. 219–233 (2003)

9. McCullagh, N., Barreto, P.S.L.M.: A new two-party identity-based authenticated key agreement. In: Menezes, A. (ed.) CT-RSA 2005. LNCS, vol. 3376, pp. 262–274. Springer, Heidelberg (2005)

10. Xie, G.: An ID-based key agreement scheme from pairing. Cryptology ePrint Archive, Report 2005/093 (2005)

11. Li, S., et al.: Towards security two-part authenticated key agreement protocols. Cryptology ePrint Archive, Report 2005/300 (2005)

12. Mitsunari, S., et al: A new traitor tracing. IEICE Trans. Fundamentals 85, 481–484 (2002)

13. Blake-Wilson, S., et al: Key agreement protocols and their security analysis. In: Darnell, M.J. (ed.) Cryptography and Coding 1997. LNCS, vol. 1355, pp. 30–45. Springer, Heidelberg (1997)

14. Cheng, Z., et al.: On the indistinguishability-based security model of key agreement protocols-simple cases. In: Proceedings of ACNS 2004 (technical track) (2004)

15. Bellare, M., Rogaway, P.: Entity authentication and key distribution. In: Stinson, D.R. (ed.) CRYPTO 1993. LNCS, vol. 773, pp. 232–249. Springer, Heidelberg (1994)

16. Cheng, Z., Chen, L., Comley, R., Tang, Q.: Identity-based key agreement with unilateral identity privacy using pairings. In: Chen, K., Deng, R., Lai, X., Zhou, J. (eds.) ISPEC 2006. LNCS, vol. 3903, pp. 202–213. Springer, Heidelberg (2006)

17. Cheng, Z., Chen, L.: On security proof of McCullagh-Barreto's key agreemnet protocol and its variants. Int. J. of Security and Networks 2(3/4), 251–259 (2007)

Implicit User Re-authentication for Mobile Devices*

Sausan Yazji[1], Xi Chen[2], Robert P. Dick[2], and Peter Scheuermann[1]

[1] EECS Dept., Northwestern University, Evanston, IL. 60208
[2] EECS Dept., University of Michigan, Ann Arbor, MI. 48109
s-yazji@northwestern.edu, peters@ece.northwestern.edu,
chexi@umich.edu, dickrp@eecs.umich.edu

Abstract. Portable computers are used to store and access sensitive information. They are frequently used in insecure locations with little or no physical protection, and are therefore susceptible to theft and unauthorized access. We propose an implicit user re-authentication system for portable computers that requires no application changes or hardware modifications. The proposed technique observes user-specific patterns in filesystem activity and network access to build models of normal behavior. These are used to distinguish between normal use and anomalous use. We describe these automated model generation and user detection techniques, and explain how to efficiently implement them in a wireless distributed system composed of servers and battery-powered portable devices. The proposed system is able to distinguish between normal use and attack with an accuracy of approximately 90% every 5 minutes and consumes less than 12% of a typical laptop battery in 24 hours.

1 Introduction

Portable computing devices such as personal digital assistants (PDAs), cellphones, and laptop computers are now used to store and access sensitive information, e.g., bank account, commercial transaction, and private emails. However, they are frequently used in insecure locations with little or no physical protection, and are therefore susceptible to theft and potential unauthorized access.

User authentication is an essential part of any security policy that grants permission to access a specified account. Currently, the most widely used authentication method is explicit authentication, i.e., authentication is performed once at start-up by asking for a password [1], a fingerprint [2], a face profile [3], or a combination. However, all these approaches are intermittent and therefore susceptible to attack, e.g., an unauthorized user can access a portable computer either by stealing a password or exploiting an open account of an authorized user.

Theft of confidential data by unauthorized users accounts for much of the financial losses due to computer crime [4]. Much of this loss could be prevented by requiring a frequent login, which would impose an unwarranted burden on

---

* This work was supported in part by the National Science Foundation under awards CNS-0347941, CNS-0720691, and CNS-0613967.

D. Zhang et al. (Eds.): UIC 2009, LNCS 5585, pp. 325–339, 2009.

the user. We propose an implicit re-authentication technique, MIA, to compliment to explicit authentication. It provides on-line protection for private data without burdening the user. Our system uses file access patterns and network activities to detect anomalous behavior. In a behavioral authentication system, the authentication module samples behavioral data and compares them with user-specific models. The comparison results are then used to identify users. Researchers have proposed using keystrokes [5] and mouse movements [6] for user re-authentication. However, they have not designed or evaluated these techniques for portable battery-powered computers.

In this paper, we describe the first implicit re-authentication technique for battery-powered wireless portable systems. This is also the first implicit re-authentication technique for portable systems based on filesystem and network activity. We describe how the framework may accept data from different authentication mechanisms to improve security. Our evaluation indicates that the proposed technique has the potential to substantially increase security and/or decrease frequency of explicit user authentication compared to explicit authentication techniques, alone. The proposed system is able to distinguish between normal use and attack with an accuracy of approximately 90% with a latency of 5 minutes.

The rest of the paper is organized as follows. Section 2 summarizes related work. Section 3 gives an overview of the proposed system architecture. Section 4 describes each architectural component. Section 5 analyzes the energy consumption of MIA. Section 6 presents the experimental setup and examines the results. Section 7 concludes the paper. Section 8 describes future work.

2   Related Work

Numerous user authentication techniques exist for portable devices. While password based mechanisms are the most used [1], they are insufficient. Therefore some researchers have proposed other techniques that rely on hardware or software enhancements for efficient authentication based on fingerprint [2], face recognition [3], and iris data [8]. Moon et al. [7] implemented a Gaussian mixture model based speaker verification module on a mobile system. However, all these approaches are used for one-time explicit authentication. In addition, most of them require application changes and hardware support. In contrast, our technique requires no application changes, additional hardware, or explicit actions by the user.

A number of previous approaches re-authenticate users by monitoring their behavior without explicitly requiring special inputs for re-authentication. Denning and Neumann [14] were the first to introduce a behavioral re-authentication system. Denning [10] proposed using audit logs for anomaly detection. Monrose and Rubin [5] proposed using keystroke dynamics for re-authentication. Lane and Brodley [9] studied a system that models the normal behavior at the command line prompt. Pusara and Brodley [15] used mouse movements for external user re-authentication. Pusara [6] built a signature-based intrusion detection system based on a combination of keystroke dynamics, mouse movements, and graphical user interface events, in which the attacker's behavior was known a priori. However, energy consumption and other metrics relevant to use in portable, battery-powered systems were not taken into account. In contrast, our technique requires no automated or manual attacker modeling: it detects attacks entirely based on models of normal user behavior. In addition, we evaluate the energy consumption of MIA when used in battery-powered mobile wireless systems.

Other techniques that use implicit re-authentication by monitoring system call traces and program execution traces have also been proposed [12,13,11].

3 Problem Definition and System Architecture

The proposed MIA architecture was motivated by the following observations: (1) different individuals have differing computer use patterns, e.g., filesystem and network access, which may be used for identification; (2) operating systems have access to a great deal of information, e.g., file access and network activities; and (3) there is a great imbalance in the cost of expending energy on portable battery-powered devices and stationary computers with easy access to energy.

It is our goal to detect whether a portable device is under attack, i.e., whether an unauthorized user is attempting to access data, or modifying the system to allow such data to be later gathered. We also have a number of other requirements: (1) to simplify deployment, application or hardware changes should not be required; (2) to avoid burdening the user, the system should not require explicit re-authentication input; (3) the latency of attack detection should be minimized; (4) detection accuracy should be maximized; (5) the power consumption and computational overhead of the technique must be low enough to permit operation on portable, battery-powered devices; and (6) the system should still be able to operate temporarily in the absence of wireless network access.

Architecture Overview. Figure 1 shows the system architecture of the proposed MIA system. The *information capturing system* consists of operating system modules and other analysis software installed on the portable battery-powered device to register user activity continuously, and to create new log file every T minutes [1]. It also consists of feature extraction and data compression processes to reduce the energy consumption of data transmission. The data captured are then sent to *information management system*, which resides on a computer with higher performance and much looser power consumption constraints than the portable system. It is responsible for periodically rebuilding models for filesystem and network access, performing anomaly detection, and transferring this model back to the portable computing system. Wireless communication between the portable device and the high-performance computer used for the information management system may be intermittent. In the absence of a wireless link, model evaluation will continue to occur on the portable computer system, allowing the detection of attack at some power consumption penalty.

---

[1] The detection latency T should be small enough to detect an attack before the attacker is capable of harming the system.

Algorithm 1. Information Management System

```
1: For each user Uₙ do the following:
2: while TRUE do
3:    Receive data from the information capturing system
4:    if NewUser = TRUE then
5:       if time < D then
6:          Add log data to the data source
7:       else
8:          Build the user's profile
9:          NewUser = FALSE
10:         Send user's profile to the client
11:      end if
12:   else
13:      Perform anomaly detection
14:      if Abnormal behavior then
15:         Take action, e.g., re-authenticate, lock client, or send warning
16:      else
17:         Continue
18:      end if
19:   end if
20: end while
```

Algorithm 1 denotes that the *information management system* consists of two major processes; the model building process, and the anomaly detection process. In order to build a behavioral model for authenticated user, data from this user needs to be captured for a training duration, D. To determine the appropriate value of D, we performed a small-scale, long-duration user study with the network-based technique and found that a D of two months results in a false rejection rate, FRR, of 2% which is the probability that the normal user will be mistakenly identified as an attacker. However, our primary full-scale multiple-metric user study is limited to two weeks to avoid undue burden on the volunteer participants, somewhat reducing the accuracy achieved in our full-scale study.

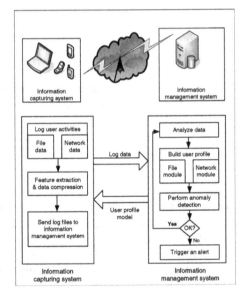

Fig. 1. MIA system architecture

Upon the completion of the data capturing phase, the "New User" flag is reset, and the user access model is built. To perform anomaly detection, the *information management system* compares the received user activity data with the same user's model. If the behavior and model are sufficiently dissimilar, the behavior is identified as anomalous and appropriate action is taken, e.g., the user is required to re-enter the password, and an alert is sent to the system administrator or the portable system is disabled.

4   User Filesystem and Network Access Modeling

The MIA system is composed of four main processes: data collection, feature extraction, model construction, and anomaly detection. In this section we will describe each process in detail.

Data Collection. To capture the files access pattern, we modified the source code of FileMon [17] to log file access events transparently in real time. We gathered timestamps, names of the process responsible for access, locations of accessed files, and operations on the file. A file access record is generated on each system call, with a time resolution of 1 ms. The file access records generated by system services, not the user, are filtered out to save transmission energy and reduce noise in classification. To capture the network activities we used the WireShark 0.995 network packet analyzer [18] to gather the following data for each real-time network access event: timestamp of each access, source IP address, destination IP address, protocol identifier, and detailed packet information. Broadcast and router-specific protocols were filtered out in order to focus on user-dependent network events for the same reasons described above.

Feature Extraction. In order to choose the most robust features to model user behavior, and to reduce the amount of data in each log file, and based on our observation that in general, a normal user tends to use a small set of processes within a small subset of directories, connects to a small subset of the available machines/sites, and performs similar activities every day, we choose the *process*, *time*, and *location* fields to build the user file access model and *destination IP*, *time*, and *protocol* fields to build the user network access model.

Model Construction. There are two major challenges to developing the MIA system: determining the best data representation and selecting the appropriate data mining algorithm.

Data Representation. Due to the limitation of the software that we use for model construction [19], we need to map some of the fields to integer values such as *location*, *source IP*, and *destination IP* fields.

The directory structure can be represented as a tree, where the leaves are files and intermediate nodes are directories. We number the directories in each level from left to right, starting from 1. We use W to represent the width of the directory tree, i.e., the largest value used to number the directories at any level of the tree. For convenience, we represent the location of a file as follows:

$$\overrightarrow{x_n} = (x_1, x_2, \cdots, x_n) \stackrel{\text{def}}{=} x_1/x_2/\cdots/x_n. \tag{1}$$

where $x_1, x_2, \cdots, x_n$ are the integers corresponding to the sub-directories encountered sequentially on the path from the top-level directory to the file location. We use the following one-to-one mapping function

$$f(x_1, x_2, \cdots, x_n) = \sum_{i=1}^{n-1} x_i \times W + x_n. \tag{2}$$

Note that distortion is unavoidable when we use linear functions to express the nonlinear relationship between file locations. To map the IP address (denoted as $A.B.C.D$) into an integer value, the following equation is used:

$$IP\ Value = A \times (255)^3 + B \times (255)^2 + C \times (255) + D. \tag{3}$$

K-Means Clustering. Although previous work used neural networks for intrusion detection [20,21], we choose K-means clustering [22] to build the models of filesystem and network behavior. This decision is based on a small-scale (four-user) three-month user study on the network-based technique. For this study, we compared the detection results based on two different data mining algorithms, a K-means clustering algorithm with the total of 8 clusters and a maximum of 20 iterations, and a three-layer sigmoid activation function neural network. With three months of training data, the accuracy of the neural network based approach did not exceed 84%, while the accuracy of the K-means clustering based approach increased to 98% within 90 days. We conclude that the K-means clustering algorithm allows more accurate prediction given a reasonable amount of training data (more than 14 days in our experiments). In addition, the K-means method is often the fastest and most energy-efficient for large data sets.

We used SPSS Clementine [19], a commercial data mining and statistical analysis software, as our model construction environment because it has built-in support for K-Means clustering. The input fields are automatically rescaled to have values between 0 and 1 before the clustering process such that each field is weighted equally.

Anomaly Detection. For an accurate anomaly detection, the main idea is to discover K clusters such that records within the same cluster are similar to each other but distinct from records in other clusters. The algorithm first selects K initial cluster centers. For each record, it computes the Euclidean distance between the record and the K cluster centers and assigns the record to the closest cluster. After all records have been processed, the cluster centers are updated to reflect the new set of records assigned to each cluster, and the records are checked again to see whether they should be reassigned to a different cluster. This record assignment and cluster update process is repeated until the change between two consecutive iterations is below a certain threshold.

One interesting problem is how to define the difference between the model and the current behavior without previous knowledge of anomalous behavior.

We define the *distribution vector* (DV) of a data set as a K-element vector, the ith element of which is equal to the percentage of records in the ith cluster. Our solution is based on the following observation: given a set of recent file access records generated by a normal user, the DV obtained from these records, i.e., $DV(evaluation)$, should be close to that obtained during the training phase, i.e., $DV(training)$, if the normal user behaves consistently during both the evaluation and the training phases. We compute the Euclidean distance[2] between $DV(evaluation)$ and $DV(training)$ and compare the result with a predefined

---

[2] We also tried using Manhattan distance but this yielded poorer accuracy.

threshold ϵ. This threshold is user-dependent and is set to a distance that results in a low false reject rate (FRR) in the training phase. If the distance exceeds ϵ, the model reports anomalous behavior. Otherwise, the current behavior is identified as normal behavior. Intuitively, a low threshold value would result in low false acceptance rate (FAR) at the cost of high FRR, while a high threshold value corresponds to a low FRR and a high FAR. In our approach, ϵ is chosen such that the FRR value does not exceed 10% during the training phase. ϵ is not determined by FAR value because we do not have access to the hacking data during the training phase in a real system with MIA deployed.

5   Energy Consumption Design Decisions

Portable systems such as laptops are usually battery powered. Since the batteries may be charged infrequently, MIA system should be energy-efficient. In this section, we analyze the energy consumption of our proposed system in a client-server architecture containing client laptop computers equipped with Intel 3945ABG WLAN cards. The parameters used for energy consumption estimation are listed in Table 1. They are measured using Power Manager, a built-in tool for power laptop consumption measurement [23], or derived from datasheets [16].

Table 1. Energy Consumption Parameters

Parameter	Explanation	Nominal Value
$P_{collect}$	average power consumption of data collection	0.15 W
P_{build}	average power consumption during model construction	17.53 W
$P_{anomaly}$	average power consumption in anomaly detection	22.45 W
P_{tr}	transmitting power for WLAN card	1.8 W [16]
E_{bat}	total battery energy	303.3 kJ
$E_{prepare}$	average energy consumption of feature extraction	4.6 J
$E_{compress}$	average energy consumption of data compression	2.8 J
E_{Total}	total energy consumption by portable device	34.675 kJ
$B_{wireless}$	uploading bandwidth of a wireless channel	1.5 Mb/s
T_{build}	time to build the user's model	540 s
$T_{anomaly}$	time to cluster new records in anomaly detection	20 s
T_{day}	total number of seconds in a day	86,400 s

Energy Consumption On the Client. When the network is available, data are sent to the server for anomaly detection. Therefore, the total daily energy consumption on the client is

$$E_{Total} = E_{collect} + E_{prepare} + E_{compress} + E_{transmission} \qquad (4)$$

When the wireless network is not available, the anomaly detection is performed on the portable device, resulting in a daily client energy consumption of

$$E_{Total} = E_{collect} + E_{prepare} + E_{compress} + E_{anomaly} \qquad (5)$$

Data Collection. The daily energy consumption for data collection is

$$E_{collect} = P_{collect} \times T_{day} = 0.15\,\text{W} \times 86,400\,\text{s} = 12.96\,\text{kJ} = 4.27\% E_{bat}. \quad (6)$$

Feature Extraction. We perform a customized feature extraction process on the client that reduces the log file size by 50% and consumes 4.6 J on average. Since the log file has to be sent to the server every 5 minutes (see Section 6), or 288 times per day, the total daily energy consumption in the feature extraction process is 1.324 kJ. This takes only 0.436% of E_{bat}.

Data Compression. We used WINRAR, a software program that uses prediction by partial matching (PPM) algorithm [24], to compress the log file. On the average, data compression reduced the file size to 11% of its original size and consumed 10.15 J every 5 minutes. Therefore, the energy consumption of the data compression process in a day is 2.923 kJ which equals 0.963% of E_{bat}.

Data Transmission. In our experiment, we used an Intel 3945ABG 802.11 WLAN card for data transmission. Our experimental data indicate that the size of raw log files associated with both filesystem and network events increases at a rate of 0.064 MB/s on average. After feature extraction and compression, the file size is reduced to 5.5% of its original value. The energy consumption per transmission is

$$E_{transmission} = P_{tr} \times \frac{File\_Size}{B_{wireless}} = 1.8\,\text{W} \times 0.055 \times \frac{0.064\,\text{MB/s} \times 8 \times 300\,\text{s}}{1.5\,\text{Mb/s}} \quad (7)$$

$$= 10.137\,\text{J}. \quad (8)$$

Therefore, the data transmission consumes 10.137 J every 5 minutes, and the total daily energy consumption of data transmission is 2.919 kJ which is 0.96% of E_{bat} per day.

In conclusion, when the network is available, the proposed technique consumes a total daily energy of

$$E_{Total} = 12.96\,\text{kJ} + 1.324\,\text{kJ} + 2.923\,\text{kJ} + 2.919\,\text{kJ} = 20.126\,\text{kJ} = 6.635\% E_{bat}. \quad (9)$$

Design Considerations. We also analyzed the energy consumption for model construction and anomaly detection to determine whether they should be performed on the server or battery-powered clients. There are trade-offs between the energy consumed during feature extraction, compression, data transmission, model building, and anomaly detection that must be considered in order to arrive at an energy-efficient design.

Model Building. If the model is built on the client, the energy consumption during model building using one week of training data is

$$E_{build} = P_{build} \times T_{build} = 17.53\,\text{W} \times 540\,\text{s} = 9.466\,\text{kJ} = 3.12\% E_{bat}. \quad (10)$$

Note that this model is built based on only one week of data. In a real system with the proposed MIA system deployed, we need two months of data to construct the model to achieve an FRR of less than 10%, which will result in a significant increase in total energy consumption. Although it might appear that building the model on the client would reduce energy consumption by eliminating the transmission of training data to the server, the same log data would still need to be sent to server every 5 minutes for anomaly detection (see Section 6). Therefore, we decided to build models on the server.

Anomaly Detection. The energy consumption by each run of the anomaly detection process is

$$E_{anomaly} = P_{anomaly} \times T_{anomaly} = 22.45\,\text{W} \times 20\,\text{s} = 449\,\text{J}. \tag{11}$$

Given 5-minute detection latency, the total daily energy consumption of anomaly detection is 129.3 kJ, i.e., 42.6% of E_{bat}. Therefore, performing anomaly detection on the server greatly increases battery life, thus motivating our design decision. However, intermittent anomaly detection on the client may still be required when the wireless network is unavailable, although this may increase energy overhead.

6   Experimental Evaluation

In this section, we evaluate the MIA system. Our experiments are designed to determine whether filesystem and network behaviors can provide sufficient information for fast anomaly detection. We first describe the experimental setup for gathering user data. Then, we explain how to generate data sets for training, testing, and evaluation. We then indicate the FARs and FRRs when we use the filesystem and network based re-authentication techniques separately. Finally, we evaluate the proposed combined technique. Experimental results indicate that we can achieve an FAR of 13.7% and an FRR of 11% with a detection latency of 5 minutes by combining filesystem and network based re-authentication techniques.

Experimental Setup for Data Collection. Since the data collection process is related to the participants' privacy, recruiting volunteers for this experiment was a challenge. We were able to recruit 16 volunteers, of which only 8 successfully completed the experiment. The filesystem and network monitoring programs were deployed on each participant's machine, which runs in the background generating log files without user intervention.

Data collection is divided into two phases: training phase and attacking phase. In the training phase, participants were asked to use their machines normally so that we could gather the training data to build a model of normal behavior for each user. We monitored the users' normal filesystem and network activity continuously for two weeks. The size of the log files generated in the training phase ranges from 80 MB to 25 GB.

The goal of the attacking phase is to obtain anomalous behavior data for each machine. Note that attacking must be done on the same set of machines used in the training phase, otherwise users and attackers can easily be distinguished because the files they access will have different file names. Before the attacking phase starts, we embedded several files that contain fake bank account information in each participant's machine, without indicating the locations of those files. Each user was assigned to attack another user's machine at random. In the attacking phase, the attacker was asked to discover as much private information on the victim machine as possible, e.g., account information, frequently visited web pages, and information about user's friends and usual contacts.

Evaluation Process. After data collection, we first partition each user's log files, generated during the training phase, into two disjoint parts: training logs and testing logs. For each user, we sampled the records in the training logs randomly, which are then used to build the model of normal behavior. We then randomly chose 20 data blocks from the training logs, each of which contains consecutive file access records generated during a T minute time window, where T was set to 2,5,10, and 20 minutes. Each data block is then used as a training data set. The testing data sets and attacking data sets (represented as *evaluation data sets*) are generated in the same way. To avoid biasing the results, we took out the records associated with the files that contain fake bank account information.

As we described in Section 4, we first build a model of normal behavior for each user along with the distribution vector $DV(model)$. After that, for each training data set associated with a given T value, we assign the records in the set to the existing clusters, which generates $DV(training)$. We then compute the Euclidean distance between $DV(model)$ and $DV(training)$ to measure how much the training data set deviates from the model of normal behavior. The comparison threshold ϵ is chosen such that the FRR value does not exceed 10% during the training phase. Finally, we calculate $DV(evaluation)$ for each evaluation data set. If the Euclidean distance between $DV(model)$ and $DV(evaluation)$ is above ϵ, the model indicates an anomaly. Otherwise, it indicates normal behavior. We compute FARs and FRRs based on the results from the 20 testing data sets and 20 attacking data sets. Based on our experiment, we concluded that $T = 5$ minutes provides the most appropriate FRR of 11%.

Using Filesystem/Network Based Technique Alone. Figure 2 shows the FARs and FRRs for eight users with an anomaly detection period of 5 minutes using filesystem and network based approaches separately. As indicated in Figure 2, the FAR ranges from 0% to 65% for the filesystem-based technique and 26.7% to 94.1% for the network-based technique. The FRR ranges from 8% to 28% for the filesystem-based technique and 0% to 20% for the network-based technique. The average FAR and FRR are 28.8% and 15.6% for the filesystem-based technique and 46.4% and 7% for the network-based technique. The results indicate that single-metric techniques have high FARs because most of users have some time periods within which there are either insufficient network or filesystem data to accurately identify an attack. For example, the filesystem model for user #7 has an FAR of 65%. A closer examination of user #7's data reveals that the corresponding attacker rarely accessed files. More specifically, 12 of the

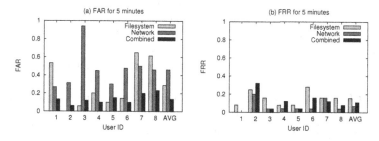

Fig. 2. (a) FARs and (b) FRRs for eight users with an anomaly detection time of 5 minutes using filesystem and network based techniques separately and jointly

20 attacking data set periods yielded no filesystem access data. This made it impossible for the filesystem activity based technique to accurately detect attacks during these periods. However, there is substantial network data for those same periods. Note that the FRRs are not significantly affected by the way we chose the evaluation data sets. In conclusion, using one technique alone results in high FARs due to intermittent use of, e.g., network or filesystem. However, using multiple metrics has the potential to overcome this problem.

Combining Filesystem and Network Based Techniques. If both the filesystem and network activity based re-authentication techniques are available, the online re-authentication manager can potentially combine them to improve detection accuracy. This improvement has two sources: (1) when the amount of data from one data source is insufficient for anomaly detection but data are available for the other source, the re-authentication manager can use the re-authentication technique with sufficient data for accurate classification and (2) when both filesystem and network are active, it is possible for the individual techniques to produce contradicting results. In this case, we may still reach the correct decision most of the time by carefully combining the decision variables derived from the two metrics.

We evaluate the combined approach for the 8 users to determine whether a multiple-metric re-authentication technique improves anomaly detection accuracy relative to single-metric techniques. Note that we ruled out the periods within which neither network nor filesystem is active because attacks generally use at least one of these. For each 5-minute period under evaluation, we first determine if only one type of data is available. If so, we use the single metric associated with that type of data, as described above. If both types of data are available, we first normalize the distance of each technique to that technique's threshold value. The aggregate distance is then computed using a weighted average of the normalized distances for the different metrics. An aggregate distance of greater than one during the testing phase (no attacks) results in a false reject and an aggregate distance less than one during the attacking phase implies a false accept. The multiple-metric re-authentication method is otherwise accurate.

Figure 2 shows the FARs and FRRs for the combined approach given 5-minute detection latency. The FAR ranges from 6.25% to 23.1%, while the FRR ranges from 0 to 32%. The average FAR and FRR are 13.7% and 11%, respectively. The results indicate that the multiple-metric (combined filesystem and network) technique reduces the FAR by a significant amount compared to using either the filesystem-based or network-based technique alone.

The data for some users shown in Figure 2 merits further explanation. Attacker #3 did not produce enough network data for identification, resulting in a FAR of 94.1% when the single-metric network-based technique was used. However, since there are sufficient data for the filesystem model to accurately detect the attack during these periods, the multiple-metric approach achieves a FAR of 11.8%. On the other hand, attacker #1 actively uses the network but has some time periods with little filesystem access. As a result, the network model achieves a better FAR (26.7%) than the filesystem model (53.3%). In this case, the multiple-metric approach also outperforms either single-metric technique, achieving an FAR of 13.3%. When both filesystem and network are active, e.g., user #6, the combined approach also improves the FAR to 10%. The FRR of the combined approach is similar to that using either single-metric technique. We conclude that the multiple-metric approach outperforms single-metric re-authentication techniques. Note that additional metrics could potentially be included in the framework without fundamental changes. Although an FRR of 11% implies that a user may need to re-enter the password every 90 minutes, this is far better than the alternative necessary to achieve the same level of security, i.e., forcing the user to manually re-authenticate every 5 minutes.

Sensitivity Analysis. When both filesystem and network are active, instead of computing the average value of normalized distances from both techniques, we can favor one technique by assigning them different weights when averaging their normalized distribution vector distances. We tried a number of different weight combinations. Figure 3 illustrates the relationship between the average FAR and FRR and the weight assigned to network-based technique (the sum of the two weights is fixed at 1). As the network weight increases from 0 to 1, the FAR fluctuates within the range from 12.3% to 18.3%, while the FRR fluctuates within

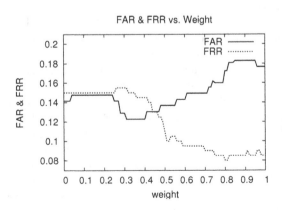

Fig. 3. Sensitivity of FAR and FRR relative to weight combinations

the range from 8% to 15%. The FAR reaches the minimum value of 12.3% with
weights ranging from 0.31 to 0.4, while the FRR reaches the minimum value of
8% with weights ranging from 0.8 to 0.81. We conclude that FAR and FRR are
not highly sensitive to weight combinations for moderate weights; using equal
weights yields good results.

System Comparison. Designing a real-time implicit user re-authentication system is challenging due to the trade-off between accuracy and detection latency.
A number of implicit user re-authentication techniques based on behavioral data
have been proposed. However, all of them have their own advantages and limitations. Table 2 lists the FAR, FRR, detection latency, and limitations of numerous
implicit user re-authentication schemes. Keystroke dynamics based techniques
usually require long training and testing times. In addition, the user is generally required to enter a particular phrase, making the technique inappropriate
for implicit re-authentication in many circumstances. Re-authentication based
on mouse movement is application-dependent because a user may have different
mouse behavior for different applications [6]. Pusara also found that combining
multiple data sources can increase authentication accuracy and decrease detection latency. However, her conclusion can benefit from additional support: it was
based on a short (four hour) training period. In contrast, we believe filesystem
and network events are appropriate data sources for implicit re-authentication. It
is difficult to conduct an attack while generating neither filesystem nor network
activity. The proposed multiple-metric network and filesystem based approach
achieves a reasonable FAR and FRR with a detection latency of 5 minutes.

Table 2. Characteristics of Different Implicit User Re-authentication Schemes

Scheme	Data Source	(FAR, FRR)	Latency	Limitation
[5]	keystroke dynamics	(N/A, 10%)	N/A	1. structured text instead of arbitrary text is favored 2. fail when the attackers do not generate keystroke inputs
[15]	mouse movements	(1.75%, 0.43%)	17.6 minutes in the worst case, 4.5 minutes on average	1. only deal with data from a single application. 2. fail for users who do not use the mouse
[6]	keystrokes, mouse movements, and GUI events	(1.78%,14.47%)	2.2 minutes	1. high FRR 2. small training data set and testing data set
Ours	filesystem and network events	(13.7%, 11%)	5 minutes	relatively high FAR for short (2-week) training period

7   Conclusions

Portable battery-powered computer systems are highly-susceptible to unauthorized access. The proposed implicit re-authentication system provides a way to
protect sensitive information on these computers from attack without inconve-
niencing the user. However, designing a system that can accurately detect attacks
on portable computers by implicit real-time monitoring of user behavior, e.g.,
filesystem and network accesses, is challenging. Portable computers have limited

battery energy, limited performance, and potentially-intermittent wireless network access. In this paper, we have proposed and evaluated a software architecture and user identification algorithms for implicit re-authentication on portable computers. The proposed system is able to distinguish between normal use and attack with an accuracy of approximately 90% with a detection latency of 5 minutes for network activity and 10 minutes for file access.

8 Future Work

Filesystem and network activities are the main data sources used for model construction and anomaly detection in this paper. Therefore, the MIA system is not valid for systems in which users don't have frequent access to the network, or are not based on the filesystem for daily activity, such as cellphones and PDAs. to overcome this limitation, we are considering the use of spatial and temporal information in addition to the filesystem and network activities to improve the accuracy and decrease detection latency.

References

1. HP iPAQ Pocket PC h5500 User Guide. Hewlett-Packard Company, http://bizsupport.austin.hp.com/bc/docs/support/SupportManual/lpia8006/lpia8006.pdf
2. Gupta, P., Ravi, S., Raghunathan, A., Jha, N.K.: Efficient Fingerprint-Based User Authentication for Embedded Systems. In: Proc. Design Automation Conf. (June 2005)
3. Aaraj, N., Ravi, S., Raghunathan, A., Jha, N.K.: Architectures for Efficient Face Authentication in Embedded Systems. In: Proc. Design, Automation & Test in Europe Conf. (March 2006)
4. Richardson, R.: 2007 Computer Crime and Security Survey. Computer Security Institute, Tech. Rep (2007), http://i.cmpnet.com/v2.gocsi.com/pdf/CSISurvey2007.pdf
5. Monrose, F., Rubin, A.: Authentication Via Keystroke Dynamics. In: Proc. Conf. on Computer and Communications Security (April 1997)
6. Pusara, M.: An Examination of User Behavior for Re-authentication. Ph.D. dissertation, Center for Education and Research in Information Assurance and Security, Purdue Univeristy (August 2007)
7. Moon, Y.S., Leung, C.C., Pun, K.H.: Fixed-Point GMM-based Speaker Verification Over Mobile Embedded System. In: Proc. Multimedia Workshop in Biometrics Methods and Applications (November 2003)
8. Gu, H., Zhuang, Y., Pan, Y., Chen, B.: A New Iris Recognition Approach for Embedded System. In: Wu, Z., Chen, C., Guo, M., Bu, J. (eds.) ICESS 2004. LNCS, vol. 3605, pp. 103–109. Springer, Heidelberg (2005)
9. Lane, T., Brodley, C.E.: Temporal Sequence Learning and Data Reduction for Anomaly Detection. ACM Trans. on Information and System Security 2(3), 295–331 (1999)
10. Denning, D.E.: An Intrusion-Detection Model. IEEE Trans. Software Engineering 13(2) (1987)

11. Wolf, T., Mao, S., Kumar, D., Datta, B., Burleson, W., Gogniat, G.: Collaborative Monitors for embedded System security. In: Proc. Wkshp. of Embedded System Security (October 2006)
12. Li, Y., Wu, N., Jajodia, S., Wang, X.S.: Enhancing Profiles for Anomaly Detection Using Time Qranularities. J. of Computer Security 10(2), 137–157 (2002)
13. Wagner, D., Dean, D.: Intrusion Detection Via Static Analysis. In: Proc. Symp. of Security and Privacy, pp. 156–169 (2001)
14. Denning, D.E., Neumann, P.G.: Requirements and Model for Ides–A Real-Time Intrusion Detection System. In: SRI International, Tech. Rep (1985)
15. Pusara, M., Brodley, C.E.: User Re-Authentication Via Mouse Movements. In: Proc. Wkshp. of Visualization and Data Minining for Computer Security (October 2004)
16. Intel PRO/Wireless 3945ABG Card Specification, Hewlett-Packard Company, http://h18019.www1.hp.com/products/quickspecs/12510na/12510na.PDF
17. Russinovich, M., Cogswell, B.: FileMon for Windows 7.04 (2006), http://technet.microsoft.com/en-us/sysinternals/bb896642.aspx
18. WireShark 0.99, http://www.wireshark.org
19. Clementine 11.1. SPSS Corporation, http://www.spss.com/clementine/index.htm
20. Ghosh, A., Schawrtzbard, A.: A Study in Using Neural Networks for Anomaly and Disuse detection. In: Proc. USENIX Security Symp. (1997)
21. Mukkamala, S., Janoski, G., Sung, A.: Intrusion Detection Using Neural Networks and Support Vector machines. In: Int. Joint Conference on Neural Networks (May 2002)
22. Hartigan, J., Wong, M.A.: A K-means Clustering Algorithm. J. of Applied Statistics (1979)
23. Thinkpad power manager, Lenovo Group Ltd., http://www-307.ibm.com/pc/support/site.wss/MIGR-61583.html
24. Cleary, J., Witten, I.: Data Compression Using Adaptive Coding and Partial String Matching. IEEE Trans. on Communications 32 (April 1984)

Lattice Based Privacy Negotiation Rule Generation for Context-Aware Service

Yonnim Lee[1], Debashis Sarangi[2], Ohbyung Kwon[3], and Min-Yong Kim[4]

[1] School of International Management Kyunghee University
Seochun, Ghiheung, Yongin, Kyunggi-do, South Korea
yonnim@khu.ac.kr
[2] Department of Mathematics, Indian Institute Of Technology Kharagpur,
Kharagpur,West Bengal, India
sarangi.iit.kgp@gmail.com
[3,4] School of International Management Kyunghee University
Seochun, Ghiheung, Yongin, Kyunggi-do, South Korea
{obkwon,andy}@khu.ac.kr

Abstract. Online privacy has consistently been a major concern for customers, growing commensurately with the growth of online commerce. Individuals often have serious concerns that their online activities are being monitored, which can prevent them from using online services. With this concern in view, service providers have started making their privacy policies more clear to customers. However, legacy systems often lack flexibility and the inability to adapt to user's interests, which are often the main reasons for inappropriate agreement. Negotiation between the service provider and user can be a possible solution to reach an agreement which seems appealing and profitable to both parties. In this paper we have developed a negotiation mechanism using the concept lattice approach. Using concept lattices in a privacy policy makes it flexible and allows both the parties to sacrifice a few interests for mutual benefits and appropriate agreement.

Keywords: P3P, Privacy negotiation, Privacy ontology, Lattice, Agent technology.

1 Introduction

Acquiring user profiles is crucial to e-commerce service providers because it is difficult to complete a transaction without revealing some personal information, such as shipping address and billing information. As shown by many empirical studies, people are very concerned about online privacy [2, 7, 12, 16, 17]. Especially on the Internet, privacy has consistently been identified as a chief user concern for more than a decade [11, 16]. As more and more user's privacy concern grows, it has become difficult for service providers to obtain correct and useful personal information. Hence developing solutions to these privacy concerns that are both technically and socially secure is important.

Many commercial web sites provide a privacy policy in practice. However, current online privacy policies have some limitations. First, only the service provider can

D. Zhang et al. (Eds.): UIC 2009, LNCS 5585, pp. 340–352, 2009.

offer a privacy policy, and the user must either accept it or reject it as a whole. The providers have typically been the ones who make the initial offer. Users perceive an imbalance of power in favor of the service provider and so privacy concerns are not diminished [4]. Understanding this problem led us to design a methodology that allows both users and service providers to represent their own privacy policy.

Secondly, typical privacy policies are static and do not provide user adaptation. Once the service provider has designed its privacy policy, it will be proposed to all users – no matter what their individual preferences are. Some users would have accepted offers with less privacy protection and would have agreed to the provider's proposal even if more personal data would have been asked.

Lastly, many privacy policies neglect the factors that underlie users' privacy concerns. In the existing literature, many researchers proposed that the "risk-benefit" tradeoff was essential to users' information disclosure decision: Individuals should assess the outcomes they receive as the risk of providing personal information to firms [3]. One recent marketing research effort found that users easily forget their privacy policies and communicate even the most personal details without any compelling reason to do so [1, 8]. This implies that users' willingness to disclose personal information might be changed by evaluating the benefits on the basis of service items.

To address the drawbacks described above, this paper proposes a privacy policy negotiation mechanism on the basis of both the individual user's privacy preferences and the individual service provider's privacy preferences. To do so, we created a privacy policy lattice, an amended form of Galois lattice, for efficiently mining dynamic privacy preference-service item correlations [9]. Using the preference policy lattice, we are able to effectively visualize privacy policies and generate privacy negotiation rules. We then propose an extended interactive P3P which enables both service providers and users to represent their privacy preference on the basis of service item - personal information trade-off. The privacy preferences are represented by using service and personal information ontologies.

The remainder of this paper is organized as follows: Section 2 presents the necessity of privacy negotiation and reviews in existing privacy negotiation mechanisms. Section 3 describes our negotiation mechanism with the extended interactive P3P. Implementation and computational experiments with an illustrative example are discussed in Section 4. Finally, in Section 5, the paper wraps up with some concluding remarks.

2 Privacy Negotiation

Among several approaches for privacy management using privacy policy and privacy preferences, the most mature model is the Platform for Privacy Preferences Project (P3P) developed by the World Wide Web Consortium [15]. P3P is a protocol that allows websites to declare their intended use of information that they collect about browsing users. It is designed to give users more control of their personal information when browsing. P3P manages information through privacy policies. When a website uses P3P they set up a set of policies that allows them to state their intended uses of personal information that may be gathered from their site visitors. When a user decides to use P3P, he sets his own policy and describes which personal information that will be allowed to be seen by the sites he visits. Then when the user visits a site, P3P will compare what personal information the user is willing to release, and what information the server wants to get. If the two do not match, P3P will inform the user and ask if he is willing to proceed to the site, and risk giving up more personal information.

However, P3P has been criticized for many reasons. For example, the Electronic Privacy Information Center (EPIC) has been critical of P3P, saying it makes it too difficult for users to protect their privacy [5]. According to the EPIC, some P3P software is too complex and difficult for the average person to understand, and many Internet users are unfamiliar with how to use the default P3P software on their computers or how to install additional P3P software.

Moreover, P3P has become widely adopted by service providers, but only allowing the service providers to offer their own privacy policy, while the users either can accept it or reject it as a whole. A negotiation process between the involved parties is not supported. Although the first drafts of the P3P specification included a negotiation mechanism, these parts were removed in favor of easy implementation and early and wide adoption of the protocol. The latest P3P 1.1 specification still does not include negotiation.

In recent years, diverse negotiation methodologies have been proposed. There are two broad streams of research. In the first, privacy negotiation is regarded as a utility maximization problem. These researches aim to maximize a user's utility. For example, researchers such as Milne and Godon proposed the economics-based model of user privacy [10]. They computed a user's utility through the trade-off between the cost of lack of services and the cost of surveillance. On the other hand, Preibusch used the user's individual trade-off between personalization and privacy to calculate a user's utility [13]. They took into account different overall sensitivity levels towards privacy and the different levels of importance one may assign to a specific privacy dimension. However, this methodology only considers a user's utility of the entire service provider's privacy policy. It ignores a user's utility of individual personal data. Privacy preferences on individual personal data are what make differences between a service provider's privacy policy and a user's privacy policy. These differences have not been considered.

At the other end of the spectrum, most researches proposed the negotiation process for making an agreement. Tumer et al. defined negotiation as "the set of activities where the user's data privacy preferences are compared with service's data request in order to reach an agreement" [15]. The negotiation process basically determines if another data element can be used in place of a "not given" but "mandatory" data element. This process continues until negotiation is achieved or one or the other party withdraws from the negotiation [14]. The aim is to determine the set of elements that can be exchanged between the parties without violating the user's privacy. However, these approaches have several drawbacks. First, they generally declare privacy preferences on personal data by using limited expressions, and then they generate negotiation rules on that basis. Their negotiation processes are thus not sophisticated enough to reflect the various user and service provider's privacy policies. Second, most negotiation rules are predefined before service providers know the exact user with who they will negotiate. This makes the negotiation process static and not adaptive. Eventually, it causes negotiation to reach inappropriate agreement.

3 Lattice Based Privacy Policy Negotiation

3.1 Privacy Policy Negotiation

Since it is not feasible to negotiate an entire privacy policy, we identified relevant and negotiable privacy policy dimensions. Based on the semantics of P3P, all non-optional parts of a P3P privacy statement are potentially negotiable privacy dimensions:

- Purpose: Describes the purpose for which the data will be used.
- Recipient: Declares the entities with whom the data will be shared.
- Retention: Defines the activity scope during which the data will be retained.
- Data: It declares what kind of data will be collected.

As shown in the empirical studies, these four generic dimensions (purpose, recipient, retention and data) reflect privacy aspects that users are concerned about. Obviously, however, the importance of each of the four dimensions—as perceived by the users—as well as their respective willingness to provide information depends on the service itself. We will focus on negotiating the amount of data to be revealed and mining dynamic privacy preference-service item correlations.

3.2 Representation of Privacy Preference

The matrix of user-item ratings for privacy preference representation contains historical user ratings on each item. Each cell (u, i) of the matrix contains a rating that indicates the evaluation of the user u to the item i, or an empty value if evaluation has not been done. Recent research has begun to examine some of the factors that underlie users' privacy concerns. More specifically, they identify the trade-offs that users are most and least willing to make when they exchange personal information for shopping benefits, such as free delivery or discounts [6]. Their findings imply that, if appropriate benefits are offered in return for information revelation, then the user's privacy preferences could be changed. Hence, our research describes a privacy preference rating matrix that takes into consideration possible trade-offs between both service (shopping benefits) and personal information. We also enable the service provider and the user to represent their privacy preferences on the basis of a service / personal information trade-off. Furthermore, to illustrate our methodology, we declare a user-item ratings matrix and a service provider-item ratings matrix which are, respectively, adopted with personal information and domain-specific service ontologies. We take a specific domain, rather than general domain, because declaring privacy preferences on the basis of service type(s) could be cumbersome or sometimes not even possible. Users may not know in advance which service they can use. Hence, we create a domain-specific service ontology and use it to inform user as to the kinds of services they can have.

In this paper, we chose services that are included in general online shopping sites as a domain and assume that an ontology for buying or additional service(s) is already available as shown in Fig. 1. In the figure, the root class "service" has two subclasses, "Purchasing" and "Additional service." Each has their own subclasses.

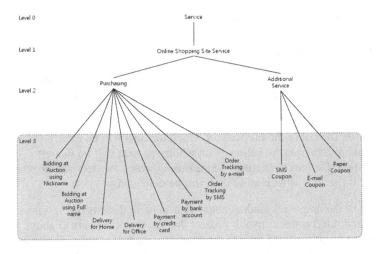

Fig. 1. Online shopping site service ontology

The ontology has a four-layered tree structure from Level 0 to Level 3. Suppose that Level 3 classes are chosen as a unit of analysis. The Level 3 classes are coded as shown in Table 1.

Table 1. Code of Level 3 classes

Buying Service (s1)	Description	Additional Service (s2)	Description
1	Bidding at Auction using Nickname	1	SMS coupon
2	Bidding at Auction using Full name	2	e-mail coupon
3	Delivery for Home	3	Paper coupon
4	Delivery for Office		
5	Payment by credit card		
6	Payment by bank account		
7	Order Tracking by SMS		
8	Order Tracking by e-mail		

Let us assume that there is ontology on demographic information and personally identifiable information, "personal information," as shown in Fig. 2. The root class "personal information" has two subclasses: "demographic information" and "personally identifiable information"; each has their own subclasses.

The ontology forms a three-layered tree structure from Level 0 to Level 2. In this paper, we chose Level 2 classes as a unit of analysis. The Level 2 classes are coded as shown in Table 2.

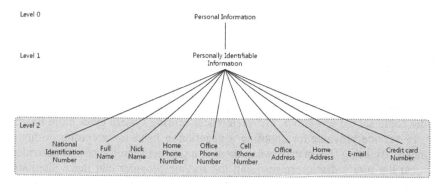

Fig. 2. Ontology for privacy preference on personal information representation

Table 2. Code of Level 2 classes

Personally identifiable information (p1)	Description
A	National Identification Number
B	Full name
C	Nickname
D	Home Phone Number
E	Office Phone Number
F	Cell Phone Number
G	Office address
H	Home address
I	e-mail
J	Credit card Number

3.3 Scoring Privacy Preference

Whether specific data items are critical can be deduced from the nature of the service transaction: It is obvious that an online bookstore cannot deliver a book if the user refuses to provide his shipping address. Our model also supports flexibility: personal data privacy preferences can be changed relative to a specific service item.

For service providers, we declare a service provider-item ratings matrix as a way to represent their privacy preferences on the basis of a domain-specific service ontology. Furthermore, the matrix presented allows service providers to declare all the preferences with a score range of 1-5, where 5 indicates mandatory data, 2 through 4 indicate optional data, and 1 indicates less useful data. How essential the personal information data is for the service to execute is judged by its score.

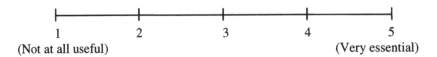

1   2   3   4   5
(Not at all useful)   (Very essential)

As an example, a service called "Delivery for Home" in Fig. 2 may require the user's home address as mandatory and a credit card number as optional. The service provider could set the score to 5. The preferences scoring system gives more flexibility to the service provider for choosing a negotiation behavior according to his requirements. By using this matrix, when there is a gap between the service provider's needs and the user's disclosure restraint, the service provider can make alternative requests according to their privacy preferences which in turn could help increase the probability of a privacy negotiation success.

Next, let us assume that we can gather the service provider's privacy preferences, shown in Table 3.

Table 3. Service provider-item rating matrix on the basis of service-personal information trade-off

	A	B	C	D	E	F	G	H	I	J
(s1, 1)	1	1	5	2	1	3	1	2	4	1
(s1, 2)	1	5	2	2	1	4	1	2	4	1
(s1, 3)	1	4	2	5	1	4	1	5	3	1
(s1, 4)	1	4	2	2	5	4	5	1	3	1
(s1, 5)	1	4	1	1	1	3	1	1	4	5
(s1, 6)	1	5	1	4	1	4	1	1	4	1
(s1, 7)	1	1	4	1	1	5	1	1	3	1
(s1, 8)	1	1	4	1	1	3	1	1	5	1
(s2, 1)	1	2	4	1	1	5	1	1	3	1
(s2, 2)	1	2	4	1	1	3	1	1	5	1
(s2, 3)	1	5	1	2	1	3	2	4	3	1

Meanwhile, as a way to represent their privacy preferences, users can declare their user-item ratings matrix using a personal information ontology and a domain-specific service ontology. The matrix allows service providers to declare all preferences with a score ranging from 1 to 5 (5, not given; 2-4, partially given; 1: given freely). The score indicates to what extent users' personal data is sharable with service providers.

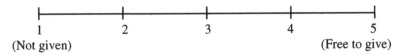

1   2   3   4   5
(Not given)   (Free to give)

As an example, let's assume that a user does not want to give her office address for an SMS coupon. She would set the score to 1. This matrix can then be used to make various negotiation contexts during the privacy negotiation process.

Next, let us assume that we can gather the user's privacy preferences, shown in Table 4.

Table 4. User-item rating matrix on the basis of service-personal information trade-off

	A	B	C	D	E	F	G	H	I	J
(s1, 1)	1	1	5	2	1	1	1	1	3	1
(s1, 2)	1	5	5	2	1	1	1	1	3	1
(s1, 3)	1	4	3	5	1	4	1	5	2	1
(s1, 4)	1	5	1	2	5	4	5	2	2	1
(s1, 5)	1	2	3	2	1	1	1	1	2	5
(s1, 6)	1	5	3	2	1	1	1	1	2	1
(s1, 7)	1	2	4	2	1	5	1	1	1	1
(s1, 8)	1	2	4	2	1	1	1	1	5	1
(s2, 1)	1	3	5	4	1	4	1	3	2	1
(s2, 2)	1	3	5	4	1	2	1	3	5	1
(s2, 3)	1	3	5	4	1	2	1	4	2	1

3.4 Visualization and Generation of Negotiation Rules with Colored Lattice

Importance of θ. To convert the data matrix to into a binary value for the privacy policy graph, privacy preferences are transformed to a digitized profile as shown in (1).

$$\text{Digitized privacy preference: } p'''(i, j) = \begin{cases} 0 & \text{, if } \overline{\overline{p}}(i, j) < \theta \\ 1 & \text{, if } \overline{\overline{p}}(i, j) \geq \theta \end{cases}. \tag{1}$$

The threshold θ implies sensitivity to the importance of the preference. Its meaning is different for the service provider and for the user. For the service provider, a θ value denotes how much an individual user's personal information he is ready to sacrifice in lieu of the services requested. For the user, θ denotes the user's reluctance provide personal information to obtain services. Generally, the service provider's θ is mainly determined by its business processes and the user's reputation. The user's θ is mostly determined by the service provider's reputation and the user's purpose and rewards.

For example, the digitized data with the service provider's $\theta = 3$ and the user's $\theta = 3$ are shown in Tables 5 and 6, respectively. Under the service provider's $\theta = 3$, if the service item is paper coupon (s2, 3), the service provider prefers full name and home address (0, 1, 0, 0, 0, 0, 0 , 1, 0, 0).

Table 5. Digitized data with service provider's $\theta = 3$

	A	B	C	D	E	F	G	H	I	J
(s1, 1)	0	0	1	0	0	0	0	0	1	0
(s1, 2)	0	1	0	0	0	1	0	0	1	0
(s1, 3)	0	1	0	1	0	1	0	1	0	0
(s1, 4)	0	1	0	0	1	1	1	0	0	0
(s1, 5)	0	1	0	0	0	0	0	0	1	1
(s1, 6)	0	1	0	1	0	1	0	0	1	0
(s1, 7)	0	0	1	0	0	1	0	0	0	0
(s1, 8)	0	0	1	0	0	0	0	0	1	0
(s2, 1)	0	0	1	0	0	1	0	0	0	0
(s2, 2)	0	0	1	0	0	0	0	0	1	0
(s2, 3)	0	1	0	0	0	0	0	1	0	0

Table 6. Digitized data with user's $\theta = 3$

	A	B	C	D	E	F	G	H	I	J
(s1, 1)	0	0	1	0	0	0	0	0	0	0
(s1, 2)	0	1	1	0	0	0	0	0	0	0
(s1, 3)	0	1	0	1	0	1	0	1	0	0
(s1, 4)	0	1	0	0	1	1	1	0	0	0
(s1, 5)	0	0	0	0	0	0	0	0	0	0
(s1, 6)	0	1	0	0	0	0	0	0	0	0
(s1, 7)	0	0	1	0	0	1	0	0	0	0
(s1, 8)	0	0	1	0	0	0	0	0	1	1
(s2, 1)	0	0	1	1	0	1	0	0	0	0
(s2, 2)	0	0	1	1	0	0	0	0	1	1
(s2, 3)	0	0	1	1	0	0	0	1	0	0

Privacy policy lattice construction. From the service provider's digitized matrix where $\theta = 0.3$, we see that to provide service (s1,2) the provider will need personal information B, F, and I. We can also look at this from the other way around; i.e., even if the user does not provide personal A, C, D, E, G, H, and J, the provider can still provide service (s1,2). We find it very useful to be able to read the preferences both ways and use this to generate privacy lattices. Turning to the user, a user's digitized matrix where $\theta = 0.3$, we say that the user is not ready to provide information on A, D, E, F, G, H, I, or J to acquire service (s1,2). Using the privacy policy lattice construction algorithm, the digitized data matrix can be transformed into a privacy policy lattice. For example, Fig. 3 and Fig. 4 show privacy policy lattices transformed from matrices in Table 5 and Table 6, respectively. The following properties of a concept lattice must be kept in mind while making the privacy policy lattice.

We take as givens a (formal) service consisting of a set of objects O, a set of attributes A, and an indication of which objects have which attributes.

A concept is defined to be a pair (O_i, A_i) such that

1. $O_i \subseteq O$
2. $A_i \subseteq A$

3. every object in O_i has every attribute in A_i
4. for every object in O that is not in O_i, there is an attribute in A_i that that object does not have
5. for every attribute in A that is not in A_i, there is an object in O_i that does not have that attribute

Rules at lattice nodes. A node in the service provider's lattice indicates an IF-THEN rule. For example, a pair (2(11), acdegj) means:

IF to provide "Bidding at auction using full name" and "Paper Coupon"

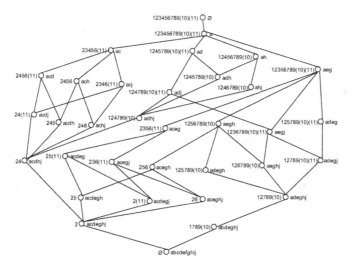

Fig. 3. Privacy policy lattice of Table 5

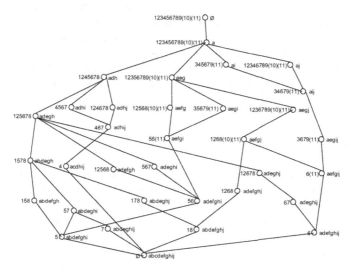

Fig. 4. Privacy policy lattice of Table 6

Table 7. Nomenclature used in the lattices

(s1, 1)	1	(s2, 1)	9
(s1, 2)	2	(s2, 2)	10
(s1, 3)	3	(s2, 3)	11
(s1, 4)	4		
(s1, 5)	5		
(s1, 6)	6		
(s1, 7)	7		
(s1, 8)	8		

THEN the user may not give "National Identification number", "Nick name", "Home phone number", "Office phone number", "Office address", and "credit card number".

Similarly a node in the user's lattice also indicates an IF-THEN rule. Thus, a total of 33 and 34 rules are generated from the lattice shown in Fig. 4 and Fig. 5, respectively.

Rule generation from service provider's privacy preference lattice. Assuming we know the set P of personal information that the user is not ready to provide, we can easily infer, from the service provider's lattice, the services that can be provided to the provider without this information. We see this by reviewing the service provider's lattice and finding the first node from the top of which the given set P of user information is a subset. Corresponding services on that node are the services which can be provided to the user without his providing information contained in set P. By increasing its θ, a user can get more services from the service provider by providing the same information.

Rule generation from user's privacy preference lattice. Assuming we know the set S of services that the user needs, we can find out very easily from the user's lattice the personal information she is not willing to share for those services. This is done by reviewing the user's privacy lattice from the bottom and finding the first node from beneath of which the given set S of services is a subset. Any personal information corresponding to this node is the information the user is not willing to share for the set of services S. By decreasing θ, the service provider will get more user information for providing the same services.

4 Conclusion

We have developed a privacy negotiation mechanism that introduces a methodology for addressing and resolving different privacy preferences between service providers and users, by using a process for negotiating privacy policies. The goal and results of these negotiations is to make an agreement between the parties that satisfies each one's preferences for the optimal amount of personal information required to complete the transaction and hence for increasing the possibility of a service match. To do so, we adopted a concept lattice construction technique that produces negotiation rules from privacy preferences.

The presented framework helps to change the imbalance of control that currently exists and hopefully helps to resolve users valid privacy concerns by providing users with a way to both tailor and quantitatively describe their own personal privacy policies. Furthermore, a user can adjust their privacy policies by using a value according to individual service instances and context. This provides flexibility and creates room for reaching an agreement through negotiation. Finally, we believe that declaring the user preferences based on standard personal information and service ontology helps address the interoperability problem. We have implemented a prototype system that follows the concept lattice construction algorithm to generate negotiation rules and have shown how to decrease the gap between the information that service providers require after privacy policy negotiation.

In the future, we will focus on the practical implementation of privacy negotiation techniques on large scale public websites. We also envision extending this approach to enable reflecting several factors which are crucial for privacy policy negotiation such as reputation, purpose, reward, etc.

Acknowledgments. This research is supported by the Ubiquitous Computing and Network(UCN) Project, Knowledge and Economy Frontier R&D Program of the Ministry of Knowledge Economy(MKE) in Korea as a result of UCN's subproject 09C1-T2-10M.

References

1. Berendt, B., Günther, O., Spiekermann, S.: Privacy in E-Commerce: Stated Preferences vs. Actual Behavior. Communications of the ACM 48, 101–106 (2005)
2. Culnan, M.J.: Consumer Awareness of Name Removal Procedures: Implications for Direct Marketing. Journal of direct marketing 9(2), 10 (1995)
3. Culnan, M.J., Bies, R.J.: Consumer Privacy: Balancing Economic and Justice Considerations. Journal of social issues 59(2), 323–342 (2003)
4. Dommeyer, C.J., Gross, B.L.: What consumers know and what they do: An investigation of consumer knowledge, awareness, and use of privacy protection strategies. Journal of interactive marketing: a quarterly publication from the Direct Marketing Educational Foundation, Inc. 17(2), 34–51 (2003)
5. Electronic Privacy Information Center (EPIC), http://www.epic.org
6. Hann, I.H., Hui, K.L., Lee, S.Y.T.: Consumer Privacy and Marketing Avoidance: A Static Model. Management science 54(6), 1094–1103 (2008)
7. Jones, M.G.: Privacy: A Significant Marketing Issue for the 1990s. Journal of Public Policy and Marketing 10, 133–148 (1991)
8. Kim, D.J., Ferrin, D.L., Rao, H.R.: A trust-based consumer decision making model in electronic commerce: The role of trust, perceived risk, and their antecedents. Decision support systems 44(2), 544–564 (2008)
9. Kwon, O., Kim, J.H.: Lattices for visualizing and generating user profiles for context-aware service recommendations. Expert Systems with Applications 36(2), pt.1, 1893–1902 (2009)
10. Milne, G.R., Godon, M.E.: Direct Mail Privacy-Efficiency Trade-offs Within an Implied Social Contract Framework. Journal of Public Policy & Marketing 12(2), 206–215 (1993)

11. Palmer, D.E.: Pop-Ups, Cookies, and Spam: Toward a Deeper Analysis of the Ethical Significance of Internet Marketing Practices. Journal of business ethics 58(1), 271–280 (2005)
12. Perri, 6.: Who wants privacy protection, and what do they want? Journal of consumer behaviour 2(1), 80–100 (2002)
13. Preibusch, S.: Implementing Privacy Negotiations in E-Commerce. In: Zhou, X., Li, J., Shen, H.T., Kitsuregawa, M., Zhang, Y. (eds.) APWeb 2006. LNCS, vol. 3841, pp. 604–615. Springer, Heidelberg (2006)
14. Shih, D.H., Huang, S.Y., Yen, D.C.: A new reverse auction agent system for m-commerce using mobile agents. Computer standards & interfaces 27(4), 383–395 (2005)
15. Tumer, A., Dogac, A., Toroslu, H.: Semantic based Privacy Framework for Web Services. In: WWW 2003 workshop on E-Services and the Semantic Web, Budapest, Hungary (May 2003)
16. Wang, P., Petrison, L.: Relationship Issues in Creating the Customer Database: The Potential for Interdepartmental Conflict between Marketing and MIS. Journal of direct marketing 7(4), 54 (1993)
17. Xie, E., Teo, H.H., Wan, W.: Volunteering personal information on the internet: Effects of reputation, privacy notices, and rewards on online consumer behavior. Marketing letters 17(1), 61–74 (2006)

Using RFID to Overcome Inventory Control Challenges: A Proof of Concept

Dane Hamilton, Katina Michael, and Samuel Fosso Wamba

School of Information Systems & Technology (SISAT), University of Wollongong,
Wollongong, NSW, 2522 Australia
hamilton.dane@gmail.com, {katina,samuel}@uow.edu.au

Abstract. Using a Proof of Concept approach, this paper examines RFID's impact on inventory control of a small-to-medium retailer. Results indicate that RFID technology can function effectively in a small-to-medium hardware environment. Also, the majority of the simulations recorded reasonable read rates even though the simulations were set up over a short period of time without a great deal of fine-tuning. Moreover, RFID could have a positive impact on the inventory-related processes of the organisation by either streamlining or formalizing them and facilitate the electronic storage of information captured in real-time, relating to the movement of stock and the amount of stock held, providing visibility to members of the organisation. Despite these encouraging findings in relation to using RFID for inventory control purposes within the small-to-medium retailer, it is recommended that other alternatives aimed at improving the inventory control practices of the organisation be investigated before committing to the implementation of RFID.

Keywords: RFID technology, proof of concept, simulation, business process.

1 Introduction

In recent years, (Radio-Frequency Identification) RFID technology has attracted the attention of the industrial community as well as the scientific community. RFID technology is a wireless automatic identification and data capture (AIDC) technology [1] that enables the identification of any tag item in real-time in a given supply chain with a minimum human intervention [2], [3], [4], [5]. A basic RFID system is composed of a tag containing a microprocessor, a reader and its antennas, and a computer equipped with a middleware program, in which business rules are configured to automate some decisions [6]. Despite the high potential of the technology as enabler of supply chain transformation, many questions remain. For example [3 p. 97]: How does radio interference by physical items impact usage of RFID in the business context? What other forms of interference may occur that prevent reading multiple items simultaneously? What is the rate of technical advancement in terms of RFID signal fidelity over longer distances? Will different industry settings require different technical capabilities from RFID systems? What limitations exist for the reading of tags in a mobile environment? How fast can an item be traveling and still achieve an accurate tag reading?

D. Zhang et al. (Eds.): UIC 2009, LNCS 5585, pp. 353–366, 2009.

What is the physical proximity margin of error? How do technical limitations impact the value achieved from this technology?

This paper is a starting point to partially fill this knowledge gap by presenting the results of RFID applications in a real world environment. More precisely, the objective of this paper is to document the results of a Proof of Concept (PoC) that examines RFID's impact on inventory control. The Proof of Concept (PoC) consists of RFID simulations as well as re-engineered business processes that demonstrate whether RFID technology can operate within a small-to-medium retailer and illustrate the anticipated impact of RFID on the business' operations. The simulations focus on issues such as tag read rates and the impact of environmental factors.

Section 2 presents related works. In section 3, the methodology used in this study, including two RFID-enabled scenarios are presented. Finally, section 4 presents the discussion and conclusion.

2   Related Works

The early works on the feasibility of RFID technology have mostly been conducted using a proof of concept approach in the laboratory or real-world setting [7], [8], [9]. Indeed, A Proof of Concept (PoC) is used to illustrate whether a proposed system or application is likely to operate or function as expected [10]. For example, [7] using data from "Wal-Mart RFID-enabled stores" over a period of 29 weeks concluded that RFID-enabled stores were 63% more efficient in replenishing out-of-stocks than stores without RFID, and thus, leading to a reduction of out-of-stocks by 16% over that 29 weeks period. [8], using a proof-of concept in a laboratory setting, demonstrated how process optimization can be achieved when integrating RFID technology into information systems applications. Finally, [9], using a proof-of-concept approach in a laboratory setting showed that RFID technology linked to the EPC network enables the synchronization of information flow with product flow in a given supply chain, and thus, provides a better level of information integration between supply chain members.

3   Methodology

The research study documented in this paper involves a case study examining a single small-to-medium retailer. A case study method has been employed as it is ideal for investigating contemporary events and is able to take into account a wide variety of evidence [11]. For this study data has been gathered through the collection of procedural documents, semi-structured interviews and a participant observation. This paper presents the data collected from the semi-structured interviews conducted with employees of the organization, as well as revealing the business process flows (through flowcharts) of the organization in order to determine whether RFID is a feasible automated data capture technology for small-to-medium retailers. An observational study was also conducted over a period of two weeks in 2007. A daily diary was kept by the participant and this data was analyzed together with full-length transcripts. A single small-to-medium hardware retailer is focused on in this paper in order to analyze and present inventory control practices.

3.1 Case Study

3.1.1 Background
The organization examined in this study is located on the south coast of New South Wales, approximately 128 kilometers from the centre of Sydney. The company employs ten staff including casuals and is classified as a small-to-medium hardware retailer. The current proprietors have operated the business since 2003.

3.1.2 Physical Layout
The premises of the retailer measures approximately 2000 square meters, with about 550 square meters of this area making up the internal shop floor. The shop floor is composed of four sheds, each with independent access. There are two small internal offices, one designed to deal with customer purchasing and Point of Sale (POS) transactions while the other is used by managers and bookkeepers for ordering, accounting and other administrative practices. The external perimeter of the organization is surrounded by an eight foot high barbed wire fence.

3.1.3 Stock and Inventory
The retailer currently possesses between $300,000 to $400,000 worth of inventory which is kept on the premises. The inventory held by the organization is estimated to consist of 5000 products lines, which are provided by 110 active suppliers. Products and other inventory are stored or displayed before purchase inside the store or outside within the confines of the premises. Items and stock within the store are positioned based on the type of product as well as the supplier. Most items kept inside the store are also shelved on racks that measure 2.1m in height. The shop floor is divided into five separate areas that include general hardware, timber, gardening, cement and building supplies. Products stored outside are generally unaffected by environmental and weather conditions such as landscaping supplies, cement blocks, treated pine sleepers and sheets of steel reinforcing. Stock is usually delivered to the store packaged at pallet, crate, carton or item level.

3.1.4 Services
The retailer provides many services to its customers primarily through the selling of hardware and other building related supplies. The organization provides a delivery service to its customers if they purchase products that are too large to be transported or products that they wish to be delivered on a certain day. Products are delivered to customers in one of the three vehicles the organization owns. A flat top truck is used for steel deliveries, a tip truck is used for landscaping supplies and a utility vehicle is used for general deliveries. The organization also has a front-end loader that it uses to load landscaping supplies on vehicles. The organization offers accounts for customers that purchase products frequently.

3.1.5 Information Technology (IT) Infrastructure

The retailer currently has limited Information Technology (IT) infrastructure and does not utilize a server, as the current operations of the business do not require a large volume storage device. The organization utilizes two desktop computers in their administration office that are primarily used to manage customer accounts through the software package MYOB Premier Version 10. At the end of each month, the organization uses the MYOB software to generate invoices which are sent out to account holding customers, requesting that they pay for the items they have purchased. The organization has another desktop computer which is used by employees to search a program that acts as an index of paint colors provided by different paint suppliers. All computers within the organization are able to access the Internet.

3.2 Interviews

3.2.1 Interviewees

Insights into the current inventory control practices at the small-to-medium retailer are based on semi-structured interviews carried out on four employees of the organization. The roles and duties of these employees are documented in Table 1.

Table 1. Employee roles and duties

ID	Job Title	Duties
1	Proprietor/Manager	Stock replenishment, capital purchasing, staff management, delivery scheduling, customer service
2	Proprietor/Part-Time Manager	Stock replenishment, staff management, delivery scheduling, delivery truck driver, customer service
3	Store Manager	Stock control and replenishment (for some of the stock), customer service, staff management, shop maintenance
4	Delivery Truck Driver	Stock delivery, stock control and replenishment (for some of the stock), customer service

As can be seen from Table 1, employees of the organization have minimal job specialization, which reinforces [12] observations of small businesses. The proprietor/manager and proprietor/part-time manager are responsible for the overall running of the business whereas the store manager is specifically responsible for shop maintenance and management. The delivery truck driver is primarily responsible for making outbound deliveries. The store manager and delivery truck driver are answerable to both of the proprietor/managers.

3.2.2 Interview Questions and the Inventory Cycle

Inventory control as defined by [13] involves "coordinating the purchasing, manufacturing and distribution functions to meet marketing needs". Coordinating these functions requires many discrete activities including ordering stock or materials and shelving or putting it in the correct position so that customer's have access to it. In this section, the inventory control process has been broken down so that the inventory practices of the small-to-medium retailer can be explored in greater detail. Fig. 1 illustrates the Inventory Cycle. It should be noted that [14 p. 21] Inventory Flow Cycle is focused on the flow of raw materials to their finished state, while this inventory control cycle has been developed based on a retailer that sells finished goods.

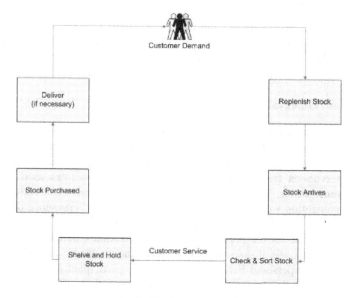

Fig. 1. The inventory cycle

As can be seen in Fig. 1, customer demand triggers the ordering or re-ordering of stock. Stock then arrives at the retailer, where it is checked and sorted before being shelved in the correct position. Stock is then purchased by a customer and delivered by the retailer if necessary.

The inventory cycle demonstrated in Fig. 1 was considered when developing questions for the semi-structured interviews. The majority of the questions asked related to the six different processes that were identified in the inventory control cycle. There were a total of twenty-eight questions included in the original semi-structured interview protocol but additional probing sub-questions were asked where the respondent was able to expand their response due to their knowledge of operations. The questions covered the background of the company case, the role of the employee in the organization, questions related to the current mode of operation to gauge the current inventory control practices and set-up, and more speculative questions regarding the transition of the organization from a manual-based system to barcode and/or RFID. For instance the proprietor was asked:

1. Can you describe the process that you use to check that orders have been delivered with the correct contents?
2. Do you keep any sort of record of how much stock you carry, either in physical or electronic form?

3. How would you describe the theft prevention measures in your workplace?
4. What triggers your organization to reorder or order stock?
5. Are there any issues affecting your adoption of automated data capture technology?
6. Do you think that RFID could be used within your business to improve inventory control?

The interview transcripts were analyzed using a qualitative approach and the findings were presented using a modular narrative style based on the steps in the inventory control cycle. The following sections summarize the findings of the semi-structured interviews.

3.3 Participant Observation

A participant observation requires the researcher to become a direct participant in the social process being studied, by becoming a member of an organization. The participant observation was carried out over a two week period with the intention of recording observations relating to the inventory control practices used within the small-to-medium retailer. This study utilizes an overt participant observation as members of the organization were already aware of the researcher's presence due to interviews being carried out at an earlier date. The overt approach was perceived to have had minimal influence on the behavior of the organization's members as they were informed that the purpose of the study was to examine inventory control practices of the retailer, not their personal behaviors. During the participant observation annotations and issues were documented through the use of a diary. Field notes were recorded during each day, and were formalized at the end of the day.

3.4 Procedural Documentation

The small-to-medium retailer's procedural documents were used to complement the semi-structured interviews and participant observation. Documentary secondary data, such as an organization's communications, notes, and other policy and procedural documents have been examined. Moreover, [15 p. 104] states that official documents, like procedural documents can be treated as unproblematic statements of how things are or were. The procedural documents have been used as evidence to support the determination of the inventory control practices of the small-to-medium retailer. The interviews conducted, participant observation and the collection of procedural documents were combined to develop the business process flows of the organization. A narrative presentation is used to bring together participant observational data and interviewee responses.

3.5 Simulation of RFID Enabled Scenarios

Eight simulations have been developed which are aimed at examining different aspects of inventory control and known RFID issues that have been documented in the literature. Fig. 2 illustrates which RFID simulations are related to stages in the inventory cycle (documented previously in Fig. 1). Each simulation is **colour-coded** (in Fig. 2 and following sections) to correspond to the relevant stage in the inventory cycle. However, within the scope of this paper, we will only present and discuss two scenarios namely the RFID-enabled-Point of Sale and the RFID-enabled- checking deliveries and invoices.

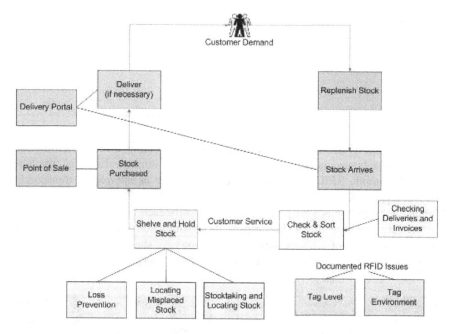

Fig. 2. The focus of the overall simulations

The results of the simulations are documented qualitatively, discussing read rates as well as any other technical issues experienced in the following section.

3.5.1 Scenario 1: RFID Enabled-Point of Sale (POS) Simulation

AIM: To simulate a Point of Sale (POS) system that utilises RFID technology to accurately identify items.

SIGNIFICANCE: This simulation should reveal how RFID can identify items compared to using a manual process. It should also reveal how visibility can be improved through recording information at POS, as purchasing history would be able to be maintained by the retailer.

APPARATUS: Symbol MC9090-G mobile computer, stock (products) and passive RFID tags.

METHOD: Ten items and products from the retailer will be RFID tagged and scanned using the mobile RFID reader prior to purchase. Multiple tagged items will be brought to the counter where they will be scanned and the tag read rates of the simulation will be recorded.

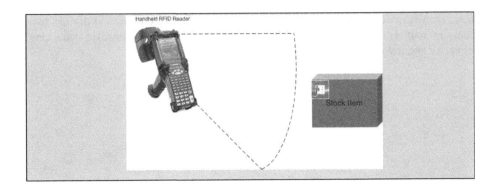

The Point of Sale (POS) simulation carried out in the retailer involved ten products and items being tagged in different arrangements. The initial test in this simulation involved the mobile RFID reader being utilised to scan or interrogate transponders located on tagged products.

Ten attempts were made with the reader to identify each tagged product individually from different orientations. This aspect of the simulation was designed to demonstrate the purchasing of a single item by a customer. Table 2 summarises the read rates experienced by the mobile reader (•= read successfully).

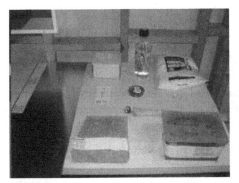

Exhibit 1. The ten tagged products (left); scanning an RFID tagged carton of nails (right)

The results revealed that the mobile reader was able to read data from all tagged items. For tagged products composed of metal, namely the flat sheet of metal and the mudguard washer, the mobile RFID reader was only able to read data from them on 40% of attempts. Larger flat items such as the cement, container of nails and the concrete paver were read on 100% of attempts, at any orientation as the tag was attached in a flat configuration. The majority of tagged items that were identified in 80% of attempts had RFID tags wrapped around these objects so that the tag was overlapping itself.

Table 2. POS single item simulation results

Item	Mobile Reader		
	Read on some (40%) attempts	Read on majority (80%) of attempts	Read on all (100%) attempts
Flat sheet of Metal 300mmx 900mmx0.5mm	•		
3/8 inch Mudguard Washer	•		
Electrical Tape		•	
Sleeve bolt Anchors 12mmx99mm (in cardboard box)		•	
76mm Zinc Eyebolt (in plastic/cardboard packaging)		•	
Wooden Hammer Handle		•	
1 Litre Methylated Spirits Litre (in plastic bottle)		•	
Concrete Paver			•
5kg Galvanised Flathead Nails 65mmx2.8mm (in plastic container)			•
4kg White Cement (in plastic bag)			•

The second part of this simulation involved attempting to read data from multiple tagged items simultaneously. Ten attempts were made with the mobile RFID reader to identify tagged products, with only four out of the ten products being successfully interrogated. The tagged items that were unable to be identified were orientated perpendicular to the reader in the majority of cases.

Exhibit 2. Delivery pallet with tagged cartons

3.5.2 Scenario 2: RFID Enabled- Checking Deliveries and Invoices Simulation

AIM: To use an RFID reader to accurately identify multiple products in a delivery which have been labelled with RFID tags.

SIGNIFICANCE: This simulation will demonstrate how RFID can improve the invoice checking process (for deliveries). The use of RFID should result in greater accuracy and improvements made in relation to time taken to carry out these processes.

APPARATUS: Symbol MC9090-G mobile computer, Symbol XR440 fixed RFID reader, Symbol AN400 High Performance Area Antenna, stock (products), a pallet and passive RFID tags.

METHOD: A mock delivery or order will be simulated by packing a variety of RFID tagged items onto a pallet as if they had just been delivered. The mock delivery will be scanned from each side of the pallet three times using an RFID reader with results being recorded and tag orientation examined to determine the effect it has on the accuracy of the reader.

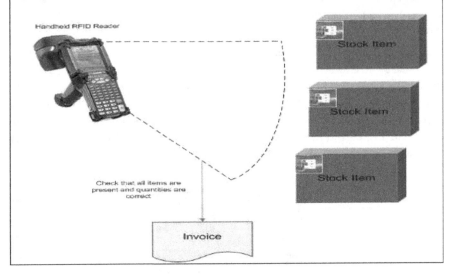

The checking deliveries and invoices simulation involved RFID tagging 24 cardboard cartons containing stock such as sponges, tape measures and crow bars from a general hardware supplier. The tagged cartons were placed on a pallet made of steel, measuring 80 centimeters in width by 1 meter in length with a metal barrier surrounding it that measured 90 centimeters in height.

In this simulation the mobile RFID reader was used to read data from tagged items, whilst standing one meter from the pallet. Fig. 3 illustrates how many tags were successfully read by the mobile reader from each side of the pallet.

The results of this part of the simulation revealed that the mobile reader was reasonably accurate at reading data from tagged cartons in the mock delivery. Majority of the tags that were not able to be identified were located the furthest distance from where scanning was conducted or the tags were orientated perpendicular to the reader.

For example, when the mobile reader was used to scan the pallet from the northern side seven tagged items were not able to be scanned; four of these tagged items were located on the southern side (far side) of the pallet. Of the other three tagged cartons that were unable to be read two of them were on the western side of the pallet, with tags orientated perpendicular to the reader and one was located in the centre of the pallet, with its tag located on the southern side (far side) of the carton.

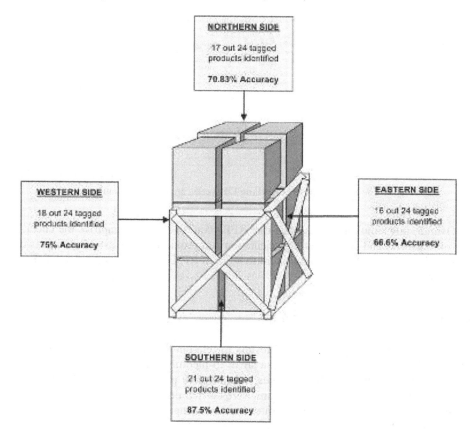

Fig. 3. Tags successfully read by the mobile reader

The latter part of this simulation involved employing a fixed RFID reader and a single antenna to scan the pallet of RFID tagged cartons to determine which reader was most accurate (Fig. 4). The antenna was fixed 1 meter above the ground and positioned 1 meter away from the pallet which resulted in less accurate read rates than those experienced with the mobile reader. Based on the scans conducted from the four sides of the pallet it was recorded that on average 58.32 % of tags were successfully interrogated by the fixed reader. As was the case in the initial part of this simulation it was observed that the majority of tagged cartons that were not identified by the reader were located the furthest distance from where scanning was conducted or tags were orientated perpendicular to the reader.

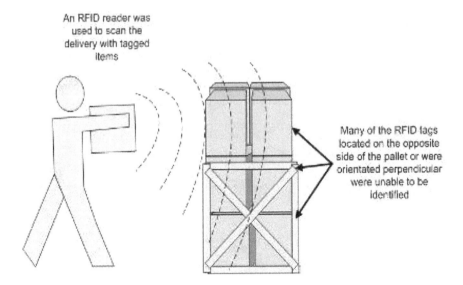

Fig. 4. The Findings of the Checking Deliveries and Invoice Simulation

Overall, this simulation illustrated that RFID could be used to improve the checking of deliveries and orders, but tag orientation and proximity were established as two factors that affected the successful identification of RFID tagged cartons in a delivery or order.

4 Discussion and Conclusion

The simulations produced promising results in relation to the successful functioning and operation of RFID technology in a small-to-medium hardware retailer. Some of the simulations yielded high read rates, while others produced only mediocre read rates. It should be noted that simulations were carried out over a brief period of time, using basic RFID equipment. Read rates could be improved if more antennas were employed (and attached to fixed RFID readers) and more attention was paid to orientation. It is perceived that RFID could improve the inventory control process of the small-to-medium retailer, but read rates would have to be improved for the technology to compete with the claimed 99.9% accuracy of barcodes in order to justify its implementation [16 p. 4]. The accuracy of RFID equipment is likely to be improved in the future as the technology is continually being refined.

The adaptability and robustness of RFID tags was demonstrated in the simulations as items with RFID tags attached to them were able to be identified successfully, even after being exposed to the elements for an extended period of time.

Even though the simulations did illustrate that RFID could be used successfully within the organisation a number of technical issues were raised when carrying out the simulations. It is perceived that if these technical issues are resolved the business case for implementing RFID within the retailer would be strengthened. The technical issues encountered are described in the list below:

- Items composed of metal that were RFID tagged could not be read as easily as items that were made of other materials. In the environment simulation it was noted that RFID tags attached to items composed of metal were only able to be identified in one of the six attempts made to read data from them.

- Tags that were wrapped around items so they overlapped could not be identified by RFID readers in the majority of cases. It was found when tags were applied in a flat configuration to items of stock they were able to be identified without difficulty.

- RFID tags that were orientated perpendicular to readers and not within a particular proximity (1m radius for the mobile reader and about 3m radius for antennas attached to the fixed reader) were not able to be identified. It should be noted however that the signal range of the readers can be varied.

- The inaccuracy and poor to average read rates experienced in the loss prevention simulation illustrated that RFID should not be implemented for a loss prevention application until read rates are improved. In this simulation the main difficulties were encountered when trying to identify concealed objects.

- Although RFID tags were able to be successfully read after being applied to pallets and other items that were exposed to environmental and weather conditions, there was difficulty experienced applying RFID labels to some of these objects, especially dampened wooden pallets which required tags being nailed to them.

The next logical step of this study is to conduct a pilot study to assess the business value of these scenarios. Furthermore, it'll be important to identify a set of key performance indicators to measure improvements from RFID. Also, it'll be interesting to use the latest generation of RFID tags in our RFID-enabled scenarios. Indeed, in some recent studies the tag reading accuracy has reached 100% [17].

References

1. Fosso Wamba, S., Lefebvre, L.A., Bendavid, Y., Lefebvre, É.: Exploring the Impact of RFID and the EPC Network on Mobile B2B ECommerce: A Case Study in the Retail Industry. International Journal of Production Economics, Special Issue on RFID: Technology, Applications, and Impact on Business Operations 112(2), 614–629 (2008)
2. Poirier, C., McCollum, D.: RFID Strategic Implementation and ROI: A Practical Roadmap to Success. J. ROSS Publishing, Florida (2006)
3. Curtin, J., Kauffman, R.J., Riggins, F.J.: Making the most out of RFID technology: A Research Agenda for the Study of the Adoption, Usage and Impact of RFID. Information Technology and Management 8(2), 87–110 (2007)
4. Huber, N., Michael, K.: Minimizing Product Shrinkage across the Supply Chain using Radio Frequency Identification: A Case Study on a Major Australian Retailer. In: The Sixth International Conference on Mobile Business, Toronto, Canada (2007)
5. Renegar, B.D., Michael, K.: The RFID Value Proposition. In: CollECTeR Iberoamérica, Madrid, Spain, June 25-27 (2008)
6. Asif, Z., Mandviwalla, M.: Integrating the Supply Chain with RFID: A Technical and Business Analysis. Communications of the Association for Information Systems 15, 393–427 (2005)

7. Hardgrave, B.C., Waller, M., Miller, R.: Does RFID Reduce out of Stocks? A Preliminary Analysis (2005), `http://itri.uark.edu/research/default.asp`
8. Bendavid, Y., Fosso Wamba, S., Lefebvre, L.: Proof of Concept of an RFID-enabled Supply Chain in a B2B E-commerce Environment. In: The Eighth International Conference on Electronic Commerce (ICEC), Fredericton, New Brunswick, Canada, August, pp. 14–16 (2006)
9. Fosso Wamba, S., Boeck, H.: Enhancing Information Flow in a Retail Supply Chain Using RFID and the EPC Network: A Proof-of-Concept Approach. Journal of Theoretical and Applied Electronic Commerce Research, Special Issue on RFID and Supply Chain Management 3(1), 92–105 (2008)
10. Webmaster Expert Solutions: Appendix A: Glossary (1996), `http://docs.rinet.ru/WebLomaster/appa.htm`
11. Yin, R.: Case Study Research: Design and Methods, 2nd edn. Sage Publications, London (1994)
12. Diamond, J., Pintel, G.: Retailing, 6th edn. Prentice Hall, Upper Saddle River (1996)
13. Wild, T.: Best Practice in Inventory Management. John Wiley & Sons, New York (1997)
14. Tersine, R.: Principles of Inventory and Material Management, 4th edn. Prentice Hall, Upper Saddle River (1998)
15. Knight, P.: Small-Scale Research. Sage, London (2002)
16. McCathie, L., Michael, K.: Is it the end of barcodes in supply chain management? In: Proceedings of the Collaborative Electronic Commerce Technology and Research Conference LatAm, Talca, Chile (2005)
17. Material Handling Management News: UHF Gen 2 RFID Delivers 100% Read Accuracy for Item Tagging (2009), `http://www.mhmonline.com/viewStory.asp?nID=5202&pNum=1`

Anticipative Wrap-Around Inquiry Method towards Efficient RFID Tag Identification

Ching-Hsien Hsu[1], Wei-Jau Chen[1] and Yeh-Ching Chung[2]

[1] Department of Computer Science and Information Engineering
Chung Hua University, Hsinchu, Taiwan 300, R.O.C.
chh@chu.edu.tw, weijauchen@gmail.com
[2] Department of Computer Science
National Tsing Hua University, Taiwan 300, R.O.C.
ychung@cs.nthu.edu.tw

Abstract. One of the challenges in designing modern RFID systems is that when more than one tag exists in an RFID environment, it may occurs collisions so that the whole system becomes inefficient and increases the time for identifying RFID Tags. To simultaneously recognize multiple tags within a reader interrogation zone, an anti-collision algorithm should be applied. In this paper, we present an Anticipative Wrap-Around Inquiry (AWAI) method, which is an enhanced technique based on the query tree protocol. The main idea of the Anticipative Inquiry is to limit number of collisions at different level of a query tree. When number of collisions reaches a predefined ratio, it reveals that density in RF field is too high. To avoid sending unnecessary inquiries, the prefix matching will be moved to next level, alleviating the collision problems. Since the prefix matching is performed in level-ordered scheme, it may cause an imbalanced query tree on which the right sub-tree was not examined due to threshold jumping. By scanning the query tree from right sub-tree to left sub-tree in alternative levels, i.e., wrap-around, this flaw could be significantly ameliorated. The experimental results show that the method of setting frequency bound and wrap-around scan indeed improve the identification efficiency in high density and randomly deployed RFID systems.

1 Introduction

In RFID system, simultaneous communications of multiple tags to reader may cause transmission collisions. Since passive tag is comprised of simple circuit that with very limit function, it could not be aware that the existence of neighboring tags and not able to detect tag collisions. Therefore, tag anti-collision protocols for passive RFID systems are of great importance to speedup tag identification.

Tag anti-collision protocols can be classified into *aloha-based protocol* [2, 8] and *tree-based protocol* [6]. *Aloha-based* anti-collision method create a frame with a certain number of time slots, and then add the frame length into the inquiry message sending to tags in its vicinity. Tags response the interrogation based on a random time slot. Because collisions may happen at the time slot when two or more tag response simultaneously, making those tags could not be recognized. Therefore, the readers have to send inquiries repeatedly contiguously until all tags are identified. Aloha-based

D. Zhang et al. (Eds.): UIC 2009, LNCS 5585, pp. 367–376, 2009.
© Springer-Verlag Berlin Heidelberg 2009

scheme might have long processing latency in *identifying large-scale RFID systems* [3]. In [8], Vogt *et al.* investigated how to recognize multiple RFID tags within the reader's interrogation ranges without knowing the number of tags in advance by using framed Aloha. A similar research is also presented in [9] by Zhen *et al.* In [2], Klair *et al.* also presented a detailed analytical methodology and an in-depth qualitative energy consumption analysis of pure and slotted Aloha anti-collision protocols. Another anti-collision algorithm called *enhanced dynamic framed slotted aloha (EDFSA)* is proposed in [4]. *EDFSA* estimates the number of unread tags first and adjusts the number of responding tags or the frame size to give the optimal system efficiency.

Tree-based protocols could achieve better read rate by using a binary search approach. RFID readers repeatedly split the set of tags into two subsets and labeled them by binary numbers until each subset has only one tag, thus the reader is able to identify all tags. The *ABS* [6] is an example in this category. The adaptive memoryless tag anti-collision protocol proposed by Myung *et al.* [5] is an extended technique based on the query tree protocol. Choi *et al.* also proposed the *IBBT (Improved Bit-by-bit Binary-Tree)* algorithm [1] in ubiquitous ID system and evaluate the performance along three other old schemes. The *IQT* protocol [7] is a similar approach by exploiting specific prefix patterns in the tags to make the entire identification process. Recently, Zhou *et al.* [11] consider the problem of slotted scheduled access of RFID tags in a multiple reader environment. They developed centralized algorithms in a slotted time model to read all the tags. With the fact of NP-hard, they also designed approximation algorithms for the single channel and heuristic algorithms for the multiple channel cases.

Although tree based schemes have advantage of implementation simplicity and better response time compare with the Aloha based ones, they still have challenges in decreasing the identification latency. In this paper, we present the *Anticipative Wrap-Around Inquiry (AWAI)* method, aims to alleviate collision problem that caused by simultaneous communications of multiple tags and to reduce tag identification delay. The main idea of the *AWAI* is dynamically adjust length of reader's inquiry message by setting a threshold of collision. When number of collisions reaches a predefined acceptable threshold, it reveals that density in RF field is too high. As a result, the identification process will be jumped to next level. In order to avoid imbalanced scan, the inquiry will proceed from left sub-tree to right sub-tree and from right sub-tree to left sub-tree alternatively in different levels. To verify the performance of the proposed technique, we have implemented the *AWAI* along with other tree-based protocol. The experiments were conducted with different network density of RFID systems. Both theoretical analysis and experimental results show that the *AWAI* technique can alleviate tag collisions under different circumstances and achieve better tag identification efficiency.

2 Tag Anti-collision with Binary Splitting

2.1 Preliminary

Binary splitting is commonly applied in solving tag collision problems; nevertheless, when tag density is higher, search duplication may occur, and that wastes the time and frequency of identification. Figure 1 shows an example of identifying RFID tags by scanning a binary tree. In such approach, RFID reader begins by sending one-bit prefix code, 1 or 0, at level 1, to all tags in its vicinity. Tags having the same prefix code will reflect the interrogation by sending its ID to this RF signal. This leads to three possibilities: no tag response, one tag response and multiple tags response, represented as *idle node, identified node* and *collision node*, respectively in a query tree. The *identified node* means that only one tag replies the reader's inquiry and thus its ID code could be identified by the reader successfully. The *collision node* represents that more than one tag match the same prefix code and replies their ID to the reader, resulting tag collision. The *idle node* shows that no tag matches the same prefix code, thus the reader could not receive any response.

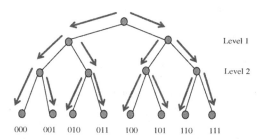

Fig. 1. Taog identification using binary splitting

Example: An RFID network consists of six tags, with ID = {A= 0000, B= 0001, C= 0011, D=1000, E= 1010, F=1011}

Figure 2 illustrates the identification of the *Query Tree* protocol (*QT*) using binary splitting. The reader starts by sending 1-bit inquiry with prefix code 0; tags A, B and C all response its ID to the reader simultaneously, which causes a collision. For prefix code 1, collision happened on tags D, E and F. To progress the identification, reader extends the prefix code by one bit, sending 00, which causes tags A, B and C collided again. On the other hand, the inquiry with prefix code 01 receives no tag's response; thus node "01" will be marked as an idle node. In the following, tags D, E and F collided with prefix code 10 while prefix code 11 results another idle node. At level 3, tags A and B response for prefix code 000, which also causes a collision. For prefix code 001, tag C will be identified. In total, the *Query Tree* (*QT*) scheme uses 14 steps to identify all of the tags.

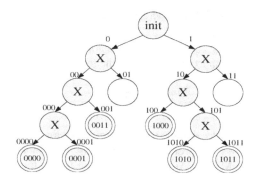

Fig. 2. Tag identification using QT scheme

In high density RFID systems, the collision might happen at most levels of a query tree. If the collision happens frequently, it's a waste of identification time. In other words, the exhaust tree search scheme is not an ideal method in minimizing number of collision nodes. To alleviate the collision problem, a reader may skip some unnecessary inquiry if it is aware that system density is high. Due to this, the frequency of collision at each level could be set with a threshold. If the frequency over threshold, the reader predicts that system density is above average; then it skips the identification at the current level to avoid unnecessary communication. Therefore, adjusting the bit-length of reader's inquiry according to actual system situation could be an optimization to reduce overall communication overheads.

2.2 Anticipative Wrap-Around Inquiry

The *Anticipative Wrap-Around Inquiry (AWAI)* is also a binary-splitting approach. Instead of scanning the entire query tree in level order, a threshold of collision frequency is set as the criterion for moving the identification to next level of a query tree. By means of the threshold to judge tag density, once the collision frequency over threshold, it reflects the network is with high density. Accordingly, the inquiry at current level will be omitted and proceed to next level. As shown in Figure 3, when number of collision exceeds the predefined threshold, the interrogation will be moved to next level (so-called threshold jumping). Through this anticipation, the frequency of broadcasting inquiries could be significantly reduced.

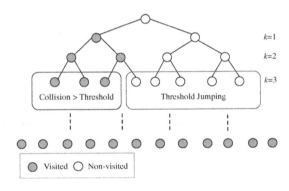

Fig. 3. The paradigm of threshold jumping

The *threshold* represents an acceptable collision frequency at different level of a query tree. It is defined as an expected ratio of the total number of tree nodes at level k.

$$Threshold = \frac{2^k}{M} \qquad (1)$$

where M is positive integer.

Let's use an example to demonstrate the methodology of anticipative inquiry scheme. Figure 4 shows the process of identifying 13 4-bits RFID tags using the threshold jumping with M = 3. At level 1, according to (1), the threshold equals to 1 (i.e., 21/3). That means the identification will be jumped to level 2 once collision is happened. At level 2, the identification will be jumped to level 3 if more than 2 (i.e., 22/3) collisions occurred; similarly, at level 3, the inquiry will be moved to level 4 if more than 3 (i.e., 23/3) collisions are raised; and so on.

The threshold jumping takes 22 inquiries to identify all of the tags. One thing worthy to mention is that although 22 inquiries is more than the amount of leave nodes at level 4 (i.e., 16), however, to directly scan leave nodes is not a feasible approach. For example, if RFID tags are with 16 bits id code, the process of scanning leave nodes will take a significant amount of inquiries (i.e., 65536). This is why the query tree based approach usually considered as feasible solution for tag anti-collision problem.

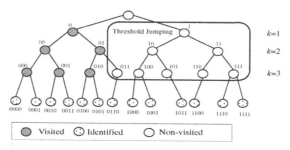

Fig. 4. Example of threshold jumping

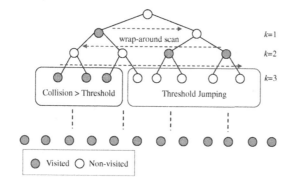

Fig. 5. The paradigm of wrap-around scan

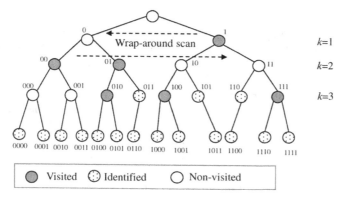

Fig. 6. Example of wrap-around scan

Table 1. Tag Identification of three different schemes

Step	Query Tree		Threshold Jumping		Anticipative Wrap-Around Inquiry	
	Prefix	Status	Prefix	Status	Prefix	Status
1	0	Collision	0	Collision	0	Collision
2	1	Collision	00	Collision	00	Collision
3	00	Collision	01	Collision	01	Collision
4	01	Collision	000	Collision	111	Collision
5	10	Collision	001	Collision	110	Identified-1100
6	11	Collision	010	Collision	101	Collision
7	000	Collision	0000	Identified-0000	100	Collision
8	001	Collision	0001	Identified-0001	011	Identified-0110
9	010	Collision	0010	Identified-0010	010	Collision
10	011	Identified-0110	0011	Identified-0011	0000	Identified-0000
11	100	Collision	0100	Identified-0100	0001	Identified-0001
12	101	Identified-1011	0101	Identified-0101	0010	Identified-0010
13	110	Identified-1100	0110	Identified-0110	0011	Identified-0011
14	111	Collision	0111	No Response	0100	Identified-0100
15	0000	Identified-0000	1000	Identified-1000	0101	Identified-0101
16	0001	Identified-0001	1001	Identified-1001	1000	Identified-1000
17	0010	Identified-0010	1010	No Response	1001	Identified-1001
18	0011	Identified-0011	1011	Identified-1011	1110	Identified-1110
19	0100	Identified-0100	1100	Identified-1100	1111	Identified-1111
20	0101	Identified-0101	1101	No Response		
21	1000	Identified-1000	1110	Identified-1110		
22	1001	Identified-1001	1111	Identified-1111		
23	1110	Identified-1110				
24	1111	Identified-1111				

The method of restricting collision frequency can effectively improve identification latency when tag density is high. However, the left-to-right level order interrogation might lead an imbalanced query tree. This because that if threshold is always fulfilled in left sub-tree, the right sub-tree will be omitted. In such way, it may waste identification time to scan right sub-tree in lower level if network density is low. This flaw can be solved through sending the inquiries with opposite direction at different level alternatively, and so-called wrap-around scan. Figure 5 demonstrates the concept of wrap-around inquiry. The level ordered scan is performed from left sub-tree to right sub-tree in all "odd" levels and from right sub-tree to left sub-tree in all "even" levels or vice versa.

Taking the same example that illustrated in Figure 4. Figure 6 shows the query tree of the *AWAI* method. It's obvious that the identification is enhanced by means of the wrap-around scan because there are three tags identified at level 3. In a total, the *AWAI* takes 19 inquiries to identify all of the tags. Table 1 shows the complete identification process of the *Query Tree, Threshold Jumping* and the *AWAI* methods. Although the *AWAI* performs only 5 steps less than the *QT* method in this example, for real practice with larger RFID systems, we could expect a significant improvement using the *AWAI* since it will have much more tags than this simple case.

3 Performance Evaluation

To evaluate the effectiveness of the proposed technique, we have implemented the *AWAI* method along with the *QT* protocol. The *identification latency* (amount of inquiry) was compared in our experiments. Length of tag ID was set 8 and 12 bits in the tests. The *QT* and *AWAI* were compared in several scenarios with different network density, different threshold ratio and different distribution of RFID tags. All of the reported results are average of 100 random cases.

Figure 7 shows the performance of the *QT* and *AWAI* methods to identify set of RFID tags under different network density. Since RFID tags are with 8-bits length, when density = 10%, it represents that there are 28 ×10% = 26 tags to be identified; when network density = 20%, the amount of RFID tags is equal to 28 ×20% = 52 tags, and so on. To model a balanced query tree, all ID codes were randomly generated in uniform distribution. This is so called balance tree, as entitled in the figure. In this test, the threshold ratio was set to 1/3. We observe that the *AWAI* method slightly outperforms the *QT* protocol in low density network. The *AWAI* gives significant improvement in high density RFID systems.

Figure 8 uses the same setup as that of Figure 7 with increasing ID length of RFID tag to 12 bits. Because of the long execution time for high density network in 12 bits length, we only report the results from density = 20% to density = 80%. In other words,

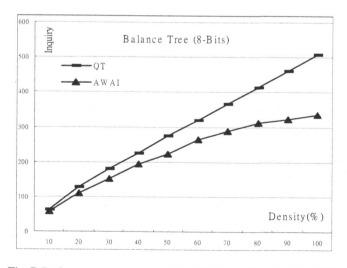

Fig. 7. Performance comparison of the *AWAI* and *QT* with 8 bits RFID tag

the number of tags in the tests was set from 212×20% to 212×80%, i.e., 819 ~ 3277. This simulation has similar observations as those of Figure 7.

The proposed technique defines an acceptable ratio of collision frequency to minimize unnecessary inquiries. Therefore, the value of threshold plays as a crucial factor to the performance of the *AWAI* method. Figure 9 investigates the effect of the threshold to the overall performance of the *AWAI* technique. Simulation setup in this test is the same as those used in Figure 7. Figure 9(a) and 9(b) gives the performance results with network density equals to 80% and 50%, respectively. Obviously, the *AWAI* uses less inquiry than the *QT* protocol, showing the identification efficiency of the *AWAI* is better than the *QT* scheme. This also proves that setting an acceptable ratio of collision frequency to predict network density can effectively avoid unnecessary inquiries. In addition, we also observed that lower threshold leads less inquiry cost. However, the inquiry will reach a lower bound when the threshold goes to a certain value that is small enough. This is because the *AWAI* will scan the entire level if the identification process goes to the lowest part of a query tree (i.e., the leave node level), which restricts the lower bound.

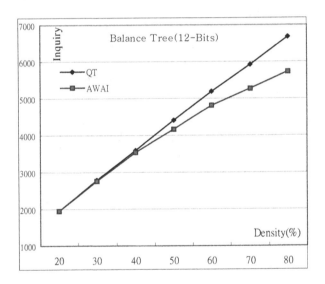

Fig. 8. Performance comparison of the *AWAI* and *QT* with 12 bits RFID tag

The last simulation was conducted to examine the effect of tag id distribution. The term *Tree Balance Factor (TBF)* shown in Figure 10 is used to indicate the percentage of tags deployed in left-subtree and right-subtree. *TBF* = 10% means that amount of tags in left-subtree and right-subtree are with the ration 1:9; similarly, *TBF* = 20% represents the amount of tags in left-subtree and right-subtree are with the ration 2:8. Since the deployment of tags in query tree is not a uniform distribution, this is so called imbalance tree, as entitled in Figure 10. The density is set 80% and threshold set 1/5 in this test. In imbalanced instances, the *AWAI* perform worse than the *query tree (QT)* protocol. This is because the *AWAI* method does not scan righ-subtree in most of levels

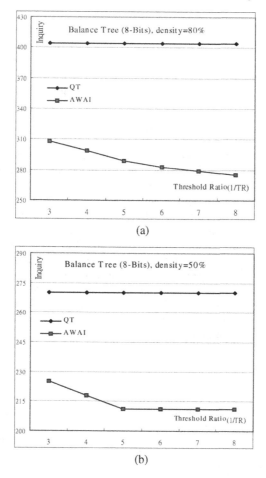

(a)

(b)

Fig. 9. Performance comparison of the *AWAI* and *QT* with different threshold ratio (a) density = 80% (b) density = 50%

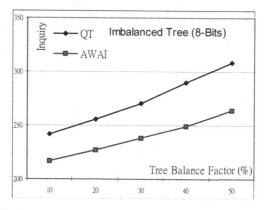

Fig. 10. Performance comparison of the *AWAI* and *QT* in imbalanced tree

in a query tree. As a result, there is no information of "collision" or "no response" in upper levels of the right-subtree. Consequently, when the identification goes to lower levels, it needs to send more inquiries. This situation usually happened in imbalanced tree. This phenomenon matches the results shown in Figure 8. For the cases of *TBF*=40% and 50%, the *AWAI* scheme could presents noticeable improvement.

4 Conclusions and Future Work

The key challenge in designing modern RFID systems is to simultaneously recognize several tags within a reader interrogation zone efficiently and correctly. In this paper, we presented an *Anticipative Wrap-Around Inquiry* (AWAI) scheme for improving the efficiency in identifying tags in high density RFID environments. The main advantage of the *AWAI* is that it can dynamically adjust length of inquiry messages at different level of a query tree. By setting a predefined acceptance ratio of collision, the interrogation with sending prefix inquiry could be advanced to lower level of a query tree. To validate the effectiveness of the *AWAI*, we have implemented the *AWAI* along with the well known *Query Tree* (*QT*) protocol. The experimental results show that the proposed techniques provide noticeable improvements in the identification latency.

There still have challenge to develop an optimal approach that would take environmental effects in order to adapt to them. We hope that the work done so far helps implementing pervasive computing environments that employ RFID systems.

References

[1] Choi, H.S., Cha, J.R., Kim, J.H.: Improved Bit-by-bit Binary Tree Algorithm in Ubiquitous ID System. In: Aizawa, K., Nakamura, Y., Satoh, S. (eds.) PCM 2004. LNCS, vol. 3332, pp. 696–703. Springer, Heidelberg (2004)

[2] Klair, D.K., Chin, K.-W., Raad, R.: An investigation into the energy efficiency of pure and slotted aloha based RFID anti-collision protocols. In: proceedings of the IEEE WoWMoM 2007, Helsinki, Finland, June 18-21 (2007)

[3] Law, C., Lee, K., Siu, K.-Y.: Efficient Memoryless Protocol for Tag Identification. In: Proceedings of the International Workshop on Discrete Algorithms and Methods for Mobile Computing and Communications (August 2000)

[4] Lee, S., Joo, S.D., Lee, C.W.: An enhanced dynamic framed slotted aloha algorithm for RFID tag identification. In: Proceedings of ACM Mobiquitous 2005 (July 2005)

[5] Myung, J., Lee, W.: An adaptive memoryless tag anti-collision protocol for RFID networks. In: Proceedings of IEEE INFOCOM 2005, Poster Session (March 2005)

[6] Myung, J., Lee, W., Srivastava, J.: Adaptive binary splitting for efficient RFID tag anti-collision. IEEE Communication Letter 10(3), 144–146 (2006)

[7] Sahoo, A., Iyer, S., Bhandari, N.: Improving RFID System to Read Tags Efficiently, KRSIT Technical Report, IIT Bombay (June 2006)

[8] Vogt, H.: Efficient Object Identification with Passive RFID Tags. In: Mattern, F., Naghshineh, M. (eds.) PERVASIVE 2002. LNCS, vol. 2414, pp. 98–113. Springer, Heidelberg (2002)

[9] Zhen, B., Kobayashi, M., Shimizui, M.: Framed aloha for multiple RFID objects Identification. IEICE Trans. on Comm. E88-B(3), 991–999 (2005)

[10] Zhou, Z., Gupta, H., Das, S.R., Zhu, X.: Slotted Scheduled Tag Access in Multi-Reader RFID Systems. In: Proceedings of the IEEE International Conference on Networks Protocols (ICNP), pp. 61–70 (2007)

A Probabilistic Semantic Based
Mixture Collaborative Filtering

Linkai Weng[1], Yaoxue Zhang[1], Yuezhi Zhou[1],
Laurance T. Yang[2], Pengwei Tian[1], and Ming Zhong[1]

[1] Department of Computer Science & Technology,
Tsinghua University, Beijing, China
wlk02@mails.tsinghua.edu.cn, zyx@moe.edu.cn,
zhouyz@mail.tsinghua.edu.cn,
{tpw04,zhong-m}@mails.tsinghua.edu.cn
[2] Department of Computer Science, St .Francis Xavier University,
Antigonish, Canada
ltyang@gmail.com

Abstract. Personalized recommendation techniques play more and more important roles for the explosively increasing of information nowadays. As a most popular recommendation approach, collaborative filtering (CF) obtains great success in practice. To overcome the inherent problems of CF, such as sparsity and scalability, we proposed a semantic based mixture CF in this paper. Our approach decomposes the original vector into semantic component and residual component, and then combines them together to implement recommendation. The semantic component can be extracted by topic model analysis and the residual component can be approximated by top values selected from the original vector respectively. Compared to the traditional CF, the proposed mixture approach has introduced semantic information and reduced dimensions without serious information missing owe to the complement of residual error. Experimental evaluation demonstrates that our approach can indeed provide better recommendations in both accuracy and efficiency.

Keywords: Collaborative filtering, topic model, semantic analysis.

1 Introduction

With the rapid development of web technologies and information publishing method, the amount of web resource is growing explosively, far beyond our manual processing ability. Therefore, it is non-trivial to design a technique which can help people find the needing information quickly and accuately. Search engine, as one such implement, achives great success in the practical use, but it has its own drawbacks: lack of personalization. Different users usually have different information needs even when they submit the same query in the seach engine, so, a technology to suggust information based on users' historial behavior, often called as personalized recommendation, can satisfy users' information needs more accurately and provide better user experience.

D. Zhang et al. (Eds.): UIC 2009, LNCS 5585, pp. 377–388, 2009.

Collaborative filtering(CF) [1] is one of the most promising personalized recommendation approach, which models the mouth-to-mouth recommending process in practical. Consider a certain user, we firstly select a group of users who have similar taste with her based on the historial ratings, then items sharing most reputation among these users would be recommended to the certain user. Collaborative filtering obtains significant success in both research and practice, and have various impressive applications, such as Grouplens [2], Douban [3] and Amazon [4].

Despite its success in various domains, collaborative filtering suffers from some inherent problems, such as sparsity and scalability [5]. To overcome these problems, many effective improved approaches are proposed. Item-based CF [6] [7] may be the most popular variation of CF nowadays, which turn to consider the problem from item-pairwise perspective rather than user-pairwise perspective, due to the observation that there are far more users than items in the practical recommendation environment. It can alleviate the sparsity and scalability in some extent, but the pairwise similarity computing is still a time-consuming task. Matrix dimension reduction methods, such as PCA [8] and SVD [9], can indeed save the pairwise similarity computing, wheras they are limited by the scalability for the inherent complexity of matrix processing. Probabilistic semantic appoaches [10] [11] [12], which view the rating prediction as a conditional probability estimation process based on the observed rating data, can provide some insightful description of the scenario, yet it is troublesome to transform the probability value to the rating value. Rating diffusion [13] [14] incorporates deep relationship between items with the help of graph mining.

In this paper, we address these issues of Collaborative filtering by introducing a probabilistic semantic based mixture approach. Probabilistic semantic analysis, such as PLSA [15] and LDA [16], has been applied in text mining, information retrieval and natural language processing for a long history. It assumes that each document constitutes of some latent semantic topics and can be seen as a probabilistic distribution on these topics, which has many advantages, such as revealing the inherent semantic structure, reducing dimention and solving the polysemy and synonymy problem [15]. With the observation that semantic mapping has some reconstruction error, we additionally use the top value part of the original vector to approxiate the residual error as a complement to the semantic mapping. Unlike the former mentioned probabilistic semantic based method, our approach only utilizes the semantic analysis result in the item similarity computing task, and completes the prediction task by accumulate similar item's ratings weighted by their similarity, just as the traditional CF does. As a whole, our mixture CF fully absorbs the advantage of probability model in semantic structure revealing and keeping the rating accuracy in the tracitional CF. Experiment results have demonstrated that our method can indeed provide better rating performance, and further alleviate the sparsity and scalability problems.

The remaining part of the paper is organized as follows. In Section 2, we introduce related works. In Section 3, we will continue to introduce our probabilistic semantic based mixture CF approach in detial. A set of practical experiments will be conducted and the corresponding results will be analyzed in section 4. Finally, conclusions and future work will be given in the last Section.

2 Related Work

In this section, we briefly present some research approach related to CF. Collaborative filtering approaches are often classified as memory-based and model-based.

Memory-based approaches construct and utilize all rating data in a large user-item matrix, just as-is into memory. In these approaches, similar users or items are selected as nearest-neighbours through the comparison between user vectors or item vectors in the matrix. Then the target rating is predicted through accumulating ratings in the nearest-neighbours weighted by neighbour similarity, which can be viewed simply as expectation of neighbours' historical ratings. Naturally, the mainstream memory-based approaches are user-based CF [1] and item-based CF [6] [7], respectively selecting nearest-neighbours from similar users or from similar items. In the practical scenario, there are often far more users than items, and items are relatively more static, so item-based CF is usually better than user-based one no matter in performance or in complexity. As a whole, the memory-based CF has less parameters to be tuned, and accordingly has less cost in the offline computing; however this method is suffered from sparsity problems severely.

Model-based approaches have to generate a model to fit the test user or the test item by the history ratings first. Then we complete the prediction task by estimating the generative probability of the target rating given the trained model, essentially given the history ratings. Many machine learning algorithms can be utilized in the model generation process, the key part of this approach, such as mixture gaussian, PLSA [15] and LDA [16]. Details about this category approaches can be seen in [10] [11] [12]. Generally speaking, model-based approaches can provide indeed insightful description, yet the rating estimation accuracy may lack of competitiveness for some generation have been made in the model fitting process.

With the development of CF, there emerges some approaches can't be simply classified into the above two categories, such as clustering-based CF and rating diffusing CF. Clustering-based CF [17] works by clustering similar users in the same class, and then computing the rating expectation in the test user's class as the prediction rating. It is effective in alleviating the scalability problem. Rating diffusing CF utilizes the graph-based technique in which nodes represents users and edges indicate similarity between two users. Prediction is produced by walking and diffusing ratings through edges. This method consider deeper relationships between users through graph walking and can solve the sparsity problems in some extent, however the extra walking and diffusing may incur serious extra computing complexity.

3   Methodology

3.1   Problem Statement

The problem of CF is to predict how well a user would like an item that he has not rated given a set of historical preference judgments for a community of users. In a CF scenario, there is a set of users $U = \{u_1, u_2, \cdots, u_m\}$ and a set of items $I = \{i_1, i_2, \cdots, i_n\}$. The rating data can be constructed into a mn user-item matrix R, with each entity R_{pq} indicates the rating of user p to item q, which is usually very sparse. Then u_p denotes the $p - th$ row of matrix R, as user vector, and i_q denotes the $q - th$ column of matrix R, as item vector. So the problem of CF could be formalized as predicting how well a user p would like an item q that she has not rated, denoted as R_{pq}, given a set of historical ratings, constructed as rating matrix R. A typical CF often contains two main phases: the model building phase and the rating prediction phase.

3.2   Our Probabilistic Semantic Based Approach

As mentioned above, memory-based CF is correspondingly better at rating prediction accuracy and in the other hand, model-based CF is correspondingly better at concaving the latent semantic insight. Intuitively, we propose an approach to combine both benefits of them, in which a probabilistic semantic model is trained in the model building phase, and similarity based nearest-neighbour rating expectation is computed in the rating prediction phase. The general overview of the approach is illustrated in the left of Fig. 1.

First of all, we train a probabilistic semantic model to fit our observed rating data. Probabilistic semantic model, also known as topic model, is a widely used method to analyze the latent semantic structure. In a typical text analysis scenario, a corpus C consists of a set of documents, represented as $\{d_m\}_{m=1,\dots,M}$, and each document d_m consists of a set of words, represented as $\{(tid_n : tval_n)\}_{n=1,\dots,N}$, in which tid_n denotes the id of $n - th$ term and $tval_n$ denotes the corresponding term count. We assume that there is a corpus-related topic sets $\{z_i\}_{i=1,\dots,K}$, each of which denotes certain semantic unit and can be represented by certain probabilistic distribution on the words space, $\{\phi_i\}_{i=1,\dots,N}$. Each document of the corpus could be viewed as a probabilistic mixture of this topic component, represented as $\{\theta_i\}_{i=1,\dots,K}$. Similarly, our CF application also could be regarded from topic perspective, in which each user could be seen as a document, and each item could be seen as a word, and correspondingly the rating of certain user to certain item can be seen as the word count in document. Topic models are numerous, such as aspect model [15] and latent dirichlet allocation [16], all of which could be employed in our model training process.

After the probabilistic semantic topic model of the rating data is trained, each user vector has been transformed to a probabilistic distribution, which can be viewed as a new user topic vector with lower dimension, often lower than 500. Then we can implement our approach just as the traditional memory-based CF does. User topic vectors' similarity are computed with vector distance metrics,

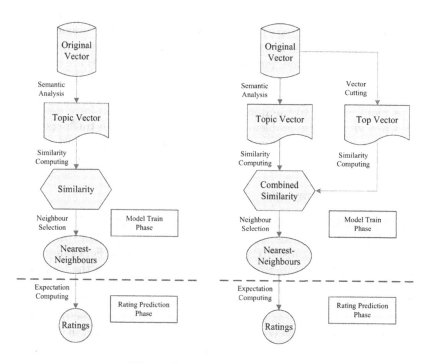

Fig. 1. Overview of our Approach

such as cosine distance and KL divergence, and we can select each user's nearest-neighbour set by ranking the distances.

At last, we can predict the target rating by average the ratings in the nearest-neighbour set to the same item weighted by neighbour similarity.

Overview the whole process, our probabilistic semantic based CF's advantages are obvious. At first, the transformed user topic vector can catch up more semantic meaning and thus can reveal deeper latent relationships between users, which could alleviate the sparsity problem in some extent. For example, in a movie CF scenario, consider a user A has high ratings on the Harry Potter 1 and Harry Potter 2, and another user B has high ratings on Harry Potter 3 and Harry Potter 4, in the typical similarity metrics, these two users may be seen having no relation, but in the semantic topic similarity metrics, they share high interest similarity for all the Harry Potter series would be absorted in the same semantic topic. Essentially, the topic in the movie CF scenario can be treat as somewhat auto-generated genre. Secondly, by the way, the dimension reduction task is achived in the topic vector transformation, for the number of semantic topic is far less than the number of items in most situation. Less vector dimension can decrease the similarity computing time and then can provide more satisfactory user experence. Further, unlike the matrix-based dimension reduction method, such as PCA and SVD, our method has no scalability problem for we can employ the model estimating in a small subset, and then carry out inference on the whole data set. At last, our method has better accuracy in the rating prediction compared to the pure model-based CF, because we just simply average the nearest-neighbours's ratings rather than estimating a generative probabilistic expectation, for the probabilistic topic models are often good at insight concaving and descripting, but are relatively weak at discriminative computing.

What is more, similar to the item-based CF, we could also have item-based topic CF when viewing the problem from item perspective. In this perspective, each item vector is seen as a document and each user is seen as a word, and thus each topic can be seen as a user cummunity sharing the same movie taste.

3.3   Our Mixture Approach

As shown in practical experience and theoretic analysis, probabilistic semantic model can effectively reveal the latent semantic relationships, but can also miss some detail information because of the probabilistic generation. For example, users with similar movie genres taste would be hard to distinguish in the topic model framework. With the observation that there exists reconstruction error between the topic vector and the original vector, intuitively we additionally incorporate the top sub-vector as an approximate complement to the topic vector. Notably, the top sub-vector refers to the vector remaining the top value part in the original vector. As a result, a mixture approach combining the topic vector and the top sub-vector has been proposed in this section to get more accurate rating prediction. The general overview of the approach is illustrated in the right of Fig. 1.

Compared to our basic approach, we measure the distance between two users by topic distance and top sub-vector distance respectively in the improved approach, namely S_t and S_i, and then combine them with a mixture factor a to get the final user distance S. The mixture factor a can be fixed by cross validation.

From a probabilistic semantic perspective, the topic vector can be seen as the reconstruction of the original user vector in the new topic space. The gap between the original vector and the topic vector is often called reconstruction error, or residual error, and it can often simply be approximated by the top value words of the document. Thus in this subsection we utilize the top value vector as a complement to the topic vector to obtain better performance. What is more, for the top sub-vector's dimension is relatively lower than the original dimension, this mixture approach can still have computing complexity advantage compared with traditional CF.

3.4   Comparison with Traditional CF

Compared with the traditional memory-based methods, such as user-based CF and item-based CF, our approach introduce a probabilistic topic model to reveal the semantic structure of the original vector, which can utilize deeper latent relationships between users and thus can alleviate the sparsity problems in some extent. Further, with the help of probabilistic topic vector transformation, we can reduce the dimension of the original vector by the way.

In the other hand, our approach employs discriminative rating prediction computing rather than the generative probability estimating compared with the traditional model-based methods. Additionally, considering that there exists residual error between the topic vector and the original vector, we utilize the top value sub-vector as the approximation of the residual error to complement the topic vector. As a result, our mixture approach can guarantee the accuracy due to the completeness of the vector representation.

4   Experiment

In this section we experimentally evaluate the performance of our probabilistic semantic based mixture CF. Traditional item-based CF is selected as our baseline method.

4.1   Data Set

We choose MovieLens data sets as the experiment dataset. MovieLens data is collected and distrubuted by GroupLens Research Group in an online movie rating and recommendting website. It contain 1,000,209 anonymous ratings of approximately 3,900 movies made by 6,040 MovieLens users who joined Movie-Lens in 2000. We randomly split the data into a training set (950,029 ratings) and a held-out test set (5,000 ratings), the former set is treated as observed ratings to build model and predict the latter set. This data set has been used in various CF methods evaluation, such as [6] [18] [19].

4.2   Evaluate Metric

For consistency with experiments in other literature, we report our evaluating result with mean absolute error (MAE), a widely used statistical accuracy metric. MAE corresponds to the average absolute deviation of prediction to the ground truth data, which can be formally represented as:

$$MAE = \Sigma_{i=1}^{N}|\widehat{r_i} - r_i|/N, \tag{1}$$

where r_i denotes the ground truth rating of an item by certain user, $\widehat{r_i}$ denotes the predict rating and N is the number of test ratings. Noted that the lower the MAE, the better the recommendation method's prediction performance.

Further, we measure the efficiency of each approach by the number of rating predicted per second, simply called efficiency per second (EPS) here. The larger the EPS of certain approach is the better the approach's efficiency is.

4.3   Result and Analysis

Firstly, we compare the overall MAE and EPS of the three approaches, Item-based CF, Topic-based CF and Mixture CF, and then evaluate the impact to

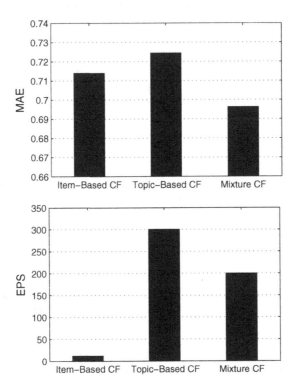

Fig. 2. Relative performance of different approaches

the performance of several important parameters, such as nearest neighbour's number (KNN), mixture factor's value (a) and top items' number (TopNum).

Figure 2 compare the three approaches' MAE and EPS. In the MAE measure, we can discover that the Topic-based CF is a little worse in MAE than baseline method, the Item-based CF, which is according to the former analysis that Topic-based CF may miss some discriminative information because of the probabilistic generation. As an improved topic-based CF, the mixture CF has better MAE. This fully demonstrates the effectiveness of semantic generation and residual error complement. In the EPS measure, our proposed topic-based CF and mixture CF are far more efficient than baseline approach, because of the dimension reduction, as an additional benefit of our proposed approaches.

Figure 3 evaluates the influence of KNN (nearest neighbours' number) to the performance. From this figure we can discover the following three properties: 1) all three approaches arrive their best MAE when KNN is around 10-20. If the nearest neighbours' number is too small, the result may be biased because of the inadequate statistics. In the other hand, if the nearest neighbours' number is too large, many neighbours included may be not so similar, thus the result accuracy may be diluted by them. 2) Compared to the other two approaches, item-based CF has deeper slope, which means the result is more sensitive to the change of KNN.

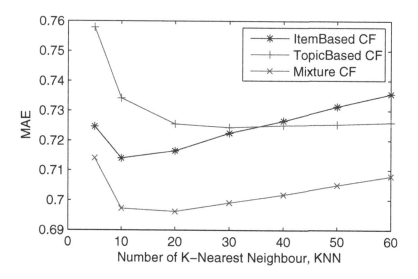

Fig. 3. Effect of Nearest Neighbour's number

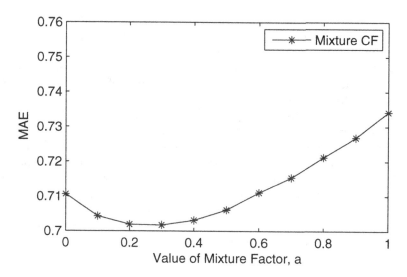

Fig. 4. Effect of Mixture Factor's value

This is caused by the fact that the variation of similarities between neighbours is more violent in item-based CF and the irrelevant neighbours will affect the result more serious. 3) Comparing the three approaches, the mixture CF has the best performance all the time, followed is the item-based CF and then the topic-based CF. Notably, the item-based CF and topic-based CF has an intersection when KNN is around 35 because of the sensitiveness of the item-based CF.

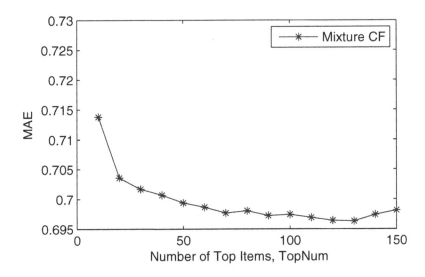

Fig. 5. Effect of Top Items' Number

Figure 4 evaluates the effect of mixture factor value (a) in the mixture CF. In fact, the mixture factor is the weight of topic vector similarity in the whole similarity value. The mixture CF will equal to a revised item-based CF, which only remains top values in the item vector, when a equals to 0 and will equal to topic-based CF when a equals to 1. The best performance of mixture CF is got when a equal to 0.3 in our experiment.

Figure 5 evaluates the effect of top item number (TopNum) in the mixture CF. In our mixture CF framework, we utilize the vector only with TopNum top values (top sub-vector) to approximate the reconstruction error of the topic vector, also known as residual error. The performance arrives extreme point when TopNum equals 120-130 in this experiment, which accords to the property of the residual error approximation. If the TopNum is too small, the top vector will contain too little information to approximate the residual error, but when the TopNum is too large, the top vector will contain too much information which seriously overlaps with the topic vector.

5   Conclusion and Future Work

Collaborative filtering gains great success in both research and practical use, but it suffers from sparsity problems and scalability problems. In this paper, we first proposed a probabilistic semantic based CF to conquer these problems, in which a topic vector is introduced by analyzing the original vector with topic model. Observing that there exists reconstruction error between the topic vector and the original vector, we further proposed a mixture CF as the improved version of probabilistic semantic based CF, in which the reconstruction error is approximately complemented. Both theoretical analysis and experimental evaluation demonstrates that our mixture CF has two benefits: 1) alleviating the sparsity problems and scalability problems because of the introduction of semantic information extraction, which can reveal and utilize deeper relationships and reduce dimensions. 2) Improving the performance, measured by accuracy here, because of the integration of reconstruction error.

One drawback of the current work is that the determination of some parameters, such as mixture factor and top item number, are through heuristic tuning. In the future we are dedicating to devise a model to estimate the rate between reconstruction value and reconstruction error automatically. Then parameters can be obtained in the model and can be dramatically adjusted. Further, we plan to develop a tool to help implement our approach in the practical application conveniently.

References

1. Goldberg, D., Nichols, D., Oki, B.M., Terry, D.: Using collaborative filtering to weave an information tapestry. Communications of the ACM 35(12), 61–70 (1992)
2. Resnick, P., Iacovou, N., Suchak, M., Bergstrom, P., Riedl, J.: GroupLens: an open architecture for collaborative filtering of Netnews. In: Proceedings of ACM 1994 Conference on Computer Supported Cooperative Work, pp. 175–186, Chapel Hill, NC (1994)
3. Douban, http://www.douban.com
4. Amazon, http://www.amazon.com
5. Adomavicius, G., Tuzhilin, A.: Toward the next generation of recommender systems: a survey of the state-of-the-art and possible extensions. IEEE Transactions on Knowledge and Data Engineering 17(6), 734–749 (2005)
6. Sarwar, B., Karypis, G., Konstan, J., Riedl, J.: Item-based collaborative filtering recommendation algorithms. In: Proceedings of the 10th International World Wide Web Conference (WWW 2001), Hong Kong, May 1-5, ACM, New York (2001)
7. Linden, G., Smith, B., York, J.: Amazon.com recommendations: item-to-item collaborative filtering. Internet Computing 7, 76–80 (2003)
8. Jolliffe, I.T.: Principal component analysis, 2nd edn. Springer Series in Statistics, 2nd edn., vol. XXIX, p. 487, 28 illus. Springer, NY (2002), ISBN 978-0-387-95442-4
9. Wall, M.E., Rechtsteiner, A., Rocha, L.M.: Singular value decomposition and principal component analysis. In: Berrar, D.P., Dubitzky, W., Granzow, M. (eds.) A Practical Approach to Microarray Data Analysis., pp. 91–109. Kluwer, Norwell (2003)
10. Blei, D.: Probabilistic Models of Text and Images. PhD thesis, U.C. Berkeley, Division of Computer Science (2004)
11. Chen, W.Y., Zhang, D., Chang, E.Y.: Combinational Collaborative Filtering for Personalized Community Recommendation. In: Proceedings of the 14th ACM SIGKDD International Conference on Knowledge Discovery and Data Mining, August 24-27. ACM, Las Vegas (2008)
12. Marlin., B.: Collaborative filtering: A machine learning perspective. Mastre's thesis, University of Toronto (2004)

13. Huang, Z., Chen, H., Zeng, D.: Applying associative retrieval techniques to alleviate the sparsity problem in collaborative filtering. ACM Transactions on Information Systems (TOIS 2004) 22(1), 116–142 (2004)
14. Zhou, D., Huang, J., Schölkopf, B.: Learning from labeled and unlabeled data on a directed graph. In: De Raedt, L., Wrobel, S. (eds.) Proceedings of the 22nd International Conference on Machine Learning(ICML 2005), pp. 1041–1048. ACM press, New York (2005)
15. Hofmann, T.: Probabilistic latent semantic indexing. In: Proceedings of the Twenty-Second Annual International SIGIR Conference on Research and Development in Information Retrieval (SIGIR 1999), California (1999)
16. Blei, D., Ng, A., Jordan, M.: Latent dirichlet allocation. Journal of Machine Learning Research 3, 993–1022 (2003)
17. Xue, G.R., Lin, C., Yang, Q., Xi, W., Zeng, H.J., Yu, Y., Chen, Z.: Scalable collaborative filtering using cluster-based smoothing. In: Proceedings of the Twenty-eighth Annual International SIGIR Conference on Research and Development in Information Retrieval (SIGIR 2005), Salvador, Brazil, pp. 114–121 (2005)
18. Herlocker, J.L., Konstan, J.A., Terveen, L.G., Riedl, J.T.: Evaluating Collaborative Filtering Recommender Systems. In: ACM Transactions on Information Systems (TOIS 2004), vol. 22(1), pp. 5–53 (2004)
19. Wang, F., Ma, S., Yang, L.Z., Li., T.: E-commendation on Item Graphs. In: Proceeding of the Sixth International Conference on Data Mining (ICDM 2006), Hong Kong 0-7695-2701-9/06 (2006)

Author Index